PROTESTANT NONCONFORMIST TEXTS
VOLUME 4

Contemporary texts are used in this volume to illustrate key themes in the history of Nonconformity in England and Wales. Although the twentieth century was in many ways a century of decline, this book shows that there was still much life in the Nonconformist tradition. It also looks at contemporary issues such as racism and the place of women. Through contemporary writings it provides an insight into the life and thought of the English Free Churches in a century in which they expected to come into their own, only to discover that they faced new challenges and the problems of decline.

PROTESTANT NONCONFORMIST TEXTS

Series editor: Alan P. F. Sell

This series of four substantial volumes is designed to demonstrate the range of interests of the several Protestant Nonconformist traditions from the time of their Separatist harbingers in the sixteenth century to the end of the twentieth century. It represents a major project of the Association of Denominational Historical Societies and Cognate Libraries. Each volume comprises a General Introduction followed by texts illustrative of such topics as theology, philosophy, worship and socio-political concerns. This work has never before been drawn together for publication in this way. Prepared by a team of twelve editors, all of whom are expert in their areas and drawn from a number of the relevant traditions, it provides a much-needed comprehensive view of Nonconformity told largely in the words of those whose story it is. The works will prove to be an invaluable resource to scholars, students, academics and specialist and public libraries, as well as to a wider range of church, intellectual and general historians.

Other titles in the series:

Protestant Nonconformist Texts Volume 1
1550 to 1700
Edited by R. Tudur Jones
with Arthur Long and Rosemary Moore

Protestant Nonconformist Texts Volume 2
The Eighteenth Century
Edited by Alan P. F. Sell
with David J. Hall and Ian Sellers

Protestant Nonconformist Texts Volume 3
The Nineteenth Century
Edited by David Bebbington
with Kenneth Dix and Alan Ruston

Protestant Nonconformist Texts
Volume 4

The Twentieth Century

Edited by
DAVID M. THOMPSON

with
J. H. Y. BRIGGS
and
JOHN MUNSEY TURNER

WIPF & STOCK · Eugene, Oregon

Wipf and Stock Publishers
199 W 8th Ave, Suite 3
Eugene, OR 97401

Protestant Nonconformist Texts Volume 4
The Twentieth Century
By Thompson, David M. and Briggs, John H. Y.
Copyright©2007 by Thompson, David M.
ISBN 13: 978-1-4982-1918-1
Publication date 2/3/2015
Previously published by Ashgate, 2007

Contents

Series Editor's Preface	xi
Preface	xiii
Acknowledgements	xv
Introduction	1

Part I: Church Life

Introduction		13
I.1	Nonconformity in London, 1902–3	18
I.2	The 'Institutional Church'	21
I.3	The Pleasant Sunday Afternoon	23
I.4	The Welsh Revival, 1904–5	25
I.5	Free Will Giving, 1906	26
I.6	Congregational Optimism, 1913	29
I.7	A Cumbrian Methodist Chapel after the First World War	30
I.8	Village Congregational Churches, 1934	32
I.9	The Future of the Free Churches, 1945	34
I.10	Evangelism after the Second World War	36
I.11	A Methodist Sunday School in the Twentieth Century	37
I.12	Methodist Decline in Youth Work in the 1950s	39
I.13	MethSoc in the 1950s	41
I.14	Rural Methodism, 1958	42
I.15	The Problems of Effecting Methodist Union, 1960	43
I.16	The Sociology of Methodism in the 1960s	44
I.17	Afro-Caribbean Churches from the 1950s	49
I.18	A West Indian Serves with an English Congregation	56
I.19	Rethinking Overseas Missions in the 1960s	58
I.20	The Urban Theology Unit in Sheffield	60
I.21	Methodism in a Multi-racial Context in London	61
I.22	Decline and Growth in the United Reformed Church in the 1970s	63
I.23	Inter-Faith Relations and Evangelism	65
I.24	Rural Baptist Churches, 1995	70

Part II: Ecclesiology

Introduction		77
II.1	The Ordination of Constance Coltman, 1917	82

II.2	Women's Ministry in the North of England	83
II.3	Women's Ministry in the Congregational Union in the 1930s	85
II.4	Ella Gordon	88
II.5	Congregational Moderators, 1920	90
II.6	Formation of the General Assembly of Unitarian and Free Christian Churches, 1928	91
II.7	The Baptist Doctrine of the Church, 1948	93
II.8	Methodist Statement on Baptism, 1952	98
II.9	The Baptist Understanding of Ordination, 1957	101
II.10	Ordination in the Methodist Church, 1960	106
II.11	Report of the Baptist Union Commission on the Associations, 1964	108
II.12	Liberty in the Lord, 1964	112
II.13	Constitution of the Congregational Church, 1966	114
II.14	The Child and the Church, 1966	116
II.15	Church Related Community Workers, 1980	119
II.16	The Community of Women and Men	121
II.17	Forms of Ministry among Baptists, 1994	123
II.18	Relating and Resourcing, 1998	128
II.19	Methodism and Episcopacy, 2000	133

Part III: Worship

Introduction		139
III.1	A Wesleyan Methodist Love Feast in the Early Twentieth Century	141
III.2	The Methodist Covenant Service	141
III.3	The Sunday School Anniversary	142
III.4	Book of Congregational Worship, 1920	144
III.5	Methodist Morning Prayer	145
III.6	Televising Holy Communion	146
III.7	Methodist Local Preachers, 1964	148
III.8	Methodist Order for Communion, 1975	149
III.9	United Reformed Church Second Order of Worship, 1989	153
III.10	Later Twentieth-Century Hymnody	155
III.11	Baptists and the Lord's Supper	160
III.12	Statement of Faith in Inclusive Language	162

Part IV: Theology

Introduction		167
IV.1	The New Theology, 1907	171
IV.2	The Jesus of History, 1917	176
IV.3	The Church and the Sacraments, 1917	181
IV.4	Grace and Personality, 1917	187

IV.5	The Baptist and Congregational Inheritance, 1928	191
IV.6	Science and Christian Belief: a Quaker View, 1929	194
IV.7	Baptist Controversy over Higher Criticism and Modernism, 1932–34	195
IV.8	A Congregational View of the Sacraments, 1943	199
IV.9	Methodist Views of the Atonement	204
IV.10	Christianity and History	206
IV.11	Unitarian Theology in Mid-Century	207
IV.12	Religionless Christianity, 1962	209
IV.13	Atonement and the Sacraments, 1988	211

Part V: Nonconformity and Politics

	Introduction	219
V.1	The Education Act, 1902	226
V.2	Nonconformists and the Liberal Landslide, 1906	226
V.3	Scott Lidgett and the Education Bill of 1906	229
V.4	Congregationalists and Education, 1909	230
V.5	Another View of Nonconformity and Politics, 1909	231
V.6	Welsh Disestablishment, 1913	236
V.7	Methodism and the Early Labour Party	237
V.8	The Enabling Bill, 1919	238
V.9	Methodism and Labour in Wales in the 1920s	238
V.10	The General Strike, 1926	239
V.11	The Revised Prayer Book, 1927	240
V.12	The Salvation Army Act, 1931	242
V.13	The Problems of the German Churches, 1933	244
V.14	Attitudes to the Jews, 1938	245
V.15	The Education Act, 1944	246
V.16	The Free Churches and the State, 1953	248
V.17	Post-War Relations with Germany	254
V.18	Concern about Africa, 1960	255
V.19	The Tercentenary of 1662	256
V.20	Methodist Church Act, 1976	257
V.21	Harold Wilson	259
V.22	James Callaghan	260
V.23	Margaret Thatcher	262

Part VI: Peace and War

	Introduction	267
VI.1	Hugh Price Hughes and the Boer War	270
VI.2	John Clifford on the Boer War	271

VI.3	The Congregational Union and the First World War	271
VI.4	Primitive Methodists and the First World War	273
VI.5	A Wesleyan Military Chaplain	274
VI.6	Churches of Christ and the First World War	275
VI.7	British Baptist Message to American Baptists, 1917	275
VI.8	Friends and Censorship in the First World War	278
VI.9	John Clifford on the End of the War, 1918	279
VI.10	The Congregational Union and Chaplains to the Forces, 1932	280
VI.11	Indiscriminate Bombing, 1937	281
VI.12	Assistance to Continental Pastors, 1945	282
VI.13	Bombed Churches	283
VI.14	Methodism on Peace and War, 1957	285
VI.15	Methodist Support for Freedom Fighting	289
VI.16	The Gulf War, 1991	290

Part VII: Social Issues

Introduction		295
VII.1	Early Twentieth-Century Teetotalism	299
VII.2	The Licensing Bill of 1908	301
VII.3	Congregational Union Distress Fund	302
VII.4	Methodist Regulations concerning Marriage and Divorce, 1948	305
VII.5	Methodism and Temperance in Mid-Century	306
VII.6	Congregationalists and Gambling, 1952	309
VII.7	Towards a Quaker View of Sex, 1963	310
VII.8	The Presbyterian View of Contraceptives, 1965	312
VII.9	Living in a Secular Age, 1964	313
VII.10	Divorce and Remarriage, 1967	316
VII.11	Abortion, 1976	317
VII.12	Social Justice, 1982	320
VII.13	Racism, 1987	322
VII.14	Commitment for Life, 1992	323
VII.15	Methodism and Gambling, 1992	325
VII.16	Methodism and Human Sexuality, 1993	328
VII.17	Baptists and Disability	329
VII.18	Marriage and Divorce, 1998	332

Part VIII: Church Unity

Introduction		337
VIII.1	Shakespeare's Vision of Free Church Unity, 1918	345
VIII.2	Overlapping of New Churches	348
VIII.3	Opposition to Methodist Union in Wesleyanism	349

VIII.4	Federal Council Response to Lambeth, 1925	350
VIII.5	Peake on Methodist Union	353
VIII.6	The Methodist Deed of Union, 1932	354
VIII.7	A Primitive Methodist in the Methodist Church, 1997	356
VIII.8	Congregational–Baptist Union Churches, 1933	359
VIII.9	The Free Church Federal Council, 1940	361
VIII.10	The Congregational–Presbyterian Covenant, 1951	364
VIII.11	Churches of Christ and Unity, 1962	365
VIII.12	Anglican–Methodist Proposals, 1963	368
VIII.13	Methodist Dissentients, 1963	369
VIII.14	Methodist Radicals	372
VIII.15	The Nottingham Faith and Order Conference, 1964	373
VIII.16	United Reformed Church Act, 1972	375
VIII.17	United Reformed Church Schedule D	376
VIII.18	Basis of Union of the United Reformed Church	378
VIII.19	Ten Propositions, 1976	384
VIII.20	The Welsh Covenant, 1975	385
VIII.21	Baptists and the Ten Propositions, 1977	386
VIII.22	The Proposed English Covenant, 1980	395
VIII.23	To Lima with Love, 1986	397
VIII.24	Baptist–Methodist Agreement on Baptismal Policy within Local Ecumenical Projects	403
VIII.25	Local Ecumenical Partnerships, 1992	405
VIII.26	The United Reformed Church and Local Ecumenical Partnerships	405
VIII.27	The United Reformed Church responds to *Called to be One*	408

Select Bibliography	411
Index of Persons	413

Series Editor's Preface

I had long felt the need of a series which would present texts from the history and thought of Protestant Nonconformity in England and Wales in such a way that the breadth of the Nonconformists' interests, the extent and variety of their activities, and the depth of their devotion from the days of the sixteenth-century Separatists onwards would become plain. When the Association of Denominational Historical Societies and Cognate Libraries was formally constituted on 23 October 1993, with the objective of sharing intelligence and facilitating co-operative scholarly activity across the several denominational boundaries, I formally proposed the preparation of a series of Protestant Nonconformist Texts to the membership.

There was unanimous agreement that a need existed which could, and should, be met. It was determined that the series should comprise four volumes covering the periods 1550–1700, the eighteenth century, the nineteenth century and the twentieth century; and that each volume should be in the hands of a co-ordinating editor assisted by two co-operating editors drawn from different church traditions. The secretaries of the member societies, with the guidance of their respective committees, nominated scholars who might be approached to serve as editors. I am pleased to say that within a month the twelve editors were mustered, and I am most appreciative of their enthusiasm for the task, and of the expeditious way in which they have carried it out. It is proper to make special and grateful mention of the late Reverend Professor R. Tudur Jones who, in addition to serving as the coordinating editor of the first volume – a task he completed within days of his sudden and much-lamented death on 23 July 1998 – also cordially agreed to act as consultant on Welsh matters to the editors of all four volumes. The sudden death of the Reverend Dr Ian Sellers, a contributing editor of Volume II, has left a further significant gap in the ranks of scholars of English Nonconformity, as has the passing of the Revd Dr Arthur Long, a contributing editor to Volume I, whose death was announced as Volumes I and IV were in the press.

The editors were given a fairly free hand in the organisation of their volumes: indeed, the nature of the materials has been permitted to suggest the lay-out of the several volumes. It is claimed that the order of each volume is clear and justifiable, even if in format one may differ slightly from another.

It is hoped that the series will prove helpful to students and interested readers, and that scholars may find it useful to have a check-list of sources which, though necessarily limited by considerations of space, is intended as an appetiser and a stimulus to further quarrying.

Above all, it is hoped that worthy tribute is here paid to those who, often at great personal cost, and in face of socio-political obstacles of various kinds, declared their faith and bore their witness. Indeed (to advert to realities, not to utter a lament), in a time of general apologetic caution, widespread doctrinal ignorance and apathy, fitful ecumenism, queried national institutions and overall numerical decline among

Series Editor's Preface

the Protestant Nonconformists of England and Wales, it may even be that forebears have something to teach those who inherit their mantle – and any others who may care to listen.

On behalf of my editorial colleagues I should like to thank Sarah Lloyd, Liz Pearce and all at Ashgate Publishing for their commitment to this project and for the care they have lavished upon it.

Alan P. F. Sell

Preface

The twentieth century witnessed the profusion of documents. The typewriter, with carbon paper and then the Roneo machine, made it possible to reproduce documents on a new scale. By the end of the century the word-processor, photocopier and computer had taken this even further. There were frequent predictions that the days of printed material, books and pamphlets were numbered. All this creates a new kind of problem for the compilation of any collection of sources. This collection, with one exception, sticks firmly to printed material in books or pamphlets as the primary sources.

The multiplication of material also increases the problems of selection. It is difficult to know how to strike the balance between the writings of individuals, reports or official statements of churches, and resolutions passed at ecclesiastical assemblies. Which can be counted as 'typical', and of what? In compiling this collection I have tried to balance the selection both of types of material and of the church traditions represented. Inevitably, extracts from books take more space than resolutions, and the balance also varies between the different Parts. Throughout I have made my selection on the basis of the relevance of the extract to nonconformity in general, either because it reflects a characteristic nonconformist emphasis or because it is significant that a nonconformist individual or church should have said something like that. This is the main reason for omitting the most interesting nonconformist contributions to twentieth-century theology in the field of biblical studies. There is also inevitably a tendency in Part IV on theology to give more space to unorthodox views than traditional ones. I am very much aware that it would have been possible to compile an equally interesting book with a completely different set of texts.

I am greatly indebted to the Revd Dr John Munsey Turner and to Professor John Briggs for supplying me with Methodist and Baptist material respectively; Janet Scott was also helpful in relation to the Society of Friends. The final choice of documents was my own.

I am most grateful to the Association of Denominational Historical Societies and Cognate Libraries for a grant towards the typing of material for this volume.

I am also grateful to the authorities in the Baptist Union, the Methodist Church, the Society of Friends, the General Assembly of the Unitarian and Free Christian Churches, and the United Reformed Church for allowing me to reproduce copyright material without charge. I wish to thank Mrs Ann Munro, formerly of the Faculty of Divinity at Cambridge, and my wife, Margaret, for helping to prepare material for the computer.

David M. Thompson

Acknowledgements

I am grateful to the following for permission to reproduce the copyright texts indicated:

The Revd Dr Ivor Jones for III.10
The Revd Dr Robinson Milwood for I.21
Mrs Ruth Micklem for III.10
The Revd Dr Colin Morris for VI.15, VIII.14(a)
Professor Edward Royle for I.2
Professor Frances Young for IV.9(b)
The Baptist Historical Society for II.7, II.9, II.14, III.11, VIII.21
The Baptist Union for I.19, I.23, I.24, II.11, II.17, II.18, VI.13, VII.9, VII.17, VIII.24
Churches of Christ Trustee Company for VIII.11
Churches Together in Britain and Ireland for I.17, VIII.15, VIII.20, VIII.21
Churches Together in England for V.16, VIII.9
Yearly Meeting of the Religious Society of Friends in Britain for VII.7, VIII.23
The Methodist Publishing House for I.12, I.14, II.8, II.10, II.19, III.2, III.7, III.8, IV.9(a), VI.14, VII.4, VII.5, VII.11, VII.15, VII.16, VII.18, VIII.3, VIII.12, VIII.13, VIII.14(b), VIII.25
The Methodist Recorder for I.13, I.15, VIII.7
The World Council of Churches for VIII.23
The United Reformed Church for I.9, I.22, II.3, II.13, II.15, II.16, III.4, III.6, III.9, III.12, IV.5, IV.8, V.14, V.15, V.17, V.18, V.19, VI.11, VI.16, VII.3, VII.6, VII.8, VII.10, VII.12, VII.13, VII.14, VIII.10, VIII.17, VIII.18, VIII.26, VIII.27
The United Reformed Church History Society for II.4, VI.12
Bryntirion Press for I.4
Cambridge University Press for III.3
Century Publishing for V.9
The Continuum International Publishing Group for IV.9(c), IV.13, VI.5
David Hyams Associates for I.7
Eyre Methuen for V.3
Harper Collins for V.22, V.23
Hodder & Stoughton for I.10
Huddersfield Local History Society for I.2
Lindsey Press for IV.11
Oxford University Press, New York for IV.10 (b)
SCM-Canterbury Press for I.16, IV.12, VIII.15
Stainer & Bell Ltd for III.10
Taylor & Francis for IV.10(a)

Urban Theology Unit for I.20
Weidenfeld & Nicholson for V.21

Every effort has been made to trace copyright owners, and apologies are extended to anyone whose rights have inadvertently not been acknowledged.

Introduction

Nonconformity entered the twentieth century confident that this would be 'their' century. There was scarcely any sense of the numerical decline that would dominate views of the century by its end.[1] In 1900 there were c. 728,000 Methodists in England, 257,000 Congregationalists, 239,000 Baptists and 76,000 Presbyterians; in 1950 there were c. 684,000 Methodists, 209,000 Congregationalists, 207,000 Baptists and 69,000 Presbyterians. By 1970 the Methodists were down to c. 572,000, Congregationalists 151,000, Baptists 173,000 and Presbyterians 59,000; and by the end of the century Methodist membership was c. 330,000 (with a Community Roll three times the size), Baptists were 137,000, the United Reformed Church 87,000 and the Congregational Federation 11,000.[2] Thus the Baptist rate of decline has consistently been the least, whereas the rate of decline among Congregationalists and Presbyterians has been the greatest. In fact, nonconformity had ceased to grow as a proportion of the population in the 1870s, though there were no numerical downturns until around 1907–8. Some voices expressed concern – the Methodist, Charles Kelly, warned of the alienation of young people from contemporary church life – but only after the First World War did anyone speak as if this represented a trend. Nevertheless the concerns expressed in the 1890s about unnecessary competition between the Free Churches, particularly in villages and new suburbs, continued into the new century; and one of the hopes for the National Council of Evangelical Free Churches founded in 1896 was that it would facilitate co-operation. There remained a substantial difference in polity and outlook between Methodism and the other Free Churches, but the Baptist and Congregational Unions continued to discuss ways of working together.

The number of men killed in the First World War obviously had an impact, though there is no evidence to suggest that the Free Churches suffered proportionately more or less deaths than society as a whole. More significantly, whereas before the war the average size of a congregation tended to exceed the number of members, from then on it was increasingly common for it to be fewer, reflecting a diminution in the fringe of adherents from which new members might be drawn. Internal discipline of members, which had been declining in the later nineteenth century, more or less completely disappeared after the war. The concentration of the Free Churches in the Midlands and the North of England, which had reflected growth in the Industrial Revolution, became more of a liability as economic depression affected the country in the inter-war years. The accelerated change of family businesses into limited liability companies removed one standard source for the large donations necessary for building new churches.[3] Nor was it so easy to keep up with a mobile population. The Town and Country Planning Act of 1948 introduced further restrictions after the Second World War.

Sunday School numbers remained relatively static in the first half of the century, but plunged from 24 per cent of the age cohort in 1960 to 9 per cent in 1980 and 4 per cent in 2000.[4] Whereas in the nineteenth century Sunday scholars tended not to be the children of members, this changed as the twentieth century proceeded; but the development of new leisure patterns and a different approach to the weekend had a more dramatic effect. If ministers in the 1890s had been worried about bicycles, the motor car made a more substantial difference, especially as ownership spread from the middle to the working classes. In the 1960s new research on religious education cast doubt on when children were 'ready for religion', and a concern for 'all age worship' offered a different justification for not providing separate activities for children. However well intentioned, the effects of this seem to have been to accelerate decline.

The increase in young people entering higher education from the 1960s meant that more of them moved away from home, often never to return. This geographical (and social) mobility, which had always been a threat to continuity of religious affiliation, accentuated the problem of retaining the children of members within the churches in which they had been brought up. Retention rates dropped. Indeed the improvements in life expectancy after 1945 probably disguised the extent to which nonconformity was losing its hold on the population, because its age structure was increasingly skewed towards the elderly. This change, coupled with the inflation that dominated the British economy between 1960 and 1990, also reduced the financial resources of church members on which the churches needed to draw, both to pay ministers and to invest in new buildings. By the 1990s a much higher proportion of ministers were being ordained after the age of 40 than had been conceivable at the beginning of the century.

The geographical and social mobility hinted at reflected a much greater integration of nonconformity into British life than had been characteristic of the nineteenth century. Asquith and Lloyd George were the first Prime Ministers to come from a nonconformist background: Asquith represented one strand of nonconformist Liberalism – from Lyndhurst Road Congregational Church, Hampstead; Lloyd George represented another – Welsh radicalism from Cricceith Church of Christ. The period 1972–90 was the longest with a succession of Prime Ministers with nonconformist origins, though the fact that this was never remarked upon at the time illustrates the perceived decline in the political importance of nonconformity. But it also shows that nonconformity was no longer a barrier to the highest office. A similar integration is reflected in many of the professions. Nonconformist ministers became Mayor's Chaplains, and the discrimination which had so irritated nineteenth-century nonconformists became a thing of the past. Furthermore in the twentieth century more nonconformists were prepared to become Anglicans. The father of Michael Ramsey, 100th Archbishop of Canterbury, for example, was a Congregational Sunday School Superintendent.

There were also significant changes in the pattern of church life as the century proceeded. In the nineteenth century the churches, particularly in the towns, were established largely as a result of preaching, and then put down roots into the community by establishing Sunday Schools and a range of benefit clubs and social activities. Such 'institutional churches' were still being commended as the way forward as the century began. But certain functions were secularised after the First, and even more after the Second, World Wars. Medical assistance, particularly for pregnant mothers, was rendered obsolete by the development of the National Health Service. Many nonconformist day schools were handed over to Local Education Authorities after 1902. Women's meetings became increasingly occupations for the retired, as the number of married women at work rose steadily towards the end of the century. Only mother-and-toddler groups grew, largely because local authorities were generally not able to afford to run them. Yet the assumption that such social activities should be the norm still remained in many churches at the end of the century. What had changed, however, was that now these tended to fill the gaps in public provision. There also remained a delicate balance between seeing such activities as the provision of a service or a means of evangelism.

A more subtle change in nonconformist life was the shift away from preaching as the central part of Sunday worship. Obviously preaching remained important, and although the frequency of communion increased it was only rarely every week. But the days when a church could gather its congregation essentially on the basis of the effectiveness of its minister's preaching have largely disappeared. This is mainly due to the changed place of the sermon in British society. The development of a popular press since the 1890s and the development of radio after the First World War and television (on a large scale) after the Second substantially changed the relative significance of sermons in the public consciousness. The same thing happened to political speeches: although still made, they are now aimed more at the wider audience to be reached through the media than the local audience on the spot. The length of sermons diminished steadily through the century; whereas 45 minutes was not uncommon at the beginning, by the end 20 minutes was the expected maximum. The style of preaching changed too, with more churches using a lectionary as the standard pattern for services; and there was closer attention to the context of the biblical text. The various series of biblical commentaries published (even in paperback) illustrated the change from the nineteenth century, though some of these began towards the end of that century. However, among some of the newer Free Churches in immigrant communities the significance of preaching is as great as ever.

Several references have already been made to the two World Wars. Their effects were both direct and indirect. Loss of life and loss of chapel buildings in the Second were significant. Polarisation of attitudes to pacifism and conscription led to bitterness and in some cases division: the treatment of conscientious objectors in the First World War was particularly harsh, and the problems caused by some members of churches who were magistrates sitting in judgement on others who took a pacifist line were considerable. Nonconformists could no longer be regarded as instinctively 'anti-war'. Some of these divisions were anticipated in the attitudes to the Boer War from 1899 to 1902, but the sheer scale of suffering in the First World War dwarfed the significance of the South African conflict. In many ways the German invasion of Belgium in 1914 – and the German invasion of Poland in 1939 – simplified the issues at stake. But in other ways it soon became apparent that Britain was engaged in a new kind of total war, which did not have a nineteenth-century precedent. The development of aerial bombardment as a routine form of warfare, described by the Presbyterian Church of England Assembly in 1937 as 'terrorism', threatened to render traditional armies almost obsolete, except as those who had to 'mop up' the enemy afterwards. Certainly this was reflected in American policy in Vietnam in the 1960s and 1970s, and in Iraq from 1990. The development of nuclear weapons also significantly changed the terms of debate after 1945, until the threat of a 'nuclear winter' as the consequence of extended nuclear warfare began to affect calculations in the 1980s. However, the end of communism in the Soviet Union also significantly changed the world scene. All this emphasised the fact that international affairs loomed much larger in the thinking of the Free Churches in the twentieth than in the nineteenth century.

There was also a more subtle consequence of the World Wars. Each of them, in slightly different ways, enhanced the power of the state vis-à-vis the individual, and many of the powers assumed by the state in wartime were not given up when peace returned. Indeed the social reforms of the post-1945 Labour government increased the state bureaucracy in a variety of ways. The lives of citizens in the second half of the twentieth century became more regulated, often to their benefit but sometimes to their irritation. In a curious way the various church bureaucracies almost imitated that governmental development, though not consciously. The number of staff in the central administration of the churches tended to increase, often but not always ministers, sometimes prompting the feeling that some of them could be more usefully engaged in serving local churches – since the decline in church membership was reflected in a decline in the number of candidates offering for the ministry.

The changing role of the state and the rise of the Labour Party also affected the relation of the Free Churches to politics. Nonconformity had never been totally identified with the Liberal Party in the nineteenth century, although the decade before the First World War probably saw a closer identification because of the 1902 Education Act and the 1904 Licensing Act. Nonconformist Conservatives were always a small minority. The collapse of political Liberalism after the First World War spread opinion more widely, with some moving to Labour, some staying with the Liberals and others becoming Conservatives. Certain social issues such as temperance receded in importance; others, such as unemployment, poverty at home and abroad, and racial discrimination, became more important; whilst issues concerned with sexual morality were never associated with one political party. By the 1950s nonconformist political opinion was much more evenly divided, and even an attempt to rally business support behind the Billy Graham Crusade of 1954 on the ground that it would stiffen British resistance to Communism failed miserably.[5] Increasingly the churches came to see themselves as pressure groups on the edge of party politics, which in truth is probably what nonconformists had been for most of the nineteenth century too. At the same time, partly because of the process of church bureaucratisation described earlier, a greater gap developed between the initiatives which churches might take locally, such as arranging regular meals for the homeless, and the language of resolution and amendment which characterised national assemblies. At the end of the century there were probably still as many nonconformists involved in politics at various levels as at the beginning, but their

Introduction

nonconformist identity was less likely to be either presented by themselves or perceived by others as a key factor in their political work.

Welsh Disestablishment in 1920 was the last move in that direction. The reunion of the Church of Scotland in 1929 left the Church as the national Church, but with few embedded privileges apart from those granted by custom; subsequent developments in Scotland demonstrated how powerful they were. The Church of England secured greater freedom to govern itself with minimal interference by parliament, first by the Enabling Act of 1919 and then more significantly by the Synodical Government Measure of 1969 and the Worship and Doctrine Measure of 1974. This implemented the main recommendation of the Chadwick Report on Church and State of 1970, and gave the Church of England freedom to change its forms of worship without reference to parliament, provided that the Book of Common Prayer of 1662 remained available. Some nonconformists resented these developments as giving the Church of England the benefits of self-government whilst retaining the privileges of establishment; others welcomed them as a recognition by the Church that parliamentary supremacy was no longer appropriate. The Church of England had four Commissions on Church and State between 1913 and 1970; interestingly there was no pressure for further consideration in the last thirty years of the century. Even the Free Churches' own Commission on the matter, which reported in 1953, acknowledged that the issue was shifting from special recognition for the Church of England to special recognition for Christianity. There never had been much enthusiasm in the Free Churches for the completely secularist French solution to the problem. The twentieth century also demonstrated, much more clearly than had been apparent in the nineteenth, that the Free Churches themselves depended on parliament for approval of crucial changes in their life and work. After the unhappy experience of the United Presbyterian Church and the Free Church of Scotland at the beginning of the century, when their union was successfully challenged in the courts by the Free Church minority, it was clear that any measure of church union required an Act of Parliament; and in different ways the Salvation Army Act of 1931 and the Baptist and Congregational Trusts Act of 1951 reflected the churches' need to involve parliament to place certain kinds of internal decision beyond legal challenge. Free Churches did not seem to be quite so free as some late nineteenth-century propaganda had suggested.

If the nineteenth century had been a time of divisions among nonconformists, the twentieth was a time when efforts were made to put things together again, with mixed success. The Bible Christians, Methodist New Connexion and United Methodist Free Churches united in 1907 to become the United Methodist Church; and this Church joined with the Wesleyan and Primitive Methodists to form the Methodist Church in 1932 – only the Independent Methodists and the Wesleyan Reform Union were left out of that union among the main Methodist Churches in Britain. The Congregational Union and the Presbyterian Church of England made a covenant with each other in 1951 after deciding that the time was not appropriate for organic union; and eventually they came together in 1972 to form the United Reformed Church. The majority of Churches of Christ joined them in 1981, and in 2000 the Congregational Union of Scotland became part of the Church as well.

However, efforts to bring the Free Churches closer to the Church of England were less successful. The conversations initiated after the Lambeth Conference of 1920 made some significant progress, but stalled over the recognition of the nonconformist ministry. The Anglican-Methodist proposals of the 1960s, which had begun as a result of Archbishop Fisher's initiative of 1946, failed to secure a sufficient majority in the Church of England in 1969 and 1972. A more comprehensive attempt to secure a covenant among the main English Churches in 1980 also failed to gain a sufficient majority in the General Synod, although a slightly differently worded covenant was signed among the same churches in Wales in 1975. At the end of the century discussions began for an Anglican-Methodist Covenant, which was signed in 2003. The British Churches were also involved in a variety of union conversations in Commonwealth territories: the earliest was the United Church of Canada (Methodist, Congregationalist, Presbyterian) in 1925; the most significant was the Church of South India (Anglican, Methodist, Congregationalist, Presbyterian) in 1947, because of the recognition offered to nonconformist ministers in a church which was to be episcopal. Other united churches were formed in Southern Africa, Zambia, Jamaica and Grand Cayman, North India (involving Baptists and Churches of Christ), Pakistan, Sri Lanka and Australia.

The increase in immigration from the Caribbean after 1948 and the development of significant student communities from Africa in the 1950s and 1960s brought black churches into Britain. To a large extent their establishment reflected the lack of welcome offered to immigrants by the traditional churches, but they also strengthened the charismatic movement which took off in the 1960s. In 1990 several of these churches joined Churches Together in England – some had been members of the British Council of Churches before. For most of the later twentieth century their growth rates were higher than those of the traditional churches. They were concentrated in towns where immigration had been greatest – London, the Midlands and the textile towns of the North of England. It remains to be seen how successful they will be in holding on to the second and third generations.

The last third of the century also saw a growth among the conservative evangelical parts of the traditional churches. Some were affected by the charismatic movement, but only a minority. Liberal evangelicals had been the mainstream, but following the fundamentalist controversies of the 1930s, which mainly affected the Baptists with some echoes elsewhere, there had been a tendency for conservative evangelicals to gather together rather than taking a leading part in the national church life of their particular churches. However, following the Keele Congress of Anglican Evangelicals in 1967, when they decided to play a full part in the life of the new General Synod, the prospects of a united evangelical front receded. Evangelical Congregational churches formed their own Fellowship in 1972 rather than join the United Reformed Church. Evangelicals had always played a significant minority role in Methodism. So the effects of the growth in evangelicalism were felt most strongly among the Baptists, and they dominated the leadership of the Baptist Union from the early 1980s. The Evangelical Alliance became once more a powerful force. It established its own Relief Fund to participate in aid to the developing world, and its influence increased under the

Introduction

eirenic and imaginative leadership of Joel Edwards, a minister of the New Testament Church of God and General Secretary from 1997.

Various explanations have been offered for nonconformist decline in the twentieth century. Alan Ruston suggested that nonconformity forgot the vital principle of not rendering to Caesar the things that are God's in the First World War, which resulted in a loss of influence in national affairs they never recovered.[6] In effect, their integration into the mainstream of British society epitomised by the war removed their distinctive identity. Others have also argued that the key lies in a loss of specific nonconformist identity, whilst locating the timing differently. Robert Currie argued that 'ecumenicalism' eliminated the minority traditions in Methodism and eventually threatened the elimination of Methodism altogether.[7] More recently Callum Brown has offered a radical interpretation for the decline of all British Christianity, with a critique of the secularisation hypothesis in general and the myths of the unholy city and the alienated working class in particular; instead he suggests that Christianity ceased to provide a narrative framework within which men understood their lives from 1800 and similarly for women from 1960. Thus people no longer turned to Christianity to interpret their existence, and the churches suffered accordingly.[8]

It is certainly true that the First World War exposed the limitations of the old nineteenth-century style voluntaryism in the context of the modern state, and that theologians in particular and the membership of the Free Churches more generally were slow to grasp the implications of this, let alone to offer an alternative view. It is also true that social and political integration, and the theological rapprochement represented by the ecumenical movement, made older points of difference and specific identity seem less relevant. However, theologians, and perhaps even church historians, have always tended to exaggerate the importance of the theological elements in the identity of the various Free Churches. The importance of the ways in which nonconformists exploited the 'them' and 'us' characterisation of particular socio-political situations, often at the expense of one another, cannot be exaggerated. In this respect differences, conventionally described in terms of social class though actually more subtle than a simple economic definition, may still be more important than some recent commentators have suggested. Undoubtedly the issue of different gendered perceptions requires more research and may yield more important new insights. New alienated or marginalised groups of the twentieth century such as ethnic minorities have retained a collective enthusiasm for a style of preaching and worship that probably has more in common with traditional nonconformity than many modern nonconformists would be happy to admit. Yet there are men and women who still attend nonconformist churches, and as we challenge the need to explain why many stay away we are confronted with the need to explain why those who go still do. Moreover, some of those who have adopted new worship styles which are in some sense 'conservative', and whose churches are growing, are also middle-class. This leaves Callum Brown's point about the power of discursive Christianity as a way of understanding one's life. Although there is a significant point here, this explanation may be more theological than the evidence warrants; nor does it explain why nonconformity suffered more than others.

In its origins nonconformity was counter-cultural. Christianity itself, at least until the conversion of Constantine, was also profoundly counter-cultural. Over nearly four hundred years the particular aspects of the culture which nonconformity sought to counter changed. No one can doubt that at the end of the twentieth century there are still many aspects of contemporary culture which need to be countered. Perhaps therefore the whole quest for 'recognition' and 'integration' (as distinct from recognition of the right to exist) was misconceived; and the problems faced by nonconformity in particular and Christianity in general in the twenty-first century lie in establishing agreement on the ways in which modern culture needs to be countered and in winning people for that stance. Jesus told his disciples that they should not expect to be popular.

So how did nonconformity stand at the end of the twentieth century? Clearly by most criteria its influence in national life was significantly less than at the beginning. This decline was greater proportionately than that of the Church of England or the Roman Catholic Church. On the other hand, the complete effects of this will not be felt for another generation, since many of those in positions of social and political leadership have been influenced by nonconformity; and a not insignificant proportion of members of the Church of England began their spiritual journey in the Free Churches. There are many lively and committed people in churches up and down the land; indeed the characteristic commitment of nonconformists in both church and society needs most emphasis. Moreover in the political life of early twenty-first-century Britain there is a continued need for a nonconformist witness, marked by a willingness to suffer the consequences, that is completely different from the personal harrassment to which some extremist protest groups have resorted. It is difficult to imagine that the Anti-Vaccination Campaign of the late nineteenth century would have been as successful one hundred years later, and when it is remembered that this was the precedent for the introduction of conscientious objection to military service in the First World War, that is a sobering reflection. The recognition that religious conviction has a priority beyond that of civil allegiance, which is also a reminder that there is a community beyond particular national borders, is something that nation states will always be reluctant to acknowledge. In a multi-faith society it raises issues which were undreamt of by nonconformists in previous centuries. But it also reminds us of those societies and periods of history in which different religious communities have lived together in a mutually enriching way – something which has not been a frequent part of British history.

Notes

1. For a deeper analysis of the twentieth century, see the essays in Sell & Cross (2003), Clements (1983), Munson (1991) and the essays by Rupert Davies and D. M. Thompson in Davies (1982).
2. Currie, Gilbert & Horsley (1977), pp. 133–5, 142–4, 149–51; Denominational Year Books.

Introduction

3. Sell & Cross (2003), pp. 266–8; Jeremy (1990), pp. 13–17; Munson (1991), pp. 14–25.
4. Sell & Cross (2003), p. 203.
5. Jeremy (1990), pp. 401–10.
6. Sell & Cross (2003), p. 263.
7. Currie (1968), pp. 296–316.
8. Brown (2001).

PART I

CHURCH LIFE

Introduction

In 1902–3 the *Daily News* conducted surveys of attendance in London churches, which were analysed by area and denomination. In many ways it is unfortunate that there should be such a detailed treatment of London and so little on other towns, since London was not typical of anywhere else in the country. Nevertheless the results are interesting. The lessons suggested (**I.1**) are the importance of preaching, the need to change the style of church buildings, the need for the churches to go to the people rather than expecting the people to come to them, and the need for the gospel to address social and political issues, which clearly go beyond what can simply be inferred from statistical analysis. But they were associated with a conviction that in many parts of London the Free Churches were better placed to take advantage of the situation facing them. In some ways the underlying situation is not unlike the situation outlined in the final volume of Charles Booth's massive survey of the Life and Labour of London, where the popular attitude to Sunday is significantly linked with 'holidays and amusements'. There the emphasis lies upon non-attendance at church (or chapel) rather than the reverse, but in the context of the multiplications of other kinds of amusement for the mass of the population, with the implication that church-going was the result of having nothing better to do.[1] What lies buried beneath both these surveys is the suggestion that the churches are holding their own rather than attracting new people, which was bound to have long-term implications for church growth.

Both these surveys endorsed the significance of the development of the 'institutional church', where a chapel had a vast range of other activities associated with it (**I.2**) – illustrated from Huddersfield, but it could have been any town – and the 'Pleasant Sunday Afternoon' movement (**I.3**), which likewise was found in most towns. Both these developments were adopted by Methodists and non-Methodists alike. They go back into the late nineteenth century but became widespread by the time of the First World War. It proved difficult to revive them on the same scale after 1918, and Stephen Yeo has demonstrated how some of the activities associated with institutional churches were secularised.[2] Certainly the football clubs that originated in association with some churches developed a life of their own quite quickly. As soon as the link between those who attended the auxiliary activities and those who attended Sunday services was broken, the auxiliaries failed to contribute to church growth as such.

Of course, traditional revivalism was still not dead. The Welsh Revival of 1904–5 (**I.4**) illustrated that. The Free Churches had organised the National Simultaneous Mission in 1901 as a way of utilising traditional techniques, and it was not unsuccessful.[3] A number of preachers, such as Rodney 'Gipsy' Smith, had a reputation for powerful preaching in such circumstances. Yet the tide was clearly turning for such efforts. Even the success of the Welsh Revival concealed the downturn in church membership in England for two or three years if totals for England and Wales are taken as the guide.

The cost of supporting church life was also striking home. In many parts of the country and in several denominations chapels had been built on borrowed money, so that the task of servicing and, if possible, reducing the chapel debt was a regular part of life. The other major cost for a congregation was payment of a minister. Some very small churches could never afford this and depended on lay preachers; but in the early twentieth century many village chapels still had their own minister. Seat rents had originally been the main source for supporting chapels, and they remained significant in middle-class churches. But the growing movement in the Church of England to remove seat rents from the 1870s affected the Free Churches also. Baptist discussion about the proposal to depend entirely on freewill offerings (**I.5**) illustrates the problem: it could produce more money, but it was also more unpredictable. After the First World War seat rents disappeared much more quickly, although the allocation of particular seats to members and their families often remained.

Nevertheless the kind of optimism that still characterised public nonconformist pronouncements is illustrated by the Congregational Union Council Report of 1913 (**I.6**). Despite the disappointments of the Liberal Governments of 1906 and 1910 (see Part V), nonconformists still hoped to achieve their rightful place in the country. And then came the war.

Norman Nicholson's description of Millom in the early 1920s (**I.7**) suggests that initially things did not change much. There were regular missions and many other activities associated with the chapel; for those who went it was still the centre of their lives. But thereafter the situation began to change rapidly. A Congregational Union survey in the early 1930s (**I.8**) described the difficulties and new opportunities for village churches. The spread of car ownership after the Second World War accelerated many of the trends there described, as it became easier to live in the country and work in the town. So the Methodist Report on Rural Churches of 1958 (**I.14**), some twenty years later, illustrated both the extent to which things were not changing and the continuing significance of village churches in the life of the Free Churches as a whole.[4] New possibilities arose from the Sharing of Church Buildings Act of 1969 and Canon B15A of 1972, which permitted Trinitarian baptised Christians in good standing to receive Holy Communion in the Church of England as guests; these led to Local Ecumenical Partnerships in many places. In 1995 Baptists emphasised that rural churches were not simply small town churches, but could do quite different things (**I.24**).

Victor Murray was still appealing for the Free Churches to come together in an address to the Free Church Federal Council in 1946 (**I.9**). In fact, Archbishop Fisher's appeal to the Free Churches 'to take episcopacy into their system', as a way of creating intercommunion without organic unity, diverted energies away from the plans for Free Church union that had been under discussion just before war broke out; and the fact that Methodism responded to that appeal, whereas the other Free Churches did not, meant that it was not until the failure for a second time of the Anglican-Methodist unity scheme in 1972 that it became possible once more to think of a way forward which would bring the Free Churches together rather than confirming their separation.

Evangelistic developments in the period after 1945 tended therefore to remain firmly denominational. Methodism tried several tactics and Donald Soper's Order of Christian Witness (**I.10**) illustrates one of them. Billy Graham made his first visit to England in 1954, and his campaigns were supported by interdenominational teams (including the Church of England) and several wealthy business men.[5]

At the same time significant changes were taking place in work with children. For more than a century the essential pattern of the Sunday School had remained unchanged. Gradually in the twentieth century Sunday schools became confined to the children of church members. This trend accelerated in the 1950s (**I.11**) when there was a sharp decline in Sunday scholars in Methodism (**I.12**). Such changes tended to marginalise the significance of new developments, such as youth clubs. Methodism put increasing emphasis on youth clubs from the 1950s and the same was true in the other Free Churches. All this was happening before the much sharper changes in youth culture of the 1960s appeared, so not everything can be attributed to cheap record players and pop music. The Free Churches had organised themselves to cater for university students: the picture of the Methodist Society at Cambridge (**I.13**) could be paralleled not only at Oxford and in London, but elsewhere; and there were CongSocs as well as MethSocs, and the Baptist Student Federation. They benefited to some extent from the increase in university students, particularly after 1961; but they were often smaller than their pre-war equivalents in a much smaller university population. In other words, nonconformity was squeezed where it hurt most – in the rising generation. The significance of the relatively smaller numbers in the 1960s became apparent by the 1980s, when the decline in nonconformist church membership became much more marked.

It is not surprising that a sense of frustration should have emerged at the difficulty in securing co-operation among the Free Churches. Even in Methodism, which had reunited in 1932, the same frustration was felt (**I.15**). Sometimes where Methodist chapels of different pre-1932 persuasions failed to join together, all of them eventually closed.

The problems of Methodism in different kinds of location are well illustrated by a sociological analysis of the 1960s (**I.16**). Suburbanisation from the inter-war period accentuated the separation of different social classes.[6] Nevertheless even in housing estates a chapel could survive because leaders who no longer lived locally travelled to support them. This residential detachment from the location of nonconformist churches, not only in city centres where it had long been true, but even in suburban settings, meant that a church might suddenly lose leadership when people reached an age where they could no longer travel so easily and there were no replacements. The survival of nonconformity depended on the ability of churches to reproduce and renew not only their membership but also their leadership in the locality where they were. Increased personal mobility as a result of greater car ownership in the second half of the century disguised the exposed situation of many chapels which had lost their roots in their neighbourhood.

The most important new development after 1948 was the increase of immigration from the Caribbean, India, Pakistan and Africa which decisively changed the religious balance in many urban areas. The failure of so many white churches to absorb even those of the same denominational allegiance from the Caribbean led to the development of black churches. A study of 1971 (**I.17**) describes two of these churches, one Caribbean, the other West African. Various reasons can be advanced for the development of separate black churches: the culture shock experienced by migrants coming from a rural economy to a competitive urban industrial one; their reaction against racial discrimination in English churches; their conformity to the pattern of English working-class absence from church; but most of all, the failure of English churches to seize the missionary opportunity on their doorstep. As race became a major issue in British politics in the 1960s, particularly due to the Commonwealth Immigrants Act of 1962, the separate development of black churches in Britain accelerated. The ecumenical reorganisation of the 1980s more thoroughly integrated them into English church life.

But it would be wrong to imply that the mainstream English Free Churches were totally unsuccessful in this area. Madge Saunders from Jamaica worked as a Deaconess at St James's Presbyterian (later United Reformed) Church in Sheffield (**I.18**). By the end of the century all the major Free Churches had some black ministers, often those who had been brought up in England as children of immigrants. Methodism has at least one black District Chairman. Such ministers had significant opportunities (**I.21**).

The end of empire forced all the Churches to think about the future of their missionary activity. In some cases the churches in colonial territories became independent of missionary control before political independence (for example, in India), but even though British missionaries usually remained after independence there is no doubt that the whole context of missionary activity was changed as a result. The New Delhi Assembly of the World Council of Churches in 1961 coined the term 'mission in six continents', and the implications of this for Baptists, as pioneers of the modern missionary movement, were explained (**I.19**). Institutionally it was reflected in the transformation of the London Missionary Society into the Congregational Council for World Mission in 1966 (the Council for World Mission after the formation of the United Reformed Church).

Political independence for former colonies also removed the privileged position of Christianity in many of those territories and increased the significance of other faiths. Immigration also increased the number of those of other faiths in Britain itself. This brought into sharp relief the relationship between inter-faith dialogue on the one hand and missionary activity on the other. The Statement from the Baptist Union Council on this theme (**I.23**) is interesting precisely because of the increasing significance of conservative evangelical attitudes within the Baptist community. It also makes clear the fact that by the end of the twentieth century it was no longer possible to adopt one strategy at home and another strategy abroad.

By the end of the century too the Free Churches were recognising that the priority for Christian mission were the poor. John Vincent and his colleagues in the Urban Theology Unit (**I.20**) were some of the first to articulate this approach. From a historical perspective this clearly demonstrated that the age had definitely gone when the constituency of the Free Churches could in any sense be assumed to be part of the poor. If the twentieth century did not turn out to be the Nonconformists' century, this was in part a reflection of their detachment from the mass of the population. This was not only, or not primarily, a consequence of numerical decline; it was a reflection of social change, as a United Reformed Church report indicated in 1979 (**I.22**). Moreover, it was still felt by many that upward social mobility was incompatible with continued nonconformist ecclesiastical allegiance. The result was a steady haemorrhage of nonconformist young people to the Church of England or to nothing at all. Institutional survival depends on either continued recruitment or sustained replenishment of members.[7] The ability of nonconformity to recruit new members was declining from the late nineteenth century; the twentieth century added to this a failure to replenish members from within their existing constituency. The resulting decline accelerated from the 1970s.

Notes

1. Booth (1902), pp. 47–51.
2. Yeo (1976).
3. Sell & Cross (2003), pp. 184–5.
4. Cf. Marshall & Lucas (1968).
5. Jeremy (1990), pp. 397–410.
6. Sell & Cross (2003), pp. 186–7.
7. Thompson (2002); Pope (2000).

Document I.1

Nonconformity in London, 1902–3

R. Mudie-Smith, *The Religious Life of London* (London: Hodder & Stoughton, 1904), pp. 6–13.

The *Daily News* religious census was taken by counting attendances at the churches of London over the year 1902–3. Mudie-Smith's summary of its lessons emphasises the continued power of preaching, especially outdoor preaching, and sees the future in terms of the institutional church (see Document **I.3**).

… I entirely agree with those who deny that, in matters pertaining to religion, statistics are either the best or the final criterion. To assert that the place of worship with the largest congregation is the most successful would be as incorrect as to affirm the opposite… On the other hand, it is indisputable that figures are unimpeachable witnesses to vigour, progress, and interest.

The outstanding lesson of the Census is that the power of preaching is undiminished. Wherever there is the right man in the pulpit there are few, if any, empty pews. By the 'right man' I do not mean a genius. On the contrary, the preacher may be 'an extraordinarily ordinary' man, so long as he possesses strong convictions, keen sympathies, and a magnetic personality. He must have a large heart, and, if he is to be believed in by the people, a small salary. Whatever may have been the case in the past, I feel sure that to-day for a minister of the Gospel to receive an income in excess of what is needed for ordinary comfort is a stumbling-stone and a rock of offence. The masses subconsciously believe that a large stipend is not in harmony with the teaching and example of Jesus Christ. Each of us must determine for him or herself whether that belief is justified. That it exists is beyond question. It will be noted that the Free Church has a larger proportion of men attending her places of worship than the Established Church. This, I think, is accounted for by the fact that in the Free Church the emphasis is laid upon the sermon, whereas in the Established Church it is laid upon the service. Men are attracted by the former, women by the latter. It is frequently urged by many that this emphasis on the sermon is misplaced; that a congregation should assemble to render homage to the Creator rather than to receive instruction from His creatures. For my own part, I fail to see the incompatibility of these two ideas. At the same time, those who lay the greater stress on the sermon have ample and sufficient warrant in the practice of Jesus Christ. Extremely little is said in the reports of His work about the service; they are almost entirely concerned with the sermon…

The worship most acceptable to God is that of character. Such worship must be perpetual, and, for the most part, unconscious. Unless this state of waiting upon God is habitual, the adoption of the attitude at set times and seasons is an empty farce. If my contention be true, it follows that the service which is most worshipful is the one that best aids the growth and development of character. In this work the sermon plays, or should play, no unimportant part. If the preacher is to apologise for his presence, Christianity will soon have to explain its absence. In the Established Church the sermon does not have the place to which it is entitled; in consequence, the preaching standard is not high. I do not think it can be denied that the average sermon in the Established Church is below the average Free Church sermon. In the latter Church the service is sometimes so little regarded that the items composing it are termed 'preliminaries.' In consequence, those who appreciate music, a true aid to devotion, too often have to endure semi-torment. No amount of grace will make singing out of time or tune enjoyable, nor need the injunction to 'shout with a loud voice' be literally interpreted. It seems to be imagined that beauty and simplicity must for ever be divorced, whereas the very fact that the Free Church service is so simple makes it all the more imperative that each item should be carried out with the utmost care...

The second lesson the Census teaches is that the buildings we erect in the future must be the antithesis of those now in existence, if the working classes, and those below the working classes, are to be found within them. Churches with cold, repellent stone walls, furnished with forbidding, divisive pews (some cushioned and carpeted, others bare and uncomfortable), badly lighted and worse ventilated, must give place to large, handsome, central halls, well lit and well ventilated, furnished throughout with seats of one pattern, which permit of no arbitrary divisions based on class distinctions. Pews with their attendant rents and proprietary rights must provide 'alms for oblivion.' In a word, the churches, instead of being built in a style which fosters the spirit of caste, must symbolise in their architecture and their adornment the universal Fatherhood of God, the universal brotherhood of Man.

This hall or institutional church must be, will of necessity be, the centre of active, aggressive, social work. Open seven days a week, it will aim at the redemption and development of body, mind, and soul, and, while seeking to transform the lives of men, women, and children, will, at the same time, be equally anxious to transform their environment. The establishment of society upon the basis of brotherhood, of labour upon the basis of justice, of commerce upon the basis of honesty, of patriotism upon the basis of charity, will be fought for as tenaciously and enthusiastically as is the salvation of the individual.

This institutional church is, I am convinced, the solution of the problem presented by closely-congested, densely-populated neighbourhoods. In the returns given in this volume these buildings shine, as regards the numbers attending them, like stars in an inky firmament of failure. I do not deny that, given an exceptionally able man, much may be done with places of worship of a Gothic character, but the work is accomplished in spite of the buildings; and as extraordinary ability is the exception and ordinary ability is the rule, it is desirable that the structures should aid, not hinder, those in charge of them. I claim for the halls in question that they attract the people instead of deterring them. The statistics for the Wesleyan Methodist Church amply substantiate this claim. The only places where, judging by figures, they can be said to be successful, are their Central Missions; these illuminate an otherwise sombre record. The three years system is, I believe, responsible in a large degree for that record. That system, however well adapted for small towns and country villages, is ill adapted for large towns and cities; for it is a sheer impossibility to build up a church in a large town or city in less than five years, whilst in London it takes ten. The returns for the Baptist Church are a further proof of my contention. Her tabernacles differ little from the Central Mission-halls of the Wesleyan Methodist Church, and witness to a like success. Both these bodies reach the masses. Apart from the Methodists and the Baptists, the only other prosperous instances are due to special men rather than special methods; and such instances, I regret to say, are few and far between.

The third lesson emphatically enforced by the Census is that even in neighbourhoods where both men and methods are alike admirable, the majority of the inhabitants remain, owing to either indifference or hostility, uninfluenced and untouched. How are these to be reclaimed? There is only one way – since they will not come to us we must go to them, and go to them with our best, not our feeblest. It is manifest from John Wesley's Journal that, under God, we owe the religious revival of the eighteenth century to the re-discovery of Open-Air preaching. To-day that divine method of winning men has fallen into desuetude and disrepute. We have thought that anything or anybody was good enough for this work. As a result, preaching in the open air is almost the monopoly of men as earnest as they are unwise. On Sunday evenings, at occasional corners, a brother may be seen and heard addressing a handful of people, the majority of whom have accompanied him from the church or mission to which he is attached. The speaker has zeal, but it is 'not according to knowledge,' and none who are jealous for the Christian religion can listen to him without pain. Either text after text is hurled at the unfortunate and unhappy auditor, without connection, rhyme, or reason; or statements are made, narrow in thought, exaggerated in language, accompanied by promises of Heaven and threats of Hell, with an intensity worthy a Savonarola and an omniscience unpardonable in a Lord Chief Justice.

I fail to understand why a method adopted so habitually and with such success by Jesus Christ and His immediate disciples should be left to those least able to make efficient use of it. ... My proposal is that during the summer months, on fine evenings, the most influential preachers should close their churches, and with their choirs and congregations, go out into the streets and lanes of the city, and compel the people to listen to them. I do not think they would need much compelling. The 'common people' would hear them gladly; the uncommon people, too, would listen to the right men....

With our present methods we preach to almost the same congregations Sunday after Sunday. Those outside do not come in – they will not come in; we must go to lanes and docks, to wharves and parks, to courts and squares, to highways and byways; otherwise we lack the true missionary spirit, nor are we treading in the footsteps of Him who, moved by a divine discontent was not satisfied with the ordinary and seasonable opportunities of worship prescribed by custom or laid down by law, but 'went about doing good,' and remains for ever the pattern and type of that ample spirit which *seeks* in order that it may save.

The fourth and last lesson I draw from the Census is that, if the future is to be more bright than the present, the gospel we preach must cover the whole of a man's life. We owe the revival of the eighteenth century to the rediscovery of the worth of the individual soul and its personal responsibility. The revival of the twentieth century we shall owe to the discovery of the worth of the entire man and the responsibilities of the community. Our forefathers were content with a Heaven after death; we demand a Heaven here. They regarded themselves as pilgrims with no continuing city, 'mere desert-land sojourners'; we are determined that this Metropolis shall become the City of God. Nothing has so alienated the people from the ministrations of the Word as the age-long opposition of the Churches to their most elementary rights as human beings. Institutions are conservative, and the Churches as institutions have almost invariably been on the side of tyranny and oppression... If the Churches are to be loved they must lead. They must be in the van, not the rear, of progress if they are to be believed in. That gospel which does not concern itself with man's body, mind, and environment as well as his soul, is a contradiction in terms, a travesty of truth, a mockery of religion; it is no 'good news,' and usurps a title to which it has no claim. If we cannot make our politics part of our religion, we have no right to cast even a vote. If we cannot take our Christianity into a Borough Council, we ourselves ought to remain outside. If the message we believe in does not rank us in eternal, vehement opposition against the sweater, the slum-landlord, the trafficker in human lives, we need not expect the masses to take seriously either it or us. If cleaner streets, better housing, sweeter homes do not come within the scope of our aim, neither will those who are convinced that they have a right to these things come within the shadow of our places of worship. If we are not for ever seeking to remove the shackles which fetter men's bodies, minds, and spirits, we have yet to learn the alphabet of the programme of Christianity. The Spirit of the Lord is not upon us unless our tidings to the poor are 'good tidings'.

Document I.2

The 'Institutional Church'

Edward Royle, *Queen Street Chapel and Mission, Huddersfield* (Huddersfield: Huddersfield Local History Society, 1994), pp. 25–7.

The development of the 'institutional church' began in the 1890s and reached its peak in the years before the First World War. It provided a complete range of activities for the community seven days a week, and all the Free Churches developed this pattern of work in towns.

William Heap took charge of the Mission in 1906. In starting the Mission, William Heap embarked on a full programme of activities on both Sundays and weekdays. Some organisations, such as the Sunday School were continued from before; others were new. The first annual report details a Wesley Guild, a Band of Hope, a Men's Reading Room, a Boys' Brigade, a Girls' Club with ninety members, and a Sunday

School with 452 scholars which had grown by 573 by 1913. Five open air meetings were held each week, six cottage meetings, an open-air anti-gambling campaign was begun, and Sunday evening service was conducted in three lodging houses. The following year a 'Gospel Van' was added and 5,000 copies of the *Queen Street Monthly* magazine were distributed by eighty voluntary home visitors. Social work figured prominently in the activities of the Mission. Some of this was of a traditional kind – for example temperance work, with 450 pledges being taken during the first year. Other work was new to Queen Street, such as the Guild for Crippled Children and the Women's Home.

Meetings for worship, social work and leisure occupied seven days a week but Sundays were particularly crowded. The main service was on Sunday evenings, when the chapel was soon reported full and even on Sunday mornings 'steadily improving' congregations numbered around 300 in 1910. Volunteers visited lodging houses on Sunday evenings to bring 'outcasts' to services, and Pleasant Sunday Afternoon services were organized to attract men. On Monday, there were Pleasant Monday Afternoons for women at which the emphasis seems to have gone beyond worship; in 1908 the membership of 120 had a series of Health Lectures from a Mrs Montgomery. Also with women in mind, a Goose Club was organized to help them manage their finances for Christmas.

Following the lead of the Salvation Army, a brass band was purchased at the start of the Mission, which was played at Saturday evening meetings in the Beast Market – 'in spite of opposition from Secularists, Romanists, and, what is far more common, from men the worse for liquor'. A further attraction was the installation of a cinematograph, about the same time that the Congregationalists of Ramsden Street began showing lantern slides at the close of their Sunday evening service in an effort to attract larger congregations. The new technology was also in evidence at one of the most successful innovations at the Mission – the Bairns Bright Hour: whereas the average attendance at the Bairns services in 1908–9 was 167, at the lantern slide evenings it was 290; and in January 1911 two slide evenings drew 585 and 668 children whereas a speaker could attract only 288; and in summer attendances were down to sixty-five.

Boys were always more difficult to attract to Mission activities than girls, one remedy for which was the Lads' Club football team formed in 1911. Some tensions remained, though, between the religious purposes of the Mission and the secular attractions, which accompanied them. In 1928 the Scouts, who had been forbidden to play games on the premises on Sundays, were excluded for some unmentioned sin, presumably breach of that injunction. But the heirs to the men who in the 1870s had prohibited a performance of *The Messiah* now generally took a more relaxed view. In 1927 it was even decided to apply for a Dramatic Licence so that entertainments in costume might be given on the premises – though this was later abandoned, not through some moral objections but because of fire regulations.

Welfare work was undertaken in many areas. A Labour Bureau was set up and during the first year of the Mission, some fifty men and women were found temporary work while seeking employment and 160 cases of need were helped with clothing. After the First World War, the Mission premises were used for a Day

Nursery until the withdrawal of Corporation funding forced its closure in 1922, and by the Poor Law Board to administer relief to the unemployed. One step in 1922, which might have earlier been considered politically controversial, was to let the school room without charge to the Education Committee of the Industrial Society (that is, Huddersfield Cooperative Society) for a lecture in aid of the 'Save the Children's Fund' on behalf of the Russian Famine Relief Fund.

One of the most important activities was the Guild for Crippled Children – later known as the Cripples Guild – which developed social work with the disabled and at one time had over 200 members. It originated as club for crippled children, which met at Queen Street on Friday evenings, but soon the work was extended to practical assistance such as the provision of surgical boots, wheelchairs, and opportunities to make excursions into the countryside. In 1910, Ada Learoyd made the Guild her life's work. A cottage was acquired at Camp Hill at which residential work was begun, transferred to a home on Lindley Moor in 1922. Here care extended to treatment and in some cases cure or the alleviation of crippling disability thanks to the help of an orthopaedic surgeon, Professor T. P. McMurray of Liverpool. If miracles were performed, they were the miracles of modern medicine. Gradually, as the number of crippling childhood diseases declined, the nature of the work changed from the care of the young to the care of the elderly and in 1947 there were only about thirty children on the Guild register. Twenty years later, though, there was still found to be need for work among the disabled despite the opening of a new local authority Welfare Centre for the Handicapped.

Document I.3

The Pleasant Sunday Afternoon

F. B. Meyer, 'How to Work a PSA', *The Free Churchman*, March 1904, pp. 55–6.

It was recognised that work among men was the most difficult. The 'Pleasant Sunday Afternoon' was one solution, and this account by a leading Baptist minister illustrates several of the problems.

If I were to begin again I think I would adopt the title 'Men's Own' or 'Men's Brotherhood', instead of P.S.A. for the Pleasant Sunday Afternoon has in many cases fallen beneath the high standard designed by its founder, and which many of us have endeavoured to maintain. Too often it has become a mixed gathering of men and women for little else than a Social Meeting in which the moral and religious elements are overpowered by solos, recitations, and other pleasantries. In my opinion these mixed P.S.A.'s have a serious defect in depleting the morning and evening congregations, and lowering the standard of religious worship…

It was agreed that the meetings should be held in the church, the consent of our trustees having been obtained, rather than in any public hall, first, because it saved expense, and secondly in order to make the men feel that they were an integral part of the Church and its operations. A man who will cross the threshold of your place of worship in the afternoon will be more likely to feel a kind of proprietorship in the place, and will almost certainly reappear at the morning or evening services...

On the appointed afternoon some 250 men entered the church, and we followed the usual programme of a P.S.A. Meeting as supplied from headquarters, and which we have subsequently improved upon. I should be happy to send to any that contemplate starting such a meeting the programme which we now follow. With unusual trepidation I took the chair, and we went forward decorously enough, until we reached the time for my inaugural address. The men clapped me when I arose. This for a moment disconcerted me, and I thought my Gothic arches gave an involuntary shudder, but I realised that probably this was the men's way of saying Amen, Hallelujah! I remembered also that it was the practice of the early Church to receive the magnificent orations of the golden-tongued Chrysostom with similar manifestations of approval; I therefore said nothing by way of reproof or restraint, and a hearty clap with which they always greet me when I enter, and the applause that follows the singing of the solo, or any striking point of the address, does more than anything to promote the good fellowship of our gathering.

Two or three Sundays after we started, a group of the men came to me at the close of the meeting, and said 'Look here, guv'nor, is this going to be a blanket and coal affair?' I said, 'What do you mean?' They said, 'Are you going to give away a lot of things?' and I said, 'Not that I know of; I am going to do my best to help you to help yourselves.' They replied, 'If that's so, we'll come right enough, but if you are going to give away a lot, our mates would roast us for coming for what we could get.' I said, 'All right, I understand.' As a result we have given nothing, but the men have helped each other marvellously. They have a Help-one-Another Society, from which they make loans; they have two or three Benefit Societies; they have got a Coal Club, where they get the best coals at greatly reduced prices. Some are bent on starting a Co-operative Society, which I believe will be of immense service to the district. For the last one or two years the income from the P.S.A. from all sources has been about £1,500. We make a halfpenny collection each Sunday, half of which goes to maintain the Institute and Club, always open in the evening, and the other half is administered by the Committee of the Brothers to relieve cases of necessity. It is very much better for them to administer relief, as they understand each other's circumstances better than men of a different station could...

I generally get some one else to give the address, but always take the chair, and speak for seven or eight minutes at the end, in the simplest and directest way possible. Hundreds of drinking men have signed the pledge, hundreds have given their hearts to God, many have handed over playing cards, and other associations of the life which they have left for ever. The tone of certain streets has been entirely altered, and a body is being formed which is pledged to promote in Borough Elections the purity, righteousness, and well-being of the district.

The most interesting incidents are perpetually transpiring, for which in this brief article we have no space; and in concluding it I will only say that it is a great mistake to think that working men desire addresses on political economy and social economics. They long for, and appreciate, simple, manly talks about Christ, interspersed with good stories, ending with a straight appeal. They do not like ranting or being preached at, or anything weak and sentimental, but an earnest utterance of the claims of Christ is always enjoyed.

Document I.4

The Welsh Revival, 1904–5

Testimony of John Penry in B. P.Jones, *Voices from the Welsh Revival* (Bridgend: Evangelical Press of Wales, 1995), pp. 30–32.

The Welsh Revival of 1904–5 was one of the last major revivals in Britain, and had a particularly powerful effect on nonconformists in Wales, with a strong emphasis on the gifts of the Spirit.

On Sunday night after the service and singing practice in Bryn-teg, we went down to Moriah at 9.30 and the place was overflowing. Evan Roberts was there. This meeting had started after the minister had closed the first meeting. After taking charge of the meeting, Evan Roberts went from seat to seat and asking everyone personally whether they were willing to stand up and confess Jesus Christ. He started at the pulpit on the right hand. I had a seat next to the door and he came to the seat and said, 'Will you stand up to confess?' 'Yes,' I said, and I stood on my feet. I said to myself, 'Why can't I? I am religious!' I stood up to confess; I was not ashamed but not everyone stood. It was now about eleven o'clock and Evan went back to the big seat and said, 'We are going to finish this meeting now for there are children here and some want to go home to their children. But I want those who can stay to stay, and after everyone who has to go has gone out, we'll close the doors. No one shall come in or go out.' The majority went out until there were about fifty young people left under forty years of age.

The doors were locked and he asked us to gather in the seats in front of the big seat and said, 'We are not going to leave this meeting tonight till the Holy Spirit is poured out. I want you each to pray this short prayer, "O Lord, send the Holy Spirit now, for Jesus Christ's sake".' We began and went from each to each until all had prayed. 'The Holy Spirit has not come,' Evan Roberts said, 'so we must ask again.' We prayed again all the way round. 'Well,' he said, 'the Holy Spirit still has not come. We are not leaving this meeting tonight until the Holy Spirit has descended. We will start again.' And as we came to halfway down the second row of chairs a young woman broke out into tears, calling on the Lord. Then someone was praying elsewhere, and then another was sighing and weeping profusely. 'That's it,' said Evan Roberts, 'the Holy Spirit has come. We can go home from the meeting happy and rejoicing.' Afterwards he went up to the sighing and weeping ones. Everyone had been dealt with by 2 or 3 a.m.

I am sorry to say I wasn't able to be in the Bryn-teg meetings the following week, on Tuesday and Wednesday evenings, because I was in work. But when I was in work I could see the chapel, and there was much excitement among the night-shift workers. They were going out every now and again to see if the lights were still on in Bryn-teg Chapel. We all of us went out in turns and there was a real stirring up of the tin-works because the ungodly were fearful and amazed to see lights in the chapel at three and four and five in the morning. It was 5.30 a.m. before the lights went out...

On Sunday morning I went as usual to the 9.30 a.m. meeting at Bryn-teg, but this Sunday there was no preacher. Mr Stephens had been obliged to stop preaching because the people who had been saved and sanctified during the week wanted to take the meeting themselves ... [There was no Sunday school that afternoon, but rather another revival meeting. At that meeting] I had a vision of Jesus hanging on the cross. My head was in my hands and I was in tears for about an hour. My sister had been blessed that week and she said, 'John, come on your knees here. Pray.' I went on my knees and prayed, 'God be merciful to me a sinner,' Sin had come home! As God sees sin, not as we see it. I rose to my feet. That's all! That's all! The tears stopped and joy came in. That night before going to the meeting I went to the bottom of the garden to pray, asking God to be in the meeting that night. As soon as the meeting started, I went to the big seat to try to tell what God had done for me that afternoon, but other people were queuing up to speak from the big seat and there was no opportunity for me to speak, yet I did tell them what happened that afternoon. I said, 'Look here! I went through a wonderful experience this afternoon. I saw myself as a great sinner and, you know, Jesus Christ has forgiven my sin and I love Him with all my heart. My heart was like flint, now it is like a lake of water. The Lord has done great things.' You know, the glory of the Lord and the joy of the Lord came into my life to such a degree as to be indescribable, until I felt I was a new man in body, soul and spirit. The only verse that came to me at that time was, 'Put off thy shoes from off thy feet, for the place whereon thou standest is holy ground.'

Document I.5

Free Will Giving, 1906

Letters on Systematic Giving (London, 1906), pp. 1–6.

This pamphlet is a reprint of correspondence in the *Baptist Times and Freeman*, which raised an issue which was to be ever more important in the twentieth century – how were the Free Churches supported. There had been a gradual move away from seat rents in the later nineteenth century, but this meant that more emphasis had to be placed on the understanding of what, after the Second World War, came to be called stewardship.

Dear Sir, For some time past the question 'How much owest thou unto my Lord?' has been pressing itself upon me, and I am now moved to write to you on the subject.

In common, no doubt, with the great majority of your readers, I am continually receiving (and especially at this season of the year) pressing appeals from the ministers and treasurers of Churches and charitable institutions for help in their work. These arrive at the rate of six or eight every week, and doubtless some of your readers receive a good many more. I for one do not complain in any way, for how else could the authors of these appeals obtain the necessary funds for the good work in which they are engaged? And yet at the end of each financial year how many of these Churches and charitable institutions find that the balance is on the wrong side, however much economy they may have exercised? How many Churches are there burdened with very heavy debts, the interest on which cripples their resources, and prevents great and good work being done for the Lord?

I have for many years past been convinced that this arises from the Church of Christ not fully realising its obligations to its Lord, and, therefore, not bringing systematically its tithes into His treasury. I firmly believe that there never would be any lack of funds for carrying on the Lord's work if every member of His Church consecrated to His service a definite portion of his income, to be decided by him after earnest prayer for guidance in this very important matter, and then most conscientiously adhered to this rule, whatever denial of self it might occasion. How often the joy of giving is clouded by the question, 'Can I afford it?' and this would be prevented altogether if the Christian Church acted upon this rule of systematic giving. The money in each home treasury would provide a fund out of which it would become a real pleasure to give for the service of the Lord.

Why should not the Baptists take a lead in this movement as they have done in many others? If a league were to be formed for this purpose, and you were willing to publish in your columns from time to time the names or initials of those joining the league, and the number of its members as they increased, I believe that great and lasting good might be done, and that our Churches and institutions would soon be relieved of very heavy burdens, and the Kingdom of Christ greatly extended.

The Church of Christ is earnestly praying for the outpouring of the Holy Spirit upon the world. We claim the fulfilment of the promise in Mal. iii. 10, that our gracious Lord would 'open the windows of heaven, and pour us out a blessing that there shall not be room enough to receive it,' but how many of us forget altogether the condition upon which that promise is made, that we should 'bring all the tithes into the storehouse that there may be meat in My house.' I earnestly trust and pray that this may be remedied in the New Year, upon whose threshold we are standing. I am, dear Sir, yours very truly,
JOHN ATTENBOROUGH.
Rosslyn, Park-road, Beckenham,
Dec. 29, 1906.

* * * * *

Dear Sir, I heartily agree with the principle of systematic giving, as advocated by my friend Mr. John Attenborough; and gladly testify to the blessing which I have derived from this practice for more than thirty years. If he were to undertake the enrolment of a list of sympathisers, I would gladly be one, and I think that the publication of the names of those who are willing to join the League would be a great incentive to others. If this practice were to become universal, we could dispense with pew-rents and have money enough for all our needs.

Yours sincerely,

F. B. MEYER.

* * * * *

Dear Sir, There has been no more important correspondence on practical religion opened in your columns than that which has been lately called forth by the letter of Mr. John Attenborough.

To us Free Churchmen the practice of voluntary offerings is not only a political necessity, but a vital part in our religion, and it would be well if in all our pulpits it were more honoured and dignified by being made the subject of systematic teaching.

Not until all our ministers gain the courage to deal faithfully with this side of the religious life can we expect the Church of Christ to overtake its great duty.

If all Christian people with any income, great or small, would begin to think about this subject, and examine what they now actually give away, and fix a proportion which they ought to give, they would be greatly startled by two things.

1. That they are giving now much less than they thought they were.
2. That they have discovered a new delight and benefit to themselves by this plan.

I should hail with pleasure the inauguration of some sort of League of Christian Stewardship, that would call for a declaration from such as are willing to join it, that they are giving to the Lord on some definite principle.

One of the good effects of this system would be to provoke the private examination of some of the payments we now make, in order to determine whether they may be fairly classified as gifts to the Lord or not. Personally I am not quite sure whether the money I pay for my comfortably cushioned corner seat, and the receptacle for my books, and the use of the umbrella stand at a certain place of worship, can be honestly described as all given to God. I confess to a natural partiality for a reserved seat in a crowded assembly, if I can secure it, but I am not perfectly satisfied that I have any right to feel particularly pious over having paid a fee to secure it. So with many things.

The past fifteen years have seen great changes in the social life of our Free Church community. It is very noticeable to those who come back to English life after living abroad. God has given a great increase of prosperity to Dissenters, and their standard of living is certainly much higher than it was a few years ago. In certain directions our religious expenditure has increased likewise, but I much doubt if on the whole we are as a community giving proportionately more than the last generation. We insist on more artistic surroundings for our religious exercises, on more costly musical arrangements, on better artificial light in our chapels, and we pay much and borrow much to secure these changes. But I am not sure that we are giving proportionately more for the education of our ministry, and the maintenance of our ordained preachers, and for the support of Christian Missions.

It is not unknown for men whose incomes have increased, to continue their former rates of offerings to God's work, on the plea that with increasing income and social status have come increasing needs. How many are there who would be willing, for the sake of being able to give a more worthy proportion of their income to the Lord, to reduce their style of living, and adopt a less pretentious appearance?

Small self-denials and gifts of loving impulse are gems of great beauty and worth, with which to adorn the Temple of God, but the real test of our love to the Saviour whose death was our life, is in the reasonable service of a systematic consecration of all He gives us.

If anyone objects that Systematic Giving would take away the charm of spontaneous benevolence, and the value of uncalculating sacrifice, it is quite easy to assure him that the man who will honestly settle with himself how much of regular income he *ought* to give away, and do it, will still have glorious opportunities of sacrificing himself in compassion for real need. And perhaps it is only at that stage of our giving that we have any right to talk of sacrifice.

Yours very truly,
C. E. WILSON.

Document I.6

Congregational Optimism, 1913

Report of the Council 1912–13, *Congregational Year Book*, 1914, p. 24.

The Congregational Union Council statement of 1913 illustrates an optimism for the future, which was to be dashed by the First World War.

In presenting this Report your Council would express the profound belief that a day of larger and brighter opportunity has dawned upon our Churches. The awakening of the democracy to a fuller consciousness of its power should of necessity be a more imperative call to us to win the people to Christ and to righteousness. The future of the state rests with these, and we must see to it that the spirit that dominates them is the spirit of our Lord Jesus Christ; only so can we hope to see our nation among the Kingdoms of our God and His Christ. The broadness of our traditions and the elasticity of our forms of worship, our freedom from either State or Episcopal control, give us an advantage that we dare not sacrifice through lack of faith in our Divine Head, or through failure of fraternal trust in one another. Your Council prays that our ministers and Churches may be kept from the secularising spirit of the age, and casting off all indolence and fear may in high courage and with devoted loyalty reconsecrate ourselves to the service of Christ and their fellows. The harvest is great; may we all feel *thrust forth*, constrained to labour for its glorious ingathering.

Document I.7

A Cumbrian Methodist Chapel after the First World War

Norman Nicholson, *Wednesday Early Closing* (London: Faber, 1975), pp. 82–6, 93–4.

This description of Wesleyan Methodist life in the period after the First World War captures the sense both that nothing had changed and at the same time that time was running out. It also makes clear the sense of differences between the various Methodist churches.

The piano, in fact, was a sign of a great change that was to come over my life, since my mother was both a pianist and the assistant organist of the Wesleyan Methodist Chapel. From now on, the once-a-month Sundays on which she accompanied the service became the twelve pillars around which the rest of the year was built. My father and I did not attend chapel in the mornings, but, on the Sunday evening, we would go down and take our seats in the rented pew – 'Mrs J. Nicholson, 2', on the little ticket; they didn't rent a place for me!

My father explained that when I entered the pew, I was to sit down and lean forwards for a few seconds, with my elbows on the hymn-book ledge and my head in my hands, and I did this at his side for several weeks, before I realised that we were supposed to be praying!

That was typical of my father's attitude to the chapel. He outwardly conformed to Nonconformity, but was inwardly detached, even rather embarrassed about it. 'We're all going to the same place,' he would say, with an air of large magnanimity, but he secretly thought that the Methodists had chosen rather a poor route. Nevertheless, when my mother was at the organ, my father could feel that he had a real share in the worship, that he was no longer just an awkward visitor from St. George's who didn't know many of the hymns, and didn't altogether like the company. So, at the end of the service, the stewards would greet us as we stepped out through the main doors to where the congregation stood about in the street, raising hats and shaking hands, reluctant to disperse...

Oddly enough, though we must often have attended chapel on Sunday evenings in summer, I remember it almost entirely in winter. From our pew, I seem always to have looked onto a gas-lit and winterly cave, with the incandescent mantles glowing in their white globes and the windows black against the outside night. We were boxed tightly into our pew, the gallery roof low above our heads, and Grandma and Grandpa Sobey in the seat behind. The chapel, if not packed, was respectably full; there was rarely an empty seat in the choir, and the boys of the congregation nudged and squinted over the gallery rail. As the service wore on and the temperature rose, the gaslight turned mistily green, the tremolo of the organ became almost visible, and the moisture oozed down the painted walls and the iron pillars that carried the gallery. The sermon lasted twenty-thirty-forty minutes – too long, often, even for the addicts – and we all settled into a hot, furtive, greenhouse doze, until the last hymn. Then suddenly, the organ sang out, the best basses and contraltos of the Millom Mixed Voice Choir tromboned into four-part chording, and every member of the congregation opened wide his mouth, until the whole baffle-board of pews and panels boomed and echoed with all the fervour of Charles Wesley's thousand tongues.

If my father had married five or ten years later, I would have missed some of the voices and much of the fervour, but, in 1922, though the high tornado of the Evangelical Revival had been dying away for at least half a century, there was still a following wind that blew through these services. Conversion, the changed life, 'the heart strangely warmed' were still at the centre of Methodist theology, even if, for many, they were now something of a formality. Indeed, few of the congregation were converts to Wesley's sense – they were children of converts, or grandchildren, or, more likely, great-grandchildren. They came from families in which, for generations, life after conversion had been the norm. Some of the preachers – more particularly, the lay preachers, or 'local preachers', as we called them – made a direct 'Come to Jesus' appeal to the congregation, but my mother found this rather embarrassing. That sort of thing, she implied, was better left to the U.Ms.

All the same, there was a formal Mission every five years or so, when a visiting Evangelist or team took over the running of the chapel, and services were held every night of the week. There were Moody and Sankey hymns, with the choir augmented by singers from other chapels, and the thumping, hand-slapping, heart-prodding tunes banged and bounced about the galleries, till the pillars shook and twanged:

> 'At the Cross, at the Cross, where I first saw the light,
> And the burden of my heart rolled away –
> *Rolled away*
> It was there by Faith I received my sight
> And now I am happy all the day –
> *All the day.*'

As the mission moved on towards its climax, and the Evangelist began to make his appeal, there was a tension and expectancy about the congregation. I think it was almost as much a sporting instinct as a religious response. They were like farmers with whippets, gathered round the last grass in a nine-tenths-mown hay-field, waiting to see which way the hares would run.

You could usually bet on who would be the first two or three to come forward – the old stagers, who could be relied on to start the pot boiling.

'It's the same crowd that gets Saved every blessed time,' my father would say, in an aggrieved voice. 'You'd wonder how they ever found time to get lost.'

And after them came the few younger people, to whom this was their first Mission. But what the congregation was waiting for was the real convert, the unexpected and unpredictable, the man to whom the decision would mean a spectacular break with his old life. For such breaks did happen, however the psychologists may choose to explain them, and there are men and women walking about Millom today whose upbringing would have been quite different, if their father or grandfather had not suddenly given up drinking, or gambling, or knocking his wife about, and turned on the snap of a response into a sober, hard-working, hard-saving, hard-praying chapel man.

To the children of the ninety and nine who felt no need of repentance, the whole event was exciting, but rather unreal. We all signed a little ticket, saying that we accepted Jesus as our Saviour, rather as if we were applying for membership at the public library. Once or twice I would have liked to have gone forward with the others in answer to the appeal, but I knew that, if I did so, my mother would accuse me of showing her up in public.

'It only makes people start wondering what you've been up to,' she would say.

What people find so hard to understand today is that most Methodists went to chapel because they enjoyed it. The chapel was not only their Place of Worship – it was their place of entertainment, their ancestral home, their music hall, assembly room, meeting house, club and gossip-shop. It came to me as a complete surprise, in my teenage years, to find that the Methodists were considered to be kill-joys, who got little pleasure out of life. For, at least up to the age of thirteen, the chapel seemed to me to be one of the happiest places in the town. I rather pitied the Church of England children who seemed to have little going on in their communion; as for the Catholics – I had been led to believe that they went about in continual fear that the priest would turn them into a nanny-goat if they missed Mass.

When I say 'chapel', I mean all the activities which took place in the chapel itself, in the two schools, in the Men's Institute and in the charmingly-named Church Parlour, where the Wesley Guild held its weekly meetings. But, of course, it was in the chapel building that the bonding process began, the welding together of the congregation into a group, a tribe, a family, a religious Trade Union or Friendly Society, all in one.

Document I.8

Village Congregational Churches, 1934

Social Service Committee Report, *Congregational Year Book*, 1935, pp. 160–62.

The problems of the village churches do not always receive the attention they both need and deserve. If we take the counties where Congregationalism has a reasonable measure of vigour we find that 291 ministers have the charge of 465 village churches, while 174 lay pastors have the charge of 273 village churches. It is true that in most districts Methodism is the preponderant Free Church witness in village life, but there are counties e.g. Essex and Hampshire, where, without Congregationalism, the Free Churches would be greatly weakened. Nor do Methodist minsters for the most part live in the villages they serve as do the Congregational and Baptist ministers and lay pastors. It is for these reasons that we regard the prosperity of the Congregational village church as a matter of the greatest importance.

Until quite recently the nation had been losing its concern for the importance of village life. The War of 1914–18 helped, however, to reveal the importance of the land and its cultivators in the nation's life, and it is increasingly evident to-day that it is for the physical, moral, and spiritual well-being of the nation that as many people as possible should be retained on the land.

Realizing these things, the Social Service Committee has given two years' consideration to the problem of securing the maximum efficiency of the village church in the religious and social life of the village. The subject has been approached from several angles and examined in two successive May Meeting Conferences, which aroused so much interest that the Committee has felt justified in devoting a large part of this year's Report to the conclusions reached.

The outstanding conclusions forced upon us by these inquiries and discussions are: (1) that village life is not getting nearly as much leadership and inspiration from the village church as are needed; and (2) that in so far as the village church is failing to lead the social life of the village, it is losing its opportunity to give its religious message.

To make the results of these inquiries accessible to the churches the Committee has compiled a pamphlet surveying the problem of the village church in a time of change. This pamphlet begins with a section describing the way in which the changes in the social and economic life of the countryside have been complicating the work of the village churches and threatening the success of their influence. It goes on to suggest ways in which some of these difficulties may be met. As these suggestions are drawn from the experience of about fifty selected witnesses it is hoped that they may prove serviceable. The following is the gist of the conclusions embodied in this pamphlet.

The Findings of the Inquiry. – Viewed from the standpoint of the village church, the most marked change that has taken place in recent years in the life of the countryside is the gradual decline in population, due partly to migration to the towns, for economic reasons, and partly to the decrease in the size of the average family. These changes in population have deprived the villages not only of their numbers, but important elements in their leadership, for the villages have in many cases lost the craftsmen and tradesmen who took a large part in leading village institutions. The cleverer children of the village tend also to be drafted more quickly into the towns. We welcome, therefore, the growing tendency to carry small industries from the town into the country and the increasing transport facilities which make it more possible for those who work in towns to live in adjoining villages.

These changes have had a marked effect upon the village church, for they have brought about altered relationships within the village itself and changes of outlook upon the world at large. We have noted many signs of the wider range of interest and knowledge possessed by the modern villager. We have noted, too, how the social unrest which has surrounded the conduct of industry in recent years tends now to invade the villages. The contact of urban and village types of mind within one village church and the clash of older and newer outlooks upon religion and the uses of leisure bring their own problems. There is thus an enhanced need to-day for the village church to be awake and efficient alike in mind and in spirit.

The evidence submitted to us goes to show that, notwithstanding many heartening reports of splendid services being rendered under severe handicaps, the influence of the village church, particularly in the life of the young people, has sadly declined. There is an increasing tendency for the old Christian Endeavour Societies, Guilds, Bands of Hope, etc., to go out of existence and not to be replaced by adequate alternatives. It is significant, however, that where Study Circles, Debates, Handicrafts, Folk Songs, and Country Dancing, Dramatic and Musical activities have been provided, with a clear understanding of the educational possibilities of these activities, in almost every case the church's spiritual influence upon the young life of the village has been high. So, too, when the village church has taken its part in the Village Institute, provided the village with a Thrift Club, organized a tutorial for the Workers' Educational Association, interested itself in rural crafts such as keeping bees or goats, or helped to promote a Farmers' Club, the position of leadership thereby gained has had its results in increased opportunity of religious influence also.

The pamphlet, therefore, pleads for a much closer relation between the village church and the life of the village as a whole, so that the church may go out beyond the confines of its own membership and bear witness for the kingdom of God in the wider life of the village. This plea is followed by detailed suggestions as to the ways in which the church may take its full part in the recreative side of village life, how it may best co-operate with the village institutions which deal with adult rural interests, how the worship and teaching of the church may be brought into closer relation with the outlook and interests of the villages, and how a succession of leaders may be raised up from among the younger people in the church.

The Committee hopes that this Report will be useful in two directions. The first is the helping of the village churches themselves in their immensely difficult and important work. The second is the stirring of interest in the town churches: some of which are near enough to village churches to give them their constant friendship and support, and all of which should be active in their support of national movements for the strengthening of the educational and economic position of the countryside.

Document I.9

The Future of the Free Churches, 1945

A. V. Murray, 'The Free Churches and the Future', *Congregational Quarterly*, vol. xxiv, no. 4, October 1946, pp. 306–7.

Victor Murray, Principal of Cheshunt College, Cambridge, gave this address at the Free Church Federal Council Assembly on 27 March, 1946, offering a challenge to greater co-operation in the future.

In this Free Church Council we are celebrating fifty years, of *what?* – *Free* Church co-operation? Can it be said that we are any more prepared today to let go our individual sovereignty than we were fifty years ago? What qualifications have we to speak the word of God to the nations when we turn a deaf ear to the word of God to ourselves? We would like some nation to make a gesture of goodwill to the others so that the whole machinery of goodwill may be got going: but what gesture of goodwill has there ever been of Methodists to Baptists, or of Quakers to Presbyterians? A willingness to talk is not a gesture, it is a substitute for it. What the world needs is action.

> And not the world only but God. Let us hear the word of God on this matter: Have that mind in you which was also in Christ Jesus, who being in the form of God counted it not a prize to be on an equality with God, but emptied himself, taking the form of a servant ... becoming obedient even unto death, yea the death of the cross.

That is the first part of it, and the application to our denominations is plain. For do they not pride themselves on being the body of Christ? 'This is my body, broken for you: this do in remembrance of me'. Is the body of Christ ready to be thus broken? Will the Methodists 'hate' *Wesley's Sermons,* as Jesus said that a man must 'hate' father and mother, in order to fulfil the prayer of our Lord that 'they might be one' with the Quakers? Will the Quakers go through the agony of giving up their liberty of theological expression that they may make union with Presbyterians easier? Will the Baptists cease to insist on their dogma of believers' baptism that they may come into line with the other churches? Will the Presbyterians relax their ordered system to allow co-operation with Congregationalists? Will all the Free Churches give up their vested interests, financial and theological, in their own individual hymn-books to produce *one* for the use of them all? Will the Churches amalgamate their colleges and have their ministers trained together, and will their missionary societies come together in a joint board to plan a joint strategy under unified control? These are the questions we ought to be asking ourselves if we are sincere.

But that is not the whole story. St. Paul continues:

> Wherefore God hath highly exalted him and given him the name that is above every name, that at the name of Jesus every knee should bow and every tongue confess that he is Lord to the glory of God the Father.

The significance of this lies in the word 'Wherefore'. It is only because Jesus went to the Cross that God highly exalted Him. His body was broken and so He Himself became the centre of loyalty for the whole world. And the power that the nations need to enable them to live together in unity will only be set free for the world by some great act of renunciation after the pattern of our Lord Himself.

The Free Churches are undoubtedly in fellowship. They recognize each other's ministries, preach in each other's pulpits, join together in common action concerning obvious social evils. They also join together to urge the claims of the State in the matter of religious education. But none of these actions really costs them anything. There is no *tension* involved in them, no plumbing the depths of sacrifice and death in order that new life may be born, no willingness to face the Cross. But the needs of the times are such and on such a scale that only faith on a similar scale can deserve the response from God that the world needs. It would be well to suspend all our competitive efforts to win the world for Christ until by some such great act we have shown that we are willing also to pay the price that He paid. We are anxious to sit on either side of Him when He comes into His kingdom: all that we can be sure of is that we are called upon to drink the cup that He drank and be baptized with the baptism with which He was baptized. That cup is renunciation. And our faith that things will come out all right is not our faith in one another but our faith in God.

Therefore, as we look into the future our next task, our primary task, is not with Rome or with the State or with the Church of England, it is with ourselves. This is the day of our visitation. If within the next ten years we have made no further progress in Free Church unity from where we are today we shall have proved unworthy of our high calling and our day will very properly be done.

Document I.10

Evangelism after the Second World War

Brian Frost, *Goodwill on Fire. Donald Soper's Life and Mission* (London: Hodder & Stoughton, 1996), pp. 181–2.

In November 1946 Donald Soper, Methodist minister at Kingsway Hall, London, founded the Order of Christian Witness (OCW) to take part in evangelistic campaigns – in some ways a development of the Christian Commandos but with more stress on community and 'pre-evangelism'. The last major campaigns were in Burslem and Bury in 1962 and 1963.

That November OCW, whose style was caught by the three words – Communication, Community and Communion – was formally inaugurated at Kingsway Hall at a Eucharist. Membership, which was ecumenical, was open to those who believed each Christian had a responsibility to witness to Christian faith by life and works; was willing to do this with others, and prepare and be available for one week-long campaign in August. In 1947, some 300 campaigners, many in their twenties, descended on Huddersfield and lived in school halls in seven 'families', led by a commandant responsible for contacts in the area designated. On the Sunday 120 services were undertaken with Donald himself preaching in the parish church. Each day started with prayer and a briefing led by Donald and for the first time there were visits to factories and to three prisoner of war camps, where the reception varied. Some also visited pubs, while others went to women's groups or spoke in the open air. At the opening meeting in Huddersfield Town Hall the Mayor pointed out that even Gracie Fields, who had recently sung there, had not drawn so many and on the last night, when Donald visited nine rallies the timing had to be stop-watched.

Cannock Chase 1948, another big campaign, involved over 300 in an area of 100 square miles, which was divided into thirty 'families' on the Huddersfield model. The ten campaigns, operating side by side, were co-ordinated each morning by Donald at the general assembly. 'Donald Soper could have a led a Crusade,' June

Strick, a member of Kingsway Hall, once observed. Now in OCW he had a modern form of it, but this time the crusade was against secular society, whose paganism continued to trouble and vex him.

Many of the commandants later held responsible positions in church life like Kingsley Turner (Chairman of District), Roy Trevithian from the City Temple (the BBC), and David Mason. Pauline Callard, too, one of the Kingsway Preachers, subsequently became Principal of Southlands College. For her OCW was contrary to her family upbringing, but the 1953 Exeter campaign broke her shackles, introduced her to teamwork and Christian fellowship at a deep level. John Stacey, and his brother David, also became involved in OCW, the former first at Cannock Chase. Though persuaded to take evangelism seriously by OCW, he found one over-riding problem existed: young campaigners were always trying to imitate Donald, 'without his ability or opportunity or persona'. Nevertheless, at Cannock Chase visits to factories, canteens, clubs, pubs, youth clubs and dances, and open-air work (Donald spoke to 500 on Pelsall Common) did have a lasting effect on the area.

Document I.11

A Methodist Sunday School in the Twentieth Century

(a) E. V. Chapman, *King Cross Methodist Church and School 1808–1958*; (b) E. V. Chapman, *The Light Still Shines*, King Cross Methodist Church, Halifax, 1878–1978.

This church in Halifax had a vigorous history of youth and community work. From 1929 to 1939 the Minister at King Cross was G. Bramwell Evens, known as 'Romany' to millions of children for his nature broadcasts and dog Raq on *Childrens' Hour*. The 1981 Census showed that Calderdale (which includes Halifax) had the highest number of over-75s in the country, 19 per cent of the population being over 65 (third highest) with the greatest number of pensioners living on their own. The range of activities in 1978 was still considerable.

(a)
The growth of the school and its offshoots is amazing. From 1894 to 1914 there was a special children's Sunday Evening Service from 6 to 7 partly to care for those whose parents were in chapel and also to get in those who would otherwise have roamed the streets. A popular visitor to these meetings was Mr Ben Cordingly, last Bellman and Town Crier of Halifax, who brought his magic lantern. But not a picture would he show without perfect discipline!

The Mutual Improvement Society where they practised debating, ready to join the Town Council or become preachers was like the Reading Society, for men only, but on Shrove Tuesday they had an annual tea. There was an interesting 'understanding' that if a man brought a girl to this tea, he had serious 'intentions'. The girls were catered for, later, by a Young Women's Christian Association and various types of Guilds have flourished at different times.

The Band of Hope had a long and vigorous history, and the King Cross

Orchestral Society was well known beyond the chapel itself. Athletics had their place. The famous King Cross Cricket Club was once King Cross *Wesleyan* Cricket Club, but there must have been trouble, for there is a minute, which reads 'the so-called King Cross Wesleyan Cricket Club shall not have the use of the school'. Other physical activities have been hockey, football and badminton clubs with tennis and table tennis in later years. Uniformed organisations were started at King Cross as early as in most schools: the Scouts date from 1914 and the Girl Guides from 1915.

In 1899 King Cross had 703 Sunday School children, the 'daughter' church Warley Road had a further 103. The 1914–18 War had a serious effect on the school. Over 200 teachers and senior scholars were serving and 30 were killed.

At the beginning of the last war (1939) there were 330 on roll but in fairness to present day figures we should note that this was not the *attendance* figure, which was below 200 on an average at that time.

Somehow the work of the school went on, under much worse difficulties than the 1914–18 War. The school was requisitioned for the use of soldiers … only the smaller rooms and the chapel remained for our use and activities were curtailed for lack of rooms. The blackout and the calling-up of both men and women teachers also hindered the work, especially as many of those left were working over, or worked on shifts or doing Civil Defence jobs as well as their daily work.

After the war a gigantic task had to be faced. The school was again entirely reorganised and fully graded. The 'House' system and many other modern methods (including teaching by visual aids – film strip projector etc.) were adopted. Teachers were encouraged to go to weekend or holiday schools to bring back new ideas to improve the efficiency of the Sunday School.

Numbers in the Sunday School:
1978 – Primary 81; Junior 69; 'Inters' 57, Young People 36.
244 on books with an average attendance of 156. Scouts and Cubs number 60, Girl Guides 30. Youth Club has 30 members who meet on Thursday and after church on Sunday evenings.

(b)
The Activities of King Cross Methodist Church in 1978

Day	Time	Activity
Sunday	8.30 am.	Holy Communion. When planned.
	10.30 am.	Morning Worship. Holy Communion monthly.
	10.30 am.	Junior Church and Creche.
	6.00 pm.	Evening Worship. Holy Communion monthly.
Monday	7.30 pm.	Church Council or Committee Meetings.
Tuesday	2.45 pm.	Women's Fellowship Meeting.
	6.30 pm.	Brownies.
	7.30 pm.	Guides.
	7.30 pm.	Modern Sequence Dancing. (Alternate weeks)
	7.45 pm.	Tuesday Women's Club. (Alternate weeks)
	7.30 pm	House Fellowship. (Alternate weeks)

Wednesday	12 noon.	Luncheon club for Senior Citizens.
	6.30 pm.	Junior Youth Club.
	7.30 pm.	Venture Scouts.
	8.00 pm.	Youth Club.
Thursday	10.00 am.	Teddy Bear Club. (Parents and Babies)
	2.00 pm.	Child Birth Trust. (Post Natal Group Therapy)
	6.30 pm.	Cubs.
	7.45 pm.	Men's Supper Club. (Monthly)
Friday	7.30 pm.	Scouts.
	7.30 pm.	Choir Practice.
Saturday	2.30 pm.	Parkinson's Disease Society. (As planned)
	7.00 pm.	Monthly Church Social.

Membership of church: 270.

Document I.12

Methodist Decline in Youth Work in the 1950s

The Way Ahead (London: Methodist Youth Department, 1961), pp. 5, 8, 12, 20.

This report from the Methodist Youth Department drew attention to the dramatic decline in the number of children and young people in Methodism which had taken place in the 1950s. Several other reports to other church bodies reflected a similar concern around 1960, for example, *Growing Christians* (BCC, 1957), *Sunday Schools Today* (FCFC, 1960), *Church, Child and School* (FCFC, 1960), which greatly influenced the thinking behind *The Way Ahead*. Later Reports like *The Child in the Church* (BCC, 1976) and *Unfinished Business, Children and the Churches* (CCBI, 1995) reflected changes in educational psychology and changing patterns of Religious Education.

The Report itself makes it quite clear that work among boys and girls is one of the urgent requirements of our time. It is only a few years since M.Y.D. could produce a leaflet describing the ONE MILLION children and young people in its care. That leaflet can no longer be used since within the past eight years the number has been almost halved. The loss of thirty to forty thousand boys and girls per annum is sufficient to show that it is conceivable for the Church to be without any boys and girls at all within the next decade.

The challenge of the Report is really very simple. Is Methodism to become a DYING CHURCH or a GROWING CHURCH? And the answer cannot be given by those who work with boys and girls. It can only be given by the Church itself — the whole Church.

It is high time for all Sunday Schools to see themselves as an expression of the Church's mission to children and young people. It is also high time for the Church realistically to fulfil its own obligations towards those children and

young people. They are to be cared for, not because they may in time become the Church of Tomorrow, but because they are here and now a part of the Church of Today…

II. THE PRESENT POSITION

The facts about the present position of work among boys and girls really must be brought home to the whole Church. Attendance at Sunday School has continued to decline throughout the post-war years. It is true that actual numbers increased between 1948 and 1953, but these numbers when compared with the increase in child population show real decreases in attendance [Cf. F.C.F.C. Report, *Sunday Schools Today*, Appendix II, p. 34]. It is also true that since 1953, not only have the actual numbers in attendance decreased, but the rate of decrease has tended to increase year by year [M.Y.D. Annual Returns: decreases reported as follows: 1953–54 1.6% decrease; 1955–56 3.5% decrease; 1958–59 5.6% decrease; 1959–60 6.6% decrease]. The Church still seems insufficiently aware of the tragic situation reflected in these declines, and of its many implications. The facts are contained in the Annual returns for Methodist Sunday Schools as follows:–

1953	815,952	scholars enrolled.
1954	802,654	" "
1955	769,733	" "
1956	742,592	" "
1957	699,494	" "
1958	664,560	" "
1959	629,080	" "
1960	587,276	" "

Since there can be no justification for continuing Sunday School work as a separate organization or as an end in itself, what should be the specific task of the Sunday School? This may be described briefly as **the keystone in a bridge which spans the life of the child at Church, at school and at home**. Those most concerned with Sunday Schools must be led to recognize the importance of that keystone; without it Sunday Schools may eventually disappear and the bridge never be built. This in turn would be disastrous for the spiritual development of boys and girls themselves.

The Sunday School, rightly understood, is the expression of the Church's concern to ensure that children shall be instructed and trained 'in the doctrines, privileges and duties of the Christian religion' so that they may grow into the 'fellowship and service' of the Church itself. Such teaching should not only include training in worship, it should itself be undertaken within the context of worship. **Valid expressions of worship within the experience of the boys and girls themselves are as important as any lessons that may be given. And leaders must be made aware that such worship is not 'worship in the Sunday School'; rather is it 'the worship of the Church' among boys and girls who are part of the Church family.** Church worship is not confined to a particular time and place.

Adults as well as children may gather elsewhere than in the church building and still be the real Church entering into fellowship and worship. This is particularly important when experiments are made in family worship, and there can arise quite unconsciously in the minds of boys and girls the idea that they worship in Church for twenty minutes or so and then go out of the Church to do something different in another place.

The greater the care exercised in the conduct of worship, the more opportunity that is given for boys and girls to experience for themselves the reality of worship, the more relevant and significant become the lessons relating to the Christian faith, and the privileges and duties involved in Christian discipleship. It is not easy to draw a line between teaching which encourages a growing faith and teaching which inoculates against an acceptance of the faith. Worship which enables God Himself to reach the boys and girls and in turn helps them to respond to Him is one sure safeguard whereby the danger of inoculation is overcome and a growing faith becomes more probable.

Document I.13

MethSoc in the 1950s

Angus Buchanan, *The Methodist Recorder*, 12 September 1991.

Methodist Societies began in universities after the First World War, and Cambridge was one of the earliest with a membership of several hundred in the 1930s. This description of the early 1950s reflects a period when decline had begun, though most people did not notice it. Professor Buchanan of St Catharine's College was later Director of the Centre for the History of Technology, Science and Society at the University of Bath.

My Methodist experience began in the course of National Service in the Army; it was then confirmed in the Community of the American Methodist Church in Singapore; and it continued in the Cambridge Methodist Society in the years 1950–1955. It was an experience of spiritual enrichment, which spilled over into other parts of my life and influenced me profoundly. The weekly cycle of church services, social activity, discussion and yet more discussion – conducted earnestly and rigorously, and with enormous good humour – determined for me the rhythm of Cambridge term-time.

I can never forget the thrill of inspired preaching in Wesley church, or the animation with which the intricate process of planning for group events was conducted, or the revelatory meditation on points of theology, especially as we ambled along the Backs on Spring mornings. With whom *did* Jacob wrestle, anyway? Above all, I am thankful that Methodism aroused in me a deep sense of fun, which provided a vital leavening to an otherwise serious and self-centred youth.

Nevertheless, as I look back over 40 years, I do have some regrets. For one thing, MethSoc created something of a distraction for me in Cambridge life, and I occasionally wonder what seminars I missed or what union opportunities I relinquished in favour of group meetings. Again, I sometimes recall with embarrassment the naive way in which we approached relationships between the sexes. The Methodist Society was certainly a wonderful opportunity for boy to meet girl, and vice-versa. But on the 'campaigns' through which we carried our enthusiasm to ordinary church congregations – and I remember with great pleasure going on two of these myself – I consider in retrospect that the response we received was not entirely spiritual, and I hope that we caused no unnecessary trouble to sensitive souls in the process.

Thirdly, and for me most seriously, I came to find MethSoc less satisfactory in its social gospel that in its personal relationships. Returning from a heady experience of the Iona Community with my wife-to-be in 1952, with a newly-stimulated awareness of social needs in a world contact, I found it difficult to readjust to the more personal preoccupations of MethSoc.

This divergence of emphasis was reinforced by our involvement with the socially-orientated industrial mission in our home-town of Sheffield, and in our commitment when we were married to the social responsibilities of a settlement in East London. I came to feel that my concerns with mission in the wider community were out of step with the more parochial interests of most church activities, and when even those communities in which I had been most heavily involved tended to become absorbed in personal spirituality I concluded, sadly, that the Church itself had been moved away from me. So for most of the past 30 years the earthly wilderness has appeared to me to be more purposeful and attractive than any ecclesiastical society.

Document I.14

Rural Methodism, 1958

Rural Methodism: A Report to the Conference, 1958, pp. 1, 5–6, 8.

The significance of rural Methodism is clearly stated here. This was one of the most realistic documents to come to the Conference, which acted upon it in 1959 with a proper scheme for the financing of ministerial travel and expenses. It also drew attention to problems for the longer term; for example, 'In only six places in twenty circuits was youth work carried on' (p. 31).

Between one third and one half of the total membership of our Church lives in rural circuits. When, in addition, one recalls the large number of town and city members who were brought up in village chapels, the vital importance of the health of Rural Methodism for the whole future of the Methodist Church is made apparent. Rural circuits vary in size from six to sixty societies. Four out of five of our 5,000 village chapels have less than 25 members, and two out of every seven societies have less than 10. To complete the picture it should be remembered that these circuits cover enormous stretches of country, the average rural circuit comprising seventeen chapels scattered over an area twenty-one miles long and eight miles wide. Some, of course, are very much larger. Every minister in the country can expect to have about seven societies in his pastoral care. For every man who has less than this, some other minister has more...

So great is the shortage of trained Local Preachers that one out of every seven services are conducted by unofficial and irregular speakers, many of whom do not believe or teach our doctrines, but whose services are tolerated by both people and minister because otherwise the pulpit would remain empty. This has opened the gates to splinter groups whose propaganda has often disrupted the peace of the churches. It moreover depresses the status of our Local Preachers and discredits the value we set on the adequate training of Local Preachers on Trial.

At the same time we have to admit that some of these, whose theology does not conform to ours, have sounded in the services they conduct, the vital note of a living experience of Christ, which has not always been heard on the lips of our accepted preachers. Some of our people respond to the warmth of this preaching, but confusing spiritual sincerity with doctrinal soundness, are thereby misled....

Methodism is already paying a heavy price for this poverty of worship and preaching, and unless there is drastic improvement it will destroy Methodism as we know it....

There are over 5,000 village Sunday Schools in Methodism, though perhaps as many as 1,000 societies are without any Sunday School, or other youth work. In some cases there are no children in the village at all – a phenomenon, which will recur more frequently in the villages with population around 200. But generally where there is no Sunday School the reason is lack of leadership. Two out of three villages Societies having Sunday Schools have no other form of youth activity.

Document I.15

The Problems of Effecting Methodist Union, 1960

Eric W. Baker, *The Methodist Recorder*, 24 July 1960.

Methodist union proved to be easier to effect nationally than locally. The Rev Dr Eric W. Baker (1899–1973) was Secretary of the Methodist Conference from 1951 to 1970 and President in 1959. In that year the Nottingham and Derby District Synod suggested to the Conference that Circuit Quarterly Meetings should be able to close a church in the circuit if it was proved to be redundant. Conference in 1961 concluded that the problem was 'large, widespread and urgent'. In 1962, the Conference Committee on the Closure of Redundant Churches reported that 'It is abundantly clear that the problem is not being taken seriously in every area where it exists and there are in many places encouraging signs of a new readiness to break with tradition, if the present age can be more effectively served.' (*Agenda*, Representative Session of Conference, 1962, p. 9.)

There is widespread impatience especially on the part of our younger people at the continued tolerance on the part of Conference of the redundancy which is steadily strangling our effectiveness – let me give two examples which are typical not exceptional.

There is one city which contains within its boundaries fifty nine Methodist Churches, considerably more than the Church of England possesses. Congregations are small and we could well do with half of them. I visited a town recently with a population of 17,000, where there were four large Methodist churches, some of which have an average congregation of fifty...

Methodist union took place twenty-eight years ago. When conference decided that union at the circuit and society level would be a matter for local action, they could never have dreamed of such a sequel. The laity of the three churches ought never to have voted for union unless they intended to consummate it locally. Ministers, of course, voted for it too but not in such numbers and they are itinerant anyhow. What can be done? I do not know. Conference has done everything in its power short of coercion and unless new powers are sought from Parliament ... can do no more. In area after area, the appeal and often the direction of Conference has been flouted. Worship of bricks and mortar has supplanted the worship of the living God.

Document I.16

The Sociology of Methodism in the 1960s

Lewis Burton, 'Social Class in the Local Church: A Study of Two Methodist Churches in the Midlands', in M. Hill (ed.) *A Sociological Year Book of Religion in Britain, 8* (London: SCM Press, 1975), pp. 15–29.

This study of two West Midlands Methodist Churches in the 1960s sheds valuable light not only on Methodism but other Free Churches as well. Parts of the West Midlands saw an expansion of Methodist membership in the period from 1945 to 1960 with the planting of several new churches. It was an area of considerable population increase and growing affluence. Some pioneering work was done among West Indian and other immigrants at this time also.

The fieldwork was carried through on two local Methodist churches of very contrasting type and situation in a West Midlands town of just over 150,000 inhabitants between the years 1962 and 1965. One church was a very large church by Methodist standards, with 537 members at the time of the study, and was judged by repute to be prosperous and successful, in popular terms. We shall call it the 'suburban church' for the purposes of this paper; it was situated in the south-west of the town in a mixed area. Most of the houses which surrounded it were the old type of town house, once occupied by fairly well-to-do families, but beginning to suffer deterioration as people moved out of housing on the town side and went elsewhere. Some of the older houses were beginning to be turned into flats and some of them had immigrant dwellers. Away from town this area consisted of solidly owner-occupied houses except for a small council housing estate, which had rather a high status among the council estates of the town. Most of the members of the church were resident in the owner-occupied part of this housing area and also in other tracts of owner-occupied housing away from town towards the south-west. This housing area we shall call the 'suburban church's neighbourhood'.

The other church was a much smaller church of 139 members in the north of the town in a very extensive corporation housing estate which had been built to a model plan for slum clearance programmes and town expansion in the years 1927 to 1933. The houses in the area were almost all rented from the council and were of two types, a 'parlour' type and a 'non-parlour' type. There was a very small proportion of owner-occupied housing. We shall call this church the 'estate church' and this area the 'estate church neighbourhood'.

... [T]hat the church is a middle class institution is confirmed in both these local churches. Not only is their social class distribution skewed when compared with that of their respective neighbourhoods, but it is also skewed when compared with the distribution of social class in the whole town on the basis of the Registrar General's statistics for the 1961 Census. One important thing to note, however, is that the situation of both churches does make a difference to their social class composition. The church in the estate has a membership, which touches social class categories much lower in the social scale than in the suburban church. The membership of the suburban church is composed of professional and lower professional occupations and to a certain extent of white-collar workers of lower grades. The estate church is composed of lower professionals, white collar workers and skilled manual grades.

Leaders

Leadership in the two churches was, on the whole, a male prerogative. There were some leadership groups, notably the trustees at the suburban church, which were exclusively male. Women featured equally with men only in the uniformed youth organizations, where division is traditionally according to sex, although there were some women in both churches among the informal leaders, the local preachers, the society leaders and the elected representatives to the leaders' meeting... When comparing the two churches, similarities between the leadership groups regarding their social class composition became plain. The trustees, for instance, are traditionally the 'men of substance' in any Methodist church. In the estate church, one or two such men had been imported in order to give the trust board some weight; they had their membership in more prosperous churches elsewhere. The distribution of social class for the trustees in both churches, confirms this. The local preachers in the estate church were few in number and so the proportions are a little misleading, but they come from the top three social class categories and two of them are in class 2. The estate church was fortunate, in fact, in having four local preachers, as most Methodist churches, particularly in this situation, have to get by with less. The suburban church with 26 local preachers was very well off, as this is more than many Methodist circuits have. The work of local preachers is at circuit level, and it is perhaps debatable how much local preachers contribute to their local church, but by virtue of their office they have seats by right on both local and circuit meetings and by virtue of their skills have a function in the pastoral and teaching work of the local church and certainly possess a status in the local church by tradition. The local preachers in the suburban church are drawn from the top three categories of social class, mainly from class 2. This reflects the fact that many of them are teachers, and it seems to be a natural tendency and one that can hardly be remarked upon that people who are trained as teachers, possibly with religious knowledge as part of their skill, should offer to use their talents for the good of the church. What should be remarked on is that the social class distributions, both of Methodist leaders and Methodist members, conceal the fact that there are certain occupations which are typical for Methodists. We have mentioned that there are many local preachers who are teachers, but there was a high proportion of teachers among the membership of both churches in this study and this was especially true of the suburban church. Methodism somehow seems to recruit or produce teachers and has them amongst its members in far greater proportion than exists among the general population. In the suburban church, occupations typical of the church members were employment in the welfare services, employment as civil servants and local government officers, employment in education and in medicine and allied services and especially employment as managers, in commerce and industry. Between the leadership groups in both churches, those who are occupied in management seem to play an influential part, though this is particularly true of the society leaders who form the group on which the responsibility for church management falls. The group of informal leaders, on the other hand, had a more even distribution between the 'typical' professions, including more of the other professions, civil servants, directors of companies, accountants, medicine, etc.

To return to considerations of social class, the youth leaders in both churches can be seen to come from rather higher status occupations than most of the others, and it was thought that this was because, as a group, they tended to be much younger than other leaders and seemed to have benefitted from educational opportunity and social mobility rather better than those who were handicapped to a certain extent by their generation. It is tempting to say that of all the leadership groups the elected representatives to the leaders' meeting from the general church meeting are the most typical of the rank and file of the church, but it is difficult to say just on this evidence that any particular levelling spirit was at work in their election. Most of the other leadership groups in Methodism are self-perpetuating bodies and rather follow oligarchical principles, but even so it will be seen that the society leaders, the main seat of authority in the local Methodist church are the leadership group in both churches who mirror reasonably closely, in their social class distribution, that of the church members in each place.

When the social class composition of leaders is compared with that of church members, …in every case, except that of the elected representatives, the leaders are of higher social class than the members.

When we compare the two churches we note in respect of leaders what was noted in respect of members in the previous discussion, that the situation of the church drastically affects the social class composition of leadership groups. The leadership groups of the estate church are higher in social status than the membership, but not as high as the membership of the suburban church, quite apart from the leadership groups there, which are higher still. The suburban church was a church of the middle class staffed by the middle class in a mixed-class neighbourhood: the estate church was a church staffed by the lower middle class for intermediate class members in a working class neighbourhood.

The fact that leadership tends to come from higher status groups than the membership and that status which is typical of the local church's neighbourhood causes problems for the local church, and proved to be a difficulty for both churches featured in this study. It was found that the leaders of both churches commuted to the church from housing areas outside the church neighbourhoods in large proportions. The difficulty for the suburban church in this respect was less for a number of reasons. For instance the problem was greater for the estate church since by and large every church of any size, large or small, needs the same number of lay leaders to staff the necessary leadership posts, and the estate church has a much smaller membership total out of which to recruit its leaders, while the suburban church had many more. One great difficulty in staffing the estate church with leaders seems to be the great desire that Methodists have to own their own house ... [A] great proportion of Methodists are owner-occupiers and ... young Methodists have a desire to own their own house rather than rent one. Thus it follows that young Methodists from the estate church, ripe for leadership positions, have to leave the estate neighbourhood if they want to fulfill their house-owning ambitions, for here there are only houses to rent, and a corporation housing waiting list to negotiate even if they are content to rent ... This process had been happening over a period of time and the estate had lost a number of potential leaders through it, though it was fortunate that some had decided to stick by the church and commute to worship and other meetings. They endeavoured to give the same kind of service as if they had lived locally and the estate church was very dependent upon them. In stressing the difficulties of the estate church, however, one must not lose sight of the fact that commuting was necessary to maintain adequate leadership in both churches.

The recruitment of leaders, the desire for house ownership and the higher social status of leaders is linked to social mobility or, perhaps to put it better, geographical and social mobility are linked for the church members.

Adherents

... [T]he term 'adherents' has been enlarged to take in all those who are members of the organizations which are sponsored and administered by the local church. Some members of the church are also members of the organizations, but by no means all... Proportions of church members in devotional, cultural and social groups were high, but proportions in the women's meeting, and almost by definition, in the Sunday School, and the youth organizations of various kinds, were low. Every 'adherent' in the sense used above makes a statistical appearance on Methodist numerical returns in the figure called the 'community roll', which is the total number of people having any kind of contact with the local church.

In both churches the distributions, which bear some resemblance to the distribution of social class in the neighbourhoods of the respective churches are those for the women's meeting, the Sunday School, and for the youth groups of various kinds. It is among these organizations that the church can be said to minister to its neighbourhood, for it is here that proportions of people coming to the church from outside the half-mile radius are lowest. The estate church has much the greater success in winning recruits to its organizations from the lower social categories, and the success of the suburban church in this matter is somewhat limited. The women's meeting is composed of a good proportion of ladies who belong to intermediate social classes on either side of the manual/non-manual line, and the youth organizations have proportions of members who come from lower social groups. The suburban church, however, had youth organizations, which tended to be dominated by children who attended the local grammar school and this is reflected in their social class composition. The social class distribution of scholars in the Sunday School is interesting. The suburban church does not seem to have much success in contacting families other than those typical of its own social class composition, but the estate church does seem to have success in recruiting into its Sunday School children of every social class. An explanation of this may be that in every social class, even in those not typical of church membership, there is a desire for or tradition of Sunday School education. When one notes the distribution of social class for the uniformed and non-uniformed youth groups in the estate church one can see the success of these organizations in contacting the working class boys and girls of the neighbourhood. Proportions are greater for classes 5 and 6 in the social class distributions of the estate youth organizations than are seen to be the case for the estate neighbourhood as a whole, ...

The church organizations, and indeed the church members, tended to be socially homogeneous and fairly exclusive groups. All the local church groups are, however, connected; by the system of authority from the leaders' meeting; by personnel who are also participants in or leaders of other groups, and who may also be church members, sharing in Christian worship and fellowship in the inner life of the church. All the church's organizations form a series of interlocking social groups with church membership as a nucleus. In social class terms the function of the church organizations is to 'bridge' the social distance between that of church members and that of the relatively lower social class status of the people who live in the neighbourhood of the church building. They provide a real link between the local church and its neighbourhood and prevent its being isolated from it. By holding each group together and through cross-fertilization, the church can display some social diversity and come to terms with the rather alien social class structure outside its walls. The system has also a dynamic aspect in that it is through contacts, which the organizations make with the neighbourhood that people of diverse class origins are drawn into the central activities of the church's life ...

Conclusions

... Having studied the class structure of the local church one can say very plainly that it is a mistake to dismiss the local church as a 'middle class structure'. The situation is more complex than that and social class within the local congregation depends on what outlook a church may have to its neighbourhood and where it is located.

Another thing that is clear is the meaning given to 'success' when applied to the local church. Our suburban church had 'success' if measured in numerical terms, but the estate church had 'success' when measured in terms of reaching the broad spectrum of social class in its neighbourhood. The people of the estate church found the going hard, as people of many other estate churches have, some feeling that things are too difficult and not worth the effort. They should be encouraged, however, for there is a 'success', which churches in suburban situations cannot match.

Document I.17

Afro-Caribbean Churches from the 1950s

Clifford Hill, *Black Churches* (London: British Council of Churches, 1971), pp. 4–13.

Clifford Hill was a sociologist who became Senior Lecturer in Sociology in the North-East London Polytechnic, as well as being a Congregational minister. He also directed the Newham Community Renewal Programme and did extensive research on issues connected with immigration and race. His booklet was published by the Community and Race Relations Unit of the BCC and reflected the early years of contact with Black Churches in Britain.

West Indian sects

There are no reliable up-to-date figures available for the number of West Indian Christian groups in Britain, neither is it possible to obtain any. This is due to the very large number of splinter groups and small independent meetings that have mushroomed into existence in every town and city where the immigrants have settled. Many of them simply meet as house groups or enlarged family prayer-meetings and the constant leadership tussles bringing fission and fusion among them reduces any kind of survey to a mere numbers guessing game.

Some idea of their rapid growth rate may be gained from early estimates. In 1962, Malcolm Calley estimated that there was a total of 77 sect congregations of all types established by West Indians in Britain. Twelve months later he estimated their number to have reached 'well over one hundred'. Less than three years later, in January 1966, I estimated the number to have reached 390. Since then, due to the rapid proliferation of groups throughout the conurbations, it has not been possible to offer further estimates.

Nevertheless in some ways the situation has become clearer than it was in the early days as since the mid-1960s there has been a strong movement among the small independent local groups to affiliate and form organised sects. Several of them now exist as national organisations with their own premises and full-time pastors and administrators. The largest of the West Indian sects in order of size of membership are:

1 The New Testament Church of God
2 The Church of God of Prophecy
3 The Apostolic Church of Jesus Christ

The growth of the West Indian sects may best be illustrated by describing the development of the largest of the sects in Britain. This is the New Testament Church of God (the NTCG), which is the oldest of the Christian immigrant sects in the UK. It began in 1953, back in the early days of West Indian migration, long before Commonwealth immigration controls began.

The first group began meeting in rented premises in a YMCA hall in Wolverhampton. By 1957 there were eleven such groups meeting in rented premises in various parts of the Midlands and the London area. In 1959 they purchased their first building – a small hall in the Hammersmith area of London. By 1963 they had increased to twenty-three congregations and had established a national administrative network with headquarters in Birmingham. During the next three years they made enormous strides both in developing their national organisation and in increasing membership. The latter was achieved both by establishing new groups and also by existing independent groups becoming affiliated to them.

The national organisation was affiliated to the Church of God, Cleveland, Tennessee, from whom they received support. The bulk of the financial resources required for their programme of expansion was provided by sect members who were making great personal sacrifices in an effort to raise funds to purchase their own buildings for worship. Thus in 1966 they had 61 congregations with a total membership of 10,500. They had 15 full-time ministers, a theological college training 20 students for the ministry, a national headquarters in Birmingham, and the whole country was divided into eight provinces each with a full-time 'overseer'. Forty-four were meeting in rented premises and 17 owned their own church buildings. These latter were purchased from one or other of the major denominations in depressed urban working-class areas where the largest settlements of West Indians were to be found. Figure 1 below shows the size of the growth since 1966.

… Most of the West Indian congregations are fairly similar in their type of worship, and although they often differ in emphasis upon particular points of doctrine, there is a large body of common characteristics… First, however, it needs to be recorded that the congregations are usually Pentecostal, that is, they believe that the Gift of Tongues received by the Apostles, and described in Acts chapter two, is still the possession of true believers in Jesus Christ. The sects also usually hold what may best be described as a conservative evangelical theological position and literalist views of Scripture as the inspired Word of God.

Figure 1

The New Testament Church of God in England – Growth 1966–1970

	1966	1968	1970
Administrative Districts	10	12	15
Full-time Ministers	15	20	24
Owned Premises	17	24	29
Rented Premises	44	45	45
Congregations	61	69	74
Baptised Membership	2,500	3,300	3,600
Adherents in regular attendance	3,600	7,000	10,000
Children and young people	4,400	5,500	7,000
Total sect membership	10,500	15,800	20,600

Source: *The New Testament Church of God, Birmingham, England*

... All the sects place a heavy emphasis on ritual, not in terms of robes and formalized prayers or the repetition of psalms and creeds, but in terms of the significance of each part of their worship. Although there is considerable scope for spontaneity, everything in the worship service is a ritual act, strictly patterned and usually Biblically-based, such as feet-washing which often precedes the celebration of Holy Communion. Although prayers are always extemporary, there is usually a similarity of expression and the language is in the mould of the Authorised Version with a high content of Scriptural quotations. Indeed, the congregations are strongly Bible-centred in their worship and practice and there is a high degree of Biblical role-play in their activities. The New Testament provides the pattern not only for the organisation of the local congregation and its activities but also for the life-styles and even the language of the members.

Baptised church members in good standing are known as 'saints' indicating their status as the chosen people of God. In the same way as Paul referred to the 'saints in Jesus Christ who are at Philippi' or the 'saints at Ephesus', so members of the NTCG regard themselves as the 'saints in Jesus Christ at Brixton', or Wolverhampton, or Birmingham ...

The worship is usually of a very uninhibited character which allows for considerable individual participation and self-expression. Individual prayers are said aloud and there is opportunity for personal testimony as well as congregational participation in singing and in response to the leader's exhortations. Most of the testimonies are of a fairly stereotyped pattern giving the impression that the speaker has said it all many times before. Each one usually ends with a quotation from Scripture or a request for prayer and is followed by the singing of a chorus.

Music forms an important part of worship, and singing and playing musical instruments are activities in which West Indians excel. Many local congregations allow anyone to bring an instrument and join in the musical accompaniment. There is a strong emphasis throughout the worship service on the full participation of the whole congregation. When the leader says 'Praise the Lord' everyone present is expected to respond immediately 'Praise the Lord'. This is often repeated time after time until the building verberates to the unison shouts of the congregation. Thus a high degree of social solidarity or 'togetherness' is engendered, the measure of which is often the criterion of a successful or fully satisfying worship service in which all the members can enter into a living experience with God and perhaps also find some emotional release from the daily frustrations of life as a black immigrant in white Britain...

Most of the sects are Pentecostal in doctrine. They believe in the extant gift of the Holy Spirit which manifests itself through the individual worshipper 'speaking with tongues'. This is an experience for which the members strive, and it is often made a test of membership. This movement of the Spirit often results in very noisy acts of group participation in the worship service which sometimes causes considerable hostility among nearby white residents. An example of this lies behind the report of a Yorkshire sect meeting which appeared in an official magazine of the NTCG:

> During the testimony service God's Spirit moved on the meeting and the sermon could not be preached for both saved and unsaved went to the altar praying, weeping and seeking God. Three were filled with the Holy Ghost, nine sanctified and also sick people were healed. Nevertheless the great stirring of the Spirit of God also caused the devil to move, and we were notified that we could no more use that hall for our worship. Please pray that we shall be able to obtain a place of our own in which to worship God in Huddersfield.

Doctrine is strongly Biblically based, with a fundamentalist or literalist interpretation...

The NTCG ... is ... a highly organised and strongly authoritarian institution. No distinction is made between men and women and all offices are open to both sexes although in practice the higher offices of the NTCG in Britain are filled by men. In ascending order of precedence the ranks within the sect are: Brother or Sister denoting ordinary baptised members; Deacon, denoting one who has some responsibility for the material attributes (buildings etc.) of the local congregation and its administration; Elder, being one who shares with the local minister certain pastoral responsibilities and spiritual duties; then Minister.

There are three orders of ministry. 1. Exhorter or lay-preacher denoting one who is licensed to preach but not to carry out the full duties of the minister or to take charge of a congregation. 2. Licensed Minister or Evangelist who is usually the Pastor of a local congregation or one who has special responsibilities at a wider district level. 3. Ordained Minister. This used to be the office of Bishop but the latter has been discarded in recent years and the ranks of ordained ministers are signified by their function within the wider sect network. An ordained minister may simply have responsibility for a local congregation or he may be a District Overseer with oversight over a whole province. The highest office of the NTCG in Britain is that of the National Overseer.

The sects are usually strongly authoritarian and hierarchical in local and national structures. Their ethic is ascetic demanding high standards of personal morality from their members. There are strict taboos on tobacco, alcohol, obscene language and extra-marital sex relationships. For women cosmetics are banned, jewelry curtailed; hairstyles and dress must be plain. Members practise tithing, usually ten per cent, often making considerable sacrifices in raising sums of money for the purchase and maintenance of their large buildings.

The social class of members varies, although there is considerable evidence to show that established sects such as the NTCG draw the bulk of their members not from the lowest classes, but from what I have elsewhere described as the immigrant 'new middle-classes'. Many sect members are houseowners and landlords, who have cars and enjoy a good standard of economic prosperity.

African sects

So far we have dealt only with West Indian groups, but the African congregations, although not nearly so numerous, are equally fast-growing. The number of Africans in Britain is very small in comparison with the number of West Indians. They come mainly from Nigeria and have settled mainly in parts of South, North and East London. There are many small independent local congregations, some no more than house-groups meeting for prayer. Some of the groups have affiliated to form such sects as the Church of the Lord in South London which is a Nigerian (Yoruba) sect. The largest of these affiliated groups in Britain, also a Yoruba sect, is the Church of the Cherubim and Seraphim which has congregations in London and the West Midlands. Its largest congregation is in Newham, East London, where it has established a church in a former co-operative hall. The members are mainly students and mainly men, which is simply a reflection of the composition of the African community in Britain...

The Church of the Cherubim and Seraphim (the CCS) is not Pentecostal although in its worship it bears many similarities to the West Indian sects. For the worship service all church members wear long white prayer gowns (like an Elizabethan night shirt) and have bare feet. Congregational singing (hymns and choruses), led by an organ or a small band with a powerful drum section plus a strong choir, is loud and rhythmical. The repetition of a chorus can sometimes bring a whole congregation to the point of extreme excitement gripped by powerful religious ecstacy which only the penetrating and persistent ringing of a handbell by the leader can bring under control in preparation for corporate prayer.

There are points in the worship service when individuals manifest phenomena similar to that of the Pentecostalists' 'speaking with tongues'. To the uninitiated observer the phenomenon may be identical, but this is the point when the aladura brethren of the local congregation prophesy or relate their dreams and visions. These dreams and visions are central to the whole belief-system, worship and practice of the CCS. If a man tells of a vision he has seen, or receives during the service, he is expected to accompany it with an interpretation. This is an essential part of the act of prophesying and without the interpretation the prophecy is considered incomplete.

Any member may prophesy during the worship service thus giving ample opportunity for individual participation, but the number of prophecies may be limited by the leader if there is a large congregation present with many members keen to take part. A further limitation on participation is that members are only allowed to prophesy if they have attended the Visioners Band during the week. This is considered central to the right exercise of spiritual gifts. Even with these limitations a large number of members may engage in public prophecy at the Sunday service and this makes the worship a lengthy act, usually of some four or five hours' duration. The CCS Newham only has one service each Sunday which begins at 1.30p.m. and will often last until 7.00p.m. On alternate Saturdays there is also a watchnight service that can sometimes last for most of the night...

The CCS is basically fundamentalist in doctrine although the sect does not give the same centrality to questions of sin and salvation as is given by European fundamentalist religious societies...

The Bible is of central importance to the CCS whose members hold literalist views of Holy Scripture as the inspired Word of God, the Authorized Version as well as the Yoruba translation being used. The Bible is extensively used in the interpretation of dreams and visions which is central to the whole doctrine and practice of the sect. Due to this particular emphasis greater importance is attached to the function of prophecy than that of preaching which is usually the main emphasis of fundamentalist sects.

The great importance attached to the gift of prophecy is reflected in the high prestige accorded to the office of Prophet. The Prophet is in fact ranked higher in the allocation of power and honour in the CCS than the Evangelist. Due to their doctrinal emphases, and the great importance attached to the correct and authoritative interpretation of visions, there are a variety of functional offices within the CCS in what is basically a hierarchical structure. Each of these offices carries its own clearly defined responsibilities as well as prestige and authority within the local congregation and within the sect network.

It may be useful at this point to note the basic organisation of the CCS in terms of the delineation of functions within the sect. The major division is between men and women for whom there are separate offices: For men the order of preference, in ascending order is: Brother or ordinary church member (baptised), followed by Aladura Brother or Prayer Brother ('aladura' simply meaning 'prayer'), then Elder, followed by Teacher then Evangelist, then Pastor, followed by Prophet and finally the office of Apostle. In the CCS in Britain the leader is an Apostle. There are two offices higher than this in the sect in Nigeria. They are Senior Apostle and the highest office of all, Aladura Father. For women, ordinary baptised church members are Sisters, then come Aladura Sisters followed by Elder Sisters, then Prophetess followed by the Lady Leader and finally the office of Mother in Israel.

The CCS is a strongly authoritarian institution with a hierarchical power structure exercising strict discipline over members...

The CCS, unlike the West Indian NTCG, has no ascetic ethic as the basis of a distinctive life-style to which members are expected to conform... The African sects adhere to the African world-view which is basically one of immanence in which the whole spirit-world is a present reality. Their practice of the Christian faith enables members to overcome the evil forces that surround them. It does not require them to practice a particular form of morality or to change social customs that are indigenous to an African way of life.

The social class of members in the CCS in England varies, but it should be remembered that almost all Africans in Britain came here as students. To be able to travel to England for higher education places them in the category of a privileged elite... Few CCS members then do come from the lowest classes. Some may come from traditional ruling families (although this would be unusual), but they all represent an educated elite. The majority appear to come from solid middle to upper-middle class Nigerian families.

Why the sects have grown

The growth of West Indian and African sects needs to be gauged in relation to the total Christian religious situation in Britain. With a few local exceptions, the major churches and denominations in Britain have been uniformly unsuccessful in attracting West Indians into their congregations. The exceptions have been where individual ministers have risked the disaffection of their white members and have gone out of their way to make their churches attractive to the new-comers. This West Indian rejection of the English churches is most remarkable since the majority of them come from three islands, Jamaica, Trinidad and Barbados, where English religious institutions embrace the overwhelming majority of the population.

An average of 69 per cent of the total population in the British Caribbean attend regularly one of the six major branches of the Christian church – Roman Catholic, Church of England, Baptist, Congregational, Methodist, and Presbyterian. But in Greater London only 4 per cent of the West Indian immigrants are regular in church attendance. Enquiries in other parts of the country indicate that a similar situation exists throughout the major cities and towns where West Indians have settled in large numbers. These figures reveal the almost unanimous verdict of rejection by West Indian Christians of the English counterpart of those churches they once supported in the Caribbean.

The African religious situation is more complex due to the large number of Muslims and adherents of other religions which make a straight comparison of church attendance figures for Africa and Britain impossible. Until more extensive research has been carried out there is no way of telling how many Africans of Christian origin have come to Britain. Close association with Africans in Britain over a number of years, however, has led the writer to the belief that the churches here have been no more successful in retaining the active participation of African Christians in worship and other church activities than they have been with West Indians.

Document I.18

A West Indian Serves with an English Congregation

Madge Saunders, *The Challenge of Service: Tenth anniversary brochure of the United Church of Jamaica & Grand Cayman, December 1965–75*, (Kingston, Jamaica: United Church, 1975), pp. 5–6.

This vivid description of church life and race relations in Sheffield comes from a remarkable woman, Madge Saunders, who served as a deaconess with the Presbyterian Church of England, and later the United Reformed Church.

December 1, 1965 was a very historic day not only in the life of the two Churches which joined to form the United Church of Jamaica and Grand Cayman, but in the lives of individuals who under God, rededicated themselves to serve their fellowmen, bringing them into an experience of the love of Jesus Christ.

I was invited by the Presbyterian Church of England, now the United Reformed Church, to serve as a deaconess to share in the Ministry at St. James Church, Sheffield, in the county of Yorkshire, with special responsibility for the West Indians in that city. In preparation for my new work the first act at the Service of Union of the United Church was to dedicate me and set me apart for my work overseas.

I arrived in England on December 31 in the middle of winter in this foreign land to find no home prepared for me in Sheffield. After three months of inadequate accommodation I found a 'flat!' As I had come to serve my people I felt this new experience of 'settling in' had prepared me to understand one of the difficult plights of my country-folk. This identity in trials soon broke down barriers and won people's confidence. It was during this time of testing that I made many lasting friendships with those of the host community. They helped me in many practical ways and encouraged and supported me in all I tried to do. It was the love of God and the challenge of what had to be done which prevented me from returning home.

While in Sheffield, with a population of more than half a million, I worked in the Community and Church among the 10,000 coloured immigrants, but in particular with the 4,000 West Indians. In that highly industrialised city with its factories of iron, steel and metal goods, a city famous for its cutlery, our people quickly settled down under great strain and tension. The natural laughter and good humour, often judged as irresposibility by those who did not know us, and our God-fearing background kept us sane and friendly. The West Indians were not and still are not afraid of hard work as they took their places in hospitals, steel works and in transport, as bus drivers and at railway stations. Later as bus drivers they won the respect and admiration of the citizens.

Much work had to be done and the need still continues in order to convince the management of retail shops, banks and other business firms that black people are capable of doing other than menial tasks. The plea to give them the opportunity to prove themselves continues with little success. Often barriers between peoples have been brought about because of fear, the repetition of rumours, misconceptions and misleading propaganda. Because of these negative attitudes, conflicts and tensions on both sides have been the result. I have been called upon at all hours of the day and night to act as mediator on numerous occasions, and although frustrating at times in the long run it had proven worthwhile.

Also I have through talks, community discussions, study groups, conferences, radio interviews, and television appearances, tried to bring about understanding and respect for the immigrants as people, who need no special treatment, only wanting to [be] treated as human beings. The culture and customs of a country are always strange to new comers and so I wrote a booklet 'Living in Britain' with all the relevant information that a new comer needs after arriving there. This was published in three different languages, English, Urdu and Gujurati. This booklet not only served the West Indians but the East Indians, Pakistani, Continentals and even the British found some of the information enlightening!

It did not take me long to discover that my services were being required not only in Sheffield, but in many parts of Britain where there were West Indians. I was on call twenty-four hours a day, sleeping with a telephone by my bed ready to help anyone in distress. Every branch of the Social Services, Police, Education and Church would call on me for advice in one way or another. In order to cope with the situation I not only tried to build up the confidence of my people but formed 'Concern Groups' in Schools, Colleges, University, friendly organisations and Churches. The British ministers of the churches who had migrants in their areas were at first not sure how to approach the West Indians and asked my advice. As a result of this need I arranged, with the help of the Council of Churches, Ministers' Fraternal, and other genuinely interested church related groups, talks and discussions which were able to help the ministers not only to serve but to gain their confidence and so share in their problems and joys.

Many invitations came from adult and youth groups who wanted to know more about coloured people. Parties, exhibitions, international food bazaars, film and coloured slide evenings were arranged for them. They in turn reciprocated and expressed genuine appreciation for the opportunity of exchanging ideas and problems, thus bringing about better understanding of each other.

As President of the Sheffield and District West Indian Association, I was able to get full support in these endeavours. Further as Vice-Chairman of the Sheffield Communuity Relations Committee and Chairman of the Education sub-Committee, I helped in the setting up of multi-racial Play groups and Language Centres, and served on School Boards and Management Committees of Junior and Infant Schools. In Pitsmoor where I lived and where there was a high concentration of coloured children as well as white childen, along with a small Committee we established a playground where the youngsters were taken off the streets and were able to express themselves freely and creatively under trained leadership.

The West Indians had and still have much to learn but also much to teach. Those who went over in the earlier days, in their gentle yet determined way changed some of the life-style of the host community for the better. They are being respected for their hard work and the care and devotion they give to their children and for their attendance at the churches under their own pastor. The St James Church to which I was attached came to be regarded as the mother Church for she had from the first critical days welcomed and served immigrants. The work had been started by the late Rev. R.C. Gillespie, the then minister of the Church and the West Indians still feel a sense of love, gratitude and devotion for him.

I shall always remember the caring and understanding of the Deaconess Committee and the Women of the Church who in the early days spared no effort to make us deaconesses feel part of the family of the Church...

As a result of my tenure in Britain ... I have been more and more convinced that the problems and opportunities of the Church will have to be faced by a united effort. The Church is more and more moving into an Ecumenical role and finding new exciting dimensions as it experiences the vitality of other Christians. This is the challenge of service which calls for humility and unselfishness. No one denomination can go it alone as we tackle the evils of racism, injustice and the moral and spiritual breakdown of our time. In many parts of Britain the B.C.C. has named areas of 'Ecumenical Experiment' and in the Pitsmoor area some of the churches have come together to form the Sheffield Inner City Ecumenical Mission. In this context I have been for these past three years sharing in the fellowship of other denominations and unitedly serving and witnessing to the community.

The challenge to serve is the true mission of the Church. People of every race, colour and occupation want to be loved and not patronised, to be treated as persons and as children of God. Not to be loved in the distance but to be respected for themselves. Let us stop looking at ourselves and behaving like privileged children, and instead looking at Jesus whose life was one of Challenge, Service and Sacrifice...

The Church has still the great task of reconciliation to bring about change in public opinion and attitudes not only on national racial issues but that of international woman-hood status. Let us not be afraid to break out of the past and venture with Him who goes before us into the future to do great things in the building up of our lives.

Document I.19

Rethinking Overseas Missions in the 1960s

Gwenyth Hubble, *Mission in Six Continents* (London: Baptist Union, 1965), pp. 3–5.

The achievement of political independence by so many former colonial territories in the 1960s carried with it a rethinking of missionary policy. Gwenyth Hubble was Principal of Carey Hall, Selly Oak from 1945 to 1960 and then spent some years working with the Division of World Mission and Evangelism of the World Council of Churches. Here she spells out what this might mean for Baptists.

'Mission not in three continents but six' – that phrase came out of the Assembly of the World Council of Churches held in New Delhi in 1961. Christ is calling his people to mission not only in Asia, Africa, and Latin America but in every area of all six continents. Everywhere there is unbelief – everywhere Christ must be preached. At the Meeting of the Commission on World Mission and Evangelism in Mexico City in December, 1963, one section report said: 'The missionary frontier runs around the world. It is the line that separates belief from unbelief, the unseen frontier which cuts across all other frontiers and presents the universal Church with its primary missionary challenge.' Everywhere the Church faces unbelief. Everywhere it is called by Christ to communicate His Gospel to men and women, in the East and in the West, unreached by the witness of the Church, be they the product of animist society in the Highlands of New Guinea, of Communist society in the U.S.S.R., or of the affluent society in North America. The whole Church is called to proclaim the whole Gospel to the whole world.

This six-continent view of mission demands that we recognize that every land, including our own, is a field of mission, a part of the whole world in which 'the whole Church is called to proclaim the whole Gospel'. In terms of missionary activity we can no longer divide the world into 'sending' and 'receiving' countries. Britain is, at least potentially, a receiving country, to which men and women of Asia or the Caribbean may be called of God as missionaries, called to work with British Christians in their task of mission in Britain, as He has called British men and women to go as missionaries to Asia and the Caribbean. Speaking at the meeting in Mexico City a church leader from the U.S.A. said that the churches in his country needed help from their 'brethren in other lands' in the urgent task in mission which they face today. He said: 'We need the help of mission workers who have experience in ministries of education and healing in hostile environments. We need the support of the prayers and offerings of churches from every corner of the earth.'

Since every church is potentially a receiving church, every church must also be potentially a sending church. We have often thought of Britain as 'the home base', from which men and women have been sent to other parts of the world. Britain is, indeed, a home base, but the home base is no longer only in Western countries, 'the home base is everywhere, wherever the Church is'. So wrote Bishop Lesslie Newbigin in 1958 in his booklet entitled *One Body, One Gospel, One World*. He further said: 'The thinking of the older churches about foreign missions has always been shaped by the fact that the ends of the earth were always "there", not "here". But from the moment that the Church becomes a worldwide fellowship, that point of view is invalidated. There are now – from the point of view of the new home base – "no regions beyond". From the point of view of a congregation in Boston what happens in Tokyo is still "the ends of the earth"; but from the point of view of the Christians in Tokyo it is not. We have entered into an era when we must simply abandon the idea that our terminology is determined by the point of view of Boston rather than that of Tokyo. From the point of view of the new home base, Boston is as much " the ends of the earth" as Tokyo. From this point of view, therefore, we can no longer speak as though what happens in Tokyo is foreign missions, and what happens in Boston is not.' We have to abandon the idea that foreign missions are the sole responsibility of churches in the West and recognize that God has given to the Church in every part of the world the responsibility to proclaim His Gospel everywhere...

To put this in British Baptist terms, we all have to recognize our calling to mission as being to the communities in which we live and in which we work as much as to Africa and Asia. For each local Baptist church mission is not only to support with concern, prayer, and giving the Baptist Missionary Society and the Home Work Fund, but to be a missionary community, whose members go out to a variety of places and relationships as witnesses to Christ. Are we, for example, truly fulfilling our missionary calling, however hard we work for the B.M.S., if we are not involved at first hand in mission where we are, thus knowing a real unity of purpose and commitment with those who are communicating the Gospel in Congo?

Document I.20

The Urban Theology Unit in Sheffield

John J. Vincent, *Five Pillars of Christianity* (Sheffield: Urban Theology Unit, 1989), p. 10.

This extract from John Vincent's address as President of the Methodist Conference in 1989 gives a sense of the kind of thinking of the Urban Theology Unit which he founded in 1970 to explore theology in and for the setting of the inner city. The Unit was now linked, as was Cliff College on the evangelical wing, with Sheffield University. It was used as a resource for ministerial and lay training; Vincent was followed by Inderjit Blogal, a Sikh immigrant from Kenya, who became a Christian through the Vicar Street Bible class at Dudley run by Bert Bissell. For the earlier stage of the Unit, see John Vincent (ed.), *Stirrings*, Epworth Press, 1976. The 'Five Pillars' Vincent suggested for the Church to correspond with the Five Pillars of Islam were: A Worldly God, A New Reality, Priority for the Poor, Journey Downwards, Things in Common.

Finally, what do our pillars mean for the Church?

1. Let's celebrate God as Worldly. Let's stop pretending to deal with metaphysical and other-worldly realities, and see our work much more as a continuation of the incarnation, as an earthly temple where earthly realities, replete with the divine, are celebrated and taken seriously. If as Jesus asserts, God receives glory by faithful disciples letting their light shine before other people. And if Jesus himself left both synagogue and temple to create sanctuaries in people's homes, then we must radically review our present concentration of resources in worship centres and our present concentration of interest on worship occasions. Our ludicrous, inappropriate, wasteful, pretentious buildings invariably totally determine what we do and are a violation of a worldly God.
2. Let's celebrate the new reality of the Kingdom. Let's set up a few 'acted parables', 'centres of Christian counter-culture', what Cedric Mayson calls 'liberated zones' and Antonia Gramsci calls 'counter-hegemonic sites'. Let's

make space for some Kingdom entrepreneurs, or groups, or projects. As it is, does what we are doing relate to the Kingdom at all, or merely service our own needs?

3 Let's really give priority to the poor. We made a good start in 'Mission Alongside the Poor', and now it will probably become part of our system. But what would happen if the poor really became the priority, above everything else, in our use of resources? And what if we asked the poor what they really need or would like? Can Christianity become Good News for the poor on their terms?

4 What about the journeys downwards? Do we need a new ecumenical Order of Sisters and Friars, to create some new models of vocation? And could we now have a few richer churches who support dozens of Methodist volunteer community workers in their 20s in the inner cities and housing estates now being pressurized to do non-vocational work? If we cannot make any journey downwards ourselves, can we pay for others who do?

5 Things in common? Not everything in common, yet. But whatever we can. Two years ago Conference decided to try to 'develop equitable systems of assessment based on income, economic status and ability to pay' and to 'find ways whereby our denominational assets can be used for the maintenance of financially poorer churches, circuits and other work.' We are still waiting.

Let's at least take our wealth seriously. Karl Marx was wrong when he said religion was the opium of the people, the poor, wasn't he? Our religion is the opium of the rich. We use it to drug ourselves to what our riches really do to us.

Document I.21

Methodism in a Multi-racial Context in London

Robinson Milwood, 'Salvation and Liberation', in Donald English (ed.), *Windows on Salvation*, (London: Darton, Longman & Todd, 1994), pp. 109–11, 114–15.

Dr Robinson Milwood was the first black West Indian to be appointed a Superintendent minister in England. Here he gives an account of the work at the Stoke Newington Mission, which includes an Educational Institute linked to Birkbeck College, Montessori Day Nurseries, and provision for Lay Training in Discipleship and a Saturday School, both led by local preachers.

I am of the firm conviction that real theology and liberation must be fully contextualised. Salvation and liberation must be the experience and expression of a particular community and its people. Salvation and liberation ought to be the testimony, along with the confession of faith, of the people in their concrete situations. This must be their experience of the liberated Christ, sharing their daily lives through the power of his resurrection. The concept of salvation and liberation is applicable where communities are confronted with inimical challenges that are impediments to their development and growth. The fulfillment of both the individual and the community is to rejoice and to live and to serve in freedom, justice, equality and peace.

Stoke Newington is a multi-racial area in composition, with a large and visible population of West Indians, Asians and Africans. The indigenous white population that existed in Stoke Newington in the mid 1950s and late 1960s has become part of its history. The area is deeply economically depressed, in that poverty is evident and part of everyday life. Disillusionment, unemployment, frustration, racism, sexism, drug abuse, prostitution and violence are the current hallmarks of Stoke Newington. At the same time, the area is politically oppressed because of the local authority's political philosophy and policy. Even within a borough where there is tremendous poverty, it seems to many residents that they further create poverty to maintain their existence. The local authority, despite its limited budget, at times appears deliberately to deny better services and facilities in order to control enterprise, expansion and development. In many ways the authority gives the impression of being anti-success and anti-progress.

It is within this context that we are beginning to see the fruits of salvation and liberation. The Methodist Church in Stoke Newington is what I call the involved church, the sharing church, the pastoral church, the church that not only speaks of salvation and liberation but seeks to live out this concept for all of God's people. At times our approach may not be the traditional and conventional one, but the things we are seeking to do, and the movement we are involved in, are the way in which we see the spirit of salvation and liberation reaching out to God's people, however hopeless their situation may appear, to give them hope and a new theology.

The Methodist Church in Stoke Newington is a traditional black Methodist Church. We use the old hymn book because it is the one that we were all brought up on… Salvation and liberation are causing people in our church to speak in tongues, to shout 'Hallelujah', 'Praise the Lord', to clap hands, to shout praises to the living God…

I see around me in Stoke Newington today young people who are mentally and emotionally unstable, and adults in their mid-forties and early fifties equally psychologically and emotionally disturbed. This is why the Mission Pastoral Counselling Unit is so vitally important. Through the Unit many have received, and are continuing to receive, the experience of inner salvation and liberation.

Over twelve months ago, a young man in his early twenties came to see me in my Counselling Surgery. He lived in Enfield and he had travelled to Stoke Newington because he had heard about our Unit. I said, 'Brother, what can I do for you?' He sat down and he paused for approximately three minutes. Then he looked at me and said, 'Reverend, I have come to you for help.' I asked him what help he needed from me. He said, 'Look at me. That is my need.' He showed me his police record. His life had been dominated by crime. He was looking like a prodigal son – rejected, disillusioned, frightened and hopeless. I read his report with pain in my heart and tears in my eyes, because as I read, it reminded me of so many other cases, of the many schools and institutions in Britain that have destroyed the future and lives of so many young people out of racial ignorance.

I said to the young man, 'If you are prepared to work with me, and to start to build a new life, I will help you.' Without any hesitation he agreed and said that all he wanted was one more chance with his life. In reading his police records, I discovered that he was a trained youth leader and I asked him if he loved children. He said he did and that he had a six-month-old child of his own. I told him that I would give him a chance in one of our day nurseries, under my own personal supervision and counselling.

In February 1994, at a staff meeting, the young man confessed that he had found a new life and that he had discovered himself anew. He had found inner peace and freedom in his soul. He is now rapidly developing as a very committed and efficient day nursery carer.

I tell this story for one simple reason: to show that salvation and liberation are not to be found in academic or theological text-books, but in people's lives, encounters and relationships, and in the act of worship in prayer and devotion of a Christian's life in the Church.

Document I.22

Decline and Growth in the United Reformed Church in the 1970s

URC, *Reports to Assembly*, 1979, pp. 37–8.

This extract from the Children's Work Committee report in 1979 gives a succinct account of the reasons for the decline in the number of children in the Church, and ways of combating it.

90 **Decline and Growth** The Assembly of 1975 drew the committee's attention to the marked decline in the number of children in our churches. Following the 1976 Assembly, three working parties were set up – in Birmingham, Dorset and Chelmsford and district. They did a thorough investigation in their own areas and we are grateful for their cooperation. The rate of decline is greater in the city than in the country (23% in Birmingham in the last five years). Reasons, however, seem to be the same in all three areas, and because it is helpful for churches to understand what is often happening to them, we summarise these. They include:

(a) the decline in the birthrate over the same period;
(b) the decline in the number of adults in the church;
(c) the higher than average age of church members, with a consequent reduction in child-bearing capacity;
(d) the closure of some churches: whereas most adult members will usuallly join other churches, children whose parents do not attend are less likely to do so;
(e) the shift in population from areas where churches are established to new

areas where churches are fewer, together with a reluctance of people (especially children) to form new attachments;

(f) the general climate of uncertainty regarding Christianity;

(g) the increase in the number of adherents of other religions;

(h) a new 'permissiveness' on the part of parents in relation to the church attendance of their children;

(j) a reduction in the number of church members willing to lead groups of children in their Christian education and to be adequately trained for the work;

(k) the failure of some churches to present themselves as communities that have a real place for children or to offer worship that seems alive or relevant to young people;

(l) a loss of nerve and enthusiasm, evident in some churches in some places.

91 This pattern of decline, however, is not the whole story. The committee have been encouraged to note that there are churches where there is considerable growth both in numbers, and, seemingly, in effectiveness. Accordingly questionnaires were sent to 36 local churches nominated by their Provincial Moderator as growing churches. While we would be hesitant to draw firm conclusions from a comparatively small sample of churches, we are able to report the following:

(a) Growth is by no means always through the transfer of members from one local church to another. In most growing churches members are joining who had no previous connection with the church or whose connection had lapsed.

(b) Sixty per cent of the churches reported growth among adults and children, whereas 11% reported growth among children only – an indication that the situation among children has a great deal to do with the situation among adults.

(c) Fifty per cent of the churches report increase among their children. In most churches the largest group of children is in the 7–10 age group.

(d) As may be expected, some growth derives from residential development in the neighbourhood of a local church; this is, however, by no means the only factor accounting for the growth.

(e) Visitation of new residents by representatives of the church often brings results.

(f) Young families attract others to the church.

(g) A major factor in every case of growth is whether the church is friendly and caring – where concern reaches out into the community through minister and members growth often results.

(h) The leadership of the minister is crucial.

(i) The educational curriculum used is not on its own a significant factor.

(j) An imaginative mid-week programme for all ages makes a real contribution.

(k) While recruitment and stewardship campaigns and the influence of the charismatic movement as such rarely seem to result in sustained growth, more sustained prayer is often given as a reason.

We draw the attention of those wishing to plan for growth to the 'Church Growth' programme organised by the British and Foreign Bible Society…

Document I.23

Inter-Faith Relations and Evangelism

Inter-Faith Relations in the Decade of Evangelism (Didcot: Baptist Union 1993).

The Decade of Evangelism in the 1990s posed sharply for the British churches the question of how they understood evangelism in a multi-faith society. This Baptist statement is particularly interesting in coming from the most evangelical group among the mainstream Free Churches.

1   **We confess** with sorrow that members of other faith communities have encountered a lack of welcome and respect, and even racism, from some British churches.

2   **We affirm** our commitment to the long-standing Baptist principle of liberty of conscience and religious practice. And we call on our chuches to recognise the presence of other faith communities in their locality and to work with them for the achievement of economic, social and racial justice.

3   **We reject** approaches to evangelism which 'target' members of other faith communities in ways which are clearly unloving and dishonouring to Christ. We endorse endeavours to witnesss to people of other faiths and none in culturally sensitive ways.

4   **We believe** that the integrity of worship of different faiths, including our own, must be respected and not compromised, whilst recognising that there are occasions when our common humanity requires us to stand alongside others. Inter-faith gatherings which meet specifically for worship are, therefore, ambiguous and inappropriate.

5   **We repudiate** the pressure, from some quarters, towards syncretism.

6   **We invite** our churches to engage in sensitive evangelism that involves:–
    a meaningful dialogue which listens as well as speaks,
    an authentic witness which testifies by actions as well as by proclamation to the love of Jesus Christ and salvation which is to be found in him alone,
    since we believe that in Jesus Christ is the unique revelation of God.

Background

The statement had its origins in a consultation, which was held at Gorsley Baptist Church on 23 June 1992, between members of the Joppa Group and others representing the Baptist Union and the Baptist Missionary Society. The consultation was hosted by the Mission Department of the Baptist Union. It followed the publication of 'A Baptist Perspective on Inter-Faith Dialogue' by the Joppa Group. Its purpose was to reflect more widely on the issues of evangelism among those of other faith backgrounds.

Participants in the consultation gladly bear witness to achieving a large measure of mutual understanding, the allaying of misgivings and fears between Baptists of very different stances, and a surprising measure of agreement.

The statement was first drafted as an expression of some of the points of agreement. It was redrafted in the light of comments received from a wider range of people and, ultimately, of comments made by the Baptist Union Council.

The specific context of the Statement is the Decade of Evangelism. The Council is aware of many other issues concerning inter-faith relationships which need further examination.

Status

The statement was adopted by the Baptist Union Council in March 1993. Consequently, it is an official expression of the opinion of the Council. It carries no legislative authority and is not binding on the churches. However, the Council commends it to the churches in the belief that it will find widespread support among them.

The Council requested that a commentary be issued with the statement as a means of explanation.

Clause 1

Many stories are told of the lack of welcome given to those of other faith communities or other ethnic backgrounds when they came to live among us. Their reception often ranged from one of coolness to outright hostility. Whilst recognising that there are glad exceptions, the churches did not distinguish themselves by giving a more positive welcome.

A particular aspect of this has been the lack of welcome given to many Christians who have settled in Britain from the Caribbean or elsewhere. Their led to the setting up of ethnic churches rather than to integration. But that is not the particular concern of this statement which focuses not on those of a different ethnic origin, but those of other faith communities.

Our behaviour, as Baptists, has often been in clear violation of God's command to welcome the stranger who lives among us (Ex 22:21; 23:9,12; Lev 19:33–34; Deut 27:19). The Bible teaches that they are to be treated with respect and dignity and that the host community should have a special care for them. Furthermore, we have neglected the teaching of Jesus as to who is our neighbour (Lk10:25–37).

We confess our sin, with penitent sorrow and apologise for our failure to live up to the teaching of our God.

Clause 2

From our earliest days Baptists have advocated liberty. In 1612 Thomas Helwys wrote, 'Our Lord the King is but an earthly king, and he hath no earthly authority as a King but in earthly causes ... Men's religion to God is betwixt God and themselves; the king shall not answer for it, neither may the king be judge between God and men. Let them be heretic, Turks, Jews or whatsoever, it appertains not to the earthly power to punish them in the least measure.'

Born out of our own experience of prejudice, we stand in a tradition that has argued not solely for our own religious liberty but for the religious liberty of all. This position is founded on a belief in the dignity of women and men as created in the image of God, God's hatred of oppression, and in the liberty of conscience of women and men before God. (Is 58:6–10; Matt 23:15; Rom 14:4, 12; 1 Pet 2:17).

We call on our churches to extend the hand of fellowship to those of other faith communities and to show courtesy and consideration in talking with other religious leaders and to invite them to appropriate events, as we do local civic leaders.

As fellow creatures of the one creator God we can join with those of other faith communities in working for economic justice, even though we may differ from them in religious beliefs.

We affirm our call to evangelism as part of the mission God calls us to, but we recognise that mission is much wider than evangelism and there is a rightful place for grappling with the concerns of justice in this world. If not, the message of the prophets and of much of the rest of the Bible makes no sense.

Clause 3

We have heard the fear expressed in some quarters that those of other faith communities are being targeted during the Decade of Evangelism in ways that are clearly inconsistent with the spirit of Jesus Christ. Whilst we affirm the right of people of all religious backgrounds, and none, to hear the good news of God's reconciling work in Jesus Christ and, whilst we affirm that Christianity is a missionary religion that has a missionary command at its heart (Matt 28:19–20), we also affirm that the methods and manner of our communicating the gospel must be respectful, gentle and sensitive (Jn 20:21; 1 Pet 3:15–16). We acknowledge that evangelism invites people to say 'Yes' to the good news of Jesus but that it also, as in New Testament days (Acts 13:42–45; 17:32–34) might meet with rejection.

We recognise that the early church lived, as we do, in a pluralistic society and yet were uninhibited in their evangelism. But we also acknowledge that there is an important difference between their situation and our own. They shared the gospel from a position of weakness. They had no position or status in the ancient world (1 Cor 1:26). We share the gospel from a position of strength. Christianity has been the religion of the old colonial powers, it is the religion of the dominant ideology and is still allied to the establishment. Furthermore, we are the inheritors of a history which has imposed the faith by the sword and which has had a long and shameful record of anti-Semitism. We need therefore to share our gospel in a specially sensitive way and to rediscover the path of Jesus which is the road of weakness and of the cross (2 Cor 13:4) and not power.

In the New Testament evangelism never took place in a cultural vacuum. The gospel was always communicated in ways that were appropriate to the culture of the hearers (1 Cor 9:19–22). We too must respect the cultures of other faith communities, learn about them and sensitively enter them if we are to be true witnesses of Jesus Christ, who was incarnate among us. We are sorry for evangelistic approaches which have been ignorant of or insensitive to these cultures.

We are aware of many white British who have either no faith or have lapsed from their faith. It is imperative that the gospel is shared with them as well. All people without distinction, should have the gospel made available to them.

Clause 4
The term 'inter-faith' worship is capable of a wide variety of interpretations and care must be taken in using it to make clear what we mean by it. Disagreements often arise because different definitions are being used. The matter deserves much wider consideration among us and readers are referred to some helpful material in the resource list for further consideration. However, since worship and evangelism are closely connected it was considerd important to make some preliminary comment on this statement.

The statement recognises that there are occasions when our common humanity binds us together, irrespective of our different faith traditions. These might particularly be occasions of human tragedy, such as occurred at the Bradford City Stadium in 1985. Grief often unites across cultural and religious boundaries (Lk 17:1–19). The Bible reports people who have experienced the grace of God in their lives continuing to worship in non Jewish settings (2 Kgs 5:17–19; Dan 4; Jonah 3–4; see also Lk 4:27). It shows God speaking to his covenant people through those from outside (Gen 14; Num 22–24; Is 45:1–7). The early Christians continued to worship in the temple and synagogue for some time before the split occurred (e.g., Acts 3:1; 13:14; 14:1).

Nevertheless, Christian worship must now be Christological. Jesus is the truth he himself spoke of in defining the worship God desires as worship 'in spirit and in truth' (Jn 4:23–24, 14:6). Any worship which implies that a route to God other than through Jesus is equally valid is likely to send out confusing signals, to imply compromise and was therefore judged by Council to be 'ambiguous and inappropriate'.

Many among us would want to argue that the Jews stand in a unique relationship with us as Christians, since our history and theology is so closely intertwined with theirs, and that therefore they are an exception to this general position. Clearly the early Christians did not initially have any difficulties in continuing to worship Jesus by attending Jewish religious institutions. And today we continue to use Jewish scriptures in our worship. Others would want to adopt a more exclusivist position with regard to contemporary Judaism. Perhaps Paul's approach to his pluralist religious context (1 Cor 8:1–6) suggests a way in which we can admit diverse opinions among us.

All would want to affirm that special respect is due to Jews in view of our common heritage, none would wish to associate with anti-Semitism in any form but rather repudiate it. All would want to stress that Jesus, whom we believe to be the Messiah was a Jew, whatever conclusion is reached about joint worship.

Clause 5
Syncretism is the attempt to unify, or the process of unifying, religions that are different. Political, civic and educational pressures exist in some quarters which seek to minimise the differences between religions and to encourage them to blend together into a religious fusion.

The Bible repeatedly warns of the error of syncretism, often in colourful language (e.g., Jdg 2:1–3; 1 Kgs 11:1–3; Ezra 9:1–15; Jer 3:6–25). Whilst repudiating the militaristic implications or imperialistic overtones of these texts the spiritual lessons are to be noted carefully. We believe that the right course is for religions to maintain their distinctiveness and for diversity to occur in the context of mutual respect and peace.

Clause 6
The final clause both summarises the significant issues of the statement and draws out their meaning further. It affirms both the necessity of evangelism (as in Clause 3; Matt 28:19–20, Rom 10:9) and the necessity of respect and sensitivity (as in Clause 3; 1 Pet 3:15–16). It further develops the meaning of Clause 3 on the means which may be used in evangelism. And it develops issues implicit in Clause 4 in reference to Jesus Christ.

Sensitive evangelism will not take place if the evangelist puts him or herself in a position of superiority above those to whom they wish to witness. Nor will it be Christ-like if communication is only one way. Sensitive evangelism will be evangelism which puts both Christians and non-Christians on level ground and that listens as much, if not more, than it speaks. Such can be seen in the encounters of Christ with people during his ministry on earth. He did not treat people as empty buckets into which to pour his good news. Rather he showed an appreciation of their unique personal circumstances and was concerned to draw them out in conversation and listen to them.

We would differ over how much there is to learn of God from those of other faiths. Mindful of our own failings and partial understandings few would want to argue that Christians have all the light whilst all others are in total darkness. Most would acknowledge in humility some light in the religions of others (Rom 2:1–16) and that therefore there will be receiving, as well as offering, in dialogue. Others would want to put it stronger and, acknowledging God's sovereign ways of speaking through those outside the covenant of Israel (Gen 14, Num 22–23, Is 45:1–7), would say there is much insight about God to be gained from those of other faiths.

Whatever position is adopted regarding this we believe that we are called not only to speak of the truth we have found in Jesus but to listen as well. We recall that, 'We do not magnify Christ by belittling others.'

Furthermore, we wish to stress that evangelism is about more than words. Again the ministry of Jesus is to be our pattern (Jn 20:21). He not only preached the word but engaged in actions of love which demonstrated the presence of the kingdom (Matt 4:23; 9:35; Mk 1:30; see also Lk 9:6). Words need to be authenticated by actions, deeds and signs. True loving evangelism will take the form of doing as well as saying.

Our evangelism is motivated by many different factors. Primary among them is the Christian belief that God has made himself known to us and made a way of salvation available to us solely, ultimately and uniquely in his son Jesus Christ (Jn 14:16; Acts 4:12; Heb 1:1–2).

The statement is commended to the churches for consideration and with the prayer that it may lead to sensitive, effective and, above all, Christ like evangelism and mission.

Document I.24

Rural Baptist Churches, 1995

Small and Rural (Didcot: Baptist Union, 1995), pp. 18–19.

This chapter by the Revd Graham Wise, Chairman of the Baptist Rural Mission Group, in a symposium produced by the Baptist Union, discusses different approaches to rural mission in the 1990s.

Some models for rural mission

A preaching team This church in a Home Counties commuter village had declined to three members plus three fairly regular worshippers and was dependent on a different lay preacher each Sunday. Holy Communion had not been celebrated for years, the property was neglected and the church seemed irrelevant to the community.

With the help of the Baptist Association a five-strong preaching team was formed who organised a planned preaching programme and re-introduced Holy Communion. Initially their families helped to swell the congregation and encourage the members. Music for services was pre-recorded and the members were also encouraged to use the gifts they had in Bible reading, welcoming others, and so on. The team were soon involved in pastoral care, began to look for opportunities in mission and began a well-advertised monthly 'family' service.

One by one and family by family new people appeared on Sunday mornings. Some were village Christians rediscovering the Baptist cause, others were incomers. Some were converted and became members, others transferred in. Decisively one of the preaching team moved into the village and he and his wife began a house group Bible study. Subsequently he was called to be the lay pastor.

By now there was a new spirit in the fellowship, it was still small but growth was a natural occurrence. It still has less than twenty members but their commitment has enabled a full-time pastor to be appointed. The buildings are now in good order and the church has a good profile in the village. From potential closure it has moved to become a strong mission-minded fellowship.

A lay pastor For many years this church, in a north-country market town, had struggled without any consistent ministry but in 1985 took the bold step of calling a lay pastor which initiated a period of new life and hope. Relevant changes to worship patterns and consistent biblical preaching enabled people to grow spiritually. Following the lay pastor's retirement in 1989 the church was challenged so commit itself to full-time ministry so that the emphasis on growth and evangelism could be continued more effectively.

A pastor was subsequently appointed and the church adopted a policy of seeking to reach out to people where they were, rather than expecting them to come to the church. Numerically the membership is still quite small but the church has clarified its vision for the future and looked for appropriate gifts within its membership. As a result a leadership team has been established alongside the pastor. House groups have been formed, there is a commitment to reaching the unchurched by relevant means and the prayer life of the church embodies a sensitive openness to the Holy Spirit's leading.

There has been no spectacular growth here but a church developing its own style under God in order to fulfil the mission to which it believes God has called it.

Using the early retired Around the large urban conurbations of the West Midlands are a number of small rural villages, many of whose inhabitants commute into the cities and even to London. In one of these villages the Baptist church is located on the parish boundary about a mile from the village centre, something which does not give is an immediate profile in the community!

In 1983 there were thirteen members, now there are over forty and the church has full-time pastoral leadership. This growth began about ten years ago when a leading elder in the church was offered early retirement and committed himself to work full time for the church, without any payment for a period of three years. With two others he sought to provide effective pastoral care and leadership, and brought a strong biblical emphasis to the preaching ministry. They also encouraged a new openness towards children in worship and the church prayed specifically for new families to come in. Such was the result that in 1988 a new building extension for youth ministry was opened.

At the end of the three years a new team of deacons and elders was elected, forming a team ministry until 1993 when the first full-time paid minister in a hundred years was appointed, since when they have all worked together as a team. The arrival of new Christian families has ensured a strong base for church life and members are actively engaged in bridge-building to the community through the annual Village Festival, Mums and Toddlers, and so on, and through involvement in local societies and organizations. Worship has moved from the traditional to something much more contemporary with participation encouraged at all levels.

The church has embraced a vision for everyone in the local community to experience the love of God and hear his message for them, and sees its mission as sharing God's good news in ways that can be easily understood and received.

Grouping rural churches Rural church groupings always appear to offer much potential but do not always achieve it. One group of five churches in the west of England has been able to provide both a presence and a ministry in some very small communities. Between them they have sixty-five members but thirty of these are in the largest centre where the minister also lives. The other centres comprise two small villages and two farming hamlets.

Expansion has not taken place in the obvious places, indeed in one of the villages the buildings are up for sale. However some growth has taken place in the main centre and, as a result of a bold initiative, in one of the hamlets where very few people live. Here the chapel has a manse attached which has been occupied by a student on placement. His presence has enabled a successful Sunday School and youth ministry to develop and he has found ready access to most schools in the area.

In small communities like these the 'presence' of the pastor is important and for many residents he, along with the vicar, is the embodiment of the church. The reward is in him being a well-known figure in all five communities. The strong base church where the pastor lives enables the others to remain viable and receive pastoral ministry so that a Christian 'presence' is maintained in communities which would otherwise have lost their place of worship years ago. Alongside the pastor is a committed team of lay preachers without whom consistent ministry would be impossible.

The existence of these churches in such small places gives a direct link to pastoral care for remote families, and the situation shows that numbers are not so important as being available to provide ministry when and where is is needed.

Secondment from a nearby church East Anglia has large numbers of rural Baptist churches and in one village close to a tourist area yet somewhat off the beaten track is a Baptist church with over thirty members but a morning congregation of about sixty adults and twenty-five children under the leadership of a recently appointed pastor.

By 1980 the church had dwindled to one remaining member who was praying earnestly for revival. A nearby town church provided a moderator and seconded three of its members to go and help in the village. A monthly 'family' service was started, shortly after which several Christians moved into the village. They committed themselves to the Baptist church which some months later was reconstituted with fourteen members. Growth continued steadily. The new life provided by these early committed Christians raised the profile of the church in the community and began to attract others to Sunday morning worship.

In 1993 growth had been such as to enable a full-time pastor to be called with Home Mission help. He has since 'door-knocked' the whole village and the church has also used a questionnaire. The church is very open to new initiatives and believes in the Willow Creek philosophy of user-friendliness. It has developed a simple mission strategy of bringing the love of Christ to the village by all possible means. Three house groups now exist, a music group leads the worship and participation in all areas of church life (including worship) is actively encouraged. Social action is a live issue and people are encouraged to be active in local affairs. The church believes it should be ready to obey God wherever he leads and takes seriously Christian commitment and service by all its members.

PART II

ECCLESIOLOGY

Introduction

The twentieth century saw a number of significant changes in nonconformist ecclesiology, both in ministry and in the structure of the Church. Some of these were consequences of moves towards visible unity, but most were initiated separately.

The most significant change was the ordination of women to the ministry.[1] Women had been accepted as the equals of men in the Society of Friends in the nineteenth century, and the Salvation Army from its beginning had women officers as the equals of men – Catherine Booth ensured that! Women had been preachers in Wesleyan and other forms of Methodism in the early nineteenth century, although the practice died out as the Methodist churches formalised their structures. But in none of these situations did women preside at the sacraments, or have exclusive pastoral care of a congregation.

The initial move came with the ordination of Constance Coltman at the King's Weigh House Congregational Church, London in 1917 (**II.1**).[2] The ordination was reported in the *Christian World*, and then the London Congregational Union had to decide what to make of it. Dr Selbie, Principal of Mansfield College, decided not to take part in the ordination because it had not been agreed in the LCU in advance. Although fortuitously one member remembered that a resolution approving the ordination of women in principle had been passed nearly ten years earlier, it is clear that the decision was that of the local church, something perfectly possible in a congregational polity but lacking the force of a collective decision – and much easier to secure. However, there were others in the years immediately following. Muriel Paulden's account of her work in Liverpool (**II.2**) does not give any clue, except to those who read the List of Contributors, that the author was a woman. When the Congregational Union reviewed the ordination of women in the 1930s, the report presented (**II.3**) almost suggested that, if it had not happened already, the committee would not be recommending it. Women's ministry was for exceptional women, with a strong suggestion that it should be for single women only; and the difficulties of finding pastorates for women in the churches were considerable. This report does not suggest that Congregationalism as a whole had accepted the ministry of women, nearly twenty years after it had first begun.

The Presbyterian Church of England General Assembly declared, in 1921, that there was no barrier in principle to the ordination of women to the ministry, but it proved much more difficult to secure approval for an actual person. When the case of Ella Gordon arose in 1956 (**II.4**) approval was given by a majority decision in the Assembly. The first Baptist to be enrolled as a Probationer by the Ministerial Recognition Committee was Edith Gates in 1922; Violet Hedger, BD, from Regent's Park College sought settlement in 1924, and the Baptist Union Council set up a Committee to consider the implications of admitting women to the

Probationers' List.[3] No objections were raised, but there was never a specific vote in the Baptist Union Assembly on the ordination of women.[4] The Methodist Church took no decision on the ordination of women until after the second failure of the Anglican/Methodist union scheme; subsequently the Conference decided positively in 1974.

A second area in which Baptists and Congregationalists moved almost simultaneously was in the appointment of ministers to oversee ministers and churches over a wide area. This happened immediately after the First World War. The Baptists called them 'General Superintendents', whilst Congregationalists used the term 'Provincial Moderator'. Interestingly, both Churches decided upon areas which were larger than the existing county or area associations, as is illustrated by the Congregational scheme as finally approved in 1919 (**II.5**). The Revd Arnold Thomas gave the address at their induction. He did not hesitate to draw a direct comparison with bishops, and this dimension of personal ministry explained the opposition which was voiced in both Churches. Despite this, there were majorities in favour in each, and the new Superintendents or Moderators established themselves very quickly. In practice they were not regarded as bishops, as Thomas supposed. This was partly because they did not have a role with power in the wider governance of the Church, and partly because they proved their value in facilitating the movement of ministers from church to church. When the Congregational-Presbyterian conversations took place in the 1960s, there was no serious thought given to abolishing them, despite the Presbyterian distrust of episcopacy; but the Presbyterians were keen to locate them in the councils of the Church, which was one of the principal reasons for the establishment of provincial synods with a set of functions more substantial than the shadowy synods of the Church of Scotland. Within Methodism there was a similar development in the office of District Chairman after 1932. Gradually this became a full-time position, with responsibilities for leadership and pastoral care.

One of the main reasons for the introduction of Moderators and Superintendents was that a polity of complete congregational independence was increasingly felt to be inadequate. This had long been recognised in the planting of new churches, where Country Unions and Associations had taken a significant part. Eventually it was reflected in new ways of thinking about the structure of the Church, and particularly local associations of churches. Historical research into the later seventeenth century showed that the associations of churches had been more important than the nineteenth-century tradition had assumed. The Baptist Union's Statement on the Doctrine of the Church of 1948 (**II.7**), though primarily prompted by Faith and Order questions, did emphasise the importance of Associations. Even the Unitarians formed a General Assembly in 1928 (**II.6**), though not without objection from those who had placed the chief emphasis in their tradition on the lack of theological tests for membership and feared that this step made them a denomination. L. P. Jacks, Principal of Manchester College, Oxford, was the most prominent exponent of such a view.

The period after the Second World War saw renewed discussion of baptism, partly because of the extent to which churches were being called upon to baptise the children of parents who were not church members, and partly because of the theological discussion provoked by Karl Barth's advocacy of believers' baptism.[5] The Methodist scholar, W. F. Flemington, defended infant baptism in his book,[6] and the Methodist Conference approved a Statement in 1952 (**II.8**), reaffirming the case for infant baptism.

Ecumenical discussions were also provoking further reflection on the understanding of ordination among the Free Churches. Among both Baptists and Congregationalists there was a 'high church' movement, which emphasised the importance of ordination to the ministry of word and sacrament with the laying on of hands. The Baptist Report of 1957 (**II.9**) reflected the development of these arguments towards the end of the 1950s. At the same time Methodism was compelled to reflect on its own understanding of ordination by its conversations with the Church of England. Whereas among Baptists and Congregationalists there was a tendency to play down the significance of ordination because of an (unhistorical) understanding of the priesthood of all believers, the Methodist problem was different. Methodist ministers began as travelling preachers, and their main difference from local preachers was the fact that they travelled further and were full time. Even among Wesleyans ordination had only begun in 1836, and none of the Methodist Churches understood ministry as primarily the pastoral care of a local congregation. The Statement of 1960 (**II.10**) linked the specifics of Methodist history with the wider history of the Church. In fact, precisely because all Methodist ministers had the pastoral care of several congregations, the Report suggested that they were the equivalent of the presbyter-bishops of the New Testament, and the ministry of Circuit Superintendents or District Chairmen was not different in kind from theirs.

The Baptists returned to the question of their Associations in the 1960s, with a Report of 1964 (**II.11**) which suggested that greater recognition should be given to the role of the Associations in a series of ways. However, it provoked a response, entitled *Liberty in the Lord* (**II.12**), from ministers and others who wished to defend the autonomy of the local church. This illustrated the difficulty of bringing about significant change which required constitutional amendment; that which could be achieved by a change in custom and practice was done. At the same time Congregationalism was involved in a similar self-examination, extending over the whole of the Church's life. One of the main practical effects of this was a change in the constitution of the Congregational Union to create the Congregational Church (**II.13**) in 1966. The Preamble and Covenant indicated the way in which the new structure was related to Congregational tradition.[7] A number of churches declined to support it and formed the Congregational Association, which eventually became the nucleus of the Congregational Federation after the formation of the United Reformed Church. Others left the Union, and formed the Evangelical Fellowship of Congregational Churches in 1966.[8] In fact, the new constitution had no legal effect, because there was no parliamentary legislation to back it up; so when the United Reformed Church Act was drafted it continued to refer to the Congregational Union. This illustrates the kind of problems involved in changing the legal status of the Free Churches (see Part V).

The problems of children and young people in the Churches have been referred to in Part I. H. A. Hamilton, Secretary of the Congregational Union Young People's Committee (1933–45) and Principal of Westhill College, Selly Oak, Birmingham (1945–54), developed the idea of 'family church' to integrate Sunday School with Sunday morning worship.[9] New thinking about child psychology and the place of religion in children's development, epitomised by Ronald Goldman's book *Readiness for Religion* (1965), led to further new approaches to the place of children in worship. Most of the Churches had reports on this topic, but the Baptist one (**II.14**) is of particular interest, because of the need to relate the place of the child to an exclusive emphasis on believers' baptism. Although the place of the child in the Church was affirmed, there were different views about the precise relationship to believers' baptism. The discussion of these issues gathered momentum in the 1980s, almost in proportion to the diminution of the actual numbers of children in the Churches.

Another challenge faced churches in areas of social change or deprivation. In 1980 the United Reformed Church approved regulations for a new ministry of Church-Related Community Workers (**II.15**). The essential tasks were very much those which Community Workers tackled in the secular sphere, but the link with the Church was emphasised.

A different issue which was coming to the fore in the 1980s was the general position of women in the churches. The World Council of Churches launched a Decade for the Churches in Solidarity with Women. After the WCC Conference on the Community of Women and Men in 1981, the United Reformed Church Assembly approved a statement on the same theme in 1984 (**II.16**).

The shifting mood within the Baptist Union is illustrated by a comparison of the 1994 report *Forms of Ministry among Baptists* (**II.17**) with the report of 1957 on ordination (**II.9**). It was now suggested that the variety of ministers, including youth ministers, lay pastors and others be included in a single Accredited List, along with traditional ministers of word and sacrament. But the concluding section on *episkope* indicated the continued wrestling with issues raised by ecumenical encounters. Finally, the report on Relating and Resourcing of 1998 (**II.18**) achieved a change in the pattern of local Associations that had been discussed at various points earlier in the century: the new Areas which were introduced corresponded to those for which Superintendents had oversight responsibility.

Methodism was also reflecting on its doctrine of the Church in the 1990s. The report, *Called to Love and Praise* (1999), set out a renewed understanding of the Church; and it was followed in 2000 by a report on Methodism and Episcopacy (**II.19**), which set out guidelines for the way in which Methodism could adopt an episcopal structure. It was part of the preparations for the formal conversations with the Church of England, which led to the Covenant of 2002.

Notes

1. See Kaye, Lees & Thorpe (2004).

Ecclesiology

2. Kaye (1988), pp. 138–42.
3. Briggs (1986), pp. 346–7.
4. I am grateful to the Revd Roger Hayden for providing me with this information.
5. Barth (1948), especially pp. 52–4.
6. Flemington (1948).
7. The Declaration of Faith may be found in Thompson (1990), pp. 198–247.
8. Cleaves (1977), pp. 20–26. For an alternative view, see Sell (2005), pp. 299–316.
9. Hamilton (1941).

Document II.1

The Ordination of Constance Coltman, 1917

The Christian World, (a) September 20, 1917; (b) October 4, 1917

Constance Coltman was the first woman to be ordained to the ministry in the Congregational Union. The first extract is a report of the ordination at the King's Weigh House Church, London, and the second is a report of the subsequent discussion of the matter in the London Congregational Union.

(a) Ordained and Married: Man and Wife as Joint Ministers

A ceremony uniting a man and a woman as ministers of the Christian Church was performed at the King's Weigh House Church on Monday evening, when Miss Constance Todd, B.D., and Mr Claud Coltman, M.A., were ordained in the presence of a large congregation. They have been called to the assistant ministry of the Weigh House, but their work will be carried on in the East End, at the Darby-Street Mission, connected with the church. The service was conducted by Dr. W. E. Orchard (minister of the church), Rev. G. Stanley Russell, M.A., (Grafton-Square Church), Rev. G. E. Dalaston, M. A., (Park Chapel, Crouch-End), and Rev. Leyton Richards, M.A.

Monday's ceremony gained additional interest from the fact that both a man and a woman were to be ordained together, and that the next day they were to beome man and wife in the same church. They were both trained at Mansfield College, Oxford, and both are graduates of London University.

To them was entrusted in the ordination ceremony – prior to which the 'Veni, Creator Spiritus' was sung – the 'ministry of reconciliation' and as Mr. Russell pointed out in a brief address, never was it so much needed as to-day. Referring to Miss Todd's ordination, Mr Russell said: 'We cast our thoughts back through the ages and realise how even in ancient Rome women held their place in the interpretation of the mysteries of religion; and as we think of the whole course of the Holy Catholic Church we realise that from the very commencement, even from the women who ministered unto our Blessed Lord, women have given up their noblest and their best to that religion which is precious to our hearts. There have been not only holy men, but holy women in every age. And we are the votaries of a religion which knows nothing of sex, but only of soul, and of the mysteries of God, who is the Mother as well as the Father of His creation. Therefore we stand here rejoicing in the fact that we have seen what may very well prove to be in that branch of the Holy Catholic Church to which we more immediately belong the beginning of a new era. A new age is travailing at the birth, and the old civilisation in which woman was the subordinate of the man has come to an ignominious end. The new civilisation which we hope to build – and not only out of its ruins, but out of new power received from on high – is one in which men and women will be in partnership.'

Rev. Constance Todd and Rev. Claud Coltman were married at the Weigh House Church on Tuesday morning, Dr. Orchard conducting the service. They intend to live in the midst of their work, and will therefore be in residence near Darby-Street, where they begin their ministry on October 1.

(b) No Sex Barrier to Ministry

On a request from the London Congregational Union for a ruling as to the admission as an accredited minister of Mrs Coltman, recently ordained at King's Weigh House Church, a long discussion ensued before it was discovered that the case had been prejudged by a recommendation of the General Purposes Committee, adopted by the Council on the case of Miss Hattie Baker. That recommendation, which became a resolution, decided that where a woman had complied with the obligation as to college training imposed on a man, she must be received on proper ordination. Mrs Coltman, on the testimony of Principal Selbie, had passed through with great distinction the full theological course at Mansfield College. Dr. Selbie had promised to take part in her ordination, but on finding that the rules with regard to consultation and arrangement with the London Congregational Union had not been complied with, he felt bound, in loyalty to the Union, to withdraw his promise. He had told Mrs Coltman, however, that he would take part in an ordination that was in accord with the regulations of the Union. Several speakers hoped that the Union would recognise as inevitable the opening of the ministry to women, and not take the line, as in some other mattters in the past, of refusing to accept an inevitability till it was no longer possible to oppose it.

Document II.2

Women's Ministry in the North of England

Muriel Paulden, 'How to Use a Down-Town Church', *The Congregational Quarterly*, vol i, no. 1, January 1923, pp. 91–3.

Miss Paulden was ordained within a year or two of Constance Coltman. This article is both a tribute to her energy and also an indication of the kind of ministry that the first women ministers undertook.

In a number of our large cities where shops, factories and offices crowd close upon one another one occasionally comes upon a Church stranded and left high and dry by the ebb of the population from that district. Sometimes such a Church struggles on – kept alive by the devoted effort of a faithful few – but more often than not it becomes derelict, and in any case its future use and purpose are a problem.

It has been said that our difficulties, if dealt with aright, may become our assets, and the Church which has lost its power largely because of its position may gain it tenfold by reason of that very position. One of the greatest needs of the Church at present is workers who are not only devoted, but equipped with the necessary knowledge, theoretical and practical, to carry on the multifarious agencies of her work – Schools, Bible Classes, Play Centres and Clubs – which in many cases fail of their purpose through lack of suitable leaders.

Berkley Street Church can hardly claim to be a down-town Church, since it is in a residential district, but the experiment which has been made there by the Liverpool and District Young People's Council might perhaps be tried with advantage by those who are seeking a solution of the 'down-town' Church problem.

In the autumn of 1919 the Council took over the church, which had been closed for some little time, and after it had been repaired and renovated, it was opened in March 1920 to serve the Liverpool and District Churches as a Training Centre and the immediate neighbourhood as a Church and Social Institute.

The Training Centre course is planned in three terms of eleven weeks, corresponding roughly to the ordinary College terms. It is open free to Congregational students; others pay a small fee. The course extends over a period of four years – each student attending one hour weekly for theoretical work, and fitting in practical work by arrangement. Since the greater number of students are engaged in business or profession all this work is done in the evening. The syllabus includes the study of the Old and New Testaments on modern lines, elementary principles of Education and Social Study.

In the first year it has been found wise to limit the groups to eight members, in order that individual difficulties may be stated and met; but in following years the work is done in lecture groups of about sixteen members. In order to develop a corporate spirit and make the centre a place of fellowship, four united meetings are arranged during the year. In October 1920 forty-six students entered the course, but by the summer term the numbers had risen to seventy-six; now the Centre accommodates about a hundred students. A preliminary diploma is gained at the end of two, the intermediate after three and the final after four years' study, provided that classwork has been satisfactory, and certain practical work done. For the final diploma a certain amount of written work is required.

A well-equipped reading-room and bookstall is an important feature of the work. Here it is possible to obtain denominational literature dealing with various subjects, and books on missionary enterprise, social welfare and education, as well as books needed in connexion with the work of the Training Centre.

Closely connected with the Training Centre, and affording an outlet where students may learn to put theory into practice, are the Social Institute, the Sunday-school and the Church, all carried on in the same building.

There are clubs for junior and senior boys, open on different nights of the week and providing amusements of many kinds – badminton, billiards, chess, ping-pong, etc. – and outdoor sports are catered for by the cricket and football clubs. The general Club is affiliated to the Liverpool Union of Boys' Clubs.

Provision is made for social work amongst girls in junior and senior clubs, meeting weekly for instruction in handwork and physical culture, music and indoor recreation; outdoor games such as net-ball and rounders are also played, and a branch of the 'Camp Fire Girls' is in being.

Boys and girls under twelve years of age attend the Play Centre.

At first the work was in charge of one person, but owing to the rapid development of the work it became necessary to appoint an assistant giving whole time service and the Committee were fortunate in securing Miss Bradley, B.A., who took up her duties in September 1921, this appointment greatly strengthening the work of the Social Institute.

An educational element is provided by the Young People's Fellowship, open to all members of the clubs of sixteen years and upwards. The fellowship meets every Tuesday evening, and its varied programme includes devotional meetings, debates, lectures, and musical evenings.

The Sunday-school has about eighty scholars, divided into lower and upper schools; the seniors are passed into the Church Guild which meets on Sunday afternoons in the church.

The teachers meet weekly to discuss organization, aims, service etc., and together plan out the syllabus which they feel to be most suitable for the school. A close connexion is kept, by visitation, with the homes from which the children come, and a definite attempt made by means of quarterly reports, parents' conferences and meetings on the school premises, to keep parents in touch with the instruction the children are receiving, and obtain their sympathetic co-operation.

It is recognised that all the clubs, societies and organizations fail of their purpose unless they help to bring the members into personal fellowship with Christ. Towards this aim weekday activities may contribute, but more is needed. A service, therefore, is held in the Church every Sunday evening, and while there is no obligation upon those who belong to the Social Institute to attend, they are heartily welcomed, along with others who have no such connexion. A few months ago it was found desirable to open a Church Membership Roll, and thus it seems that a Church will be built again where once it flourished.

It is not easy to describe a scheme which is yet only in its early stages, but the response with which the whole work has met so far encourages its supporters to feel that it is helping to meet one of the needs of our time, and will fully justify its continued existence.

Document II.3

Women's Ministry in the Congregational Union in the 1930s

Report of the Commission on the Ministry of Women, *Congregational Year Book*, 1937, pp. 91–3.

The Congregational Union set up a Commission to review the Ministry of Women in 1934, which reported in 1936. Its scope was much broader than the ordained ministry, but its discussion of that is particularly interesting in the light of nearly twenty years' experience. The tone of the report is intriguingly ambiguous, recommending no change in the principle but not offering much encouragement to women to offer for ministry.

In turning to the task which has been quite erroneously assumed as our sole concern, the question of women ministers, we may here quote the paragraph in the Report of the Commission of Inquiry as clearly indicating the reasons for our appointment:

'There are women already among our recognized Ministers, and they are doing good service, but their number is very small. When we have regard to the great part taken by women in the life of our Churches and the greatness of the contribution which it is in in their power to make to the teaching and pastoral care of our people, we cannot be satisfied with the present state of affairs. It seems clear that our Churches are not often disposed to invite women to undertake the duties of the regular pastorate. It may be that there are reasons for this which ought to be overcome. It may be that we ought to discover other forms of ministerial service for women, prepared by other kinds of training than that now given to men in our Colleges, through which we might more effectively employ their powers for leadership in our Churches.'

The number of women who have been ordained since 1917 to the home pastorate is 17; of these 13 are now in pastoral charge. A wide-reaching inquiry has been made by correspondence and interviews. It is on what may claim to be adequate knowledge that any judgments or proposals made in this Report rest.

(1) It may be fitting first of all to summarize what these ministers have reported about their work.
   (a) There is general agreement that they have not experienced any special difficulties on account of their sex, although at least one woman admits that in dealing with men and boys she has found it advisable to call in the assistance of some of the men on the diaconate, while two others have found that a sense of chivalry gave them an advantage in gaining a personal influence over boys up to the age of eighteen. Several of the women bear witness to the value of consultation with male colleagues on problems of the work, and the need of the co-operation of men and women in the common service.
   (b) All the women ministers testify to the friendly and helpful relations which they have experienced with their brother ministers, with the male deacons and with the members of the church.
   (c) While in some cases a difficulty in securing a settlement was experienced owing chiefly to the reluctance of women members, yet in other cases a call was received before the end of the College training.
   (d) All are agreed that the training should be the same as for men, and in the same College with men, as a preparation for the work among men in the pastorate. Some express themselves very grateful for and satisfied with their College course; one suggests that it might have been more practical.
   (e) In view of a common opinion that women are specially qualified for pastoral work, it deserves record that all the women, without denying that assumption, lay stress on their love of preaching and the necessary preparation for it, and one or two even express a preference. The danger of neglect of adequate preparation, due to absorption in practical service,

Ecclesiology

is by some recognized. It is evident that these women at least would not be satisfied with any form of ministry which deprived them of the privilege of preaching to which they feel themselves called.

The general impression conveyed by the evidence is that on the whole the experience of these women has been a happy one, and that their ministry has proved effective and valuable.

(2) Evidence from other sources confirms this impression, although all women have not been equally successful in their ministry. Of the ministry of most of the women very favourable reports have been given, in two cases at least failing causes have been revived, and decided progress in all respects has been made. But, on the other hand, there is a general testimony to a widespread and strong unwillingness among the churches to consider a woman as a candidate in a vacancy, so that much greater difficulty in settling a woman is experienced by the Colleges unless she is of exceptional ability, and that in several cases women have received calls because the church was in financial difficulties and could not offer an adequate salary to a man.

(3) On the basis of the evidence before them, and the personal experience of the members, the Commission feels justified in recording the following convictions:

(*a*) Despite the difficulties and disappointments which have been indicated, the measure of success which has attended the ministry of most of the women now ordained, excludes even the suggestion that the principle of the eligibility of women for the ministry of the Congregational churches should be challenged.

(*b*) Owing to the state of feeling and opinion in our churches the difficulties and disappointments, however, are so great as to forbid the encouragement of women generally to enter the ministry at present; but where a woman has shown tried capacity for such service, has exceptional ability, and is so certain of her vocation that she is prepared to run all risks, it would not be right to put any obstacle in her path, and she would have a claim to all necessary help. For it is only as women are able to prove their distinctive worth that any change of attitude and action can be expected. Should the proposals for the grouping of churches be widely adopted among the two or three ministers placed in charge, it would appear desirable that an appropriate sphere for a woman minister might be found.

(*c*) While endorsing the judgment of the women ministers that the training should be the same as that of men, and in the same College, the inconvenience of having one or two women in a College among a large number of men has proved such that, if women are to be admitted, some arrangement among the Colleges would seem to be necessary, so that all women candidates would be brought together in one of the Colleges.

(*d*) Without passing any adverse judgment on existing settlements of women in churches offering a smaller salary than what would be proper for a man, as the special circumstances have offered some justification, it would be deplorable if the practice became general, and the churches were led to believe that they could secure the services of a woman at a lower salary than those of men, and it is a matter for serious consideration whether County Unions or Colleges should give any encouragement to any tendency to offer less than the minimum salary, while recognising there may be exceptional cases.

(e) As it is at least doubtful whether a woman could physically sustain the strain of ministry to the same age as a man, the question arises as to whether women should be admitted as eligible for the Superannuation Fund under exactly the same conditions as men.

(f) It does not seem desirable for a woman to continue in a pastorate after marriage as the claims of the pastorate would not seem to allow such discharge of the duties of the home as necessarily fall on a wife and mother. The new obligations need not, however, prevent a continuance of the ministry of preaching.

In conclusion, we invite the consideration of the Colleges to (c), of the County Unions as well as the Colleges to (d), and of the appropriate Committee of the Union to (e).

Document II.4

Ella Gordon

Arthur Macarthur, 'Ella Gordon (1909–1999)', *JURCHS*, vol 6, no. 4, 1999, pp. 296–7.

Although the Presbyterian Church of England General Assembly approved the principle of the ordination of women to the ministry in 1921, it was not until 1956 that the first woman was ordained. Ella Gordon was appointed a Church Sister at St Columba's, North Shields, in 1952, and Arthur Macarthur, later General Secretary, describes the background to her ordination.

... Quickly she won the affection and warm support of the parent church and of the still tiny company at West Chirton. There, her industry and care for people moved mountains. Nine baptisms one Sunday afternoon were only one sign of her influence and I had no worries about the degree of preparation they had involved. My real worry was that I might let her down by baptising them by wrong names. It registered with me that she was already a real pastor and that I was a fifth wheel to the coach, present only because I was a minister and she was not. If she felt that it was never evident.

Leading members of our national Church Extension Committee came up to look at us. They agreed that the site already ear-marked should be bought. It was our practice for that to be done by the Church at large, but the local building operation had to be financed locally. A 'two-way' church as we then called it, with the hall separated from the chancel by a curtain, was designed by architects from

St. Columba's and money raised mostly by its members. It is impossible to say how much of even that was due to Ella's presence and the confidence she had evoked.

One day she arrived at the manse with a sheet of paper. It was her application to be received into the ordained ministry of the Presbyterian Church of England. That church had gone on record in 1921 as authorising the ordination of women to the eldership and delaring that there was no theological bar to their entrance into the ministry. No doubt the First World War with its immense casualty list had left all the churches wondering where their men had gone. Women in many cases carried the life of the churches during that awful time. Women elders began to appear and by 1956 had become a natural and an accepted part of the life of nearly all our congregations. But in the thirty-five years that had passed several gifted women had tested the waters with regard to ministry. For one reason or another the time was never right. At least one of them joined the ranks of the Congregational ministry and made a real place for herself. So, what should I do with Ella's application? It was carefully drafted with a full *curriculum vitae*, including her training, the story of her overseas service and of her work in North Shields. Its tone was right because it was genuine. Stressing that the nature of the pastoral relationship required entry to the full ministry she went on to say: 'I feel quite unworthy of that high calling, but frankly it is not on the grounds that I happen to be a woman.'

Warning her that she might very well suffer the same disappointment that had come to previous applicants, I took her application to the appropriate Presbytery Committee. She had of course become known and esteemed in the Presbytery and when her record was read out, I recall the Chairman of the Committee, Allan Whigham Price, commented to the (male) ministers present that we had better not lay ourselves open to comparison. The Presbytery debated, and when put to the vote the decision to forward the application to the Assembly saying that it 'heartily approves and endorses her application' was carried by fifty-six votes to one, with five abstentions.

The Assembly proved more cautious. Two well-known and respected ministers moved that the 1923 decision should be re-examined and the principle reviewed. They had substantial support but when their amendment was put to the votes it was lost by 123 votes to 229. The original resolution was then put and carried, 253 voting for and only twenty-five against.

Ella Gordon was thus declared to be eligible for a call. It was clear that if we were to ordain a woman we would never have better candidate. She was outstanding in ability, experience and personal grace of character. She was obviously delighted but responded without any triumphalism, as she had accepted her previous standing without any bitterness.

A call followed speedily to the nearby church of High Howden. She was ordained there in November 1956. Apart from making undue demands upon herself, her service there for the next five years was beyond praise. It was not a strong church but she nourished its life and won the affection of her people and high regard in the community...

Document II.5

Congregational Moderators, 1920

Congregational Year Book, 1921, pp. xxx–xxxi.

The Scheme for Provinces and Moderators was initiated as a result of a resolution of the Council of the Congregational Union in 1917 and prepared by a Special Committee of 12. The proposals were adopted by the Council in November 1918 and by the Assembly in 1919 and 1920 (the only significant change being the omission of the provision that Moderators' stipends should be not less than £500 p.a.

Scheme for Provinces and Moderators

I   That provinces be formed by the grouping together of County Unions, and that to such provinces moderators be appointed. It is hoped that such provinces will as soon as possible become administrative areas.

II The general duties of such moderators shall be:–
   (a) To stimulate and encourage the work of the denomination within their own provinces, and to act as friends and counsellors of ministers and Churches.
   (b) To act as superintendents of Church Aid and Central Fund Committee Administration.
   (c) To assist Churches and ministers in all matters connected with ministerial settlements and removals by personal action and by constant and regular conference with one another.

III To make the work of the moderators effective they should act in co-operation with the County Union Executives. To secure this it is highly desirable that each moderator be elected a member of the County Union Executive concerned.

IV The appointment of moderators shall rest with the Assembly of the Congregational Union of England and Wales – acting, for purposes of nomination, through a Central Committee of Nine, to be appointed ad hoc by the Council on the nomination of the General Purposes Committee.

V   For the purposes of the first appointments each Country Union in the several provinces shall send one representative to act with the Central Committee as to the nomination to be forwarded to the Council. No province to have fewer than five representatives, such representatives to have the same powers as the representatives of the Congregational Union.

VI In any subsequent appointment the Central Committee shall act in co-operation with the Provincial Committee, the members of which shall have the same power as the provincial representatives in Clause V.

VII The General Purposes Committee shall have the general administration of the scheme.

VIII Moderators shall be appointed for periods of five years.

IX In each province a Provincial committee shall be formed consisting of representatives of all the County Unions in the group – such Committee to be for the purposes of general consultation and co-operation with the moderator and to secure so far as possible a uniform policy throughout the County Unions.

No Provincial Committee is to exceed fourteen in number, and each County Union in the province is to have at least one representative.

LIST OF PROVINCES
North-West Province – Lancs, Cheshire, Westmorland, Cumberland.
North-East Province – Northumberland, Durham, Yorks.
Eastern Province – Cambs, Essex*, Herts, Suffolk, Norfolk.
East Midland Province – Derby, Lincs., Leics. and Rutland, Notts, Northants, Hunts., Beds.
West Midland Province – Staffs., Salop, Warwick, Glos. and Hereford, Worcs., Oxford, Bucks, Berks.
Southern Province – Kent, Surrey, Sussex, Hants.
Western Province – Cornwall, Devon, Somerset, Dorset, Wilts.
London Province – The Area of the London Congregational Union.
Wales and Monmouth Province

*The Essex Area being that of the Essex County Union

Document II.6

Formation of the General Assembly of Unitarian and Free Christian Churches, 1928

Year Book of the General Assembly of Unitarian and Free Christian Churches, 1929, pp. 23–4.

The British and Foreign Unitarian Association celebrated its centenary in 1925, and it was suggested that it might merge with the Triennial National Conference of Unitarian, Liberal Christian, Free Christian, Presbyterian and other Non-subscribing or Kindred Congregations to form for the first time a directly representative assembly. A Joint Delegation with ten representatives of the two bodies and their secretaries met in 1926–27 and sent out a circular with proposals for amalgamation. The majority of replies expressed approval and this Constitution was approved by Special Meetings of the two bodies on 29 and 30 May 1928.

1 Name.
   This Assembly shall be called 'THE GENERAL ASSEMBLY OF UNITARIAN AND FREE CHRISTIAN CHURCHES'.

2 Objects.
The objects of the Assembly shall be:–
   (a) To promote pure Religion and the Worship of God in Spirit and in Truth.
   (b) To carry on and promote the work and principles of the British and Foreign Unitarian Association and of the National Conference of Unitarian, Liberal Christian, Free Christian, Presbyterian, and other Non-Subscribing or Kindred Congregations, as shown in their respective rules and practice; provided always that nothing in this clause shall be construed as limiting the complete doctrinal freedom of the constituent Churches and Members of the Assembly.
   (c) To promote union, sympathy and co-operation among those who reject for themselves and others the imposition of creeds or articles of theological belief as a condition of association in religious fellowship.
   (d) To meet for consultation on matters affecting the well-being and interests of the Congregations and Societies which form the Assembly, and to take such action thereon as may be considered advisable.
   (e) To help in the founding and maintenance of Congregations which do not require for themselves or their Ministers subscription or assent to any doctrinal articles of belief.
   (f) To publish and circulate literature dealing with religious, theological, and other subjects.
   (g) To do all such other lawful things as are incidental to the attainment of the above objects, or any of them.

3 Membership
The Assembly shall consist of:–
   (a) Congregations and societies approved by the Assembly who are willing to be included in its membership, acting through their appointed representatives, viz:– One Lay Delegate from each Congregation having less than fifty members, and two Lay Delegates from each Congregation having fifty or more members above the age of eighteen years on the Church Roll; and one delegate from each Society.
   (b) The Minister or Ministers of any Congregation in the membership of the Assembly, and Ministers not in charge of Congregations, whose names appear in the 'Essex Hall Year Book', or other Year Book approved by the Assembly, issued last prior to its Annual Meeting.
   (c) All Honorary Officers and members of the Council and Committees.
   (d) Associate Members. Life Members of the British and Foreign Unitarian Association at the date of the formation of the Assembly, and individuals subscribing not less than five shillings annually to the funds of the Assembly, shall be Associate Members and shall have the right to be summoned to its meetings but not to vote on any matter except the election of their Representatives on the Council.
   (e) Honorary Members. The Honorary Members of the British and Foreign Unitarian Association who were specially elected at the Centenary

Meetings of the Association in 1925 shall be Honorary Members of the Assembly; and also any other person who may be expressly elected at an Annual Meeting of the Assembly; and they shall be entitled to the same privileges as the Associate Members.

4 Officers
The Honorary Officers of the Assembly shall be a President, the ex-President, and a Treasurer, who shall be ex-offico members of the Council. The President and Treasurer shall be elected at the Annual Meeting of the Assembly and shall hold office until the close of the following Annual Meeting.

5 Meetings of the Assembly
The Assembly shall meet regularly once in each year; and at least once in every three years the meetings shall be held outside London. The Council shall have power to summon a special meeting of the Assembly.

[Further clauses dealt with the business of the Assembly, Finance, the Council and its meetings, By-Laws, and amendment of the Rules.]

Document II.7

The Baptist Doctrine of the Church, 1948

The Baptist Doctrine of the Church in Roger Hayden (ed.), *Baptist Union Documents* (London: Baptist Historical Society, 1980), pp. 4–11.

The discussions provoked by the Lambeth Conference of 1920 within England and Wales and more widely by the Lausanne and Edinburgh Conferences on Faith and Order in 1927 and 1937 challenged the Free Churches to articulate their understanding of the Church. Among Baptists and Congregationalists there was increasing emphasis on associations of churches as well as the independence of the local congregation. This Statement approved by the Council of the Baptist Union of Great Britain and Ireland in March 1948 was also a response to Archbishop Fisher's Cambridge sermon of November 1946, and is the most complete Baptist statement of the twentieth century.

1 The Baptist Union of Great Britain and Ireland represents more than three thousand churches and about three hundred thousand members. Through its membership in the Baptist World Alliance it is in fellowship with other Baptist communities throughout the world numbering about thirteen million, who have accepted the responsibilities of full communicant membership ...

The structure of local Baptist churches

3. *(a)* It is in membership of a local church in one place that the fellowship of

the one holy catholic Church becomes significant. Indeed, such gathered companies of believers are the local manifestation of the one Church of God on earth and in heaven. Thus the church at Ephesus is described, in words which strictly belong to the whole catholic Church, as 'the church of God, which he hath purchased with His own blood' (Acts xx, 28). The vital relationship to Christ which is implied in full communicant membership in a local church carries with it membership in the Church which is both in time and in eternity, both militant and triumphant. To worship and serve in such a local Christian community is, for Baptists, of the essence of Churchmanship.

Such churches are gathered by the will of Christ and live by the indwelling of His Spirit. They do not have their origin, primarily, in human resolution. Thus the Baptist Confession of 1677 ... uses phrases which indicate that local churches are formed by the response of believing men to the Lord's command. Out of many such phrases we may quote the following 'Therefore they do willingly consent to walk together according to the appointment of Christ.' Churches are gathered 'according to His mind, declared in His word'. Membership was not regarded as a private option, for the Confession continues 'All believers are bound to join themselves to particular churches when and where they have opportunity so to do.'...

(b) The basis of our membership in the church is a conscious and deliberate acceptance of Christ as Saviour and Lord by each individual. There is, we hold, a personal crisis in the soul's life when a man stands alone in God's presence, responds to God's gracious activity, accepts His forgiveness and commits himself to the Christian way of life. Such a crisis may be swift and emotional or slow-developing and undramatic, and is normally experienced within and because of our life in the Christian community, but it is always a personal experience wherein God offers His salvation in Christ, and the individual, responding by faith, receives the assurance of the Spirit that by grace he is the child of God. It is this vital evangelical experience which underlies the Baptist conception of the Church and is both expressed and safeguarded by the sacrament of Believers' Baptism.

(c) The life of a gathered Baptist church centres in worship, in the preaching of the Word, in the observance of the two sacraments of Believers' Baptism and the Lord's Supper, in growth in fellowship and in witness and service to the world outside. Our forms of worship are in the Reformed tradition and are not generally regulated by liturgical forms. Our tradition is one of spontaneity and freedom, but we hold that there should be disciplined preparation of every part of the service. The sermon, as an exposition of the Word of God and a means of building up the faith and life of the congregation, has a central place in public worship. The scriptures are held by us to be the primary authority both for the individual in his belief and way of life and for the Church in its teaching and modes of government. It is the objective revelation given in

scripture which is the safeguard against a purely subjective authority in religion. We firmly hold that each man must search the scriptures for himself and seek the illumination of the Holy Spirit to interpret them. We know also that Church History and Christian experience through the centuries are a guide to the meaning of scripture. Above all, we hold that the eternal Gospel – the life, death and resurrection of our Lord – is the fixed point from which our interpretation, both of the Old and New Testaments, and of later developments in the Church, must proceed

The worship, preaching, sacramental observances, fellowship and witness are all congregational acts of the whole church in which each member shares responsibility, for all are held to be of equal standing in Christ, though there is a diversity of gifts and a difference of functions. This responsibility and this equality are focused in the church meeting which, under Christ, cares for the well-being of the believing community and appoints its officers. It is the responsibility of each member, according to his gifts, to build up the life of his brother and to maintain the spiritual health of the church (Rom. xv, 14). It is the church meeting which takes the responsibility of exercising that discipline whereby the church withdraws from members who are unruly and have ceased to share in her convictions and life.

The church meeting, though outwardly a democratic way of ordering the affairs of the church, has a deeper significance. It is the occasion when, as individuals and as a community, we submit ourselves to the guidance of the Holy Spirit and stand under the judgments of God that we may know what is the mind of Christ. We believe that the structure of local churches just described springs from the Gospel and best preserves its essential features.

(d) The Christian doctrine of the Trinity asserts a relationship of Persons within the Godhead, and God has revealed Himself in the Person of His Son, our Saviour Jesus Christ. Thus the Gospel is the basis of the Christian evaluation of men and women as persons. Behind the idea of the gathered church lies the profound conviction of the importance of each man's growth to spiritual maturity and of the responsibility which, as a member of the divine family, he should constantly exercise.

(e) Although each local church is held to be competent, under Christ, to rule its own life, Baptists, throughout their history, have been aware of the perils of isolation and have sought safeguards against exaggerated individualism. From the seventeenth century there have been 'Associations' of Baptist churches which sometimes appointed Messengers; more recently, their fellowship with one another has been greatly strengthened by the Baptist Union, the Baptist Missionary Society and the Baptist World Alliance. In recent years, General Superintendents have been appointed by the Baptist Union to have the care of churches in different areas. Indeed, we believe that a local church lacks one of the marks of a truly Christian community if it does not seek the fellowship of

other Baptist churches, does not seek a true relationship with Christians and churches of other communions and is not conscious of its place in the one catholic Church...

The Ministry

4   A properly ordered Baptist church will have its duly appointed officers. These will include the minister (or pastor), elders, deacons, Sunday school teachers and other church workers. The Baptist conception of the ministry is governed by the principle that it is a ministry of a church and not only a ministry of an individual. It is the church which preaches the Word and celebrates the sacraments, and it is the church which, through pastoral oversight, feeds the flock and ministers to the world. It normally does these things through the person of its minister, but not solely through him. Any member of the church may be authorised by it, on occasion, to exercise the functions of the ministry, in accordance with the principle of the priesthood of all believers, to preach the Word, to administer baptism, to preside at the Lord's table, to visit, and comfort or rebuke members of the fellowship.

Baptists, however, have had from the beginning an exalted conception of the office of the Christian minister and have taken care to call men to serve as pastors. The minister's authority to exercise his office comes from the call of God in his personal experience but this call is tested and approved by the church of which he is a member and (as is increasingly the rule) by the representatives of a large group of churches. He receives intellectual and spiritual training and is then invited to exercise his gift in a particular sphere. His authority, therefore, is from Christ through the believing community...

Ordination takes place when a man has satisfactorily completed his college training and has been called to the pastorate of a local church, appointed to chaplaincy service or accepted for service abroad by the Committee of the Baptist Missionary Society. The ordination service is presided over by either the Principal of his college, a General Superintendent or a senior minister and is shared in by other ministers and lay representatives of the church. Though there is no prescribed or set form of service, it invariably includes either a personal statement of faith or answers to a series of questions regarding the faith. From the seventeenth century onwards, ordination took place with the laying on of hands: in the nineteenth century this custom fell into disuse, but is now again increasingly practised.

The Sacraments

5   ... Following the guidance of the New Testament we administer Baptism only to those who have made a responsible and credible profession of 'repentance towards God and faith in the Lord Jesus Christ'. Such persons are then immersed in the name of the Father, the Son and the Holy Spirit. Salvation is the work of God in Christ, which becomes operative when it is accepted in

faith. Thus we do not baptize infants. There is, however, a practice in our churches of presenting young children at a service of public worship where the responsibilities of the parents and the church are recognised and prayers are offered for the parents and the child. Baptists believe that from birth all children are within the love and care of the heavenly Father and therefore within the operation of the saving grace of Christ; hence they have never been troubled by the distinction between baptized and unbaptized children...

We would claim that the baptism of believers by immersion is in accordance with and sets forth the central facts of the Gospel ... As a matter of history, however, the recovery of the truth that baptism is only for believers preceded by some years the return by Baptists to the primitive mode of baptizing by immersion, and it is a credible and responsible profession of faith on the part of the candidate for baptism which we hold to be essential to the rite ...

Membership of our local churches is normally consequent on Believer's Baptism, but differences of outlook and practice exist amongst us. 'Close Membership' Baptist churches receive into their membership only those who have professed their faith in Christ by passing through the waters of baptism: 'Open Membership' churches though they consist, in the main, of baptized believers, receive also those Christians who profess such faith otherwise than in Believers' Baptism.

Similar differences are to be found amongst us on the question of those who may partake of the Lord's Supper. 'Close Commnunion' churches invite to the Lord's table only those baptized on profession of faith. 'Open Communion' churches welcome to the service all 'who love the Lord Jesus Christ in sincerity'. These differences do not prevent churches of different types from being in fellowship one with another nor from co-operating in the work of the Baptist Union, the Baptist Missionary Society and the Baptist World Alliance. They are united in the conviction that, in New Testament teaching, personal faith in Christ is essential to the sacraments of the Gospel and the membership of the Church.

Church and State

6   Our conviction of Christ's Lordship over his Church leads us to insist that churches formed by his will must be free from all other rule in matters relating to their spiritual life. Any form of control by the State in these matters appears to us to challenge the 'Crown Rights of the Redeemer'. We also hold that this freedom in Christ implies the right of the church to exercise responsible self-government. This has been the Baptist position since the seventeenth century, and it appears to us that the growth of the omnicompetent state and the threat to liberty which has appeared in many parts of the world today make more than ever necessary this witness to spiritual freedom and responsibility which has always been characteristic of the Baptist movement...

Document II.8

Methodist Statement on Baptism, 1952

Statement on Holy Baptism, 1952, in *Statements of the Methodist Church on Faith and Order 1933–1983*, 2nd edn (Peterborough: Methodist Publishing House, 2000), pp. 33–7.

This Statement on Baptism is a fuller defence of Methodist practice than had been offered in the immediate post-union period and is on the one hand a response to the theological challenge to infant baptism offered by Barth and on the other a reflection on the pastoral issues raised by those not in regular contact with the church who sought baptism for their children.

Preamble

In issuing this Statement the Conference Committee does not seek to impose on the Methodist people any one of the varying interpretations of the Sacrament of Baptism which have been held amongst us. It is no dogmatic definition that is offered in this document; still less is it a Confession of faith by which orthodoxy or loyalty might be tested. Our purpose is primarily practical. This document moves forward to certain practical recommendations at the end. The purpose is to make sure that the use of this Sacrament shall never be casual, thoughtless, or unenlightened; to enable the Methodist people to appreciate the meaning of Baptism, as the practice emerges in the Primitive Church; and to face the fresh problems arising when parents who have only a nominal connection with the Christian Church present their children for Infant Baptism.

(I)   The Obligation of Baptism for the Methodist People

The Methodist Conference, since the Union of 1932, has by no means left the Methodist people without guidance on the obligation of Baptism. The Deed of Union itself declares as one of our doctrinal standards, that 'The Methodist Church recognizes two sacraments, namely, Baptism and the Lord's Supper as of divine appointment and of perpetual obligation, of which it is the privilege and duty of Members of the Methodist Church to avail themselves.' It also states: 'According to Methodist usage the Sacrament of Baptism is administered to infants, and regular oversight should be given by the local Church and its Minister to all who have been dedicated to God by this sign.' Among the Committees appointed by the Uniting Conference was one to revise the Book of Offices, and another to prepare a special Statement on Infant Baptism. Both Committees concluded their work in 1936, when their documents were finally approved by the Conference.

'The Order of Service for the Baptism of Such as are of Riper Years' begins with the Lord's Prayer and the Apostles' Creed, and declares in the words of Scripture that Baptism is unto the remission of sins, and promises the gift of the Holy Spirit. One of the questions asked of the candidate for Baptism is: 'Thus having pledged yourself to Christ, will you seek to fulfil the ministry He appoints you in His Church as a member of His Body?' Immediately after the Baptism the Minister says: 'We receive this person into the congregation of Christ's Church'; and this is followed by a prayer 'that he may have grace to build up the Body of Christ.'

The Order of Service for the Baptism of Infants repeats the promise of Christ's redeeming grace 'to you and to your children, and to all that are afar off', and the promise of the Holy Spirit. At the climax of the service the Minister declares that we receive the person baptized into the congregation of Christ's flock.

Both services are therefore services of reception into the One, Holy, Catholic and Apostolic Church. The Statement on Infant Baptism of the Conference of 1936, however, declares that the child's membership is necessarily incomplete, but that by Baptism the child is brought into the household of faith, and should be regarded as remaining therein, in the hope and expectation of the time when he will personally receive Jesus Christ as his Saviour and Lord. The statement concludes:

'We assert in common with the general body of the Church of Christ, that a solemn obligation to Christ, the Church, and the child, rests upon parents to present their children to Christ in Baptism, and thus to honour the ancient ordinance whereby they are joined to the visible community of Christ's people.'

There can, therefore, be no reasonable doubt that every member of the Methodist Church is under a solemn obligation to submit in penitence and faith to the ordinance of Christian Baptism, if for any reason he has not been baptized, and also to bring his children to be baptized.

The spread of unbelief, indifference to religion, and nominal Christianity in Western Europe has created a difficult situation in relation to the administration of Infant Baptism. The mixed character of a community which is neither Christian nor pagan gives rise to acute practical problems. It is notorious that many parents who do not themselves attend Church, seek baptism for their children, often with the most vague and erroneous ideas about its meaning, and with no intention of accepting the solemn obligation involved.

We are called to proclaim that the Gospel is for all men, that in Christ all were created and in Him all have been redeemed. When non-Christian parents bring their children for Baptism we are presented with an evangelical opportunity which we may not neglect. Yet we dare not pass lightly over or omit the solemn responsibilities involved in Holy Baptism. Therefore the Methodist Church in this country offers Baptism to all, and denies it to none, whose parents or guardians, after due instruction in their meaning, are willing to make the solemn promises contained in the service of Holy Baptism in the Book of Offices.

(II) The New Testament Doctrine of Baptism and its Vital Connexion with Justifying Faith

From the Day of Pentecost onwards Baptism was the symbol of entry into the Church of Christ [Romans vi. 3–7, Galatians iii. 27]. There is insufficient evidence for the assertion that infants were baptized in New Testament times, but on the other hand it is nowhere stated that their baptism had to be postponed until they became believers in the full sense. In any case those writers from whom we learn the New Testament's doctrines of Baptism clearly have the Baptism of believers in mind …

The New Testament plainly teaches that we are justified by the grace of God through faith [Romans iii. 22–4, 5 Ephesians ii. 8 etc.]. It is apparent, too, that in New Testament teaching and practice, faith in Christ is followed by Baptism [Acts ii. 38; viii. 36; xvi. 31–3, etc.]. This faith (itself a divine gift), is, in the New Testament linked with Baptism in the most intimate possible way [cf. Romans ii. 21–8 with v. 3–6]. Yet in this Sacrament of the Gospel it is God's action which is primary. In it God comes and gives Himself to us, and claims us for His own. Our action is the answer of faith, but the emphasis must always lie not on what we do, but on what God has done and is waiting to do for us in Christ. Christ Himself is the minister in Baptism, and the Sacrament is made effectual through the gracious working of God, whereby what He accomplished once for all in the death and resurrection of Christ is more and more realized in the life of those who increasingly make the divine gift their own [cf. Romans vi. 3–8 with Ephesians ii. 4–6].

(III) Infant Baptism and the Grace of God

The New Testament doctrine of Baptism is primarily concerned with the Baptism of believers. In what sense is it possible to understand the riches of the promises which in the New Testament are comprised in Baptism, when the recipient of these promises is an infant?

These spiritual benefits are summed up in the word 'Grace'. Grace should never be understood as a mere quality or disposition, but as the redeeming activity of God in Jesus Christ our Lord, through the fellowship of the Holy Spirit. The essential mark of the gospel sacrament is not what we do, but what God does. Just as Jesus welcomed the little children in the days of His flesh, so in Baptism now He receives them into His company. Baptism is God's authoritative acknowledgement of them as His children. In Baptism Christ Himself through His Church takes the children in His arms and declares what He has done and what He will do for them. Thus they come to belong to His people and receive access to the teaching, the worship, and the example of Christians. In this sense they have entered the realm of grace. Grace is the Love of God, spontaneous and unearned, active in Christ, and therefore in His Church, for the redemption of all men from the habit and bondage of sin.

Grace comes before faith, and awakens faith. In that sense it is always 'prevenient'. The Sacrament is never administered without the response of faith, the faith of the assembly of believing people, who dedicate the child to Him. Baptism signifies the act of God, whereby He shows Himself graciously calling forth the faith of His Church, and setting the Child amongst them as an inheritor of His promises. But the conscious response in the infant is always delayed. This fact should not prevent us from recognizing that the love of God, active and redemptive, is the thing signified and present in the sacrament of the Baptism of infants, and will be accessible to every child brought up in the fellowship of believing people. The practice of Infant Baptism is in itself an impressive witness to the truth that the Grace of God comes before our response, and it wholly apart from our deserts.

Ecclesiology

But though the child baptized in infancy is an heir to the promises of God, he does not always or inevitably claim his inheritance. As he comes to riper years, a continued working of the Holy Spirit is necessary, if he is to give any conscious response. He must see his sin and his need. He must put all his trust and confidence in Christ, both for his life here and for his hope of life everlasting. This full response, this saving faith, he cannot produce in his own unaided strength. It is the work of God, the Holy Spirit, and is essential to life in Christ. Whether this work is called 'Conversion' or 'the New Birth', whether it is regarded as sudden or gradual or as both process and crisis, it is true that without the gift of saving faith those baptized in infancy can never attain to their privileged life as sons of God. While Methodists recognize that Christ is the true Minister of Baptism and that therein Christ sets the child in the company of His people, they also declare that the personal appropriation of the promises of Christ by the child should be prayed for and expected.

Both Sacraments point forward to the end, to the final consummation. As we partake of the Lord's Supper we proclaim the Lord's death 'until He come'. So, according to St. Paul, Baptism proclaims the death and burial of the old self with Christ, and our rising again with Him to a new life in which we ever look forward to His final manifestation in glory. This promise is not only for those who are of riper years. It is also for little children.

The Methodist Church believes the Baptism of Infants to be in accordance with the mind of Christ. Not only is it sanctioned by the practice of the Church since very early times; it proclaims and offers the grace of God, who is eternally active for the salvation of all men, and receives even the youngest into that realm where His promises are gloriously fulfilled. Sin is not simply a matter of individual wrongdoing; each one of us is also involved in the sin of the world, in the community of evil. When an infant is baptized, he is received into the new Israel of God, which is God's answer to the community of evil.

Document II.9

The Baptist Understanding of Ordination, 1957

The Meaning and Practice of Ordination among Baptists, reprinted in R. Hayden (ed.), *Baptist Union Documents* (London: Baptist Historical Society, 1980), pp. 74–81.

This Baptist Union Statement on Ordination of 1957 indicates Baptist thinking on the nature of ministerial distinctiveness in the late 1950s.

IV   The Meaning of Ordination

47   The following form of words is offered as a definition of ordination. The subsequent paragraphs are an elaboration of this definition in which suggestions are made concerning some of its implications.

Ordination is the act, wherein the Church, under the guidance of the Holy Spirit, publicly recognises and confirms that a Christian believer has been gifted, called and set apart by God for the work of the ministry and in the name of Christ commissions him for this work.

48   (i) The Call of God is fundamental.

Consideration of ordination must begin with the recognition that Christian ministry depends upon the call of God and is His gift in Christ to the Church (Ephesians 4, 11–12).

It is given by Christ and derives its sanction from Him who is Himself the Head of the Church. No man can take upon himself any such task except at the imperative and irresistible call of God (Gal. 1, 1). This fact is basic to our understanding of the ministry and to our interpretation of ordination (see par. 20 [not reprinted]).

49   (ii) Ordination is an act of the Church.

The work of the Ministry is not personal service rendered by the individual in his own right, nor is a minister a free lance 'prophet' exercising his ministry in a private capacity. He is a leader within a fellowship, viz. the Church (Acts 14, 23; 15, 22; Romans 16, 1; 1 Cor. 12. 18, 28, etc.). He speaks in the name of God; but in so doing he speaks within the witness of the Church and in its name; and so his work of ministry must be an act of Christ and of the Church. Ordination signifies the setting apart of the minister for this work both by Christ and the Church.

In view of the responsibility which the Church undertakes in thus commissioning a man to the work of the ministry it is clearly right that the man concerned should be properly tested before this commissioning takes place. (See further par. 58.)

50   (iii) What is meant here by the Church?

In the section on the New Testament (par. 21 [not reprinted]) it is stated that the New Testament speaks of both the Church and the churches and that the local church is a manifestation in Corinth or Rome of the Body of Christ. Among Baptists it has been customary for the word 'Church' in regard to ordination to be interpreted as meaning the local church in which a man is to exercise his ministry. We accept this interpretation, but it is our conviction that the New Testament teaching, as well as much Baptist practice in previous centuries, would suggest the view that the local church is not an isolated unit, but shares in a fellowship in which the churches are members one of another, and that therefore the local church must act in the closest fellowship with all the churches of its denomination through their representatives. Hence it seems to us proper that at the Service of Ordination there should be represented the Baptist Union, the Association, the College and neighbouring Baptist churches. The whole Baptist community is thus acting through its members, the arrangements for the Service of Ordination being the responsibility of the local church.

It is also true that the Church is now divided into separate communions, and in this situation each denomination has developed its own practice of ordination. Although it is difficult to speak simply of an act of the Church or a ministry of the Church it is desirable that an Act of Ordination should include members of other denominations as a witness to the inherent unity of the Body of Christ.

51 (iv) By the work of the ministry we mean what is frequently called 'the ministry of the Word and Sacraments'.

This work is more fully described in the New Testament section (par. 10–11, 14–16 [not reprinted]) where it is suggested that ministerial function implies leadership of the Church's worship, the administration of the ordinances of Baptism and the Lord's Supper, the proclamation of the Gospel and the teaching of the faith, the work of pastoral care and Christian service. This work may or may not be the minister's sole activity; but it will be his primary activity to which he devotes most of his time.

52 This ministry will normally be exercised within a local church, but it need not be confined to the local church. A man may exercise ministerial functions within the total life of the Church in other spheres of service, e.g. Superintendencies, Colleges, Chaplaincies, etc. We are not prepared to make a specific list of such spheres of service, but we would emphasise the point that only service which demands that a man shall exercise some of the ministerial functions mentioned in par. 51 may be regarded as within the scope of ordination.

Most of these spheres of service fall within a man's denomination, but the development of inter-denominational spheres of service is characteristic of our day. We believe that any ministerial function in these spheres of service is within the scope of ordination and in this connection we note that among the British Free Churches there is a widespread mutual recognition of one another's ministries.

53 (v) How does the Church 'recognise, confirm and commission'?

A church, in quest of a minister, after certain enquiries and consultations, invites a man to conduct public worship on one or two occasions; thereafter the members meet together in the Church Meeting and, after individual and corporate prayer in which the guidance of the Holy Spirit is sought, they invite the man to be their minister. In so proceeding the church is recognising and confirming 'that a Christian believer has been gifted, called and set apart by God for the work of the ministry', and by committing to him the pastoral oversight it 'commissions him for this work'. Ordination is thus implied in these acts and in the man's response to them. The elements of ordination are already present in the process of divine call, recognition, confirmation and commissioning by the church.

Whilst it is true that the elements of ordination are already present in this process, nevertheless it is most fittingly expressed in a particular Act designed to recognise the fact of God's call to the ministry, to confirm that call, to commission His servant, to invoke the help of the Holy Spirit and to ask God's blessing on his work. In such a Service ordination receives its natural and most impressive expression.

54 (vi) What is conferred by ordination?
It is not possible to define precisely what is conferred by ordination, but three things are clear. First, the Service of Ordination is an occasion of blessing to all who share it, and especially to the person ordained in response to the prayer of the congregation. Secondly, the local church being assembled, together with representatives of the wider fellowship, publicly acknowledges the person ordained as being one called of God to the work of the ministry the exercise of which is recognised throughout the churches (see par. 20 [not reprinted]). Thirdly, this acknowledgment and recognition give him the right to be regarded both by other Christian communions and by secular authorities as one set apart for the work of Christian ministry.

These statements do not imply that ordination confers upon a man a status which belongs to him of right for life. The recognition is in regard to the exercise of ministerial functions in the Church, and comes to an end when a man no longer exercises those functions as his primary activity (cf. par. 23–26, 37, 38, 51 [only 51 reprinted]).

55 (vii) The relation between ordination and induction.
In the course of time the word ordination has changed its meaning within our denomination (see Appendix I [not reprinted]). Whereas formerly 'ordination' related to the induction of a pastor to his pastoral office in a particular local church, today the word is used to refer rather to the public acceptance by the ordinand of a ministry of the Word and Sacraments (which phrase is used to include generally pastoral functions) and approval of that acceptance by the churches of our faith and order represented by the gathered congregation. The term 'induction' which is of fairly recent innovation, applies to the specific induction to a particular local sphere of service (which may not necessarily be in a local church). In considering the relationship between ordination and induction we intend by our definition of ordination to imply that before any public Service of Ordination can take place there should be an acceptance of a specific realm of ministerial activity. This in turn would seem to imply what is in fact the common custom, whereby both the Act of Ordination and of Induction occur at the same time, but this does not appear to us in principle to be essential. As long as the ordinand has already accepted a specific sphere of service there should be no objection to the Services of Ordination and Induction being separated by a short space of time. Ordination is not, however, complete until induction has taken place...

V   The Practice of Ordination

57 (i) Who should be ordained?
The simple answer to this question can be given in the words of our definition of ordination. It is for those who are 'gifted, called and set apart by God for the work of the ministry'. Confirmation of a man's sense of call is normally sought from his own home church, his College Committee, his local

Ecclesiology

Association, or the denomination in which he seeks to exercise his ministry, as well as by the conviction of the local church or other body by which he is to be commissioned. The test will be on a number of grounds – on his Christian experience, his moral standing and character, his gifts for preaching and pastoral work and on his readiness both to learn and to teach.

The devotion, of such men to the work of the ministry will be demonstrated in their willingness to pursue such training as may be required by the denomination, and then in their strong intention to continue in the ministry.

The foregoing statements refer to men and women without distinction of sex.

The language used might be interpreted so as to apply to deaconesses, but we have in fact regarded the whole question of the status of deaconesses as lying outside the scope of this Report (see Appendix 4 [not reprinted]).

The questions raised by the entry of ministers of other communions into the Baptist ministry are many and complicated; although it is the practice among Baptists not to require re-ordination, we feel that so large a subject is outside the scope of our Report.

58 (ii) When should the Service of Ordination take place?

At present missionary ordinands are ordained at the conclusion of their training and before proceeding to the field, and ordinands for the home ministry at the time when they begin their first pastorate. We have considered whether or not the Service could be at the conclusion of the probationary period. Our considered view is that, in regard to the collegiate candidate, it should be held on entrance to his first sphere of ministerial service after the satisfactory completion of his College course; in regard to the non-collegiate candidate it should be held at the time when the ordinand's name has been placed on the List of Probationers, because he has then completed a time of testing and preparation which may be considered equivalent to that undertaken by a collegiate candidate.

59 (iii) Where should the Ordination Service take place?

In our view the Ordination Service should take place within the fellowship of the local church and in the presence of those indicated in paragraph 50. In the case of a man not taking up pastoral charge, the work to which he is being commissioned should be represented. The place where the Service is to be held may depend upon individual circumstances (e.g. whether a man is called to serve abroad or to chaplaincy work, etc.)...

60 (iv) Who should participate in the Ordination Service?

In paragraph 50 we state our opinion that there should be present at the Ordination Service representatives of the Baptist Union, of the Association, of the College and of neighbouring Baptist Churches. It appears to us fitting therefore that the conduct of the Service should be in the hands of some or all of the following persons: the College Principal, the Area Superintendent or an officer of the Association, the minister of the ordinand's home church or some other senior minister in good standing. In addition to these ministers the ordinand himself and a representative of the work to which he has been called will participate in the Service. Our suggested Order of Service indicates what share in the Service each of these persons is likely to have.

61 (v) Should ordination be with the laying on of hands?

The ... imposition of hands in association with ordination may be supported by Scriptural passages and by frequent custom among Baptists during the seventeenth and eighteenth centuries, though there is no suggestion in this evidence that the practice can be regarded as an essential element of a Service of Ordination.

To some Baptists, the imposition of hands is justified both on account of the evidence already mentioned and as an impressive symbolic act widely used in the Christian Church, expressing the solemnity with which the Church through its representatives declares that Christ has chosen and ordained His servant; with this attitude the majority of the group would agree. Other Baptists judge that in Christian history the imposition of hands has been associated with doctrines of the ministry and of grace that Baptists do not accept and therefore this practice should not be used at Services of Ordination among Baptists.

When the imposition of hands is practised, it is suggested that the act should be a corporate one in which those persons mentioned in paragraph 60 should share. A corporate imposition of hands is justified both by Scripture and by Baptist history; it well expresses the truth that those who are engaged in the act stand as representatives of the Church so that, in fact, it is the whole Church which thus by prayer and the imposition of hands seeks the blessing of God upon the minister-elect and declares him to be ordained to the Christian ministry.

It is now the frequent practice among Baptists to ask a layman to share in the corporate imposition of hands. It is doubtful whether this practice can be supported by reference to Scripture and it was not known among Baptists in previous centuries; but it may be accepted on the ground that the declaration of ordination and the commission to the work of the ministry is an act of the whole Church and not of any section of the Church.

Document II.10

Ordination in the Methodist Church, 1960

Ordination in the Methodist Church, in *Statements of the Methodist Church on Faith and Order 1933–1983*, 2nd edn (Peterborough: Methodist Publishing House, 2000), pp. 104, 106–7.

This Statement by the Methodist Church, approved only a few years later than the Baptist Statement in the previous extract, makes an interesting comparison. For Methodism the crucial act was Reception into Full Connexion and before union in 1932 only the Wesleyans had invariably used the laying on of hands in ordination.

Ecclesiology

The Ministry in Methodism

… The present Methodist ministry is heir to the traditions of all these Conferences, and it may fairly be said that Methodist Ministers are both travelling preachers in the Methodist Connexion and Ministers of the Word and Sacraments in the Church of God. They have authority to preach the Word and administer the Sacraments and they normally exercise pastoral care in a number of local congregations. They thus constitute a ministry which corresponds to that of the presbyter-bishops of the New Testament. Some of the 'charismata' of the Holy Spirit which in the New Testament period were widely distributed over the members of the Church are now ordinarily exercised in Methodism by the ordained ministry, but they are also bestowed by the Spirit on those who are outside the ordained ministry. The Reformation office of 'deacon', closely corresponding to the New Testament 'diaconos', is held among us by the various kinds of 'stewards', who are called to perform their stewardship to the glory of God and the building up of the Church. Chairmen of Districts and Superintendents of Circuits, though they have additional functions to those of the ordained ministry in general, have the same ministry as the rest.

The Ordination Service

… The act of making a man a Minister is performed by the Methodist Conference, by its standing vote in the Reception into Full Connexion and through its appointed representatives in the Ordination Service; it is not performed by individuals, or a group of individuals, acting in their own capacity…

By reception into Full Connexion and Ordination the office of a Minister and Pastor in the Church of God is conferred. The ordained Minister enters fully upon the status, duties and privileges of the Methodist ministry. He is called to be a Steward in the household of God and a Shepherd of His flock, and the exercise of this ministry is his sole occupation (CPD p. 265). But the distinguishing mark of a Methodist Minister is not simply that he is a full-time worker in the Church. Others, not ordained, are also full-time workers in the Church. The ordained Minister has also a principal and directing part in those spiritual activities, preaching the Word, and pastoral care, which he shares with lay members of the Church. In the office of a Minister are brought together the manifold functions of the Church's ministry, and it is his privilege to exercise them as the servant of Christ and of his fellows in the Church as a whole, as the Church under the guidance of the spirit shall appoint him; for this he is set apart at the call of Christ, and commits himself to the Church's discipline, that he may give himself wholly to the demanding and yet glorious 'work of the ministry, unto the building up of the body of Christ' (Eph. iv. 12).

The ordained Minister has full authority to administer the Sacrament of Holy Communion. Deaconesses, Probationers, Lay Pastors, Local Preachers and other laymen are entitled to administer this Sacrament only when especially authorized by a temporary Dispensation of the Conference.

The Methodist Church is committed to the view that the ordained Minister does not possess any priesthood which he does not share with the whole company of

Christ's faithful people. But the doctrine of the 'priesthood of all believers' is that we share, as believers, in the priesthood of our great High Priest, Jesus Christ Himself. As our High Priest He sacrificed Himself, a faultless offering in utter obedience to God and infinite love for man, for the cleansing of our sins and our reconciliation to God; His sacrifice was made once for all, but it is for ever efficacious, and He for ever makes intercession on our behalf. Into that priesthood of Christ we are taken up by faith, and we in our turn, and in self-identification with Him, offer ourselves in utter humility and obedience as a living sacrifice to God. We are 'priests unto God', and therefore 'take upon ourselves with joy the yoke of obedience', as we are enjoined in the Covenant Service. So the doctrine does not mean that every Christian has the right to exercise every function and administer both sacraments. For it is not an assertion of claims, but a declaration of our total obedience. A Methodist Minister is a priest, in company with all Christ's faithful people; but not all priests are Ministers.

Ordination is never repeated in the Methodist Church.

A Minister is Christ's ambassador and the representative of the whole people of God. Called of God to his high and responsible office, equipped by the Spirit with the gifts necessary for its fulfillment, and supported by the prayers and confidence of the Church, he is charged with a special responsibility for guarding the truth of the Gospel and communicating it to others; for this he is trained and prepared by his work in College and by his continued study of the Bible and the Faith throughout the years of his ministry. He is the confidant, often the sole confidant, of his people in many kinds of trouble, and he mediates to them the pity and the care of God.

Document II.11

Report of the Baptist Union Commission on the Associations, 1964

The Report of the Commission on the Associations (London: Baptist Union, 1964), pp. 10–15.

This Report emphasised the crucial role of the Associations in Baptist life, following the lead in the 1948 Statement on the Church. However, no radical change resulted at this time.

3. The Purpose of the Associations.

... [P]articular matters ... express the nature of church life in association, demonstrating ... that an Association is no mere administrative unit, and that its activities are not simply a repetition of what belongs to the life of the local church. The Commission has given thought to the following :–

Ecclesiology

A. Mutual Inspiration and Evangelical Encouragement

The Association manifests the reality of Christian fellowship between churches of different types and sizes, between the large city church and the small village company. Baptists have always recognised that membership of the Church of Jesus Christ becomes real in membership of the local church. It is for this reason that stress is laid upon the effective functioning of the local church. The Association exists to aid this functioning. It is the churches working together for the encouragement of each. There is therefore a responsibility upon all churches to share in the Association fellowship, for through it there is not only the encouragement of the struggling cause but also the making aware to the prosperous church that such causes do exist and belong to an Association. Out of such knowledge there springs the possibility of aid and a pinpointing of particular challenges to the church's evangelism. Many smaller churches are encouraged and aided by Association assistance to undertake evangelical enterprises which would be out of the question for them to face up to alone.

B. Christian Education

Christian education becomes more and more the responsibility of the Association as it is the Association which finds it possible to arrange courses for deacons, lay-preachers, Sunday School and youth workers, and others serving the local church. Only a few churches have the personnel and facilities to undertake organised training within their own fellowship and thus Association programmes of education assume an ever greater importance. The need for trained leadership within the local church is acknowledged as most urgent, and Associations are probably in the best position to meet this need.

C. Christian Citizenship

In an age in which society has largely abandoned Christian codes of behaviour, the matter of Christian Citizenship assumes very great importance. Faced with practical problems, the local church often finds itself lacking both experience and influence. It has already proved to be of great value if such a local church can draw on the experience already gained by other churches in similar circumstances or on the considered conclusions arrived at through the studies of citizenship groups in the Association or Union, and call for joint action by the churches of the Association. Associating churches are also able to make a stronger impact on the community in the matter of training in Christian Citizenship as they act together.

D. Support of Wider Baptist Witness

Both the Baptist Missionary Society and the Baptist Union recognise the vital importance of the Association unit as a channel for information to the churches and also as the collecting unit of gifts. Although the Baptist Missionary Society has Missionary Auxiliaries – and these are not always linked satisfactorily to Association Missionary Committees – the Association Missionary Secretary is often rightly a key figure in the local situation. The Baptist Union Home Work Fund is even more clearly and closely related to the Association unit, with the

Association Treasurer usually acting as the link between the local churches and the Baptist Church House, and the Home Work Fund providing a refund to finance the Association. The causes of the apparent failure of the Association line of communication as it affects both the Baptist Union and the Baptist Missionary Society are matters to which we return later.

E. The Ministry
As the pattern of ministerial recognition has developed over the past years, Associations have been given more and more a vital role to play. This, in itself, is enough to raise the question of the relationship of the Association to the Union, for as things stand at present it is the Union which finally grants ministerial accreditation. When it was desired that all candidates for the ministry should have a local commendation beyond that of their local church, it was the Association which was asked to supply it, so that now all candidates for the ministry have first to appear before the Association ministerial recognition committee. In a similar way the Association also has the responsibility of commending men seeking to pass from the Pre-Probationers' stage to the Probationers' List before they are interviewed by the Baptist Union Ministerial Recognition Committee.

The matter of the settlement of ministers and possible Association involvement in such a settlement is often raised. With an inadequate supply of ministers, the settlement of men becomes a matter of even greater importance. The General Superintendent is usually closely involved in settlements and brings a wider viewpoint to bear than that of the local church. A properly functioning Association is also in a position to see the over-all need. Consultation in which General Superintendent, Association Officers, and the local church are involved is suggested by some as a desirable preliminary in ministerial settlements. This question raises vital issues of the relationship of the local church to the Association as well as the Association to the Union and must be looked at separately.

F. The Strategy of Church Extension
It is now generally accepted that church extension projects must be of wider concern than that of the local churches promoting them. Such practical matters as finance for building, allocation of sites, Home Work Fund Grants for the ministry take extension immediately into the purview of the Association. But in any case, as a matter of principle, if the idea of 'associating' has any content at all, any new church extension contemplated should be recognised as requiring Association consideration before being proceeded with seriously. This matter is becoming increasingly more complicated by the relatively large numbers of people who are 'on the move.' New towns have, for example, already sprung up where villages once stood, and populations have increased in a few years from a thousand or so to upwards of sixty thousand. There is evidence to suggest that the movement of population will be even greater in the next twenty years ... There is a suggestion that the population of N. Bucks. will be increased by 350,000 chiefly by the establishment, in the next twenty years, of a monorail city with an estimated population of a quarter of a million. This sort of development presents Associations

in reception areas with problems beyond their resources. In fact the need is now clearer than ever for church extension to be developed as a national policy rather than leaving it to local churches and Associations. This could mean a pooling, for the benefit of all, of Association resources of thought and foresight as well as of finance. In our judgment the formation of a denominational policy for church extension is urgent.

G. Church Closure

We are inevitably brought face to face with this problem. From time to time evidence has been produced of churches holding on in situations where reason suggests, and evangelical strategy demands, closure. Whilst it is true that reversionary clauses in Trust Deeds sometimes make it difficult, if not impossible, to release money from the sales of redundant churches for church extension, this statement is sometimes made an excuse for doing nothing and, in any case, the very sight of Baptist churches situated close to one another or left isolated by the moving tide of population scarcely proclaims the Gospel of enthusiasm and evangelical strategy. The matter of redundant churches is one of utmost urgency. But the total responsibility of the Association in this matter remains still to be defined. Certainly the Association has the task of surveying the church building position within its territory, out of which survey certain things will become clear. Taking action on the results of such a survey depends again upon the decision about the Association-local church relationship.

H. Grants Administration

All applications for grants made by the Home Work Fund must have the recommendation of the Association in which the church making the application is situated. This places upon the Association the need for intimate and up-to-date knowledge of the condition of each such church and the opportunities that lie open to it.

The thinking of the Commission has been governed by the question as to how these defined responsibilities may be carried out in the light of the known situation to-day and the anticipated situation to-morrow. This has led to a discussion of denominational organisation as it affects the Association as well as consideration of the structure of the Association itself. It has also been found necessary to take serious note of the evident truth that an effective Association can result only from effective local churches. Yet beneath all these points lies the fundamental truth that no fellowship can ever function where there is not mutual trust. At heart the effectiveness of the Baptist Association life – and indeed of the Baptist Union life – depends upon there being a spirit of mutual trust amongst us.

Document II.12

Liberty in the Lord, 1964

Liberty in the Lord (London: Baptist Revival Fellowship, 1964), pp. 46–8.

The Report on the Associations provoked a vigorous response from those who felt that the independence of the local congregation was under threat, possibly accentuated by the contemporary developments in Congregationalism. The evangelical authors of this pamphlet produced by the Baptist Revival Fellowship felt that scriptural principles were at stake.

IV Some Immediate Conclusions and Suggestions

(i) Baptists must be alerted to the pace and direction of these modern trends and to the seriousness of the situation we face. We are approaching a point of crisis in our denominational life which will involve us all in heart-searching questions and difficult decisions. We need to do much more clear theological thinking before this crisis breaks upon us.

(ii) Our attitudes, judgments, decisions, and policies must always be firmly based on doctrine and not on mere expediency. We must recognize clearly the premises that underlie the 'practical' changes which are being suggested, and evaluate them, and, if need be, revise them on theological grounds.

(iii) We urge ministers to give their people doctrinal teaching that they too may be made aware of the Scriptural principles at issue.

(iv) We re-affirm our belief in the concept of the gathered church. This we understand to mean that 'Each local church is to be a "gathered community" of regenerate believers, living in fellowship with all believers within the one body of Christ, and having "liberty under the guidance of the Holy Spirit, to interpret and administer His laws", and is thus sufficient under Christ for the ordering of its life in obedience to His will'. We hold that this is true to the New Testament teaching about the church and rests upon sound and fair New Testament exegesis. We dare not give up or compromise this important New Testament doctrine and principle.

(v) We do not believe that an inter-dependency, construed in terms of connexional church polity, involving legislative and executive authority for Associations and National Assembly, will remedy the spiritual malaise of our churches. Further, we believe such a change of polity would bring many new dangers which outweigh any administrative advantages.

(vi) One clause of the 'Declaration of Principle of the Baptist Union' reads:
'The basis of this Union is:
1. That our Lord and Saviour Jesus Christ, God manifest in the flesh, is the sole and absolute authority in all matters pertaining to faith and practice, as revealed in the Holy Scriptures, and that each church has liberty, under the guidance of the Holy Spirit, to interpret and administer His Laws ...'

Ecclesiology

We therefore believe there should be no fundamental change of denominational polity without:
(a) Consultation with all local churches in the Baptist Union.
(b) Presentation of all positions, and opportunity for the fullest open debate in assembly.

(vii) We affirm that the church is never more powerful spiritually than when she is spiritually pure in membership, character, and strategy.

(viii) Ministerial and church settlement problems may be reduced by giving greater power to Superintendents and associations, but will be ultimately *solved* only by an increase of sensitivity to the Holy Spirit in both ministers and churches.

(ix) We recognize that in many of our churches there is a paucity of spiritual leadership. We consider this can be remedied only by the re-establishment of the Eldership in our local churches. (We gladly note one or two Association Reports also suggest this and we realize that many deacons are now already exercising the functions of elders in their churches.) To this end we believe we must pray the Head of the Church by His Spirit to bestow gifts of 'Elder qualities' on men and so raise up elders in every church – whose appointment, office, and work would be quite distinct from that of the deacons. We note that some of our churches are reaching out after this. In our judgment the New Testament contains no evidence for placing the functions of eldership for the local church in the hands of a representative synod or a group at Association level, or in the hands of one man at local church level, and there is much evidence to the contrary.

(x) There may be some cases, in our judgment, where small causes should be united. Then we believe New Testament principles indicate that, for example, three present village churches should become one church with one eldership, one diaconate, and one church meeting with one Pastor, and not a circuit of three churches (*i.e.*, not three churches managing with one Pastor, but working as one church). We regard these as vital distinctions.

(xi) We fully accept some recent words of Dr. E. A. Payne: 'Faith and Order issues are inescapable and are becoming increasingly pressing within every Christian denomination as well as between them.' We suggest that the Baptist Union officers immediately initiate discussions between those whose viewpoint is represented in this Report and those of the other theological viewpoints in the denomination.

(xii) We repudiate isolationism as contrary to the spirit and practice of the New Testament and we affirm that all believers should have fellowship with one another on a wider scale than the local church, seeking always an adequate basis of doctrine and experience for such fellowship and provided always that its purpose is not legislative, but for mutual consultation and edification.

Document II.13

Constitution of the Congregational Church, 1966

Congregational Year Book, 1966–67, pp. 40–41.

Congregationalists were thinking about the same issues as Baptists at the same time; but in their case the result was a new constitution for a Congregational Church based on a covenant made among the member churches. The Preamble (particularly §5) and Covenant explain the thinking behind the new constitution. Not all churches accepted it.

Preamble and Covenant

1 According to the Scriptures, the purpose of God from the beginning was to gather all people to Himself in fellowship. He covenanted with the people of Israel that they might be the agents of this purpose. In the fullness of time God sent Jesus Christ his Son to make a new covenant not with a nation but with all who believe in Him. Thus, through God's redeeming act, a community of believers, the Church of Jesus Christ, was called into being to be the new agent of His unchanging purpose. By the continuing presence of Christ and the power of the Holy Spirit God gives new life to His Church in every generation.

2 Congregational (or Independent) churches were first gathered at the time of the Reformation. They acknowledged that they had been called by God's grace into a covenant relationship with Him. The members of these early churches entered into a relationship with one another the essential spirit of which was of grace rather than of law, and they believed it to be right to use the word covenant to express this relationship. Although in early days it was usual for the terms of the covenant to be set down, there have been times when the terms have tended to be implicit rather than explicit, but the notion of covenant has never been wholly lost. The formation of these churches as covenanted fellowships under Christ was based upon what was believed to be the truly Scriptural character of the Church's life, worship and forms of government. Congregationalists claim unity with all those who, through the centuries of Christian history, have acknowledged the Lordship of Christ in His Church and have sought to be obedient to the leading of the Holy Spirit.

3 A Congregational church is a fellowship of those who, believing in God as heavenly Father, and accepting Jesus Christ as Lord and Saviour, and depending on the guidance of the Holy Spirit, have covenanted with one another to live in God's presence according to all that He has made known or will make known to them. They know that such life is possible for them only because Jesus Christ has redeemed them and the Holy Spirit continually inspires and directs them, giving them all that is necessary for life in the Church. They have the Scriptures to nourish them, the sacraments of Baptism and the Lord's Supper to sustain

Ecclesiology

them, and ministries to serve them. Under the guidance of the Holy Spirit, each church is called to live in direct response to the Lordship of Christ.

4 Such a covenanted fellowship accepts its calling to be an agent of the continuing ministry of Christ. It has power and responsibility as His Church to formulate its covenants and affirmations of faith; to order its worship; to adopt its constitution; to provide and maintain property; to raise and administer funds; to prepare, receive, nourish, transfer and discipline members; to attend to the education of the whole family of the church; to elect elders or deacons to call, uphold, support ministers, and to accept or effect the termination of a pastorate; to share with the fellowship of Congregational churches in the ordination of ministers; to live in active fellowship with other Christian Churches; to witness to the Lordship of Christ in every sphere. All these duties properly belong to each local Congregational church; they may be shared or delegated only by its own decision.

5 From the time of their formation Congregational churches have had fellowship with one another and this has found increasing expression in County and National Unions. In such fellowship the churches have found more than a means of consultation and co-operation; they have found guidance similar to that known in the local church meeting. Together the local churches have expressed their oneness in Christ; have formulated, but not imposed, covenants and affirmations of faith; have adopted constitutions; have worked for the spread of the Gospel at home and abroad in every relationship of life; have exercised a ministry of friendship and encouragement among the churches; have provided and maintained property; have raised and administered funds; have prepared, accredited, and supported ministers and shared in their ordination and their induction; have commissioned lay pastors; have recognized lay preachers; and have fostered ecumenical relationships.

6 The experience of this fellowship has led Congregational churches in England and Wales to covenant together, acknowledging themselves to be one communion within the whole Church of Christ.

7 Both the local church and this covenanted body are under the same authority – the Lordship of Christ. Both are pledged to discern the mind of Christ for themselves and to listen to the testimony of others as to what the mind of Christ is. In the local church and in the covenanted body alike, the fundamental principle is Christ's rule in his Church. Thus, as in the local church no member is excluded if on conscientious grounds he cannot accept a judgement of the church, so no church shall be excluded from the covenanted body if on conscientious grounds it cannot accept a judgement of that body.

8 That they may obey the will of Christ as they discern it, Congregational churches express this covenanted relationship in the following terms or

substantially to the like effect:

'We, the members of .... Congregational Church, accepting the word of God made known in the Scriptures of the Old and New Testaments as the supreme authority for the faith and conduct of all God's people,

> acknowledge one God, Father, Son and Holy Spirit, within whose covenant of grace we all stand;
> acknowledge ourselves to be, with other Congregational churches, one communion within the whole Church of Christ;
> affirm that Christ is Head of the Church, and each local church and each association of churches is subject alike to His authority;
> rejoice in our fellowship with the whole Church;

and therefore, as a church, covenant with other Congregational churches
> to form the Congregational Church in England and Wales;
> to join with them in seeking the mind of Christ;
> to make common witness with them to His Gospel;
> to serve His purpose in all the world;

and we commit ourselves to God in the confidence that He will never leave us nor forsake us.'

Document II.14

The Child and the Church, 1966

The Child and the Church, reprinted in Roger Hayden (ed.), *Baptist Union Documents* (London: Baptist Historical Society, 1980), pp. 210–12.

Alongside the problems surrounding children's work in the 1960s, new thinking about a child's approach to religion was going on in educational and church circles. This Baptist report of 1966 is particularly interesting, because the practice of believers' baptism forced Baptists to reflect on how they understood the relation of children to the Church.

… The New Testament recognises that the whole truth of a child's humanity is not expressed in terms of Adam. The humanity which the child bears is the humanity in which Christ has become incarnate. The child is as much involved in Christ's incarnation as he is in Adam's folly. Paul sets side by side the mortality inherited from the first Adam and the salvation and life won by the Second Adam (1 Cor. 15:21–22; Romans 5:12–21). It is the one race that is enslaved by the first and liberated by the second. Furthermore, the epistle to the Ephesians sees a cosmic significance in Christ in whom all things are to be gathered up (chapter 1). Our group differed on the conclusion to be drawn from this teaching, but all were agreed that its presence in the New Testament could not be escaped. Simply to speak of the human race as fallen, in isolation from the work of Christ, is to violate the witness of the New Testament. Man is certainly confronted with decision, there is acceptance or rejection, and yet, whatever his responsibility as an individual, he is a member of a race redeemed in Christ.

The tension between these two insights is felt most acutely when we are dealing with responsible agents. When men and women are confronted with the Gospel they are faced with the decision which is unavoidable and personal. The New Testament recognises that men reject or accept Christ whether it be by responding to what they hear, as in the parable of the Sower, or responding to the claims of compassion as in the parable of the Last Judgment. Whether in our preaching of the Gospel we exhort men to turn from what they are or to become what they are, the cutting edge of the Word, demanding decision, remains the same. In the case of an infant, however, where response is not possible, the tension hardly exists. We recognise the infant, regardless of his parentage, to be a member of Adam's race redeemed in Christ. This is not because his parents are Christian but because he is a human being. If he is baptised as an infant it can only be to declare what he is and not to give him a 'status' that he does not already possess.

In our opinion, it is clear that the child of a Christian home does not stand in any position of privilege in relation to God's redemptive work in Christ. He is nevertheless born within the sphere of the Church and from his earliest years, he will encounter Christ and will be caught up in the worship and service of the Church. He receives all these mercies not by any imparted status but simply because this is the sphere in which his family lives. He is not a member of the Church, nor does he possess the fullness of 'a man in Christ'. There is a line of demarcation between believing parents and the child which is part of the catechumenate, but it is important that this line be defined.

The line of demarcation between the believing parent and his children cannot be understood apart from reference to the wider context of the demarcation between Church and the world.

In traditional Baptist terms the Church is a fellowship of believers. It is divided from the world by the personal faith of its members in the atoning work of Christ; it is a committed community. Stated thus boldly it is clear that children can have no place in such a body. They cannot exercise the faith by which they become members. Yet the definition 'fellowship of believers' remains an abstraction unless it is related to the on-going life of the local church and here, manifestly, the Church is not simply a fellowship of believers. At its heart is the fellowship of believers, but around that nucleus are children and adults, akin to the 'God-fearers' of the Jewish synagogues in the ancient world, who are at varying stages of progress towards faith in Christ. They participate in the congregational life of the Church, they share in the worship of the Church, and they are recipients of the teaching of the Church. Any complete doctrine of the Church must take account of these. The children of believers will be numbered among this circle that lives about the fellowship of believers. Therefore the line of demarcation between the parent and the child is not that between Church and world.

The difficulties which such a view presents will depend upon the understanding of the nature of the Church. The distinction between believer and non-believer is sometimes made synonymous with 'saved' and 'unsaved'. The logical consequence of excluding a child from the Church, so understood, is to exclude him from salvation. In such a situation baptism at birth becomes an act of obvious compassion. But, as has already been noted, even Churches that practise infant baptism do not all think of it in these terms. There is a recognition by most that the salvation won in Christ is given to every infant regardless of his parentage or his baptism. The Church is not simply a community that benefits from the atonement over against a world that does not. The New Testament separates the Church from the world and at the same time speaks of the work of Christ upon the Cross as being effective for all mankind. It is clear that the basis of that division is not a clear-cut one between saved and unsaved. The reformers recognised this by their doctrine of the 'visible' and the 'invisible' Church.

The line of demarcation is most clearly seen in baptism. In baptism a man is identified with the cross-resurrection event by which mankind has been redeemed and it gathers up his response in faith and commitment to Christ as Lord. He is made a member of the body of Christ in order that he might serve Christ in the life of Church and world. He is now part of the servant body of Christ in the world. He has recognised the salvation won for him in Christ, he has accepted the Lordship of Christ as a man must when he recognises the salvation that Christ has given him, and now he is committed to the mission of the Church to the world in the Name of Christ. It is a mission that proclaims what God in Christ has done once for all, and embodies that proclamation by priestly service in the life of mankind. The line of demarcation is here drawn at the sacrament of baptism. It is between those who recognise Christ's Lordship and those who do not, and those who are serving the world under Christ's Commission and those who are not.

On this understanding a child is separated from his Christian parents by all that is expressed in believers' baptism. He is part of the Christian community and his place and part within it is constant witness that the Church is not a self-enclosed 'saved' community, but a Body whose raison d'être is the salvation of mankind. He becomes a member of that Body by his personal recognition of the salvation won for him in Christ and his own commitment to the Lordship of Christ. All this is gathered up in baptism, which holds together the redemptive act of God in the cross and resurrection and the candidate's response to it in faith and his personal commitment to Jesus as Lord.

There was within our group a tension between two views of the work of Christ that could not be resolved. We were all in agreement that the work of Christ was for all mankind, and that infants before the age of reason were in some sense included in God's purpose of salvation. We parted company when considering persons who had attained the stage of responsibility. Half the group wished here to emphasise the nature of baptism as a personal transition from death to life, following a conversion in which a man was made what hitherto he had not been. The remainder felt that we can only talk in salvation terms about infants because we speak in these terms of mankind. The salvation of infants rests upon their place in the human race in which Christ has become incarnate and which, in His incarnation, He has redeemed. We did agree that in neither case is the evangelical demand of the Gospel thwarted. We also felt that the theological crux of our discussion lies here, but that is a study of

Ecclesiology

such magnitude as to lie outside the terms of reference of this group. A thoroughgoing theology of childhood however must wrestle with all the problems of which, through our discussions, we became aware.

Document II.15

Church-Related Community Workers, 1980

URC, *Reports to Assembly*, 1980, pp. 52–4.

In 1980 the United Reformed Church introduced a scheme for the selection, training and appointment of Church-Related Community Workers in places of social need. The aim was to bridge the gap between Community Workers associated with the Social Services departments of local authorities and traditionally trained ministers in local churches. By the end of the century there were nine in post and sixteen on the roll.

Need and Opportunity

63   Some parts of Britain are becoming increasingly subject to stress because of urban renewal, chronic unemployment, broken families, homelessness and the need for integration in those communities with a high immigrant population.

64   In such places there easily develops among disadvantaged groups a sense of injustice, helplessness and alienation; conflict between various sections of the community can exist. The Gospel of reconciliation has much to contribute to those living in such conditions.

65   Unfortunately, it is often in these places that our churches are weakest in membership and see their role more in terms of survival than of mission. They need trained leadership to help them turn the problems into creative opportunities.

66   Through the centuries the Christian Church has provided many types of community service – in education, medicine, welfare, etc. The British Council of Churches 1976 report on 'Community Work in the Churches' has drawn attention to a new way in which the churches can make an important contribution to a growing need.

Community Work

67   Community work in this context is characterised by the principle 'of work with people rather than for people – encouraging them to act collectively in order to identify their own community needs, and to make their contributions to the meeting of these needs.'

68   The World Development Movement has laid stress on this distinction in policy, and in Britain for some years a number of approaches to achieve this

aim have been followed, chiefly in secular contexts, through community development, community action, community organisation, community education, community relations and community care.

69 There are a number of our churches where there is a great need and opportunity for such an approach and the appointment of a trained community worker is desirable. Such Church Related Community Workers would help lead and strengthen the local church's mission to the community through the promotion of community development, in an area where an additional lay member of a team would provide specialist help to meet unusual needs.

Selection

70 The URC cannot guarantee that candidates accepted for training will be found appointments.
71 Candidates must be members of the United Reformed Church showing capabilities for leadership. They must be willing and able to undergo specific training in preparation for their service.
72 Candidates for the Church Related Community Workers scheme will be required to go through the following selection procedures:–
   i) to obtain the commendation of their own local church through Elders and Church Meetings;
   ii) to be commended by the District Council;
   iii) to be accepted by the Provincial Synod;
   iv) to be accepted for training by Westhill College and St Andrew's Hall, or similar institutions.

Training

73 Church Related Community Workers would be required to hold a Certificate in Community and Youth Work, or its equivalent (we recommend the 2 year course in the Community and Youth Studies Department of Westhill College, Birmingham, which also leads to the award of the Certificate of Qualification in Social Work (CQSW) for those students who are at least 20 years of age on entry to the course).
74 An additional year, either before or after completion of the CCYW course would be required to be spent at St Andrew's Hall to study the theological insights and resources which provide a Christian basis for community work, or the one year Certificate course 'Training in Mission'.

Administration

75 **National** The Supplementary Ministries Committee will be responsible for the training of Church Related Community Workers in consultation with the Principal of St Andrew's Hall, Selly Oak, Birmingham.
76 **Provincial** Provincial Synods will be responsible for:–

Ecclesiology

   (a) the acceptance of candidates as CRCW as outlined above under Selection;
   (b) examining situations where the appointment of a CRCW is desirable and encouraging or promoting such an appointment;
   (c) the oversight of all candidates by annual report and interview.
77 **District Council**   District Councils will be responsible for:–
   (a) taking initiatives in examining situations where the appointment of CRCW's are desirable and encouraging or promoting their appointment;
   (b) commending suitable candidates for training;
   (c) in consultation with the local church arranging the appointment, commissioning and oversight of CRCW for a stated term, which may be renewed.
78 **Local Church**   The local church will be responsible for:–
   (a) the encouragement of suitable gifted members to offer to be trained as CRCW;
   (b) the invitation of a CRCW to serve in the local community and/or to work in a team with the minister/s of the church or a group of churches.

Finance

79   Church Related Community Workers will be financed through Local Authority grants, ecumenical schemes, trusts, etc. No provision is being made from the Central Funds for the maintenance of CRCW's.
80   Assembly 1979 agreed that 'any funds given for the Deaconess service, when no longer required, shall be available to the Supplementary Ministries Committee to help fund CRCW's. The SMC have requested from the Finance and Administration Department a sum of up to £1,500 for 1980 for training grants.
81   In cases of need (where LEA grants are not available) churches/Districts/Synods may be able and willing to contribute to a candidate's costs during training.

Document II.16

The Community of Women and Men

URC, *Reports to Assembly*, 1984, pp. 57–8.

The United Reformed Church set up a Working Party on the Community of Women and Men in 1982 following the Sheffield Consultation on the same subject organised by the World Council of Churches. Although the Church had deliberately not established a national committee to co-ordinate women's work when it was formed in 1972, this report and its reception showed that there was still some way to go before the equality of women and men in the Church was accepted as a practical reality, with all its implications.

40 We share our findings and concerns with the General Assembly in the following terms:

1 'In Christ there is neither male or female'. Christ has set us free from stereotypes and prejudice so that we can accept and value one another as individuals. As a church we rejoice in this and are always open to new ways of deepening and giving fuller expression to our oneness in Christ. Are we not 'united' and 'reformed'?
We must therefore
  – continue to explore the relationships between men and women in the light of both Scripture and contemporary experience, believing that God guides us through both;
  – enable everyone to use to the full the gifts that God has given them for the building up of the Church;
  – ensure that cooperation between the sexes is shaped, not by domination but by a reciprocity which reflects the relationship of mutual love between Father, Son and Holy Spirit.

2 To those who do not see this as an issue, and to those who feel that the URC has already achieved a right relationship in this area, we say
  – there is a real hurt and frustration among both men and women in the URC. We must be careful lest we miss 'the beam in our own eye';
  – there is a need to show our solidarity with fellow Christians in Churches which do not yet ordain women to the Ministry of Word and Sacrament, and a responsibiity to share our experience with them;
  – moreover the examination of the relationship between men and women is part of the continuous effort needed to build and maintain true community within the Church, as part of our Christian witness. 'The world will not come to believe because of what we say, but because of the quality of our life as a reconciling, loving and inclusive community in Christ';
  – and the BCC has asked member denominations to respond to the issues raised by the 1981 World Council of Churches Conference on the Community of Women and Men in the Church.

3 We have a vision of the Church which offers
  – positive support to all, whether in the Church or not, who are trying to find their identity as human beings created in God's image;
  – a place for deep and searching dialogue about different patterns of marriage and family life, about sharing power and responsibility and about where authority lies in these areas;
  – a practical sign of hope that women and men can progress together towards human wholeness.

4 As a Reformed Church, claiming to follow Scripture, the URC must be prepared

Ecclesiology

- to face up to the generally 'patriarchal' tone of the Bible, and the difficult texts in the Epistles which subordinate women to men;
- to ask ourselves whether we are doing justice to the richness of the Biblical image of God which on the one hand includes both feminine and masculine characteristics and on the other hand transcends both;
- to make clear through the language we use that the people of God comprises both men and women.

5 The role of existing women's groups in the Church has been much debated. These are valued by many and can play a useful part in building confidence and teaching leadership skills needed by the wider Church. It can also be helpful for men and women to discuss separately what it means to be male and female today in the light of their faith. We recognise, however, that it is no more acceptable for women to acquire confidence and freedom at the expense of men, than it is for men to exercise leadership roles at the expense of women.

6 Many people, particularly women, find their ability to contribute their talents restricted by practical considerations. Synods, District Councils and committees could help, for example, by changing times of meetings, seeking to remove obstacles in the way of those who would otherwise take part, offering training opportunities, and by including appropriate questions on visitations.

7 These issues are threatening and sometimes make us feel defensive or react defensively, but we have discovered that it is through experiencing the hurt and working through the insecurities produced by the changing role of women and men that we can make a new creative dimension to our life together, in the URC and beyond.

Document II.17

Forms of Ministry among Baptists, 1994

Forms of Ministry among Baptists (Didcot: Baptist Union, 1994), pp. 19–27.

This Report may be compared with the earlier Report on Ordination of 1957 (**II.10**) to indicate thinking at the end of the century, with a greater emphasis on the ministry of the whole people of God and ministries that fall outside traditional patterns.

II. Two approaches to the question of spiritual leadership

5. Offices of ministry

We may distinguish two distinct views about the basis for particular forms of spiritual leadership in the Church. The first is the conviction that Christ has established certain 'offices', or appointments to ministerial leadership, alongside the exercise of gifts by all members of the church. So both Particular and General Baptist Confessions of the 17th Century declare that 'a particular church consists of officers and members'. Being set aside for these offices has been called 'ordination' since the beginning of Baptist life in Britain (with a breach in the tradition in the 19th century), the word expressing both the sense of 'appointment' and of an 'ordinance' created by Christ himself for the health and good order of the churches.

This view of ministry proposes that while these offices may well take different shapes in different social contexts, there is a stable underlying pattern of office which can be discerned from the New Testament and from the experience of the Spirit by the Church in its life through the ages. As can be seen from the historical material collected in Appendix II [not reprinted], until the latter part of this century Baptists have for the most part affirmed a constant 'two-fold office' of Pastor (or Minister, Elder or Bishop) and Deacon.

This two-fold office has usually been understood to reflect the two-fold pattern of

a) Bishop or Elder (episkopos and presbuteros being taken as equivalent) and
b) Deacon (diakonos) as found in I and II Timothy and Philippians 1:1.

While a haze of uncertainty surrounds their appointment and functions, it seems that at least by the time of the Pastoral Epistles, leaders had emerged in some churches who were charged either with pastoral oversight of a congregation (*episkope*) or with particular pastoral service (*diakonia*). Modern New Testament scholarship has brought to light the variety of church life in the early period, and the prominence in some places of the exercise of spiritual gifts (*charismata*) over appointments to leadership, so that it can hardly be claimed that this two-fold office was universal throughout the early congregations, as Baptists had formerly supposed. However, those who hold to this basic pattern will place weight upon its survival and firm establishment in the post-New Testament period, as indicating continuing guidance of the churches by the Holy Spirit.

Some General Baptists in the 17th and 18th centuries held to a 'three-fold office' of Bishop (or Messenger), Elder and Deacon with the Bishop exercising various kinds of inter-congregational ministry, and it has been claimed that the 20th century Area Superintendent revives this earlier office. This would put Baptists more in line with the Catholic, Anglican and Orthodox traditions, who look to the development of the office of Bishop in the second and third centuries of the Church. In its modern form, however, the Superintendent is to be seen as an extension of the function of the congregational minister, rather than being a distinct third office. In Baptist understanding, the local pastor is 'bishop' (*episkopos*) of the flock as well as 'elder' (*presbuteros*), and so exercises a leadership in not only caring for, but 'overseeing' the Body of Christ in its needs and its mission. The Superintendent exercises the *same kind of* 'episcopal' ministry of pastoral oversight as the local minister, but among a group of churches rather than in a single congregation.

This first approach to the question of spiritual leadership therefore looks for forms of *episkope* and *diakonia* which the Spirit of God has created, and is creating among the churches. While Baptists have a distinct contribution to make to the ecumenical process in their view of the 'episcopal' ministry of the local pastor, this approach does have obvious links with ecumenical concerns and can get conversation going. The WCC Faith and Order paper *Baptism, Eucharist and Ministry* (1982), for example, discusses ministry in terms of a three-fold order. The response from the Baptist Union of Great Britain made clear that the 'heavy insistence' on a three-fold form (bishop, presbyter, deacon) was a matter of 'deep concern'; it commented, for example, that the more flexible approach of discerning 'diaconal functions' had been tightened up implicitly into 'diaconal functionaries' placed in a three-fold structure. However, it is only possible to have this kind of conversation if there is some conviction about the presence of diaconal and episcopal functions in the Church at all.

6. Gifts and calling must shape structures

A rather different approach has developed among Baptists in recent times, although we observe that it is more present in Britain than among Baptists in either the USA or the rest of Europe. This moves away from a presupposition about the existence of 'offices', and rather looks to see what gifts Christ through his Spirit is actually giving to the churches, and what forms of service he is calling people to in the present day. Structures of ministry and forms of ministerial leadership should, it is urged, flow from this gifting and this calling. We should indeed recognise and honour spiritual leadership, but its forms cannot be trapped within the traditional pattern of 'minister and deacons'. We must be open and flexible, ready to make new structures of recognition, training and support for the forms of ministry that the Spirit is actually raising up. Suspicions about the words 'ordination' and 'office' that first emerged among Baptists in the 19th century in reaction to the high church movement have thus re-appeared in our day in a very different context. There is a fear that singling out one kind of ministry as the 'ordained ministry' not only suppresses the ministry of the whole people of God in their daily life in the world, but also fails to give proper recognition to other kinds of service in the church to which people are called to give their *primary* commitment – for example as a youth worker or evangelist.

On the local scene this kind of conviction sometimes lies behind the creation of 'eldership' in a local church, cutting across the traditional two-fold pattern of office with new forms of leadership. In a different way, and on a national level, we also find echoes of this second approach to ministry in the two sets of papers at present before the BU Council. Though dealing with different issues (Youth Specialists and 'Lay Pastors'/'Lay Preachers'), they have a similar concern to extend to other ministries the kind of national recognition given at present to those whom we call 'ministers'. The paper on Youth Specialists urges that the significance of this particular ministry calls for a process leading to recognition which is 'comparable' with that applying to those seeking accreditation as ministers. It proposes accordingly that those recognised for this specialist ministry 'will be accorded benefits similar to those currently accorded to those on the accredited list', including entry to the *Baptist Union Directory*, membership of the Assembly, eligibility for HMF grants and use of the settlement process. The papers on Pastors and Preachers advise Association Ministerial Recognition Committees that many of the criteria for assessing the fitness of someone for denominational recognition as a pastor/preacher correspond to the criteria which apply to those seeking inclusion on the Baptist Union accredited list.

We can only warmly commend the guidelines in these documents about training, self-discipline, standards and the fostering of Baptist identity. However, we notice that the effect of these documents is to break down distinctions presently existing between those on the 'accredited list' and those exercising other ministries, and what this implies needs to be grappled with theologically. There also needs to be theological reflection on the relationship of these ministries to what we have traditionally called 'the ordained ministry'. As a committee we have had conversations with representatives from the Mission and Ministry Departments which have made clear that there is a widespread desire to work towards having a single accredited list containing those recognised for different kinds of ministry – including, for example, Youth Specialists and 'Pastors' (formerly 'lay pastors').

Those who take this second approach to ministry may be motivated by a worry that the present 'ordained ministry' can easily acquire the characteristics of a 'priestly class', and also by the desire to affirm and encourage those who believe they are called to new kinds of ministry in our day. But it seems that above all they are concerned that proper recognition by the whole community of the church should be given to ministries that are called into being by the work of the Holy Spirit of God. Practically, it is necessary to afford such recognition so that persons can move from one church situation to another in a mobile society, and that churches may know that these men and women enjoy the confidence of the Union in their skills and calling. Theologically, divine calling must always be discerned by more than the individual privately; a person needs the testing and recognition of the whole community to confirm a personal sense of vocation.

7. A proposal

We suggest that there is a need to combine the best insights of both approaches to the nature of ministerial leadership. Both are grounded in aspects of the New Testament witness, and in a Baptist understanding of a balance between order and freedom.

On the one hand, we believe that a distinction between a ministry of 'pastoral oversight' (*episkope*) and that of 'pastoral service' (*diakonia*) is still a useful one, in distinguishing between the activity of 'the minister' and that of 'other ministries'.

On the other hand however, these terms need a good deal more qualification than our Baptist forebears supposed. We should recognise that *episkope* and *diakonia* are dimensions of ministry that are not sealed exclusively into two offices. The boundary between them is a moving one, and both need to be understood in the context of the ministry of the whole church to which is corporately entrusted both *diakonia* and *episkope*. We also need to envisage the range, training, national accreditation and ordination of pastoral service in a way that bursts the old wineskins of what we have previously regarded as 'diaconal' ministry (ie simply the service of deacons in the local church). We believe that this will meet the challenge we are facing, adequately to recognise new gifts and new forms of ministry for a new age...

9. The key idea of *episkope*

We are well aware that criticism has recently been levelled by some in our churches against an appeal to the concept of *episkope*. The significance of 'pastoral oversight' has been affirmed in the recent report on *The Nature of the Assembly and Council* and in the guidelines given to the Commission on the Nature of the Superintendency, as well as in this present paper. We believe that the unease felt by some about this trend is understandable, but misfounded.

There is some suspicion, for example, that when applied to the service of Area Superintendents it is moving us towards the kind of notion of Bishop that obtains in the so-called 'Episcopal' church traditions. It is urged that congregational leaders in New Testament times were called not only by the Greek title of *episkopos* but by the Jewish title of 'elder' (translated into Greek as *presbuteros*), and that there is thus no good reason to concentrate on the concept of *episkope*. We should observe, however, that the two titles soon became synonymous in the early church, and that *episkope* expresses the *function* of the elder/presbyter (see Acts 20:28) in a way that the word presbuteros itself cannot. In the English translation 'to watch over', the word was in fact a key one in early Baptist descriptions of ministry: while all members enter into covenant to 'watch over' each other spiritually, some are especially charged with this office:

> And as Christ for the keeping of this Church in holy and orderly Communion, placeth some speciall men over the Church, who by their office are to governe, oversee, visit, watch; so likewise for the better keeping thereof in all places, by all the members, he hath given authoritie, and laid duty upon all, to watch over one another. (*The London Confession*, 1644)

Thus *episkope* is a concept that helpfully embraces corporate as well as individual spiritual care. Since the whole community has a commission to 'watch over' its members and to find the mind of Christ for its life, oversight is held corporately in at least three spheres: by the local church meeting, by the Association Council and by the Assembly and Council of the Union. But oversight is also focused in individuals in each of these three spheres of church life – in the local ministers, in the Area

Superintendents and officers of the Associations, and in the group who are formally called the 'Senior Management Team' at Baptist House, but who should be understood to be the Pastoral Team which guides the Union. *Episkope* flows back and forth between individual leaders and community, characterised not by ruling but by the gaining and giving of trust. Pastoral oversight can never be a matter of requiring obedience; the only authority can be that of the winning of trust from others, through service offered in imitation of the self-giving of Christ.

The concept of *episkope*, or pastoral oversight, thus links Baptist to wider ecumenical discussion, while we have a distinctive understanding of it which may actually contribute to the development of new forms of *episkope* in partnership between churches.

Document II.18

Relating and Resourcing, 1998

Report of the Task Group on Associating to the Baptist Union Council, 1998, pp. 3–10.

Unlike the *Report on Associations* (II.11), this Task Group's recommendations for the restructuring of the Baptist Union were accepted, possibly because by the 1990s it was the Baptist Union Council rather than the Assembly which had the power to take decisions. The result was the most radical changes in Baptist life beyond the local congregation for more than a century.

2 Relating and Resourcing: Crucial Distinctions and Foundations

2:1 The terms of reference invited the Task Group on Associating (TGA) to 'encourage a deeper understanding of the need for Associating, and further experimentation in new patterns of Associating', to 'explore the importance of Associating for promoting the mission of the local church' and to 'consider ways of deepening spirituality through Associating'. Moreover, we were invited to set out what is meant by associating, its basis in 'covenant commitment' to one another and its purposes in 'mission, resourcing, envisioning, inspiring'. An embryonic theology of associating is therefore already present in the terms of reference.

2:2 It is as well to formalise at this point a distinction which has already gained currency in this discussion and which is crucial for this report, namely that between *associating* and *association*. By associating we mean that spiritual and social reality whereby churches and their pastors relate to each other in committed, intentional relationships for the purposes of mutual support, encouragement and accountability in the service of mission. By *association* we mean those historic institutional and legal agencies which aim to serve, resource and benefit their member churches in the work of mission. This

Ecclesiology

distinction is reflected in the title of this report. *Relating* is of the essence of *associating, resourcing* is of the essence of *association*.

2:3 To distinguish between these two elements is not to divide them. They exist in mutual interaction. Associations grew out of associating in the first place and are able to provide a framework within which relationships can be built and established. However, it is crucial to affirm that associating/relating has priority. *Associating does not primarily consist of churches relating to a central institutional agency whether this be association or Union. It consists of churches relating co-operatively and directly to each other.* This we sense to be an important statement since a 'good association church' has often been taken to be one which does its duty, especially financially, by the central institutional structures, whatever the quality of its relations to other churches. Moreover, it cannot be assumed that local Baptist churches will necessarily find their primary inter-church relationships with other Baptist congregations. Many will, while many others will find their most natural relationships with churches in other traditions.

2:4 The report *Transforming Superintendency* very helpfully began its reflections with the mission of the Triune God and moved from this to affirm the nature of the church as a community sharing in God's mission: a community of persons gathered together in local congregations, and a community of congregations serving the mission of God as the one people of God. To the people of God as a whole, God gives ministries to build up the church as a whole and enable it to fulfil God's mission.

2:5 Baptist accounts of the church have been inclined to begin their reflection by stressing the local fellowship of believers gathered together with Christ in the midst. Sharing in the priesthood of all believers and having the mind of Christ imparted to each congregation the local church has both power and competence to appoint its own leaders and govern its own affairs (See e.g. Article 36 of the *London Confession* of 1644). For this reason, all theologies which presumed power over a congregation and imposed leadership or government upon it were rejected. This instinct remains close to the heart of Baptist identity. It was balanced in early confessions by a willingness to recognise that although no church had the right to impose its will upon any other, churches might in fellowship or by freely associating together be of mutual benefit in 'peace, increase of love and mutual edification' (*Second London Confession*, 1677 and 89, articles 14, 15). Furthermore, the discussions surrounding the founding of the Abingdon Association in 1652 require close attention. After affirming that churches should hold 'a firm communion with each other', the argument is advanced that there is the same relationship between one church and another as there is between the members of one church. As each believer should be part of a church for the purpose of mutual support and correction so churches should manifest the same care for each other (B R White, ed., *Association Records of the Particular Baptists of England, Wales and Ireland to 1660. Part 3: The Abingdon Association*, pp. 126–7). The logic here suggests that as membership of a church is a freely chosen act so churches might and should freely choose to join a communion of churches.

2:6 It can be claimed with justification that the early Baptist understanding of the relation of particular churches to the wider church is 'independence in regard to power but not in regard to communion' (cp. R C Walton, *The Gathered Community*, London, 1946, pp. 89–91). This is the balance we are required to strike: the forming of a fellowship of churches in which power is owned by autonomous congregations but where fellowship is widely and constructively pursued. There are those who hesitate to describe the relations between the churches as 'covenantal', but provided this is understood as a free covenant of love in which the participants retain their freedom there should be no objection to the use of the word. Similarly, fears are sometimes expressed about the alleged desire to transform the Union into a 'Church' in which power is centralised. This report in no way supports such a move. But it does recognise that in gathering together as churches and committing ourselves to each other we are giving expression to important aspects of 'being church'. The Body of Christ is not confined to local churches but finds expression in the relations between churches as well as within them.

2:7 The Baptist understanding of the local church is rooted in the belief that 'where two or three come together in my name there am I with them' (Matthew 18:20). Belief in the competence of the local church derives from this sense of the presence of Christ among his people. Yet such a belief is often misunderstood. It is not a claim that local churches do not need anything or anybody else. The local church may be competent, but it is scarcely omnicompetent. And if Christ is present in the local church he is also present in the wider church which is the 'fullness of him who fills everything in every way' (Ephesians 1:23). No local church is complete of itself and does well to seek for that of Christ which is expressed in the wider Body. This impinges upon both mission and spirituality. To fulfil the mission of Christ, churches have to do it together that they may make up for each other's lacks and set forth the whole Christ. To grow into spiritual fullness requires us to tap into the spiritual insights, wisdom and vitality of the wider Body. These considerations provide the spiritual and theological foundations for the rest of the report.

2:8 We take the key issue at stake in this report to be the discovery, or re-discovery of a new quality of relationship between congregations. The Statement of the Denominational Consultation referred to 'relationships of trust'. At the end of the day these can only be found where they are desired and earnestly pursued. We have borne in mind that we stand in a 'voluntarist' tradition: spiritual acts and exercises are only deemed to have value if they are freely willed and entered into. What this report will call for therefore is more than can be achieved by means of constitutional or institutional reform. It requires a work of God and active response from God's people. However, in order to encourage the quality of associating which is being called for, the challenge of institutional change cannot be shirked since association life can both enable and hinder effective associating. As *Transforming Superintendency* indicated, the church is 'a movement of God rather than an institution of our making' (p.13). Institutions are not to be devalued, but they are to be kept flexible in order to serve the purpose of this moment rather than a past one. Accordingly, the report makes recommendations concerning the revision of our relating to one another and of the resourcing agencies which could do much to encourage this into being.

2:9 Relating to the broader church of Christ must inevitably reach beyond the boundaries of Baptist churches alone. Relating between churches will include other Baptist congregations but it is inevitable and desirable in the present climate in which denominational boundaries have been blurred that different churches will relate in different combinations according to the realities of their situation. We view this positively. It does mean that there will be no straightforward formula which can be applied across the board of churches in the Baptist Union. Granted the fact of diversity, we do not believe that it is in the interests of churches to have purely nominal ties to the Baptist Union of Great Britain. Even where the primary focus of associating is elsewhere, there will continue to be help and resources, a sense of connectedness and the perspectives of an historic Free Church denomination from which churches might continue to benefit. However, diversities of associating will lead to diverse levels of participation in the life of associations and Union. This is, of course, in principle no different from the present, but should the recommendations of this report be implemented our awareness of it may increase.

2:10 The Task Group has been asked to respond to the discussions arising out of *Transforming Superintendency*. Our response chiefly concerns the definition of the primary task of the superintendents. It will be clear from what is recommended that we understand the role of superintendents to be primarily that of leaders in mission with a particular responsibility to ensure that the ministers of the churches are adequately supported and cared for. If associating is to become a renewed and widespread reality the leadership given by the superintendents is a crucial factor. Furthermore, if we are calling the churches to a new quality of associating it becomes imperative that those who are involved at levels of senior leadership within the life of the Union should themselves practise and model a high quality of relating towards one another in the service of the Union's mission.

2:11 The TGA was further charged with determining 'a method of annual renewal of commitment between churches, Associations, colleges and the officers and staff of the Union'. As we have discussed this within and beyond the TGA we have become persuaded that an annual renewal of commitment is impracticable and would swiftly become a formality. However, we do believe there is value in a renewal of commitment focused on the millennium and with the initial decade of the new millennium in view. We have given serious consideration to the view that we are living in a 'post-denominational' age and that people are no longer willing to be tied too closely to a denominational identity. Much more important for many believers in their choice of a church seem to be the vibrancy of worship or the inspiration of the preaching or the style of mission. However, while many believers are no longer denominationalist in approach we judge the more decisive factor to be post-institutionalism. In every aspect of life, centralised and impersonal structures are instinctively distrusted, however unfairly. There is evidence that people do still wish to belong to a movement with a definable ethos, a clear vision and trusted leaders. A vision statement could assist the Union in defining itself as a missionary movement...

4 Recommendations and Explanations

The TGA makes the following recommendations. R1 and R2 should be seen as foundational to all the others.

R1 We recognise through church meetings, the Baptist Union Council, Assembly, Association Assemblies and in our college communities that although we possess institutional forms of association we have largely lost the reality of associating. We need as a matter of urgency to rediscover this dimension of the church's life for the sake of our own spiritual health and for the proper fulfilment of the mission to which we are called.

R2 Since this rediscovery can only take place as the churches of the Union desire it and seek it out, we recommend the Council to
- **call our churches to a new start in this regard,**
- **urge them to identify those other churches with which in particular they are able to build mutually supportive relationships, clusters and networks and to take appropriate initiatives to rediscover the reality of associating,**
- **assure them of our support and encouragement in this process,**
- **urge them to see the continuing value of larger structures in regional and national forms acting as sources of missionary vision and challenge, and as providing resources, support and the means for remaining connected to one another at wider levels.**

Explanation: We have already noted that the rediscovery of effective associating is likely to take a diversity of forms. It will involve for some churches closer forms of ecumenical associating, and for others patterns of associating which cross the boundaries of existing associations. We believe that a viable vision for future patterns of associating will involve smaller clusters of churches working more closely together while belonging to wider networks providing fellowship, accountability, resources and recognition. However, the key to all of this is the will to associate with other churches which can only be generated from within the churches themselves. As we are a Union of churches, associations and colleges, the importance of the colleges is recognised in Rl and they also are invited to explore their part in strengthening relationship both within and beyond their communities. We hope this will be further considered by the Union/Colleges Partnership Task Group.

R3 To enable us more effectively to fulfil our task of serving and supporting effective associating in the service of mission we recommend that existing associations undergo substantive reform, including:
R3:1 the overall recasting of association structures to form 'regional associations'. This will be achieved by merging the existing 29 geographical associations in England and Wales and the 12 Baptist Union 'areas'. We envisage initially approximately 16 regional associations as the outcome. We recommend this taking place by 1 January 2001 at the latest.

Document II.19

Methodism and Episcopacy, 2000

Episkopé and Episcopacy in Statements and Reports of the Methodist Church on Faith and Order, 1984–2000, vol. ii (London: Methodist Publishing House, 2000), pp. 407–10.

Following the approval of the Report, *Called to Love and Praise*, which was a Statement on the Methodist doctrine of the Church at the end of the century, the Faith and Order Committee prepared a report on *Episkopé and Episcopacy*, which was accepted by the Conference of 2000. These are the recommendations of the Report:

H. GUIDELINES

114. The Faith and Order Committee proposes that the following Guidelines be adopted as a summary statement of the Methodist Church's position on episkopé and episcopacy.
1 The Methodist Church recognizes that *episkopé* is exercised within its life in communal, collegial and personal ways.
　　a. **The Methodist Church values communal *episkopé*, exercised by representative bodies throughout the Church's life.**
　　The Conference and the District Synod, in their representative sessions, Circuit

Meetings and Church Councils are examples of the exercise of communal *episkopé*.

   b. **The Methodist Church values collegial *episkopé*, and its tradition of expressing collegiality, not only among members of the same order of ministry, but also among lay persons and ordained persons.**

Examples of such collegiality include the Ministerial Session of the Conference, which is made up of ministers, and Local Preachers Meetings and local church Pastoral Committees, where collegial oversight is shared by ordained and lay persons.

   c. **The Methodist Church values personal *episkopé* in every part of the Church's life, but believes that such *episkopé* should be exercised within a collegial or communal context.**

It is important that personal *episkopé* be allowed for within connexional structures in ways consonant with its exercise in Circuits and Districts. Because the *episkopé* exercised by individuals within the life of the Methodist Church is derived or representative oversight, it is important that those who exercise personal *episkopé* remain accountable to the wider Church. It must be recognized that the need to be accountable and the need to maintain proper confidentiality may sometimes be in conflict.

2. The Methodist Church is a connexional Church and all *episkopé* should be exercised within this context. In the development of any structures, due consideration should be given to their impact upon the life of the whole Church. There is a proper balance to be maintained between, for example, Circuit and District or District and Connexion.

While recognizing the value of a diocesan model, the Methodist Church would be uneasy about the development of any models of personal *episkopé* which isolated Districts from the whole Church.

3. The Methodist Church began as a missionary movement and continues to have mission at its heart. Methodists believe that a key function of *episkopé* is to enable and encourage the Church's participation in God's mission.

The missionary imperative was an important consideration in the introduction of 'separated' Chairmen. The experience of some Methodist Churches, including the United Methodist Church, which have adopted episcopal systems of oversight provides encouraging precedents for expressions of *episkopé* that are mission-led.

4. In the furtherance of the search for the visible unity of Christ's church, the Methodist Church would willingly receive the sign of episcopal succession on the understanding that ecumenical partners sharing this sign with the Methodist Church (a) acknowledge that the latter has been and is part of the one holy catholic and apostolic Church and (b) accept that different interpretations of the precise significance of the sign exist.

As to (a), this was something that the Conference asked of the Church of England in 1955 as the 'Conversations' began. Many people in our partner churches would themselves be anxious to ensure that nothing done in the uniting of ministries should imply that previous ministries were invalid or inauthentic.

As to (b), Methodism has previously insisted that there should be freedom of interpretation as to the significance of the historic episcopate. The concept that episcopacy is a 'sign but not a guarantee of the apostolicity of the Church' may be widely acceptable, as a testimony to its symbolic witness to links across time, while testifying too to the obvious truth that bishops are not automatically and invariably wise or faithful.

5. The Methodist Church, in contemplating the possibility of receiving the sign of the historic episcopal succession, expects to engage in dialogue with its sister Churches to clarify as thoroughly as possible the nature and benefits of this gift.

In considering the introduction of the historic succession to Methodism in the sort of circumstances outlined in Guideline 2, the Methodist Church recognizes the need to explore its potential for complementing and enriching the Methodist Church's present experience of *episkopé* and for enhancing Methodism's sense of communion within the one holy catholic and apostolic Church.

6. The Methodist Church would be unable to receive the sign of Episcopal succession in a context which would involve a repudiation of what the Methodist Church believed itself to have received from God.

An obvious and important example of what is meant by this Guideline is the ministry of women. Since women were ordained to the presbyterate in the Methodist Church, every office for which male ministers are eligible has been open also to women. In its preliminary consideration of the scheme for an Ecumenical Bishop in Wales, the Conference was extremely concerned by the statement that the first such bishop would necessarily be male, and it gave its approval for further work to be done on the scheme on the understanding that serious efforts would be made in the ongoing discussions to ensure that such a restriction should not obtain in relation to any subsequent appointment.

7. The Methodist Church, in receiving the sign of episcopal succession, would insist that all ministries, including those of oversight, are exercised *within* the ministry of the whole people of God and at its service, rather than in isolation from it and in supremacy over it.

In earlier conversations, the Methodist Church has emphasized the value which it would place on the pastoral office of bishops, and on bishops having leadership responsibilities for mission and a representative role in community affairs. The view has been expressed that they should know and be known at many levels, and that they should exercise authority with gentleness and be humble servants of God.

As the survey of styles of *episkopé* and of episcopacy indicated, Methodists should not fear that the adoption of episcopacy would, of necessity, involve the adoption of a hierarchical model. Increasingly, in episcopally ordered churches, emphasis has been placed on the pastoral, teaching and missionary roles of the bishop. As Commitment to Mission and Unity insists:

> The office [of a bishop] is relational in character and must be exercised in, with and among the community which it is called to serve. The office should not be so overburdened with bureaucratic demands that bishops are prevented from being alongside their people, or that their collegiality with their fellow bishops, presbyters and deacons is diminished. It is a ministry of service which requires an appropriate lifestyle and pastoral demeanour.

RESOLUTIONS

711. The Conference adopts the Guidelines set out in this report as a summary statement of its position on *episkopé* and episcopacy.

712. The Conference affirms its willingness in principle to receive the sign of episcopacy on the basis of the Guidelines set out in this report.

PART III

WORSHIP

Introduction

Nonconformist worship probably changed more in the twentieth century than in the previous two.[1] Of course, many things remained the same. The distinctive characteristics of the Methodist Love Feast (**III.1**) and the Covenant Service (**III.2**) survived some modernisation of wording. The latter gained a wider following outside Methodism as a result of ecumenical encounter, though the former declined in significance as the century proceeded, partly because of an increased frequency of celebration of Holy Communion. One institution that virtually disappeared was the Sunday School anniversary (**III.3**), largely because of the collapse of the traditional Sunday School. The description here from a Methodist church would have been true of the other major Free Churches.

The principal change was undoubtedly the relative decline of extemporary prayer and the greater use of set liturgical forms. When Methodism united in 1932 it was emphasised that the tradition of using the Anglican forms of Morning and Evening Prayer in many former Wesleyan chapels would continue alongside extemporary prayer, but this was a practice in decline (**III.5**). The *Book of Congregational Worship*, published by the Congregational Union in 1920 (**III.4**), also included a significant collection of prayers and various orders of service for worship, including congregational responses. This was the first 'official' book of its type among Baptists and Congregationalists, and it was followed by others after the Second World War.

A different issue which affected the churches after the war was the question of televised religious services. By and large the churches had welcomed broadcast services between the wars, after an initial nervousness that they might tempt people to stay at home rather than come to church. Television introduced a new element into the situation and the Presbyterian Church of England took an early stand against the televising of Holy Communion in 1949. An attempt to revise the policy in the early 1950s failed and was followed by a further discussion in 1958 (**III.6**). By then two things had become clear: the focus of broadcast services had definitely switched to those who did not regularly attend church; and other churches, not least the Church of Scotland, did not share the Presbyterian Church of England's reservations. The Committee's recommendation for a change of policy was approved by the General Assembly, though not without dissent.

The decline in the numbers in the Free Churches was accompanied by a decline in the number of ministers. With a general tendency to standardise conditions of service including stipends this meant that village churches were particularly exposed to the loss of a minister of their own, even if they retained a share in one as part of a group of churches. This in turn increased the significance of lay leadership of worship, which had always been a feature of nonconformist life. Local Preachers had always had a vital role in Methodism. This was illustrated in the restatement of Local Preachers' responsibilities in 1964 (**III.7**). By the end of the century a significant proportion of them were in business or the professions.[2] The same responsibilities fell to Lay Preachers among Baptists and Congregationalists, but were not articulated so systematically.

The Free Churches were also affected by the liturgical movement more generally after the Second World War. It was not until the 1960s that there were any attempts to modernise the language of liturgy in either the Free Churches or the Church of England. (The shift is illustrated by a comparison of the language of the New English Bible in 1961/70 with the Revised English Bible in 1989.) But the liturgical revisions of the 1960s and 1970s, both Anglican and Free Church, shared many characteristics. The new Methodist Order for Holy Communion of 1975 (**III.8**) may be compared with the United Reformed Church's Second Order of 1989 (**III.9**); both include the Sursum Corda, which would not have been expected in the traditions making up the United Reformed Church half a century earlier. The second includes separate prayers of thanksgiving for the bread and the wine, reflecting the traditions of Churches of Christ, which became part of the United Reformed Church in 1981. There was also a greater openness to a wider understanding of Holy Communion itself, indicated by the Baptist, Michael Walker (**III.11**). The greatest change, however, was probably the end of the practice whereby Communion was 'tacked on' to a normal Sunday service, after a short break which allowed some people to escape if they did not want to stay.

The second half of the century also saw an explosion of new hymnody in the Free Churches, particularly from Congregationalist and Methodist authors. This included a readiness to use 'you' for God, and a move away from a special 'religious' language, rather like the use of plain English in Wordsworth's *Lyrical Ballads* (1798). Examples from the leading authors have been included from *Hymns and Psalms* (1981) and *Rejoice and Sing* (1991), which were new hymn books for Methodism and the United Reformed Church respectively (**III.10**).

The final stage of the movement in language in the last twenty years of the century was increased sensitivity to the use of masculine nouns and pronouns to refer to women and men collectively, and also to God. Both *Hymns and Psalms* and *Rejoice and Sing* attempted to provide hymn texts in inclusive language. There were similar attempts in relation to common liturgical texts, for example, the elimination of 'men' in 'for us men and our salvation' in the Nicene Creed. But the really difficult area was in language about God. The United Reformed Church produced a version of its Statement of Faith in inclusive language, which was approved by the General Assembly in 1997 (**III.12**), though not without some controversy.

These developments in language were largely ignored by evangelicals in both the Free Churches and the Church of England. New evangelical hymnody retained the more traditional language of the New International Version of the Bible, and there was less interest in modernised forms of liturgy. On the other hand, there was greater enthusiasm for music and choruses in traditional revivalist style.

Notes

1. An excellent discussion of this topic is found in Sell & Cross (2003), pp. 102–31.
2. Field (1995).

Document III.1

A Wesleyan Methodist Love Feast in the Early Twentieth Century

Kenneth Young, *Chapel* (London: Eyre Methuen, 1972), pp. 108–9.

This description of a Wesleyan Love Feast is from the history of Mount Tabor Wesleyan Chapel, Halifax, 1920–1920. George Sutcliffe was a chemistry teacher and a local preacher.

The love feasts at which members of the congregation gave their testimony to the power of God in their lives were also times of great blessing. An unusual feature of these meetings was the partaking of refreshment. Two large cups of water and baskets containing buns were passed round. At one time admittance was obtained only by the production of the ticket of church membership. So popular were these services that the chapel gallery where they were held was usually crowded to overflowing. Collections were made for the poor of the district.

G. Sutcliffe, who belonged to this same chapel from 1891 onwards, writes that love feasts were in those days held on the first Sunday of the month in place of the normal evening service. No preacher in charge. Class leaders responsible. Hymns and choruses often struck up by some person in the pews – popular ones included 'There are angels hovering round' with reference to Mary and Martha having just gone along. Testimonies and prayers were made as those participating felt led.

During the meeting two large porcelain drinking cups inscribed with the words 'Love Feast' were passed from pew to pew each person present drinking from them of the water they contained. A shallow basket of buns was also passed round.

Document III.2

The Methodist Covenant Service

The Book of Offices (London: Methodist Publishing House, 1936), p. 57.

The Covenant Service has been part of the Methodist worship tradition from the beginning. Prefaced by modern prayers of adoration, thanksgiving and confession, the Covenant still echoes the Puritan sources and John Wesley's adaptation.

THE COVENANT

Here, the People standing, the Minister shall say,
And now, beloved, let us bind ourselves with willing bonds to our covenant God, and take the yoke of Christ upon us.

This taking of His yoke upon us means that we are heartily content that He appoint us our place and work, and that He alone be our reward.

Christ has many services to be done; some are easy, others are difficult; some bring honour, others bring reproach; some are suitable to our natural inclinations and temporal interests, others are contrary to both. In some, we may please Christ and please ourselves, in others we cannot please Christ except by denying ourselves. Yet the power to do all these things is assuredly given us in Christ, who strengtheneth us.

Therefore let us make the Covenant of God our own. Let us engage our heart to the Lord, and resolve in His strength never to go back.

Being thus prepared, let us now, in sincere dependence on His grace and trusting in His promises, yield ourselves anew to Him, meekly kneeling upon our knees.

Here shall the Minister say in the name of all:
O LORD God, Holy Father, who hast called us through Christ to be partakers in this gracious Covenant, we take upon ourselves with joy the yoke of obedience, and engage ourselves, for love of Thee, to seek and do Thy perfect will. We are no longer our own, but Thine.

Here all the People shall join:
I AM no longer my own, but Thine. Put me to what Thou wilt, rank me with whom Thou wilt; put me to doing, put me to suffering; let me be employed for Thee or laid aside for Thee, exalted for Thee or brought low for Thee; let me be full, let me be empty; let me have all things, let me have nothing; I freely and heartily yield all things to Thy pleasure and disposal.

And now, O glorious and blessed God, Father, Son and Holy Spirit, Thou art mine, and I am Thine. So be it. And the Covenant, which I have made on earth, let it be ratified in heaven. Amen.

Document III.3

The Sunday School Anniversary

David Clark, *Between Pulpit and Pew: Folk Religion in a North Yorkshire Fishing Village* (Cambridge: Cambridge University Press, 1982), pp. 95–8.

The Sunday School Anniversary was a distinctive feature of the year in all nonconformist churches, only rivalled by the Chapel Anniversary, although the Sunday School often had a broader outreach into the community. This is a picture of Methodism in Staithes near Whitby, based on research done in the 1970s. More recently it has been overtaken by the decline in numbers, 'all age' worship and a sense that children should not be 'exploited' in this way.

Large congregations in the chapel on the Sunday evenings mark the highpoint of the Sunday School Anniversary weekend. At each of the chapels I observed attendances in the region of 120 to 150 people. These included members, who in some cases were often poor attenders Sunday by Sunday, as well as those who were nominally affiliated, such as former scholars and the parents of children taking part. A notable feature of this latter group was the high proportion of fathers present to watch their children perform; these men in particular were normally distinguished by their non-participation in chapel matters, but for the Sunday School Anniversary were very much in evidence, albeit frequently looking ill at ease. Older people are also well represented at the service, often in the capacity of grandparents as well as of long-standing supporters of the chapel.

A special platform is erected for the evening service in front of the pulpit, which extends out over the front pews. Children taking part are seated on this platform, dressed in their best clothes. At Wesley there is a strict rule that girls must wear white, though at the other two chapels this tradition has fallen foul of the dictates of fashion, so that many girls now appear in long party dresses. Most parents seat themselves in the gallery of the chapel, from where they can obtain a better view of their children on the platform. Sunday School Anniversaries and funerals were the only occasions upon which I saw the gallery contain more than a handful of people.

The service commences with a hymn sung by the entire congregation (the Wesleyans print a special sheet of anniversary hymns which are sung during the course of the weekend). Thereafter the children dominate the proceedings with a series of recitations and songs. In solos and group items the children work their way through a variety of poems and musical interludes. The poems, both from the smallest children and the teenagers, frequently have no religious content whatsoever, but are usually anecdotes about animals ('Old Rover', 'Little Mouse'), the seasons or, in the case of older boys, the sea – lengthy sagas of disaster and shipwreck being a particular favourite. Most of the children clearly find performing a matter of some discomfort, something to be rushed through at a rapid rate, and in which an iron-like metre leaves little room for personal expression. This, coupled with the size of the congregation, the formality of the occasion and the wearing of one's best clothes, combine to make the experience somewhat traumatic. Most of the children on the platform have a manifest air of bewilderment mixed with excitement and fear. Despite all this the congregation delights in the performances and is totally indulgent of unintelligibility, errors and inaudibility. In fact the songs, poems and general spectacle seem to please the adults far more than they do the children. After the service, for example, typical overheard comments might refer to a particular child's performance or the attractiveness of the girls' dresses. Whatever the balance of enjoyment between adults and children, there is no doubt about the lasting impression which 'standing on the platform' makes on the child. Many adults made reference to their memories of the occasion, some recounting, not with a degree of pride, how after appearing in the anniversary for the seventh time, they received their own bible, a practice which still persists today.

Celebrations continue on the following day, Monday, when in the afternoon members of the Methodist chapels parade around the village, carrying the chapel banner and singing their anniversary hymns. Paying particular attention to singing outside the homes of their own brethren, especially the sick and infirm, the group tours the yards and streets of the village before making their way back to the chapel Sunday Schoolroom for tea.

The final event in the Sunday School Anniversary celebrations takes place on Monday night, when the children repeat their performance of the previous evening. Once again they run through the poems and songs, though this time in a rather more relaxed manner and in an atmosphere of greater levity. Unlike at the previous service, which takes place upon the Sabbath, applause is permitted and encouraged. The Monday night service provides yet another opportunity for money raising. Collections are held throughout the weekend and a charge is made for the anniversary tea which, since it relies entirely upon donated foodstuffs, incurs no drain on chapel funds. As a result, the Sunday School Anniversary constitutes one of the largest single contributors to a chapel's trust funds.

The Sunday School anniversary stands out as perhaps the most important annual event in the religious life of the village. There are a number of reasons for this. Many people who do not attend a chapel at all during the course of the year, including the young married men, will be present for the Sunday evening service. The anniversary draws in even those with extremely weak nominal ties as well as the more sporadic Sunday attenders. All come together for a service which reaffirms the strength of the chapel. In so doing each chapel is able to present a picture of success and continuity through large congregations, the presence of 'old scholars' and a platform filled with Sunday School members. Problems of finance and attendance are temporarily masked by a collective statement of institutional vigour. The choice each year of the same preacher, ironically the same person for both Wesleyan and Primitive chapels, further affirms the desired image. The preacher can be relied upon to idealise the role of the chapel in village life and point to its continuing relevance. The sense of continuity between past and present is no mere illusion, however.

Document III.4

Book of Congregational Worship, 1920

Book of Congregational Worship (London: Congregational Union of England and Wales, 1920), pp. 7–8.

Wesleyan Methodism had always had a *Book of Offices*, but this book was the first collection among Baptists or Congregationalists with official status, as distinct from collections published by individual ministers, notably John Hunter's *Devotional Services*, which went through five editions from 1880.

The desire for a Book of Services for public worship providing for the use of liturgy has found such wide and increasing expression, that the Council of the Congregational Union of England and Wales now issue this *Book of Congregational Worship* for optional use in the Churches...

The Committee has drawn freely on forms consecrated by centuries of usage, and with equal freedom has utilized modern prayers such as no man out of his 'extemporal wit' could devise. At the same time, in accordance with the inheritance and genius of the Free Churches, an essential place has been given to extemporary prayer in each Order of Worship. The fervour of personal appeal informed with the impulses of the hour and pleading the hour's needs is frequently charged with sympathetic force such as no printed forms can supply.

They trust that by following this course they will promote reverence, lead to more general congregational participation in worship, and contribute to the richness of Divine service in all the Free Churches that avail themselves of this book. It serves to deliver a congregation from what is called 'the tyranny of the pulpit', and it delivers the minister from the tremendous drain on his spiritual resources involved in the unaided conduct of the devotions of his Church.

Document III.5

Methodist Morning Prayer

E. D. Bebb, *Trinity Methodist Church, Wolverhampton* (Wolverhampton, 1951).

Between 1902 and 1951, when Dr Douglas Bebb wrote, many churches in the Wesleyan tradition gave up using Morning Prayer. Dr Bebb's account typified the growth in Methodism in the 1950s. By the mid-1970s that particular church closed after the possibility of an Anglican church joining Trinity on their site was abandoned.

Trinity was opened on 30th June, 1863, and is therefore ninety-one years old. It was built largely under the leadership of Lord Wolverhampton, as an offshoot from Darlington Street Church; and we shall soon start looking forward to our centenary in 1963.

Trinity is one of the very few Methodist churches in which the Sunday morning service follows the Anglican Prayer Book, as slightly modified by John Wesley, while the evening service is of the usual Free Church order. As a result, we find that both those who have been used to the 'free' form of service and to the liturgical, have their needs met in our regular Sunday worship, while many find the contrast in form between the morning and evening most helpful. We notice that many who have hitherto been used to only one form of service, discover that their worship is enriched by this contrast between the morning and evening services.

During the past two or three years we have seen our net membership grow from 230 to nearly 300. At the same time, the average attendance at the morning service has increased by about 75%, and the average at night by some 25%, while the number of those attending Holy Communion has increased by 50%. Half-a-century ago, attendances on Sunday were larger than now, but the membership was considerably less, and the attendance at Holy Communion in those days much less than now, nor did they have then the multitude of week-day activities to which we are accustomed.

Document III.6

Televising Holy Communion

Committee on Public Worship and Aids to Devotion, *Reports to PCE General Assembly*, 1958, pp. 467–9.

The question of broadcasting church services raised a number of questions, particularly when Holy Communion was involved. The Presbyterian Church of England General Assembly discussed this on several occasions between the late 1940s and the late 1950s before eventually agreeing to the recommendation contained in this report of 1958.

Televising the Communion Service

In accordance with the instruction of last Assembly, the Committee has carefully considered this matter. The decision whether or not to allow ministers to accept invitations to conduct a Communion Service on television is one which cannot be taken in isolation; it needs to be considered in the context of the great and increasing influence of this new medium. An important factor to be borne in mind is the recent change in sound and television policy at the level of religious programme-planning. Since the inception of sound broadcasting, most time on the air has been devoted to 'overhearing' a local congregation at worship. Religious talks, discussions and feature programmes have been presented from time to time, and some services have been experimental in form (for example, those with 'dramatic interludes,' first introduced by Dr. W. A. L. Elmslie); but the staple religious diet for listeners has consisted either of broadcasts of ordinary congregations at their normal worship or studio services which have mostly followed the traditional patttern. In future, however, the number of Church services will be drastically reduced until these form a minor element in the programme. The religious producers, both in sound broadcasting and television, propose to concentrate upon experimental features – talks, discussions, films of the Church actually at work in society (such as the TV portrayal of the Luton Industrial Mission, the 'House Church' scheme, etc.) – which have more chance of making real contact with those outside the Church. In other words, there has been a shift in emphasis from catering mainly for the Church member to using the new media as instruments of evangelism, beginning from subjects which can interest and grip the not-very-religious person. It was on this basis that the religious advisers of television (both of the B.B.C. and the companies operating under I.T.A.) approved the use of time during which Church services are being held; hitherto those times have always been carefully avoided.

From this change in policy it is clear that the Church is faced with a wholly new development, which calls for important decisions. Since the number of actual services is to be dramatically reduced, and since those presented will therefore probably be reserved for ministers who can be relied upon to attract the widest audience, opportunities for ministers of this particular Church to conduct acts of worship will in future be few and far between. Of those services, celebrations of

Holy Communion will be fewer still, and those allocated to the Presbyterian Church of England even more rare – probably as infrequent as one in two or three years. The Assembly must, therefore, decide, first, whether it is sufficiently impressed with this chance to reach the non-churchgoer that it is willing to seize every opportunity extended to it; or whether, alternatively, it is prepared to accept only some invitations and to reject others (for example, any invitation to televise the Communion Service), even if this limited and conditional co-operation might mean that eventually the programme-planners, weary of refusals, turn to other churches when they are in search of help.

The Committee adheres unanimously to the view that Holy Communion is, in Calvin's phrase, a 'visible word' (something very different from a mere 'spectacle'), and that there can be no objection to the presence of 'non-churchmen' as spectators which does not equally apply to the traditional practice of allowing children or non-communicating visitors to remain in fellowship with the congregation, while not receiving the Elements. Those viewers who have no interest in such a service will simply switch off, as they do with all ordinary services at present. It is interesting to note that following the first two celebrations of Communion in the Church of Scotland which were televised, a large number of appreciative letters were received, some from lapsed members who declared their intention of resuming active membership as a result of their viewing. While acknowledging that our Church is not bound to follow the practice of others in this matter, the Committee feels that this experience of the Church of Scotland is worth recording as part of the evidence upon which to form a judgment.

The Committee feels that the Church should accept, thankfully, all invitations to co-operate in the use of this new and immensely influential medium; and a resolution to that effect will be brought before the Court. Certain problems would remain to be settled; for example, what precise form should the first televised Communion Service take? The resolution seeks to meet this difficulty by suggesting that whoever be invited to conduct such a service (and the B.B.C. has always reserved the right to select its own preachers, a practice which I.T.A. will certainly follow) should consult with the Committee, which would be summoned specially for the purpose, if necessary. It is because the Committee is convinced that a wise decision can be taken only within the wider context, that the resolution has been drafted in the terms in which it will be found, and not in terms of 'approval' or 'disapproval' of televising the Communion Service alone. The Church is privileged to be allowed to participate, from the start, in this medium which will come to affect the lives of people more and more. We believe that Presbyterianism has a real and distinctive contribution to make to the religious life of England, not least in its interpretation and practice, of the Lord's Supper.

Document III.7

Methodist Local Preachers, 1964

The Place and Functions of a Local Preacher (1964), in *Statements and Reports of the Methodist Church on Faith and Order, 1933–1983* (London: Methodist Publishing House, 1984), p. 135.

The circuit system in Methodism meant that Local Preachers played a crucial part in the worship of congregations from the beginning. This statement of the Conference in 1964 on 'The Place and Functions of a Local Preacher' reflects the understanding of the office in the later twentieth century. G. Milburn and M. Batty (eds), *Workaday Preachers* (London: Methodist Publishing House, 1995), tells the story of the place of Local Preachers in Methodism.

1. When a Local Preacher is publicly recognised as such he openly avows his belief that he has been 'inwardly moved by the Holy Spirit to preach the truth revealed in the Holy Scriptures as the Word of God, and to make known the glorious Gospel of Salvation through Jesus Christ'. The proclamation of God's Word is his primary function, and requires wholehearted devotion to study and prayer for its effective fulfilment.
2. He is not concerned with preaching only, but also with the preparation and conduct of worship. There has been a revival of worship in many parts of the Church, and the Local Preacher has a large part to play in fostering and expressing this. He will need to give attention to the insights concerning worship which have been granted anew to the Church, as well as to fill the established modes of Methodist worship with the richest possible meaning.
3. A Local Preacher is committed to being available in all normal circumstances for appointments in his own Circuit, to attendance at the Local Preachers' Meeting and to acceptance of its discipline. If he fails at any of these points he impoverishes his preaching, and damages the fellowship of Local Preachers through the Connexion.
4. A Local Preacher needs to have his roots in the life of the local Church, and to receive there the ministry of the Word and Sacraments, even though it is necessary for him to be absent from time to time and in some cases very frequently, from worship in the Society to which he belongs.

    These matters all belong to the work of a Local Preacher as it is laid down in the Standing Orders of the Church. Two others also need his careful attention.
5. Many Local Preachers are Class Leaders too, and in that capacity have a definite pastoral task. But even when they are not, the opportunity may occur for them to help the Minister and the Class Leaders in caring for people, especially in small Societies where pastoral care is not close at hand. In any case, a pastoral attitude of mind is an essential mark of the preacher.
6. The task and influence of a Local Preacher extend far beyond the bounds of Sunday worship in Church. Because of his special knowledge and experience, his fellow-Christians look to him for a lead in offering a Christian witness at

Worship

their place of work and in other spheres of social activity. He can command the Gospel and the Church as effectively there as in the pulpit.

Document III.8

Methodist Order for Communion, 1975

The Methodist Service Book (London: Methodist Publishing House, 1975), pp. B12–B17.

In 1936 *The Book of Offices* was published with two styles of services for Holy Communion. The basic service was the traditional Wesleyan adaptation of the Prayer Book of 1662; the alternative service was intended for congregations not used to a liturgical or responsive style. For a time it was quite widely used, following a Preaching Service. *The Methodist Service Book* of 1975 reflected the renewal of biblical theology, the ecumenical movement and the liturgical movement, which led to much convergence in the basic 'anaphora' or Prayer of Thanksgiving in the Service of Holy Communion. The anaphora is here set out in full. *The Methodist Worship Book* of 1999 has nine eucharistic services and a great deal of prayer material for every possible event.

THE THANKSGIVING

All stand.

21   The Minister says the great prayer of thanksgiving:

Lift up your hearts.
We lift them to the Lord.

Let us give thanks to the Lord our God.
It is right to give him thanks and praise.

Father, all-powerful and ever-living God,
it is indeed right, it is our joy and our salvation,
always and everywhere to give you thanks and praise
through Jesus Christ your Son our Lord.
You created all things and made us in your own image.
When we had fallen into sin, you gave your only Son to be our Saviour.

He shared our human nature, and died on the cross.
You raised him from the dead, and exalted him to your right hand in glory,
where he lives for ever to pray for us.
Through him you have sent your holy and life-giving Spirit
and made us your people, a royal priesthood,

to stand before you to proclaim your glory
and celebrate your mighty acts.
And so with all the company of heaven we join in the unending hymn of praise:

Holy, holy, holy Lord,
God of power and might,
heaven and earth are full of your glory.
Hosanna in the highest.
Blessed is he who comes in the name of the Lord.
Hosanna in the highest.

We praise you, Lord God, King of the universe,
through our Lord Jesus Christ,
who, on the night in which he was betrayed,
took bread, gave thanks, broke it, and gave it to his
disciples, saying,
'Take this and eat it. This is my body given for you.
Do this in remembrance of me.'
In the same way, after supper,
he took the cup, gave thanks, and gave it to them, saying,
'Drink from it all of you.
This is my blood of the new covenant,
poured out for you and for many, for the forgiveness of sins.
Do this, whenever you drink it, in remembrance of me.'

Christ has died.
Christ is risen.
Christ will come again.

Therefore, Father, as he has commanded us,
we do this in remembrance of him,
and we ask you to accept our sacrifice of praise and thanksgiving.

Grant that by the power of the Holy Spirit
we who receive your gifts of bread and wine
may share in the body and blood of Christ.

Make us one body with him.

Accept us as we offer ourselves to be a living sacrifice,
and bring us with the whole creation to your heavenly kingdom.

We ask this through your Son, Jesus Christ our Lord.

Through him, with him, in him,

Worship

**in the unity of the Holy Spirit
all honour and glory be given to you, almighty Father,
from all who dwell on earth and in heaven
throughout all ages. Amen.**

THE BREAKING OF THE BREAD

22   The Minister breaks the bread in the sight of the people, in silence, or saying,

EITHER:

   The bread we break is a sharing in the body of Christ.

   **Though we are many, we are one body
   Because we all share in the one loaf.**

OR:

   The things of God for God's holy people.

   **Jesus Christ is holy, Jesus Christ is Lord
   to the glory of God the Father.**

OR, from Easter Day to Pentecost:

   Alleluia, Christ our Passover is sacrificed for us.

   Therefore let us keep the feast. Alleluia.

23   Silence, all seated or kneeling

THE SHARING OF THE BREAD AND WINE

24   Lord, we come to your table trusting in your mercy
     and not in any goodness of our own.
     we are not worthy even to gather up the crumbs under
     your table, but it is your nature always to have mercy,
     and on that we depend.
     So feed us with the body and blood of Jesus Christ,
     your Son, that we may for ever live in him and he in us.
                                                  Amen.

25   The Minister and any who are assisting *him* receive the bread
     and wine and then give them to the people.
     The Minister may say these or other words of invitation:
     Draw near with faith. Receive the body of our Lord

Jesus Christ, which was given for you, and his blood,
which was shed for you; and feed on him in your
hearts by faith with thanksgiving.

26 The bread and wine are given EITHER with these words:

> The body of Christ given for you.
>
> The blood of Christ shed for you.

OR with these words:

> The body of our Lord Jesus Christ, which was given
> for you, keep you in eternal life. Take and eat this in
> remembrance that Christ died for you, and feed on
> him in your heart by faith with thanksgiving.
>
> The blood of our Lord Jesus Christ, which was shed
> for you, keep you in eternal life. Drink this in
> remembrance that Christ's blood was shed for you,
> and be thankful.

The communicant may reply each time: Amen.

27 The Minister covers what remains of the elements with a white cloth.

THE FINAL PRAYERS

28 Silence

29 Let us pray.

> **We thank you, Lord,**
> **That you have fed us in this sacrament,**
> **united us with Christ,**
> **and given us a foretaste of the heavenly banquet**
> **prepared for all mankind. Amen.**

30 Hymn

31 The blessing of God, Father, Son, and Holy Spirit,
    remain with you always. **Amen.**

32 Go in peace in the power of the Spirit
    to live and work to God's praise and glory.

> **Thanks be to God.**

Document III.9

United Reformed Church Second Order of Worship, 1989

Service Book: The United Reformed Church in the United Kingdom (Oxford: Oxford University Press, 1989), pp. 26–9.

The United Reformed Church published a second *Service Book* in 1989, and the Second Order for Holy Communion reflects the Churches of Christ tradition of having separate prayers of thanksgiving for the bread and wine.

8   The Approach to Communion

As we gather at this table, we remember
that Jesus was born of Mary;
he lived our common life on earth;
he suffered and died for us;
on the third day he rose again;
and he is always present through the Holy Spirit.
In his presence,
and in the company of all the people of God,
past, present, and to come,
we celebrate the Supper of the Lord.

'Behold, I stand at the door and knock; if anyone hears my voice and opens the door, I will come in to him and eat with him, and he with me.' (*Rev. 3:20*)

or

How shall I repay the Lord for all his benefits to me?
I will take the cup of salvation,
and call upon the name of the Lord.
I will offer you a sacrifice of thanksgiving,
and call upon the name of the Lord. (*Ps. 116:11–12; 16*)

or

Blessed are those who hunger and thirst to see right prevail for they shall be satisfied. (*Matt. 5:6*)

9   Narrative of the Institution

Hear again the words of institution of this feast as they are given by the Apostle Paul: For I received from the Lord what I delivered to you, that the Lord Jesus on the night when he was betrayed took bread, and when he had given thanks, he broke it, and said, 'This is my body which is for you. Do this in remembrance of me.'

In the same way also he took the cup after supper, saying 'This cup is the new covenant in my blood. Do this, as often as you drink it, in remembrance of me.' For as often as you eat this bread and drink the cup, you proclaim the Lord's death until he comes. (*I Cor. 11: 23–6*)

10 Thanksgiving and Sharing

Lift up your hearts.
We lift them to the Lord.
Let us give thanks to the Lord our God.
It is right to give our thanks and praise.

We give thanks to you, O God,
that from the earth you cause the grain to come
for the making of bread.
We praise you for Christ, the bread of life,
whose body was broken for us.
By your Holy Spirit sanctify us and this loaf,
that the bread which we break may be to us
the communion of the body of Christ,
and that we may be made one in him.
As of old you fed your people in the wilderness,
so feed us now that we may live to your praise;
through Jesus Christ our Lord.
Amen.

The minister breaks the bread saying:
When Jesus had given thanks,
he broke the bread and said:
'Take, eat: this is my body which is given for you.
Do this in remembrance of me.'

The distribution takes place

We give thanks to you, O God,
that you cause the vine to yield fruit.
We bless you for Christ, the true vine,
whose blood was poured out for us.
By your Holy Spirit sanctify us and this wine,
that the cup which we bless may be to us
the communion of the blood of Christ,
and that through abiding in him
we may bear fruit that shall last.

Worship

As we share the sufferings of Christ, so give us grace
that we may know the power of his resurrection;
through Jesus Christ our Lord.
Amen.

The minister pours the wine and distributes it saying:
When Jesus had given thanks,
he gave the cup to his disciples and said:
'Drink this, all of you;
for this is my blood of the new covenant,
which is shed for you and for many,
for the forgiveness of sins.
Do this, as often as you drink it in
remembrance of me.'

[The service concludes with a prayer and the blessing.]

Document III.10

Later Twentieth-Century Hymnody

Hymns and Psalms (London: Methodist Publishing House, 1983); *Rejoice and Sing* (Oxford: Oxford University Press 1991).

The later twentieth century saw a rich flowering of hymnody in Methodism and Congregationalism, which moved decisively away from traditional language but remained within traditional metres. This contrasted with the burgeoning number of new hymns following a more popular style of music, but often retaining traditional language. The Methodist hymn book, *Hymns and Psalms* (1983), and the United Reformed Church hymn book, *Rejoice and Sing* (1991), contained some of the best of these. Dr Ivor Jones was Principal of Wesley House Cambridge and Convener of the *Hymns and Psalms* editorial committee; his hymn was written in 1969. Fred Pratt Green was a Methodist minister and poet who came to hymn-writing comparatively late; this was written for a church in Texas in 1978. Fred Kaan's hymn is a variant on the harvest theme, written while he was minister at Plymouth in the 1960s. Brian Wren's hymn, written in 1973, was intended as a restatement of Wesley's 'And can it be'. Caryl Micklem's hymn was written for the inauguration of the Council for World Mission in 1977. Alan Gaunt's hymn was written in 1985.

Hymns and Psalms, 75

1   CHRIST, our King before creation,
    Life, before all life began,
    Crowned in deep humiliation
    By your partners in God's plan,

Make us humble in believing,
And, believing, bold to pray:
'Lord, forgive our self-deceiving,
Come and reign in us today!'

2 Lord of time and Lord of history,
Giving, when the world despairs,
Faith to wrestle with the mystery
Of a God who loves and cares,
Make us humble in believing,
And, believing, bold to pray:
'Lord, by grace beyond conceiving,
Come and reign in us today!'

3 Word that ends our long debating
Life of God which sets us free,
Through your body recreating
Life as life is meant to be,
Make us humble in believing,
And, believing, bold to pray:
'Lord, in us your aim achieving,
Come and reign in us today!'

               Ivor H. Jones (1934–)

Hymns and Psalms, 653

1 GOD is here! As we his people
Meet to offer praise and prayer,
May we find in fuller measure
What it is in Christ we share.
Here, as in the world around us,
All our varied skills and arts
Wait the coming of his Spirit
Into open minds and hearts.

2 Here are symbols to remind us
Of our lifelong need of grace;
Here are table, font, and pulpit;
Here the cross has central place.
Here in honesty of preaching,
Here in silence, as in speech,
Here, in newness and renewal,
God the Spirit comes to each.

Worship

3   Here our children find a welcome
In the Shepherd's flock and fold;
Here as bread and wine are taken,
Christ sustains us, as of old;
Here the servants of the servant
Seek in worship to explore
What it means in daily living
To believe and to adore.

4   Lord of all, of Church and Kingdom,
In an age of change and doubt,
Keep us faithful to the gospel,
Help us work your purpose out.
Here, in this day's dedication,
All we have to give, receive:
We, who cannot live without you,
We adore you! We believe!

            F. Pratt Green (1903–2000)

Rejoice and Sing, 33

1   Eternal God, your love's tremendous glory
cascades through life in overflowing grace,
to tell creation's meaning in the story
of love evolving love from time and space.

2   Eternal Son of God, uniquely precious,
in you, deserted, scorned and crucified,
God's love has fathomed sin and death's deep darkness,
and flawed humanity is glorified.

3   Eternal Spirit, with us like a mother,
embracing us in love serene and pure:
you nurture strength to follow Christ our brother,
as full-grown children, confident and sure.

4   Love's trinity, self-perfect, self-sustaining;
love which commands, enables and obeys:
you give yourself, in boundless joy, creating
one vast increasing harmony of praise.

5   We ask you now, complete your image in us;
this love of yours, our source and guide and goal.
May love in us seek love and serve love's purpose,
till we ascend with Christ and find love whole.

            Alan Gaunt (1935–)

Rejoice and Sing, 89

1. Now join we, to praise the creator,
   our voices in worship and song;
   we stand to recall with thanksgiving
   that to him all seasons belong.

2. We thank you, O God, for your goodness,
   for the joy and abundance of crops,
   for food that is stored in our larders,
   for all we can buy in the shops.

3. But also of need and starvation
   we sing with concern and despair,
   of skills that are used for destruction,
   of land that is burnt and laid bare.

4. We cry for the plight of the hungry
   while harvests are left on the field,
   for orchards neglected and wasting,
   for produce from markets withheld.

5. The song grows in depth and in wideness;
   the earth and its people are one.
   There can be no thanks without giving,
   no words without deeds that are done.

6. Then teach us, O Lord of the harvest,
   to be humble in all that we claim;
   to share what we have with the nations,
   to care for the world in your name.

Fred Kaan (1929–)

Rejoice and Sing, 339

1. Great God, your love has called us here
   as we, by love, for love were made.
   Your living likeness still we bear,
   though marred, dishonoured, disobeyed.
   We come, with all our heart and mind
   your call to hear, your love to find.

2. We come with self-inflicted pains
   of broken trust and chosen wrong,

Worship

    half-free, half-bound by inner chains,
    by social forces swept along,
    by powers and systems close confined
    yet seeking hope for humankind.

3   Great God, in Christ you call our name
    and then receive us as your own
    not through some merit, right or claim
    but by your gracious love alone.
    We strain to glimpse your mercy-seat
    and find you kneeling at our feet.

4   Then take the towel, and break the bread,
    and humble us, and call us friends.
    Suffer and serve till all are fed,
    and show how grandly love intends
    to work till all creation sings,
    to fill all worlds, to crown all things.

5   Great God, in Christ you set us free
    your life to live, your joy to share.
    Give us your Spirit's liberty
    to turn from guilt and dull despair
    and offer all that faith can do
    while love is making all things new.

                      Brian Wren (1936–)

Rejoice and Sing, 582

1   Thanks be to God, whose Church on earth
    has stood the tests of time and place,
    and everywhere proclaims new birth
    through Christ whose love reveals God's face.

2   Thanks be to God, whose Spirit sent
    apostles out upon his way;
    from east to west the message went;
    on Greek and Roman dawned the day.

3   Thanks be to God, whose later voice
    from west to east sent back the word
    which, through the servants of his choice,
    at last in every tongue was heard.

4 Thanks be to God who now would reach
   his listeners in more global ways;
   now each will send the news, and each
   receive and answer it in praise.

5 Thanks be to God, in whom we share
   today the mission of his Son;
   may all his Church that time prepare
   when, like the task, the world is one.

      Caryl Micklem (1925–2003)

Document III.11

Baptists and the Lord's Supper

M. Walker, *Baptists at the Table* (Didcot: Baptist Historical Society, 1992), pp. 203–5.

Although Michael Walker's book is a treatment of Baptist sacramental theology in the nineteenth century, the issues raised in his final chapter relate very much to the end of the twentieth, and show that Baptists also had been affected by the liturgical movement.

Recognition of the spiritual and theological wealth of the wider church has led to a renewed depth of understanding of the doctrine of baptism. It is only a similar recognition that will unlock for Baptists the wealth of the Lord's Supper. Sacramental theology ... is inseparable from the dialectic of scripture and tradition by which it has been formed. There is no access to a scriptural theology of the sacraments that bypasses the theological tradition of the church ...

Their own hymn writers, the Stennetts, provided vibrant, powerful and lovely images of the presence of Christ in the supper. The anonymous author of the 'Sacramental Meditations' showed that it was possible both to be a Baptist and to believe that God gave his people something infinitely precious at his table. Spurgeon's warm and eloquent preaching encouraged them to come in the belief that they would find Christ there. The Calvinist tradition from which they came taught that the bread and wine were the means by which the Holy Spirit raised believers into the presence of Christ where spiritually they might feed upon him. Luther took with utter seriousness the words of Jesus, 'This is my body', and taught a real eating and drinking of the body and blood of Christ that, significantly, was not dependent upon the priestly intervention of an episcopally ordained president. The further they fled from any of these alternatives the less remained to Baptists of a sacramental theology with any real content. The 'safe house' of Zwinglianism provided them, as it provided many of their Protestant contemporaries, with temporary shelter. But, for Baptists, it was less safe than it was for others.

Zwinglianism's ambivalent attitude to matter and spirit, sign and thing signified, offered too many temptations for those tempted into the far country of the radicals, the *Schwärmerei*, the seekers after perfection. Affirming a faith that could dispense with baptism, identifying the Lord's Supper with the material side of religion above which men might rise in the onward and upward march of the spirit, they left themselves clutching the inedible ashes of a non-sacramental theology.

A doctrine of the Lord's Supper that has no place for the real presence of Christ, however, understood, has substituted a meritorious act, a pious spiritual exercise, for the sacrament of grace in which the Father gives his Son again to his people in the fellowship of the Spirit. We have seen that there have always been Baptists able to affirm with the apostle Paul that the cup which we bless is a participation in the body of Christ. The question of the real presence is inescapable if the supper is to be seen as an act of God and not a rite of man, if the attention of the church is to be upon what God in Christ has done for us and not what we, in our response of faith, do for him. Baptist theology has been inhibited from grasping the issue, threatened as it has felt by the ubiquitous spectre of transubstantiation. The real presence is, however, a mystery, and Baptists have no need to flee from that mystery nor to be ashamed of the efforts that some of their forefathers made to come to terms with it. Nor can they elude it by leapfrogging across history and tradition into the pages of the New Testament. It was to those pages that the stabbing finger of Luther pointed as he defended his eucharistic doctrine against Zwingli at the Marburg Colloquy. If Baptists are to have a viable eucharistic theology then they have to retrace their footsteps along the paths they took at the Catholic revival and come again to a place where they can listen to the testimony of the wider family of the church. And, perhaps, they should listen to the testimony of their own people who used to come to the Lord's Supper singing:

> Here at thy table, Lord! we meet
> To feed on food divine:
> Thy body is the bread we eat,
> Thy precious blood the wine ...
>
> His body torn with rudest hands,
> Becomes the finest bread,
> And with the blessing he commands,
> Our noblest hopes are fed.
>
> His blood that from each opening vein,
> In purple torrents ran,
> Hath filled this cup with generous wine,
> That cheers both God and man.

Document III.12

Statement of Faith in Inclusive Language

URC, *Record of Assembly*, 1997, p. 27.

When the United Reformed Church decided to put its Basis of Union into inclusive language in 1986–87, the Statement of Faith in paragraph 17 was not amended, since this was a historical statement about a declaration made in 1972. An alternative version of the statement in inclusive language was therefore adopted by the General Assembly in 1997.

1 We believe
 in the one and only God,
 Eternal Trinity,
 from whom, through whom and for whom all created things exist.
 God alone we worship;
 in God we put our trust.

2 We worship God,
 source and sustainer of creation,
 whom Jesus called Father,
 whose sons and daughters we are.

3 We worship God
 revealed in Jesus Christ,
 the eternal Word of God made flesh;
 who lived our human life,
 died for sinners on the cross;
 who was raised from the dead,
 and proclaimed by the apostles, Son of God;
 who lives eternally, as saviour and sovereign,
 coming in judgement and mercy,
 to bring us eternal life.

4 We worship God,
 ever present in the Holy Spirit;
 who brings this Gospel to fruition,
 assures us of forgiveness,
 strengthens us to do God's will,
 and makes us sisters and brothers of Jesus,
 sons and daughters of God.

5 We believe
 in the one, holy, catholic and apostolic Church,
 united in heaven and on earth;

Worship

    on earth, the Body of Christ,
    empowered by the Spirit
    to glorify God and to serve humanity;
    in heaven, eternally one with the power,
    the wisdom and the love of God in Trinity.

6   We believe
    that, in the fullness of time,
    God will renew and gather in one
    all things in heaven and on earth through Christ,
    and be perfectly honoured and adored.

7   We rejoice in God
    who has given us being,
    who shares our humanity
    to bring us to glory,
    our source of prayer and power of praise;
    to whom be glory, praise and adoration,
    now and evermore.

PART IV

THEOLOGY

Introduction

In the twentieth century nonconformist theology became an integral part of English theological development. It ceased to be relevant for the appraisal of a book that its author was a nonconformist. Theologians in nonconformist colleges were increasingly writing for a national rather than a denominational audience and were received as such. The Departments of Theology at the provincial universities which became independent in the early twentieth century were often mainly composed of the staffs of the local nonconformist theological colleges, whereas Oxford, Cambridge, King's College, London and Durham retained an Anglican predominance. There nonconformists (and indeed lay people) were only appointed to university posts in Theology in any number from the 1970s. Significantly the first area in which this happened was biblical studies:[1] C. H. Dodd, a Congregationalist, was the first nonconformist to hold a chair at Cambridge in 1935, and George Caird, from a similar background, was the first to hold a biblical chair at Oxford nearly forty years later. Nevertheless, six of the eleven members of the Old Testament panel for the *New English Bible* were nonconformists, two of the seven on the Apocrypha panel, and three of the nine on the New Testament panel.[2]

At the beginning of the century R. J. Campbell, minister at the City Temple, London, attracted much controversy by his preaching – and considerable crowds. His book, *The New Theology*, was published in 1906 (**IV.1**). The emphasis on the Kingdom of God in the preaching of Jesus, almost to the exclusion of the Church, on the one hand represented the re-reading of the New Testament in terms of the message *of* rather than *about* Jesus; on the other hand, it reflected contemporary enthusiasm for commitment to social action – exactly what the author of *Nonconformity and Politics* deplored (**V.5**). Campbell's second book in 1907 on *Christianity and the Social Order* developed those themes further. He provoked many critics, notably Bishop Charles Gore in the Church of England (who received him into that Church in 1916) and P. T. Forsyth in Congregationalism, whose book, *The Person and Place of Jesus Christ* (1909), was a response to Campbell.

A different approach came from T. R. Glover, a Baptist layman and classical scholar, whose *The Jesus of History* (1917), emphasised that theology rather than history provided the decisive clues to the identity of Jesus (**IV.2**). Hence Glover argued that the Bible alone could not tell us who Jesus was, which is why he was classed as a liberal in an atmosphere where biblical authority was increasingly coming under scrutiny. Thus Glover was criticised not so much for his conclusions about who Jesus was, which are essentially orthodox, but for the grounds on which he based those conclusions.[3]

P. T. Forsyth was Principal of Hackney College from 1900 until his death in 1920, and was probably the greatest nonconformist theologian of the first half of the century. His *Lectures on the Church and the Sacraments* (1917) affirmed that the

Free Churches needed a more positive understanding of the Church (**IV.3**), and he also discussed the issue of Church v. Kingdom, raised by Campbell. He criticised the deficiencies of an exclusively congregational understanding of church polity more from theology than history.

John Oman, a Presbyterian who taught at Westminster College, Cambridge from 1907 to 1935, wrote in a different area. Scholars disagree about which of his works count as the greatest: *Vision and Authority, Grace and Personality, The Natural and the Supernatural, Faith and Freedom, The Church and the Divine Order*. But *Grace and Personality* was described by F. R. Tennant as 'one of the major treasures of theological literature'. His understanding of the nature of grace had implications for the Church and the Kingdom of God (**IV.4**). The work as a whole represented a new attempt to look at the meaning of grace in the context of the contemporary understanding of human nature.

Another Cambridge personality was B. L. Manning, a Fellow and later Bursar of Jesus College, and also a Congregationalist; like Glover, he was a layman and a historian. His principal period of interest was the late Middle Ages, but he wrote also about the origins of dissent in the post-Reformation period. His address of 1928 (**IV.5**) was also concerned with the nature of the Church and the place of scriptural authority within it. Manning was another Congregationalist with 'high church' views, like those associated with Mansfield College at the same time, and he was a strong critic of fundamentalism.

A rather different theological concern was the relation of religion and science. Sir Arthur Eddington was yet another Cambridge don, whose lecture, *Science and the Unseen World* (1929), reflected the thoughts of a prominent member of the Society of Friends and a distinguished astro-physicist, who was actively involved in scientific research (**IV.6**).

The Baptists were those most affected by fundamentalist controversy in the first half of the century. There were strands of conservative resistance to biblical criticism in all the churches, but the most public controversy broke out in the Baptist Union.[4] A pamphlet suggested, on the basis of a series of events between 1930 and 1932, that the Union had been taken over by 'liberals', but would not admit the fact (**IV.7**). The crisis passed, but the conservative evangelical voice had been heard.

Nathaniel Micklem, Principal of Mansfield College, Oxford, and his colleagues were in the vanguard of defending a catholic understanding of Congregationalism. His chapter on 'The Ministry and the Sacraments' (**IV.8**) was an excellent illustration of that. It drew on Forsyth, but even more on Luther and Calvin, thereby affirming the fundamentally Reformed nature of its theology. Micklem drew out the rich meaning of the sacraments, whilst also affirming an underlying relationship with the Word; hence the emphasis was placed on the objective action in them rather than subjective experience.

Traditionally, nonconformist theology had tended to emphasise the atonement rather than the incarnation. Dr Vincent Taylor, a leading Methodist scholar of the first half of the century, wrote a trilogy on the Atonement – *Jesus and His Sacrifice* (1937); *The Atonement in New Testament Teaching* (1940) and *Forgiveness and Reconciliation* (1941). His conclusion (**IV.9a**) was that all the traditional interpretations of the atonement had to be kept in mind, not least because the Church has never authorised a definitive interpretation which goes beyond the statement in the creed that 'For our sake he was crucified under Pontius Pilate'. From a later generation of Methodist theologians Professor Frances Young expounded some of the rethinking of the doctrine since the Second World War (**IV.9b**).

A rather different Methodist contribution came from Herbert Butterfield, Regius Professor of Modern History at Cambridge, in his writings on Christianity and History (**IV.10**). His book of that title, first published in 1949, was one of the early Fontana paperbacks. Butterfield was writing when the Second World War and its consequences had destroyed the nineteenth-century confidence in progress, such that history threatened to be meaningless. Although a layman and a secular historian, his interpretation affirmed the importance of the fact that Christianity was a historical religion.

Those same developments threatened the tenability of a traditional liberal theology, and characteristically these problems were tackled by the Unitarians. Gordon Bolam's essay of 1959 (**IV.11**) was a good illustration of their response.

German theologians like Dietrich Bonhoeffer had begun to question whether Christianity was best understood as a religion, and picked up some of the issues raised by the Danish writer Søren Kierkegaard a century earlier, when he suggested that Christianity put a question mark against traditional understandings of religion. Although the popularisation of these ideas in Britain is usually associated with John Robinson's *Honest to God* (1963), most of them were raised by the Congregational theologian, Daniel Jenkins, in his book, *Beyond Religion* published a year before (**IV.12**). The phrases 'religionless Christianity' and 'holy worldliness' came from Bonhoeffer; significantly Jenkins emphasised that problems begin when the Church becomes an end in itself and clerical elites seek to defend their position.

All these themes are brought together in the final extract from Colin Gunton's *The Actuality of Atonement* (1988) (**IV.13**). Gunton, also originally from a Congregational background and a minister of the United Reformed Church, was Professor of Theology at King's College, London, and the first nonconformist to give the Bampton Lectures at Oxford. He was the most significant nonconformist systematic theologian in the second half of the century, and his premature death in 2003 was a tragic loss. His discussion of church and sacraments was set in the overall context of an examination of the doctrine of the atonement, and how it can be understood in an age when so many of the metaphors on which it depends have lost their currency, both in the theological and the secular worlds. Gunton moved in the same world as Forsyth and Micklem, but the voice was significantly different.

It is particularly difficult to give an adequate picture of the diversity of theological views in relatively short extracts, and the choice of significant voices does not result in denominational equality. But all the writers represented appealed to a national readership, and were taken seriously by Anglican and Roman Catholic scholars.

Notes

1. Sell & Cross (2003), pp. 1–32.
2. Ibid., p. 31.
3. A fuller treatment of Campbell and Glover is found in Clements (1988), pp. 19–48, 107–29.
4. See Bebbington (1990), pp. 297–326.

Document IV.1

The New Theology, 1907

R. J. Campbell, *The New Theology* (London: Chapman & Hall, 1907), pp. 232–56.

'The New Theology is an untrammelled return to the Christian sources in the light of modern thought.' So wrote R. J. Campbell in the opening chapter of his book. As minister of London's City Temple in his twenties, his preaching was controversial. This extract from the penultimate chapter argues that the Kingdom is prior to the Church.

... What is the Church? Where did the idea spring from? What had Jesus to do with it originally? What is the Kingdom of God, and how do the various Christian societies which call themselves Churches stand in regard to it to-day? To answer any of these questions we must try to place ourselves to some extent in the intellectual and moral atmosphere of those amongst whom the ideas first arose. Let us take the kingdom first.

At the time when Jesus came every person of Jewish nationality was looking for the establishment of what had come to be called the Kingdom of God. For many generations the Jews had been a subject race. There had been one brief period of national splendour and prosperity, namely, the reigns of David and Solomon ... Israel always looked upon herself as in a special way a theocratic kingdom – a chosen of God. At its best this idea was a fine one, it led to the thought of a special spiritual vocation for the sake of the other nations of the earth; at its worst it meant the assertion of national privilege and contempt for everything which was not Jewish ... Hence there grew up a firmly held conviction that God would some time raise up a prince born of David's line, who with supernatural help, and with a strong hand, would drive out the invader and establish a kingdom which would outshine even that of David himself. This was the root idea of the Kingdom of God, as we meet it in the New Testament, and as it is described in some of the most beautiful passages of the Old...

But we should do an injustice to the subject if we failed to allow for the fact that, according to the prophetic ideal, this kingdom was to be a blessing to the world, and to abolish all violence and oppression; the Kingdom of God was to be a kingdom of universal peace and joy, a kingdom of righteousness based on social justice. It was because of this widespread expectation that the austere preacher John the Baptist obtained his hearing in the wilderness of Judea... It is clear ... that, in the opinion of the man who has now come to be regarded as the forerunner of Jesus, the Kingdom of God was to be an earthly kingdom, was to come suddenly, and was to be inaugurated by a sort of general judgment or clean sweep of all the elements that made for oppression, cruelty, foul living, and pretentiousness of every kind. It had not the remotest reference to a world to come or a Divine Redeemer whose principal duty it should be to suffer and die in order to secure a blessed immortality for those who believed in Him.

How far Jesus shared these ideas at the commencement of His own ministry it is impossible to say, but it seems clear that He was attracted by the moral earnestness of John, and wished to associate Himself with those who were looking for a kingdom of God which should mean the establishment and realization of the moral ideal in all human relations. But at the baptism a purpose long forming in His mind appears to have taken definite shape. He felt Himself called to preach the good news of a kingdom which could begin at once in the heart of any man who was willing to become the instrument of Divine love and the expression of the ideal of human brotherhood ... As time went on, however, Jesus came to see that it would not be realized as quickly as even He had thought. Men could not or would not understand; they were looking for a kingdom which should mean plenty to eat and drink, and universal dominion for the sons of Abraham. Even His most immediate followers were unable to divest themselves of this notion, and it is plain enough that they went on hoping even to the end that Jesus would head a revolt and establish a kingdom in which they themselves would hold positions of dignity and importance: 'Grant that we may sit, the one on Thy right hand, and the other on Thy left, in Thy kingdom.' The striking rebuke which Jesus administered to these pretensions, by setting a little child in the midst of the jealous men, will never be forgotten while the world lasts. Jesus did believe in an earthly kingdom of righteousness, peace, and joy, but it is evident that He would have nothing to say to violence as a means of realizing it. He even believed that the kingdom had already come in the heart of any man who was desirous of being at one with God and man and denied himself in the effort to do it...

An important fact, which I do not think is generally recognized, is that the first Christians thought almost precisely what the Jews did about the Kingdom of God. Most people are accustomed to think of Christianity as having been from the first a religion which had principally to do with getting men ready for the next world. We can hardly think about it apart from ecclesiastical buildings, choirs, baptisms, confirmations, prayers for the sick and dying, and so on. So much have we been accustomed to think of it in this way that the average man reads his New Testament with these assumptions in the background of his mind. But this is certainly not New Testament Christianity. The apostles and their followers believed, like the Jews, in the sudden establishment of an ideal commonwealth upon earth. This was how they understood the Lord's prayer: 'Thy kingdom come, Thy will be done on earth as it is in heaven.'...

All the earnestness and enthusiasm of the first Christians were centred upon the belief in the near advent of a Divine kingdom upon earth, with Jesus as its head. This belief even affected the practice of these early Christians in regard to the disposal of their property ... They had no organized economic system; no one was compelled to give anything, but under the pressure of the new spirit they willingly gave everything. What did it matter? they thought; they were only like pilgrims within sight of home, or watchers waiting for the morning.

Where, then, did the idea of the Church come from? It is as plain as anything can be that the primary interest of early Christianity was the Kingdom of God. It took the conception over from Judaism with a deeper moral content derived from the preaching and the life of Jesus. Its first adherents did not even know that they had a new religion; they only thought they had found the true Messiah, although the Jewish nation as a whole had rejected Him. What they wanted above everything was to see the kingdom come upon earth, and we now know that they were mistaken in imagining that it would be established speedily and suddenly by the visible second coming of Jesus on the clouds of heaven. But seeing that they were thinking of it in this way, how did the Church arise, and why?

It is doubtful if Jesus ever used the word 'Church,' for the two verses in Matthew, in which He is credited with it, are probably of late date, and point to a time when the ecclesiastical organization was fairly well established. Still, the word itself has an interest and a history of its own, apart from its Christian use. The *ecclesia,* as most of my readers may be aware, was the assembly of the citizens of any Greek city-state ... It was quite natural that the primitive Christians should have come to adopt this word, and to an extent this very idea, as a convenient description of the new Christian community. After the departure of their Master, the Christians held together, and wherever their missionaries went new communities sprang up, animated by a spirit of loyalty to Jesus and a desire to realize His ideal for mankind...

But how far did Jesus foresee and intend this? It is difficult to say; but His choice of twelve apostles, whom He carefully trained to continue His work, is evidence that He contemplated the formation of some kind of society to give effect to His teaching. The number twelve points to the probability that He thought of this society as a kind of new Israel, a spiritual Israel, which should do for the world what the older Israel had failed to do, that is, bring about the kingdom of God ... Broadly speaking ... there are two outstanding views as to the scope and function of the *ecclesia* or Church of Jesus. One is the sacerdotal, and the other is what, for want of a better name, I may term the evangelical. In outline the former is as follows: Before Jesus finally withdrew His bodily presence from His disciples, He formally constituted a religious society to represent Him on earth. This society was to be the ark of salvation, the 'sphere of covenanted grace.' Its principal work was to call men out of a lost and ruined world and secure for them a blessed immortality; those who were members of this Church, and only they, were certain of heaven. Membership therein was clearly defined; the gateway was baptism. Those who were baptized in a proper way, even though they were unconscious infants, were members of the Church of Christ, and all others were outside. Within this sacred society souls were to be trained in rightness of living, and, to an extent, made fit for heaven. The Holy Spirit abiding in this society would sanctify the individual members and guide them into all the truth. It is even held that Jesus definitely appointed the way in which this Church was to be governed. Its affairs were to be managed by a threefold order – bishops, priests, and deacons...

This sacerdotal view has exercised enormous influence in Christian history, and I have sufficient of the historic imagination to be able to say that at certain periods it has undoubtedly worked on the whole for good. But did Jesus really found a Church of this kind? I am quite sure He never thought of such a thing, and historical criticism of Christian origins does not leave the sacerdotalist much to stand on.

Jesus appointed neither bishop nor priest, and never ordained that any merely mechanical ceremony should be the means of admission to the Christian society or be necessary to the eternal welfare of any one. In the early Church the bishop or elder was the president of the little Christian society meeting in any particular locality. Primitive Christian organization was anything but rigid and formal, and was as far as possible from the sacerdotal model...

The other view of the meaning of the word 'Church,' to which I have already referred, is that it is the totality of the followers of Jesus. Under this view organization is a secondary matter. There are many reasons why Christian societies should organize themselves differently from one another. Temperament plays a great part in the matter. But theories of Church government have ceased to be the burning question that they once were. Most sensible men are now satisfied that forms of government matter much less than the kind of life which flourishes in the society itself.

... Two inconsistent views of the work of the Church, as well as of the constitution of the Church, have come down the ages together, and exist side by side in the world to-day. The first is that the chief business of the Church is to snatch men as brands from the burning and get them ready for a future heaven. The Fall theory has had much to do with this. The assumption behind it is, as we have seen, that the world is a city of destruction, as Bunyan calls it. It is a ruined world, a world which has somehow baffled and disappointed God, a failure of a world which, when the cup of its iniquity is full, will be utterly destroyed at a general judgment. When that dreadful day comes it will be bad for all those who are outside the fellowship of Christ, for, like those who have died without availing themselves of the means of salvation, they will be relegated to everlasting torment in the world unseen. This view of the fate of the world ... is still implied in most of our preaching and in the hymns we sing ... [O]n the whole, it has been thoroughly mischievous, and there is nothing which is acting as a greater hindrance to the spirituality and usefulness of the churches to-day. It is based on an entirely false idea as to the relation of God and the world.

But alongside of this view a far higher and nobler one has been present to the minds of Christians in every century – namely, that the work of the Church is to save the world and to believe that it is worth the saving. If what I have already said be true, this is the idea which was in the mind of Jesus when He founded His *ecclesia*. To Him the purpose of the *ecclesia* was to help to realize the Kingdom of God by preaching and living the fellowship of love. Ever since His day those who have been nearest to Him in spirit have been going forth into the dark places of the earth trying to win men to the realization of the great ideal of a universal fellowship of love based on a common relationship to the God and Father of us all ... I maintain that the Church has nothing whatever to do with preparing men for a world to come. The best way to prepare a man for the world beyond is to get him to live well and truly in this one. The Church exists to make the world a Kingdom of God, and to fill it with His love...

Judged by this standard, where are the Churches to-day? We have seen that the only gospel which Jesus had to preach was the gospel of the Kingdom of God;

everything He ever said can be included under that head. His Church, or Christian society, or whatever else we like to call it, has no meaning unless it exists for the realization of the kingdom of God. We cannot state this too strongly. The whole of the other-worldism of the Churches, the elaborate paraphernalia of doctrine and observance, is utterly useless, and worse than useless, unless it ministers to this end. Unless it can be shown that I am wrong in this supposition – and I think that will be pretty hard to do – a fairly good case could be made out for burning down most of the theological colleges in the land, and sending the bright young fellows in them to do some serious work for the common good. For it must be confessed, as I said at the beginning, that the Churches are to a large extent a failure. We cannot but recognize, for one thing, that our modern civilization, with all its boasted advance on the past, is still unchristian. It puts a premium upon selfishness. Modern industrialism is cruel and unjust, and directly incites men to self-seeking. The weak and unfortunate have to go to the wall. Little mercy is shown to the man who is not strong enough to fight his way and keep his footing in the struggle for existence. We are all the time making war upon one another, man against man, business against business, class against class, nation against nation. We talk of our freedom; but no man is really free, and the great majority of us are slaves to some corporation, or capitalist, or condition of things, which renders the greater part of life a continuous anxiety lest health or means should fail, and we should prove unequal to the demands made upon us. ... I do not mean, of course, to make the foolish statement that present-day industrialism is unrestrainedly individualistic; thank God, it is not that. But the principle of competition still exercises a sway so potent as to stamp modern social organization as unchristian. We may just as well recognize that fact and state it plainly. The glaringly unequal ownership of material wealth is anti-social; it is good neither for the rich man nor for the poor, for it is to the interest of every man that the body politic should be healthy and happy. That so large a number of our total population should have to exist upon the very margin of subsistence is a moral wrong. We have no business to have any slums or sweating-dens, or able-bodied unemployed, or paupers. Poverty, dulness of brain, and coarseness of habit are often found in close association. Some amount of material endowment is required even for the development of the intelligence and the training of the moral faculties. Wealth possesses no value in itself; it only possesses value as a means to more abundant life. If there is one thing upon which Christianity insists more than another, it is the duty of caring for the weak and sinful; but at present this duty is only recognized to a very limited extent.

... There is no blinking the fact that the standard of Christ and the standard of the commercial world are not the same. Our work is to make them the same, and to that end we must destroy the social system which makes selfishness the rule, and compels a man to act upon his lower motives, and we must put a better in its place. We must establish a social order wherein a man can be free to be his best, and to give his best to the community without crushing or destroying any one else. In a word, we want Collectivism in the place of competition; we want the Kingdom of God. Charity is no remedy for our social ills and their moral outcome; the only remedy is a new social organization on a Christian basis. I do not believe that any form of Collectivism, as a mere system superposed from without, can ever really make the world happy; it must be the expression of the spirit of brotherhood working from within. Neither do I feel much faith in any sudden and cataclysmic reformation of society ... But at least we can recognize the presence of the guiding Spirit of God in all our social concerns, and work along with it for the realization of the ideal of universal brotherhood. We can show men what Jesus really came to do, and, as His servants, we can help Him to do it ... I deplore the fact that, for the moment, the main current of the great Labour movement which, perhaps more than any other, represents the social application of the Christian ideal, should appear to be out of touch with organized religion. This cannot continue, for I observe that the men who lead it are men of moral passion, and often men of simple religious faith ... In fact, the Labour Party is itself a Church, in the sense in which that word was originally used, for it represents the getting together of those who want to bring about the Kingdom of God.

The New Theology, as I understand it, is the theology of this movement, whether the movement knows it or not, for it is essentially the gospel of the Kingdom of God. No lesser theology can consistently claim to be this; systems of belief, which are weighted by dogmatic considerations, have not and cannot have the same power of appeal. This higher, wider truth, which sweeps away the mischievous accretions which have made religion distasteful to the masses, is the religious articulation of the movement towards an ideal social order.

Document IV.2

The Jesus of History, 1917

T. R. Glover, *The Jesus of History* (London: SCM Press, 1917), pp. 219, 222–3, 224–5, 226–35, 237–9.

T. R. Glover was the son of a Baptist minister, University Lecturer in Ancient History and Fellow of St John's College, Cambridge. This book was based on lectures given in India in the winter of 1915–16, and largely written there. It was published with a warm commendation from the Archbishop of Canterbury, and became a best-seller which made the fortune of the SCM Press. Whilst Glover did not hesitate to incorporate the results of historical criticism, he also appealed to experience, and thus the whole history of the Church as evidence, thereby in practice abandoning *sola scriptura* as the basis for the Church's teaching. His concluding sentences are something of an echo of Schweitzer's *Quest of the Historical Jesus* (1906; Eng. trans. 1910).

Jesus Christ came to men as a great new experience. He took them far outside all they had known of God and of man. He led them, historically, into what was, in truth, a new world, into a new understanding of life in all its relations. What they had never noticed before, he brought to their knowledge, he made interesting to them, and intelligible, In short, as Paul put it, 'if any man be in Christ, it is a new creation' (2 Cor. v.17) ... Why has Jesus meant so much? Why should all this be associated with him?

Theology

... We may classify the records of the Christian exploration roughly in three groups. In the early Christian centuries, we find endless thought given to the philosophical study of the relation of Christ and God. It fills the library of the Early Church, and practically all the early controversies turn upon it. The weak spot in this was the use of the *a priori* method. Men started with preconceptions about God – not unnaturally, for we all have some theories about God, which we are apt to regard as knowledge. But knowledge is a difficult thing to reach in any sphere of study; and men assumed too quickly that they had attained a sound philosophical account of God...

Our second group is represented roughly by the Hymn Book. The evidential value of a good hymn book will stand investigation, Of course a great many hymns are mere copies, and poor copies; but the Hymn Book at its best is a collection of first-hand records of experience. In the story of the Christian Church doxology comes before dogma ... The order is experience, – happiness and song – and then reflection. The love and the cleansing, and the joy, supply the material on which thought has to work ... Philosophy and theology do not give us our facts. Their function is to group and interpret them.

Our third group of records is given to us by the men of the Reformation. We have there two great movements side by side, There is Bible translation, which means, in plain language, a decision or conviction on the part of scholars and thinkers, that the knowledge of the historical Jesus, and of men's first experiences of him, is of the highest importance in the Christian life. The whole Reformation follows, or runs parallel with, that movement. It is essentially a new exploration of what Jesus Christ can do and of what he can be...

So far our records. Today we are living in an era when great scientific discoveries are made, and more are promised. Geology once unsettled people about *Genesis*; but closer study of the Bible and of Science has given truer views of both, and thinking people are as little troubled about Geology now as about Copernican Astronomy. At present heredity and psychology are dominating our minds – or, rather, theories as to both; for, though beginnings have been made, the stage has not yet been reached of very wide or certain discovery ... However, all these modern discoveries and theories are, to many men's minds, a challenge to the right of Christians to speak of Jesus Christ as they have spoken of him, a challenge to our right to represent the facts of Christian life as we have represented them – in other words, they are a challenge to us to return to experience and to see what we really mean...

The old problem returns upon us: Who and what is this Jesus Christ? We are involved in the recurrent need to re-examine him and re-explore him.

There are several ways of doing so, Like every other historical character Jesus is to be known by what he does rather than by *a priori* speculation as to what he might be. In the study of history the first thing is to know our original documents. There are the Gospels, and, like other historical records, they must be studied in earnest on scientific lines without preconception. And there are later records, which tell us as plainly and as truthfully of what he has done in the world's history. We can begin, then, with the serious study of the actual historical Jesus, whom people met in the road and with whom they ate their meals, whom the soldiers nailed to the cross, whom his disciples took to worshipping, and who has, historically, re-created the world.

The second line of approach is rather more difficult, but with care we can use Christological theories to recover the facts which those who framed the theories intended to explain. We must remember here once more the three historical canons laid down at the beginning. We must above all things give the man's term his meaning, and ask what was the experience behind his thought. When we come upon such descriptions of Jesus as 'Christ our Passover' (I Cor. v.7), or find him called the Messiah, we must not let our own preconceptions as to the value of the theories implied by the use of such language, nor again our existing views of what is orthodox, determine our conclusions; but we must ask what those who so explained Jesus really meant to say, and what they had experienced which they thought worth expressing ... To explain Jesus, his friends and contemporaries spoke of him as the Logos, the Sacrifice, "Christ our Passover", the Messiah, and so forth. Of those terms not one is intelligible to us today without a commentary. To ordinary people Jesus is at once intelligible – far more so than the explanations of him. Historically, it is he himself who has antiquated every one of those conceptions, and, so far as they have survived, it has been in virtue of association with him ...

The inner significance of each term will point to the real experience of the man using it. He employs a metaphor, a simile, or a technical term to explain something. Can we penetrate to the analogy which he finds between the Jesus of the new experience and the old term which he uses? ...When we look at the terms, we find that the essence of sacrifice was reconciliation between God and man (we shall return to this a little later) – and that the Messiah was understood to be destined to achieve God's purpose and God's meaning for mankind and for each man. We find, again, that the inner meaning of the Logos is that through it, and in it, God and man come in touch with each other and become mutually intelligible. Reconciliation, the victory of God, the mutual intelligibility of God and man – all three terms centre in one great thought, a new union between God and man. That, so far as I can see, is the common element; and that is, as men have conceived it, the very heart of the Christian experience.

In third place, we can utilize the new experiments made upon Jesus Christ in the Reformation and in other revivals, They come nearer to us; for the men who report are more practical and more scholarly in the modern way; they are more akin to us both in blood and in ideas. Luther, for example, is a great spirit of the explorer type. He went to scholarship and learnt the true meaning of *Metanoia* – that it was 're-thinking' and not 'penance' – and he grasped a new view of God there. From scholarship he gained a truer view of Church History than he had been taught; and this too helped to clear his mind. Above all, as 'a great son of fact' (Carlyle's name for him) his chief interest was the exploration of Jesus Christ – would Christ stand all the weight that a man could throw upon him without assistance? And Luther found that Christ could; and he at once turned his knowledge into action as the world knows. 'Justification by faith' was his phrase, and he meant that we may trust Jesus Christ with all that we are, all that we have been, and all that we hope to be;

that Jesus himself will carry all; that Jesus himself *is* all; that Jesus is at once Luther's eternal salvation, and his sure help in the next day's difficulty – his Saviour for ever from sin, and his great stand-by in translating the Bible for the German people and in writing hymns for boys and girls. *Nos nihil sumus*, he wrote, *Christus solus est omnia*. In the case of every great revival – the Wesleyan revival, and smaller ones in the United States, in the north of Ireland, in Wales, – in every one we find that, where anything is really achieved, it is done by a new and thoroughgoing emphasis on Jesus Christ. It may be put in language which to some ears is repulsive, in metaphors strange or uncouth; but whatever the language, the fact that underlies it is this – men are brought back to the reality, the presence, the power and the friendship of Jesus Christ; they are called to a fresh venture on Jesus Christ, a fresh exploration: and again and again the experience of a lifetime has justified the venture.

This brings us to the most effective and fundamental method in the exploration of Jesus, in some ways the most difficult of all, or else the very simplest, The Church has been clear that there is nothing like personal experiment, the personal venture. It is the only clue to the experience. The saying of St Augustine (*Sermon* 43, 3), *Immo crede ut intelligas*, is to many of our minds offensive – I think, because we give not quite the right meaning to his *Credo*. But, if the illustrations are not too simple, swimming and bicycling offer parallels. A man will never understand how water holds up a human body, as long as he stays on dry land. In practical things, the venture comes first; and it is hard to see how a man is to understand Christ without a personal experience of him ...

The change that Jesus definitely operates in men, they have described in various ways – rebirth, salvation, a new heart, and so forth. What they have always emphasized in Jesus Christ, is that they find he changes their outlook and develops new instincts in them. ... This new life is at all events all the evidence available, and how much it means is very difficult to estimate without some personal experience.

Here again the great theories of Redemption will help us to recover the experience they are to explain; and once more we may note that they are not the work of small minds or trivial natures, however badly they have been echoed. Substitution implies at any rate some serious confession of guilt before God, some strong sense of a great indebtedness to Christ. The theory of Sacrifice implies the need of reunion with God ... When we look at the New Testament, we find that the emphasis always lies on God seeking reconciliation with man (*cf.* 2 Cor. v.19). The theory of ransom – a most moving term in a world of slavery – implies the need of new freedom for the mind, for the heart and the whole nature, from the tyranny of sin. All these are similes; and tremendous structures of theory have been built on every one of them – and for some of these structures, simile, or, in plainer language analogy, is not a sufficient foundation. It is probably true that all our current explanations of the work of Christ in Redemption have in them too large an element of metaphor and simile. Yet Christian people are reluctant to discard any one of them; and their reluctance is intelligible. There is a value in the old association, which is found by new experience. Every one of these old similes will contribute to our realization of the work of Christ, in so far as it is a record of experience of

Christ, verified in one generation after another. We shall make the best use of them, when we are no longer intimidated by the terminology, but go at once to what is meant – the facts.

We come still closer to the facts in the less metaphorical terms of the New Testament. For example, there is the New Covenant. The writer of the Epistle to the Hebrews went back to a great phrase in Jeremiah, and by his emphasis on it he helped to give its name to the whole New Testament – 'I will make a new covenant with the house of Israel and the house of Judah' (Heb. viii. 8–12; Jeremiah xxxi. 31–34). Using this passage, he brings out that there is a new relation, a new union, between God and man in Jesus. He speaks of Jesus as a mediator bringing man and God together (Heb. viii.6) – language far plainer to us than the terminology of sacrifice, which he employed rather to bring home the work of Jesus with feeling and passion to those who had no other vocabulary, than to impose upon Christian thinkers a scheme of things which he clearly saw to be exhausted. Then there is Paul's great conception of Reconciliation (2 Cor. v.18–20). Half the difficulties connected with the word 'Atonement' disappear, when we grasp that the word in Greek means primarily reconciliation. As Paul uses the noun and the verb, it is very plain what he means – God is in Christ trying to reconcile the world to Himself. These attempts to express Christ's work in plain words take us back to the great central Christian experience – to the great initial discovery that the discord of man's making between God and man has been removed by God's overtures in Christ; that the obstacles which man has felt to his approach to God – in the unclean hands and the unclean lips – have been taken away; and that with a heart, such as the human heart is, a man may yet come to God in Jesus, because of Jesus, through Jesus …

This brings us to the central question, the relation of Jesus with God – the problem of Incarnation. After all that has been said, we shall not approach it *a priori*. We are too apt to put the Incarnation more or less in algebraic form:

$$x + y = a,$$

where *a* stands for the historical Jesus Christ, and *x* and *y* respectively stand for God and man. But what do we mean by *x* and y*?* Let us face our facts. What do we know of man apart from Jesus Christ? Surely it is only in him that we realize man – only in him that we grasp what human depravity really is, the real meaning and implications of human sin. It is those who have lived with Jesus Christ, who are most conscious of sin; and this is no mere morbid imagination or fancy, it rests on a much deeper exploration of human nature than men in general attempt. Not until we know what he is do we see how very little we are, and how far we have gone wrong. It is his power of help and sympathy that teaches us the hardness of our own hearts, our own fundamental want of sympathy. Again, until a man knows Jesus Christ, he has little chance of even guessing the grandeur of which he himself is capable, A man has, as he says, done his best – for years, it may be, of strenuous endeavour; and then comes the new experience of Jesus Christ, and he is lifted high above his record, he gains a new power, a new tenderness, and he does things incredible. We do not know the wrong or the right of which man is capable, till we know Jesus Christ. The *y* of our equation, then, does not tell us very much.

When it comes to the x, is it not very often a mixture – an ill-adjusted mixture – of the Father of Jesus, with the rather negative 'beyond all being' of later Greek speculation, and perhaps the Judge of Roman Law? ... But, in fact, is it not true now that we really only know God through Jesus? For it is only in and through Jesus that we take the trouble, and have the faith, to explore and test God, to try experiments upon God, to know what He can do and what He will do. It is only in Jesus that the Love of God (in the New Testament sense) is tenable at all ... It is only in Jesus that we can live the real life of prayer, in the intimate way of Jesus. All this means that we have to solve our x from Jesus – not to discover him through it. The plain fact is that we actually know Jesus a great deal better than we know our x and our y, the elements from which we hoped to reconstruct him. What does this mean?

It means, bluntly, that we have to re-think our theories of Incarnation on *a posteriori* lines, to begin on facts that we know, and to base ourselves on a continuous exploration and experience of Jesus Christ first. The simple, homely rule of knowing things before we talk about them holds in every other sphere of study, and is the rule which Jesus himself inculcated. We begin, then, with Jesus Christ, and set out to see how far he will take us. Experience comes first. 'Follow me,' he said. He chose the twelve men 'that they might be with him,' and he let them find out in that intercourse what he had for them; and from what he could give and did give they drew their conclusions as to who and what he is. There can be no other way of knowing him.

Document IV.3

The Church and the Sacraments, 1917

P. T. Forsyth, *Lectures on the Church and the Sacraments* (London: Longmans. Green & Co., 1917), pp. 5–6, 7–9, 10–12, 13–15, 17, 24–5.

P. T. Forsyth was the greatest nonconformist theologian of his generation, of whom Karl Barth said, 'You did not need me; you had Forsyth.' He responded to R. J. Campbell in his magisterial *The Person and Place of Jesus Christ* in 1909. This late book on the Church and the Sacraments was essentially lectures to his students, and this extract from chapter 1, 'Holy Church and Free Church', illustrates his critique of many of the popular Congregational conceptions of his day.

The Free Churches need to cultivate a sense of the great Church, if their freedom is not to lose all its greatness, and they are not to go down in corporate egoisms or social programmes. This is a historic sense (to lose which is to turn fantastic gnostics or fancy sectaries); but it is still more an evangelical sense (which to lose is to become fractious individualists). It is the sense and faith of the common Word of grace. And here there is much to learn, and much to do.

One recognises heartily the unspeakable service of the Free Churches to local and personal religion. But, in the first place, they have been much too *atomist*. The independence of each congregation or each member has been overdone. This is a fertile source both of their practical overlapping and their theological confusion. Their multiplication paralyses them in many a place ... Each single Church is entitled by the Gospel to no more independence in the great Church than each individual man has in the small, where they are all members one of another. And each Church has the right to live only in virtue of the contribution it makes to the great Church.

In the second place, they are apt to be too *negative* in their note. Protestantism finds it hard to get over the first oppositional tone forced on the Reformers by the situation of their day. It is too much engrossed with the note of challenge and of suspicious vigilance. It suspects even the early creeds and their atmosphere ... It is in danger of overdoing its protest against a false Church, of spending more on that protest than on realising a true Church, of denouncing a priestly Church till it lose its own sense of the essential priestliness of the Church. The ministers of the Churches it opposes are, on the whole at least, as earnestly spiritual as they ... We protest *against* much – what do we protest *for?* Is it for liberty, or for the truth which makes liberty? Liberty for what? Some are actually afraid for liberty if we state the belief which makes liberty. Does that not mean that their liberty is not created *by* truth, and is not spiritual, but is natural liberty applied to truth? To this point I will return.

§

... The real strength of a Church is not the amount of its work but the quality of its faith. One man who truly knows his Bible is worth more to a Church's real strength than a crowd of workers who do not. If we ask the preacher, he will tell us among whom he finds his real strength. Our poverty is not in the amount of our work, but in the quality of our religion. Our religion does not make us do what patriotism does – sacrifice and die for it; else the work would be more productive. And that is not denying the passion and sacrifice that many of us do make for our Church. But is it for *the* Church?

If we are preoccupied as we should be with the One, Holy, Catholic, and Apostolic Church of the saving Word, there is a very present danger which we shall escape. We shall not be the slaves or the caterers of the public. We shall serve it, but not follow it. We shall not treat the Word as the vassal nor as the colleague of the world. We shall not look upon a Free Church merely as the religious side of the democracy. That is the most recent form of Erastianism, and the particular form of it from which the Free Churches are liable to suffer most subtly. The old Erastian position regarded the Church as the nation on its religious side. Now the Free Churches are in no danger from that view. They have existed to protest against it. And it is a view which has no longer real vitality, though it is the hollow root of an Established Church, and makes the anachronism of it. But there are other ways of establishing a Church than by law ... The Free Churches ... may come to care more for social work than for public worship. A Church may be on quite happy terms with the world; and its Christ may be made welcome chiefly because He is 'so human,' or so democratic, or His worship is the correct thing. Thus a Church becomes established by the world even when it is not by the State. It does become so if it has no distinctive message over against the world; if it treat itself but as the consecrated part of the world; if its chief object is to affect and serve the world rather than to worship and glorify and commune with God; if it cease to regard its fundamental relation to the world as miraculous; if it regard its Gospel merely as the consummation of the best spiritual instincts of Humanity and not as a new creation; if its Word is simply the gathering up of the best in other faiths; if it make its final appeal to the courts of comparative religion; if it cherish the principle that its most precious thing is what unites it with other faiths and other movements, instead of what makes it different and commanding; if it is supremely concerned to have the *cachet* of the general heart, reason, and applause. What makes Christianity Christian is that grace of God which marks it off from other creeds, makes it descend on the instincts of man instead of rising from them, and seeks from them absolute obedience as truly as sympathetic recognition.

What I have just described may be called the rationalist establishment of the Church. But the Church succumbs to the democracy especially when it is tempted to forget its Holy Word, and trim it down to the happy world and the ideals of an age and culture. It is exposed to the peril of the newest phase of Socialism, in which the Church would be not the nation on its religious side, but democracy suffused by religion ... In such a state of things the minister would become ... the pastor of the people instead of the minister of the Gospel, the organ of the human fraternity rather than the oracle of the divine Word. He would be not so much the organ of God's grace and God's demand to the people as the tribune of the people's cause, the advocate of their rights, lending a divine sanction to their ideals, their grievances, their programme ... His effect, and therefore his value, would be gone when he went out of favour with his public. He would not be free to rebuke them in God's name, nor to call for their repentance as a first condition of the Kingdom. (It is the Church's call for repentance that is the deep source of its disfavour with the democracy.) ... He would popularise his Gospel till he secularised it ...

§

... The great antithesis of Christianity in the world is 'civilisation.' The World, the mere mastery of nature and of man, is the chief obstacle to Christianity in the world. Well, democracy is but a phase of civilisation on its way to the Kingdom of God. It is nearer the Kingdom than the rest, perhaps not far from the Kingdom, but yet of itself not in it. To say that the Christian Church is but the religious side of democracy is to say that it is human nature turned pious – which is certainly no description of New Testament Christianity. And now that civilisation has gone to pieces in the great war, is it that part of it called democracy that is to regenerate Society?

Besides, no society, which gives Christ the regal place the Church does, can be a democracy. It is an absolute monarchy. Less might be said by us about freedom, and more about obedience in the spirit of freedom. The Church is much more bound up with the obedience of the democracy than with its triumph – its obedience, not indeed to the Church, but to Christ, His Kingdom, and His Gospel. No triumph of democracy weighs with the Church in comparison with its obedience to Christ, and to the whole, full Christ, the holy Christ crucified, and risen, and reigning, and *saving.* For this purpose of submission the *character* of Christ is quite inadequate; and even the *Person* of Christ is not enough. We must be broken to a grateful submission to the *Cross,* in which the Person of Christ comes to a head and has far more than an ideal, aesthetic, or hallowing power; it has its judging and saving, its humbling, miraculous, and new-creative power. That is the element which gives Catholicism its strength ... The fundamental difference between a Church and a democracy lies thus in the principle that no numbers can create a real authority such as the Church confesses, whereas democracy as such will listen to no authority but what its numbers and majorities do create.

So, if we ask why the Church does not at once attract the democracy, we must answer that its faith is not democratic. It demands a ready and willing and absolute submission to authority, it demands obedience, which a democracy gives but partially, grudgingly, critically, or temporarily. The Church does not win the democracy because it is not a democracy. It is not based on natural right, or natural fraternity, or natural ideals. It is based on total surrender to an absolute monarch and owner in Christ, which is not natural and not egoist, and not easy ...

When we have to choose among social systems, truly it is the democracy that lies nearest to our heart and hope. It is not the Kingdom (indeed it must be taken in hand by the Kingdom), but it offers most possibility for the Kingdom if taken in hand. But, if Church or Gospel should identify itself with the democracy in the sense of giving itself up to its natural ideals, it would commit the same error in principle as when it staked itself upon a dynasty or an aristocracy ...

... If a rebuking and demanding Church must be an unpopular Church, then the Church must accept its unpopularity. It must be prepared to go into the wilderness with Christ; it must suffer outside the camp; it must show itself independent of the world it would chiefly save and bless, and perhaps be crucified by it. The Free Churches are not in so much danger from men who, in the name of religion, openly exploit the public; but they are from its caterers, from the men who follow and humour it, who minister to its ideals and sympathies at the cost of any holy discipline to its conscience.

The form of Christianity which founded modern democracy and its liberties, laid more stress on the holy demand of God than did all the tyrannies which deduced the king's right from God's. Democracy was made by a Calvinism which did not humour human nature, and did not believe in it till God had done with it. It was the Arminians, the human-naturists who stood by the Stuarts, and the divine right of such kings.

§

... If the democracy hates hard Church, it despises soft Church. But such has been the tendency of much recent religion in its reaction from hard Church. What has dropped out of our creed is the element that compels respect, the element of noble demand and solemn judgment. And that loss comes to a head in our view of the

Cross. As our Cross is, so will our Church be, such will our Gospel be, and such will be our control. And if we drop from the Cross any satisfaction of God's holy demand, any reference to His holy judgment, we lose the royal thing from our moral centre. We lose what makes faith a controlling power. We are left with no more than an exhibition of love, or an apotheosis of sacrifice, which only cheers man by showing him himself at his best, instead of humbling and quickening him by the salvation of his worst.

The Church will be for the world just what it is made by its theology of the Cross. And a theology which leaves us at the mercy of our religious subjectivity, a theology which canonises a mere spiritual experience regardless of its supernatural content, a theology which just makes sacrifice divine, will leave us in the end with a Church which would simply be a sycophant of the public heart, and a waiter upon the providence of the crowd ... The laicising of the ministry is one of our chief perils. Let us especially beware of that laicity of mind which never experiences soul-disease and its healing, but lives only in a religiosity of interest or of feeling, whose faith is a sympathy and not a salvation, whose piety is mindless temperament and not intelligent conviction ... The once-born are the chief spiritual peril in the Church, the religious-minded without the religious experience, with a taste for religion but no taste of it, who treat Christianity as an interpretation of life rather than a recasting of the soul, and view the Church as the company of the idealists rather than the habitation of the Spirit ... The danger of the hour is to mistake the aesthetic for the spiritual, and the spiritual for the holy. A choral service may be so enjoyed that we think we have been engaged in an act of worship ... And we may think that to be *like Christ* is really to be *in Christ*. But the best of the spirits must be tried whether they be of God's historic Christ.

§

Many who have a wide knowledge of the Churches are impressed with their spiritual powerlessness, their decay in virility, moral and mental, their loss of influence with the world because of their attempt to conciliate the world by a colourless and inexigent creed. They are depressed by the world's poor opinion of the *personnel* of the Church's ministry, and its poor respect for the influence of its membership...

The remedy for the existing state of things is not one which affects primarily either individuals or congregation, but the whole type and staple of belief ... A new baptism we need; meaning by that, however, not a new piety, a new subjectivity, a mere revival. We need a new Spirit, but in the sense of *a recovered Word.* For our present belief hardly supplies us with a Word. What Word we inherit we cannot translate into the mental and moral speech of our time. Yet the new Word does not mean a new revelation except of itself. If we could only reach a truer interpretation and deeper grasp of the old, make a revised version of the old Word, and put a new accent into the old truth. It is not a new theology we need so much as a renovated theology, in which orthodoxy is deepened against itself, and not pared away. It is a new touch with our mind and conscience on the moral nerve of the old faith. We have had many new theologies in the last hundred years. Theological enterprise has been turning them out freely. But the vein of liberalism, which thus followed on the old Orthodoxy, has been worked out for the preacher's purpose. It is now exhausted of religious ore…

§

… Independency has for its principle liberty, and, while it was weak enough in the eighteenth century through the abeyance of that principle, its peril today is in its excess and abuse.

But it will protect us from much misunderstanding if we are clear at the outset about what the principle really is. However democracy may mean the principle of the nation and its liberty, that is not what Independency means. It does not mean religious liberty in the sense of freedom to be *franc-tireurs,* free-lances, or atomic weights, entitled to hold any opinion about God or none. That is liberty with which in its civic form Independency has had much to do, but it is not its own principle. It is but civil liberty on one side of it. It is liberty in the State, and not in the Church. In the Church mere latitudinarian liberty is not the principle. No Church can survive on the liberty to hold any views we think fit about religious matters so long as they are held in a religious spirit, or subject to the 'great general truths of religion.' They may make any groups they please on such a basis, but these would not be Churches, nor have any moral right to the property or the position of Churches. A Church has a historic and positive base. And in so far as Independency claims to be a branch of the true Church, its principle is not rational liberty, nor spiritual liberty, but evangelical liberty, which is the true Catholic tradition. It is a liberty not intrinsic to us but to which we must be redeemed and reborn. It is liberty for all thought or action which is compatible with the genius and finality of the Gospel Word, however traditional custom or theology may be affected. It is liberty for all that is created by that Gospel with its central, social, and entire Redemption. It is not merely a liberty which the Gospel does not impugn, which it finds and consecrates; it is liberty which the Gospel creates, in speech, act, or thought. The liberty of Christ is the fulness of the new man in Christ. It is not civil liberty on its religious side. It is not spiritual liberty *sans phrase.* It is not liberty, either civic or mystic, *for* Christ. But it is liberty *in* Christ, and Christ's work for the race. It is an experienced liberty which grows out of an authority, and, as its authority is, so will its liberty be. The first interest of liberty is authority.

Document IV.4

Grace and Personality, 1917

John Oman, *Grace and Personality*, 3rd edn (Cambridge: Cambridge University Press, 1925), pp. 174–82.

John Oman was on the staff of Westminster College, Cambridge, from 1907, and Principal 1922–35; he also held a University Lectureship in the Philosophy of Religion. Originally based on articles in the *Expositor* in 1911–12, the book was profoundly influenced by the First World War since the fact that such sorrow and wickedness could happen in the world forced him to reconsider his whole religious position. Essentially the grace of God is regarded as more significant than any attribution of omnipotence.

From a fellowship which would express the relation of a personal God to us as moral persons, so that He is gracious in all our experience, all arbitrary dealings are ruled out. Righteousness and truth and joy in spiritual things are the very Heaven in which our Father dwells, which, so far from being outside of our present experience, shows itself real as it turns the perpetual change of our earthly life increasingly into one purpose of God, so that uncertainties on which nothing could be built are shown to be themselves a building of God.

Of the fellowship which would thus embody the conception of grace as a gracious relation of God to His children in all things, four characteristics also may be distinguished.

1. It is a fellowship which has no frontiers except those it exists to remove: and in that task it must acknowledge no failure except what is due to the moral independence necessary for the truly personal relation to a gracious God it exists to manifest.

By the nature of grace as God's gracious personal relation to His children, response to which must be won and cannot be compelled, all its limitations are determined. It is a fellowship of persons who realise their relations to one another through their relation to God and who find their relation to the Father realised in their fellowship with His children; and it takes the form of a society, working under historical conditions, because an understanding of God through human relations requires a common use of experience. But it is a special society only because it rests exclusively on a blessed dependence on an absolutely gracious God, impossible to realise except in freedom and moral independence, which is not the basis of any other society. This may set a severe limit to success, but it is not arbitrary, being imposed only by God's respect for the liberty of His children, and by the nature of His Kingdom as a family and not merely a federation. Arbitrariness is impossible for a gracious God, but, on the other hand, compulsion is equally impossible.

2. It has no means of grace except what enables us to use the world as God's world, in fellowship with men as children of God, and in peace through His rule of truth and righteousness, because it interprets God's gracious relation to us in all experience. Its means of grace must be real means for bringing home the nature of

reality to minds made in the image of God, which is to say, they must impress only as they persuade. The Apostle's ideal was, 'By manifestation of the truth, commending ourselves to every man's conscience in the sight of God.' The appeal is by truth alone to the common human conscience and to it alone. Yet no limit may be set for the variety of the manifestation, so long as it is truly in the sight of God and not an appeal to mere human suffrage. It may draw from us sublime poetic utterance and stateliness of presentation, or it may drive us to the utmost simplicity of speech and worship. Both will be right in their place, if they spring from the vision of spiritual realities. But, also both will be wrong, not manifesting but obscuring, if they are used as substitutes for consent of the soul, to sweep men along without freedom or insight.

Prayer, Word and Sacrament are still the means of grace, yet only as they are means of manifesting the truth to every man's conscience, and not merely as they are devices or vehicles or impressive doings. Except as means of persuading they cannot help to manifest God's gracious personal relation to His children, for as devices to wring blessings out of God or as vehicles to convey something to man, however individual they may be, they would not, in any strict sense, be personal.

Prayer is not bombarding God for acts of omnipotence which, otherwise, he might withhold, but is the intercourse of the family of God, wherein our brethren are included as well as our Father. And it manifests a gracious relation, whereby all things work together for our good, its chief task is in everything to give thanks; and, though our needs may require special petitions, it is because, being straitened in ourselves, we need God's help to receive to profit, and not because God forgets to be gracious until He is urged.

Speech is the natural mode of communication between persons, because it enables both to think the same thought, each as his own thought, being a word only as it is spoken with the understanding to the understanding. The Word, as a means of grace, is, therefore, the utterance of what we have been enabled to see of God's dealing with us, to minds made like ours in the Divine image, that they also may see. Therefore, it must commend itself, not merely to the liking for the pleasant or even for solemn and impressive utterance, but to the conscience of right which can enable men to interpret it as a word of God to themselves.

The Sacraments solemnly employ water, and bread and wine – the common things in daily use – to express and, as it were, give the concentrated essence of the sacrament of life. They presuppose that there is more in nature than an appeal to the senses, and more in every gift of food than to eat of the loaves and be filled and that we ought therein to see the miracle of a gracious God manifesting Himself in goodness. The miracle is extended in these rites to all God appoints for us. The special rite which connects this sacrament of life directly with the Cross, forbids us to rule out any part of experience, and teaches us to find in agony and shame and death the manifold wisdom and measureless love of God. This is the message by which it becomes pre-eminently the sacrament of reconciliation.

3. This leads to the next mark, which may be described as the secular quality of its religion.

The special rites of the special fellowship, having distinctive sacredness, not by remoteness from things secular, but by penetrating deeper into their true meaning and true uses, teach us not to use the sacred shrine as a shelter from the secular world, but to make all things sacred, and so, in the right way, to abolish the distinction between sacred and secular, till the world is our spiritual possession as much as Cephas.

Our Lord's religion was in a pre-eminent degree secular. From the day-labourers, farmers and fisher-folk, he demanded a righteousness beyond that of the recognised ministers of religion, a demand made reasonable by removing righteousness from the sphere of sacred observances into the sphere of our common life, through faith in the Father exercised amid our daily tasks and trials. All His own ministry was simply the absolutely religious handling of the incidents that arose for Him in His intercourse with the ordinary people who met Him, as we should say, by accident. His teaching abounds in illustrations from secular life, but there are only two from the ecclesiastical religion – the Pharisee praying in the Temple with himself alone, and the Priest and the Levite passing by on the other side. Moreover, most of what he says to the Scribes and Pharisees applies to the dangers of outward organised religion at all times.

4. The final mark is the relation of the fellowship to the Rule of God, the sense in which the Church is the Kingdom of God. Catholicism identifies the Church with the Kingdom as far as it outwardly extends, and Evangelicalism only as far as it inwardly succeeds, and the difference is deep and wide; yet they are at one in regarding the Rule of God in both as fundamentally mystical and traditional. Grace, that is to say, is a swaying of individuals, of which the individual may be conscious, but is so immediately the work of God that he may not; and its manifestation in history is merely the handing down of the accumulated results of individual operations of grace, so that we are founded upon the apostles and prophets and Jesus Christ is the chief corner-stone purely by traditional guarantees, for which our moral freedom is no necessary condition.

But in the society which embodies a gracious relationship to God of all men, in all things, at all times, the Kingdom of God is manifested religiously – or we might say apocalyptically – and ethically, and not mystically and traditionally.

The Kingdom of God is the Rule of God, and not, in any sense, mere moral progress of man. Our reliance is on God, and not on our freedom, and there is a place only for trust and gratitude, and none for merit, yet the essence of God's Rule is that it is not content with obedience except in the blessedness of moral independence. All his dealings with us, from first to last, concern our freedom, not, indeed, as if we were free, but always to make us free. Were we free, we should be already saved, and we are only being saved; but what we are being saved into is the liberty of the children of God. Wherefore, God's Kingdom has come, not in so far as individuals have been made the vehicles of absolute truth or holiness, or even in so far as mankind grows in truth and righteousness, but in so far as men are willing in the day of God's power, in so far, in short, as being reconciled to God, they find in His will alone their blessedness.

This society of the Kingdom of God is necessarily historical, but is not traditional. The blessedness of God's Rule is God's most unmerited gift, introduced wholly by the finger of God, yet is so personal that even God cannot impose it except by enabling us to accept it; and the essential thing to see is that it is not less, but more God's personal gift, because it takes the trouble to pass round by way of our own personal acceptance and co-operation. Hence this amazing, varied, suffering, joyous world, with some success but much frustrated endeavour, much knowledge laboriously won but with more darkness we cannot by any effort dispel, and much gladness of living but ever arrested by pain and shadowed by death. And hence also the supreme significance of those who, in fellowship, have, from age to age, interpreted to their brethren the Divine rule it displays. These are the prophets who, since the world began, have been preparing for the fullness of the time when it might be perfectly manifested in teaching and service and poverty and all the agony and contumely which could increase the terror of death, and the apostles who have since interpreted the fullness of the manifestation. On this foundation of the apostles and prophets, with Jesus Christ as the chief corner-stone, we are to build, not in slavish subjection to the past, but in the freedom of God's children, who are also themselves apostles and prophets.

Instead of regarding the rest of experience as mere scenery for operations of grace which are canalised in special channels, whether priest or evangelist, we see nothing less than our whole varied experience can suffice for making souls truly in God's image, free and not restrained, knowing as He knows, loving as He loves, choosing as He chooses, blessed as He is blessed, sons and not subjects. If this be the high goal we can understand the necessity of the labyrinthine by-ways towards truth, with blind alleys that admonish us to seek anew the true road, with agonies and disasters to warn us of our mistakes and our sins, with the necessity of bitter penitence and sympathy evoked by suffering. Then the Church, if it be interpreting to mankind the mind of God, has its convincing place, however small it may be, or however divided on other matters. But, otherwise, what is life but a mockery and a despair, and what is the largest, most united church, as a mere refuge in the midst of it, save a poor kind of device at best, wholly inadequate as the work of a goodness which, with the resources of omnipotence, can compel man as it will?

Mankind is often weary of the long and arduous and circuitous way, and constantly takes shorter cuts than God's way of personal faith and moral freedom. Often the Church which should stand only for God's order, is inveigled into the service of organised compulsion and becomes the most eager and successful advocate of mental pupillage and moral subjection: and then, men are put back under the discipline of what the Apostle calls the Law. Yet God is not weary and soon He burns up the wood and hay and stubble with which men build, often in vast calamities and desolating conflicts, till men are taught that a mere order of subjection is, in the last resort, mere anarchy, and that the Divine way of the insight of our own faith and the consecration of our own wills, through our own recognition that in all things God is gracious, is alone the abiding order of reality, which evil can neither tempt nor terrorise.

Document IV.5

The Baptist and Congregational Inheritance, 1928

B. L. Manning, *Essays in Orthodox Dissent* (London: Independent Press, 1939), pp. 95–101.

B. L. Manning was a historian, specialising in the late Middle Ages, and a Fellow of Jesus College, Cambridge. This is part of an address given to a Joint Assembly of the Hertfordshire Baptist Association and the Hertfordshire Congregational Union in their jubilee year on 18 October 1928. Like Forsyth, but from a different perspective, Manning emphasises that the freedom of the Free Churches is freedom *for* as much as freedom *from*, and this positive understanding of free churchmanship is essential.

Now our inheritance is freedom. But freedom, to be of any use to us, is not freedom from Archbishop Laud or from the Athansian Creed or even from the New Prayer Book. We want freedom from the evils of our own time, and we have it. We are (do you realise it?), if we know how to enter into our heritage, free, gloriously free, from the twin horrors of Fundamentalism and Modernism, from the venomous uncharity of the one and the arid superficiality of the other. The problems of Fundamentalism and Modernism do not arise for a Church endowed with our heritage. As by our sacrifice of position in the State we have secured freedom for the intenser and more independent life of our Church, freedom from those humiliating controversies that have vexed the Establishment through the Prayer-Book discussion, so by sacrificing the desire for a supreme and infallible authority on earth we have secured freedom from the degrading controversies of Fundamentalist and Modernist. Our first and last and middle word to them is: 'A plague on both your houses.' Stand fast, therefore, in the liberty wherewith Christ has made us free and be not entangled with *their* yoke of bondage.

That is one side: there is another. Part of our inheritance is the knowledge of the unique position and value of Holy Scripture in the Faith. Do not set that aside as the old-fashioned conventional assertion. It is a living issue. Muddled by rumours and misunderstandings of the results of historical criticism many even of our own people are losing all sense of the unique treasure that the Church has in the Bible. People repeat as a parrot phrase that the Bible is an historical document 'exactly the same as any other' until they miss entirely what that means. The Bible *is* an historical doument, but no historical document is like any other. Documents vary in their importance for human life according to what they contain. It is precisely because the Bible is an historical document, with a particular historical content, that it is unique and has a unique value for our faith. It is, in the New Testament, the most immediate record we have of the impact of the Incarnate Word on human life. It is, in the Old Testament, the record of the preparation in people and place for that impact. There is no history *like* that. To say that there is as much reason for reading the historical records of England or Italy as the historical books of Israel in a religious service is to betray a total lack of the historical sense.

To make of the Bible a book of moral lessons and human experience, with precisely as much authority and importance as any other record of human experience, may be a legitimate secondary use of it, but overlooks its primary quality. If the value of Bible history is to provide the same sort of lessons as may be drawn from the story of the Armada it has practically no value; for the more a man knows of history the less he is prepared to say what it teaches. 'When I hear a man say *All history teaches*,' confessed a great historian, 'I prepare to hear some thundering lie.' The Bible is not a useful scrap-book of illustrations for our own ideas or of snippets for devotional use. It has a value of its own. The Written Word contains and shows forth the Incarnate Word. Modern study of the Bible as an historical document underlines our inherited conviction of the unique position of Holy Scripture in the Church. The prominence which our traditions give to expository preaching needs no apology. It needs respect.

A third part of our inheritance is more definitely theological. It is two-fold. Calvinism and Evangelicalism are the two lines of thought which converged to make modern Dissent. They are historically the two main currents in our thought, and though in theory in antithesis to one another they have in common the fundamental quality. They provide a more than adequate basis for that intensity of which I spoke first. They turn our eyes away from ourselves and our fellows to the great things in our faith, to the things that God does: to His Will, His Grace, His Passion. They emphasise at once the objectiveness of our religion and the direct immediate contact that it gives between the soul and God. Coming from this is the note of certainty and finality and joy. The ultimate truth about the religious life, as we have received it, is not that it is a pilgrimage, a development, an education, a struggle, in which we must take our part with such help as we can get. It is Good News. Whom He did predestinate, them He also *has* called. God *was* in Christ reconciling the world unto Himself. The powers of the new age are here. We have tasted the heavenly gift. We are more than conquerors through Him that loved us. The rapture of certainty about something already done for us, not waiting for us to do, is part of our inheritance.

I have no time in which to speak of our inheritance in practice. Let me make two points. First, our inheritance is a full but pure churchmanship, churchmanship without clericalism. Here, if I may say so with respect and affection, our inheritance differs from, and is fuller than, that of the other great group of Free Churchmen, the Methodists. For the Methodists were not in origin or essence or intention a Church. They were, and so they called themselves till a time within living memory, a Society in a Church. They were members of the Established Church, but the fellowship from which they drew the best of their religion was not their Church. There was a divergence between their spiritual experience and their churchmanship. They thought of the Church as something other than the most sacred brotherhood. They prayed:

> Let us for each other care,
> Each the other's burden bear;
> To Thy Church the pattern give,
> Show how true believers live.

'Thy Church' and 'true believers'; not synonyms but in antithesis. It is the traditional Anglican idea of the Church as the whole of society, shot through now by an intenser experience. Of course the Methodists came in time to recognise that the Society which gave them the grace of God in the Word and the Sacraments was itself the Church.

Now I mention this not in derogation of the great Methodist Church, but to show you how august is your inheritance. We Congregationalists and Baptists have never been able to conceive of a churchless Christianity, a private sect, a Christian experience that is not also an ecclesiastical experience. We have always asociated the grace of our Lord Jesus Christ with the communion of the saints. That great vision of the Church, unbroken through all our history, is our inheritance and it marks us as specially privileged above all other Christians. The Anglicans have been prepared to make of the Church something less than the free Bride of Christ which knows only His sovereignty. The Methodists supposed that apart from the Church they could best find the Lord. The Society of Friends does not even know the value of some essential parts of churchmanship enough to care to claim them. The Romanists, like ourselves, have always recognised the supreme place of the Church in Christ's religion, but they have legalised and Judaised the conception almost beyond recognition. I make bold to claim that in the despised Bethels of our denominations and in the Churches of the Presbyterians alone has the fullest inheritance of churchmanship been preserved; emphasising equally the independence of the Church from all secular powers, the necessity of the Church for the means of grace, and the freedom of the Church under grace from clericalism, that is from Judaic legalism.

It suffices to remind you that there has never been a time when the world needed this inheritance of ours more than to-day. To-day the great mass of Christians in the world have almost no choice but between an inadequate and a false conception of churchmanship. On the one hand is a conception of the Christian Society that makes of it something less than a true Church, at best only one help among others to the religious life, desirable but not essential, and with this conception inevitably goes the failure to understand the importance of the sacred Ministry and the Sacraments; on the other hand is a conception of the Church right indeed in the place that it claims for the Divine Society, as the very essence of Christianity, but marred almost to the point of being unrecognisable by what Lord Salisbury, with that blistering irony of his, used to call the 'chemical theory of Orders', turning free grace into something like private magic. It is the bane of almost all Europe that it is offered a choice between a clerical Church and no Church at all, and as the worst of Fundamentalism is that it begets Modernism, the worst of clericalism is that it begets anti-clericalism. The steady triumph of the Latin party in the Established Church brings even this country nearer and nearer to the hateful dilemma: clericalism or anti-clericalism. What can save us? Nothing, *nothing*, but your inheritance of a full and free and pure churchmanship. Your Jubilee is a call that you hold fast this inheritance alike in its fullness and its purity.

Document IV.6

Science and Christian Belief: a Quaker View, 1929

Arthur S. Eddington, *Science and the Unseen World* (London: George Allen & Unwin Ltd, 1929), pp. 53–6.

Sir Arthur Eddington, Plumian Professor of Astronomy at Cambridge from 1913 and Fellow of Trinity College, was one of the most distinguished theoretical physicists and astrophysicists in the early twentieth century. He came from a committed Quaker family and was an active member of the Society throughout his life. His Swarthmore Lecture for 1929 was an account of how he related his religious belief to his science. This is the Conclusion, which was included in the 1960 edition of *Christian Faith and Practice in the Experience of the Society of Friends*.

In its early days our Society owed much to a people who called themselves Seekers; they joined us in great numbers and were prominent in the spread of Quakerism. It is a name which must appeal strongly to a scientific temperament. The name has died out, but I think that the spirit of seeking is still the prevailing one in our faith, which for that reason is not embodied in any creed or formula. It is perhaps difficult sufficiently to emphasise Seeking without disparaging its correlative Finding. But I must risk this, for Finding has a clamorous voice that proclaims its own importance; it is definite and assured, something that we can get hold of – that is what we all want, or think we want. Yet how transitory it proves. The finding of one generation will not serve for the next. It tarnishes rapidly except it be preserved with an ever-renewed spirit of seeking. It is the same too with science. How easy in a popular lecture to tell of the findings, the new discoveries which will be amended, contradicted, superseded, in the next fifty years! How difficult to convey the scientific truth of seeking which fulfils itself in this tortuous course of progress towards truth! You will understand the true spirit neither of science nor of religion unless seeking is placed in the forefront.

Religious creeds are a great obstacle to any full sympathy between the outlook of the scientist and the outlook which religion is so often supposed to require. I recognise that the practice of a religious community cannot be regulated solely in the interests of its scientifically-minded members and therefore I would not go so far as to urge that no kind of defence of creeds is possible. But I think it may be said that Quakerism in dispensing with creeds holds out a hand to the scientist. The scientific objection is not merely to particular creeds which assert in their own outworn phraseology beliefs which are either no longer held or no longer convey inspiration to life. The spirit of seeking which animates us refuses to regard any kind of creed as its goal. It would be a shock to come across a university where it was the practice of the students to recite adherence to Newton's laws of motion, to Maxwell's equations and to the electro-magnetic theory of light. We should not deplore it the less if our own pet theory happened to be included, or if the list was brought up to date every few years. We should say that the students cannot possibly realise the intention of scientific training if they are taught to look at these results as things to be recited and subscribed to. Science may fall short of its ideal, and although the peril scarcely takes this extreme form, it is not always easy, particularly in popular science, to maintain our stand against creed and dogma. I would not be sorry to borrow for our scientific pronouncements the passage prefixed to the Advices of the Society of Friends in 1656 and repeated in the current General Advices:

> 'These things we do not lay upon you as a rule or form to walk by; but that all with a measure of the light, which is pure and holy, may be guided; and so in the light walking and abiding, these things may be fulfilled in the Spirit, not in the letter; for the letter killeth, but the Spirit giveth light.'

Rejection of creed is not inconsistent with being possessed by a living belief. We have no creed in science, but we are not lukewarm in our beliefs. The belief is not that all the knowledge of the universe that we hold so enthusiastically will survive in the letter; but a sureness that we are on the road. If our so-called facts are changing shadows, they are shadows cast by the light of constant truth. So too in religion we are repelled by that confident theological doctrine which has settled for all generations just how the spiritual world is worked; but we need not turn aside from the measure of light that comes into our experience showing us a Way through the unseen world.

Religion for the conscientious seeker is not all a matter of doubt and self-questionings. There is a kind of sureness which is very different from cocksureness.

Document IV.7

Baptist Controversy over Higher Criticism and Modernism, 1932–34

The Crisis in the Baptist Churches and the Default of the Baptist Union (Taunton: Hammett & Co., c. 1934), pp. 2, 7–8, 9–11.

For the most part the British Churches escaped the kind of fundamentalist controversy in the 1920s and 1930s that afflicted the USA. The Baptist Union was criticised here for a series of events in the 1920s, culminating in a furore over a pamphlet published by T. R. Glover at the end of 1931, entitled, perhaps provocatively, *Fundamentals*. Both sides remembered clearly the 'Down Grade' controversy of 1887–88, which led to the withdrawal of C. H. Spurgeon from the Union.

No harsh feeling prompts the writer of the ensuing examination of the serious situation in the Baptist Denomination; but only solicitude for the witness of the great fellowship of Churches in which his life has been mostly spent, at a time when it is urgently needed. To those who are acquainted with the history of the Baptist Union it will appear plainly enough that the crisis in the matter of Evangelicalism is only the natural development of the policy adopted many years ago as to the basis of its fellowship.

To very many people who think of these matters earnestly, the composition of the Baptist Union as it has appeared during the modern controversy on Higher Criticism and Modernism, has presented a difficult problem. The Union has spoken with two voices. It has never been possible to think of it as standing for any definite leadership in an evangelical direction, albeit it has kept up the profession of Evangelicalism – and in some of its units with truth. But it has included many whose sympathies are known to be with the new attitude to Scripture, and whose influence seems to be ever increasing. It has been made as a consequence almost impossible to conscientiously maintain one's relation to or position in the Union, if one adheres to the old belief as to the Scripture and the great Christian doctrines ...

The wonderful thing is that this position is regarded as the true expression of the ideal of the Christian Church: the 'personal following of Christ' being substituted for a definite theological belief. *Of such an ideal, the New Testament Church provides no illustration*, and its consequence is seen in the anchorless state of the Churches that lean to it. The modern story of this development in the Baptist denomination may be swiftly sketched. After the time of Chas. Haddon Spurgeon, the regime of Dr. John Clifford familiarised the community with the loosening of the Divine authority of the Holy Scriptures: that of Dr. J. H. Shakespeare saw the material expansion and aggrandisement of the Denomination – the Church House was built – the World Alliance instituted: and the great Funds subscribed which initiated the super-organisation that is neither Independency nor Connexionalism, but an amalgam of both. From that time the denomination has been unable to escape the entanglements and features that are inseparable from commercialised institutions. *Modernism breeds in materialism, not in spirituality.* Can anyone say that the Baptist denomination has increased in spirituality since it sacrificed its doctrinal boundaries for corporate advancement? Every man's conscience can be left to answer the question. The criticism applies not only to the Baptist Union ...

Events during recent years have demonstrated the weak position of the Baptist Union as to Christian doctrine. During the War a movement to effect the closer federation of the Free Churches was promoted, the Joint-Committee proposing a colourless basis. In the Baptist Assembly in 1918 Dr James Mountain opposed this as 'unsatisfactory owing to its ambiguity as regards the Divine authority of the Bible as the Word of God, and inadequate in omitting all reference to the Virgin Birth of our Lord: His infallibility as Teacher: His sinless Life: His bodily Resurrection: His High-Priesthood and intercession: and other fundamental doctrines'.

The opposition to this was led by Dr. John Clifford, and Dr. T. R. Glover, and *another step was taken away from the affirmation of the distinctive beliefs of Christianity.* 'The honoured leaders' of the denomination led it into a humiliating surrender to those who were unwilling to be bound by the doctrines of the New Testament.

In 1922–3 a crisis arose in connection with the exposure by Mr Watkyn Roberts and the Rev. Wright Hay of the false teaching being given in India by certain missionaries of the Baptist Missionary Society – and the resignation of other Missionaries from the society owing to its condonation by the London officials. The

Rev. Dr. G. Howells was impeached for his general teaching, and especially for his book *The Soul of India*. Quotations were given showing Dr. Howells to be not only *an extreme member of the Rationalistic critical school*, but also as holding pernicious views about accommodating the presentation of the Gospel to Hindu culture and prejudice. A lamentable attitude was adopted by the officials of the Baptist Missionary Society, who declined to recognise this as departure from the Faith, in the presence of overwhelming evidence. A pamphlet by Rev. C. E. Wilson sought to minimise the heresies in Dr. Howell's book by quoting passages that seemed less wide of the mark. This reply was felt to be unsatisfactory by a great body of supporters of the Society, who were entitled to a clearer indication of its Evangelicalism, and much support was withdrawn – especially as it became known that Missionaries were not required to subscribe to any form of Belief.

Yet another episode, still fresh in the memory, occurred in connection with the Union in 1929–30 which illustrated again the folly and peril of the non-doctrinal basis and *raised the grave question of the unscriptural teaching being favoured in some of the Baptist Colleges*. It was shown that a certain outside Candidate for the Baptist Ministry had been subjected to injustice and disability in consequence of his refusal to accept the theological rationalism of Dr. A. C. Underwood of Rawdon College. A outcry was raised against the Professor's attempt to infringe the student's right of private judgment, and it was urged upon the Baptist Union Council that it should reserve the right to scrutinise the books appointed for outside candidates for the Baptist Ministry and should also *refuse to accept Ministers on the Accredited List from Colleges known to be under modernist control*. It seems obvious that if the members of the Council were unequivocally faithful to evangelical beliefs, these actions would be a matter of course.

The answer usually made by the Council to such appeals for action is that it has no control over the Colleges and no responsibilty corporately for the opinion and views expressed by any of its members. An examination of this plea will show it to be in the main fallacious. The independence of the Colleges of any control by the Baptist Union is understood, but inasmuch as an arrangement exists by which their students are accepted for the Ministry of Churches in the Union, and inclusion in its accredited List, *it is absurd to suggest that the Union has no power to discriminate against students who do not hold evangelical views*. In the regretted absence of any doctrinal criterion in the Union, the Council is nevertheless charged with the duty of maintaining the Baptist Faith which is known to be Evangelical and Biblical. On this ground it has a definite duty of discrimination. Could there be anything feebler than the position of a Union having forced upon it Ministers from Colleges outside its jurisdiction, and exercising no right of selection?

On the other aspect, when all has been said of the lack of a doctrinal standard in the Union, nothing whatever has been taken from *the full responsibility of the Council as a popularly-elected body to those who elect it – the representatives of the Churches*. Year by year the Council is elected and delegates are co-opted from various quarters, and it is invested statutorily with powers to act and devise policies on behalf of the entire Denomination. In this respect there is no difference between it and a Trade, or any other, Union. The Churches pay an annual affiliation fee to belong to it just as a working man to his Union. All federations are voluntary, and the fact does not weaken the mutual guarantees and responsibilities between the members and the elected Council. *What the Council does the Denomination does –* the Denomination is ultimately responsible for all its actions, until and unless it repudiates them. Only those Baptists who are outside the Union escape this responsibility. For all its own actions therefore the Council is strictly responsible and must presumably be guided by the fact of the biblical and evangelical character of the Baptist Denomination.

What then becomes of the pretence so often indulged in by the Editor of *The Baptist Times*, that the Union is not responsible for the views expressed in its own publications? There may certainly be individual writers for whom the Union could not be held responsible. But if the Council officially orders, accepts, and approves any writing, *it involves itself and the Denomination in the views expressed.* The recent pamphlet by Dr. T.R. Glover is a case in point. According to *The Baptist Times,* October 15th, 1931, the Council requested Dr. Glover to produce this publication, and in the same issue it reported that they gave him a warm expression of thanks for doing so. They are therefore responsible for it, and to the Denomination for asking Dr. Glover to write it. Yet when the anti-christian and semi-Gnostic tenets of this pamphlet were exposed, the Editor of *The Baptist Times* declared that:

> 'The publications of the Baptist Union Publication Dept. are issued upon the authority of the writers ... the Union does not take responsibility in the matter of doctrine ... no member of the Baptist Union other than the writer is responsible'.

What a shameful and unworthy subterfuge! The question is not that of the publication of the pamphlet, but of its being written at the request of the Council, for use in the 'Discipleship Campaign' of the Baptist Union. If all is as it should be, why the anxiety to disown responsibility for its publication? The fact of its adoption still remains. The action of the Council, reported in *The Baptist Times* of March 10th, 1932, deciding not to withdraw this pamphlet, but to issue another containing other Doctrine, suggests that Christian doctrine is a matter of choice, and illustrates the confusion to which compromise has reduced the Baptist Union Council.

The only deduction is that the denomination must itself safeguard its Evangelical Faith, and the Assembly is justified in demanding the suppression of this and all such subversive literature, as contrary to the Baptist Faith and against the spiritual well-being of the community. *If the Council shirks its responsibility, the court of appeal is the Assembly, and we should awake to its need of action...*

Document IV.8

A Congregational View of the Sacraments, 1943

N. Micklem, *Congregationalism and the Church Catholic* (London: Independent Press, 1943), pp. 53–60.

Nathaniel Micklem, Principal of Mansfield College, Oxford, had already written on 'The Sacraments' in the collection of essays, *Christian Worship* (1936), written by members of the College to celebrate the fiftieth anniversary of the move of Spring Hill College from Birmingham. This is an extract from Part IV of a book published during the Second World War to present key themes of the Congregational heritage for a future generation. Micklem drew on Forsyth, as well as Calvin and the Reformers.

The Apostolical Succession

The witness of the Church has been continuous throughout the ages. We have sometimes forgotten that. We have been so conscious of the fresh start made at the Reformation that we have tended to think of the early catholic Church or the great mediaeval church as alien to us; we are like high-placed ecclesiastics who seem to forget that their grandparents were Presbyterian or even Methodist. We can change our opinions but not our ancestry. We have stressed, and sometimes over-stressed, the break which is marked by the Reformation. The dominant school among the Anglicans today emphasizes, often too imaginatively, the continuity. Hence they insist upon 'the Apostolic Succession', while we sometimes declare it to be of no interest and unspiritual. But they are right. The Apostolical Succession is essential to the Church. Only we must be sure that the Succession is authentic.

Their theory is that the first apostles laid their hands upon the first bishops in consecration; they in turn on their successors, and so in unbroken practice from the apostolic age to the Anglican bishops (and, of course, the Roman bishops) of today. It is a moving thought and may, in some sense, be true, though it cannot be proved. But we are rebuked when we see in it sentimental value only; we are told that it is of profound theological and religious significance. The 'historic episcopate', so continuously consecrated, is said to be the symbol and in some way the guarantee of the Church's unity, of the Church's continuity, of the validity of the Church's sacraments and of the authenticity of the Church's doctrine. Never let us smile at this theory as if unity and continuity, doctrine and sacraments, were matters of indifference to us.

We have our own theory of the Apostolical Succession, and a recent Pope has answered the Anglican. He has declared that the true Succession requires continuity not only of touch but of intention, and that the English Church has known no continuity of intention to ordain priests in the mediaeval or modern Roman sense. We may hope that later Popes will have the courage to take the matter further and deal satisfactorily with the intention of the first apostles! But those who have filched the name 'Catholic' and used it for party purposes are insisting upon vital issues we have too much neglected. Bishops do not guarantee the church's unity; they can only express it when it is there. Again, if bishops should be custodians of the apostolic tradition, they have proved insufficient in their task; Popes themselves have embraced heresies, and episcopacy is patently no guarantee of sound doctrine. Moreover, a theory which implies that the church of Rome in Spain, for instance, is an integral part of Christ's church visible on earth, and the church of Scotland is not, does not rest upon any spiritual judgment. No, this theory is unimpressve; we answer it with a better.

We say that by the faithful preaching of the Word, the believing celebration of the sacraments and the exercise of Gospel discipline the Church is kept in the doctrine and fellowship of the apostles and stands in the true succession. 'There is an unbroken succession,' said Bernard Manning, 'from the Apostles down to you and me today, the true apostolical succession of men and women who have received the Word and celebrated the Sacraments ever since the first Easter Day. The true apostolical succession is in the whole church which continues to find Christ where it always has found him – in the means of grace; in his Word, in prayer, in the Sacraments. It is not the ministry – whether with or without bishops – which guarantees the Word and Sacraments. It is the Word and the Sacraments, given by Christ, which guarantee the ministry.'

The Spirit is present with the Church to reveal to it the things of Christ, and, if we be asked how we know that we are led by the Spirit and not by some will o' the wisp, we answer that our guidance is to be tested by the Scriptures and by the testimony of the saints and fathers. The rebirth of the Church from age to age by the ever renewed miracle of regeneration is the work of the Spirit; it rests upon the promise of God; it can have no external guarantee. The strongest external safeguard of the Church's continuity and purity is the public and private study of the Scriptures, for though there may be many vagaries of private interpretation, yet the general sense of Scripture is not obscure, and Scripture is the fountain and inspiration of reform and renewal from age to age. We claim that, except where we have been unfaithful to our calling, we have stood 'in the doctrine and fellowship' of the apostles. That is the true Succession in the Church.

In the doctrine and fellowship – the fellowship not less than the doctrine. The churches that have arrogated to themselves the name of 'Catholic' have their guilds and religious houses and associations, and are not without fellowship in Christ, but that fellowship of the Church which is expressed in our church meeting – the fellowship of different ages and different interests, of men and women in covenant relation with one another and with their Lord, bearing one another's burdens and conferring, ministers and laity together, upon the concerns of the Lord's work, evoking each other's spiritual gifts and worshipping in the intimacy of brotherly love – this is an experience which is little known in the churches of a different order. We claim to stand in the true succession, which is the doctrine and fellowship of the apostolic Church.

Theology

Baptism

In other matters also we are apt to take a negative, instead of a constructive, attitude to the pretensions of the Establishment. In reaction to those in other churches who lay exclusive stress upon holy Baptism, deeming all baptized persons to be members of the Church and the unbaptized to be outside the church, there are some amongst us who boast aggressively that there are unbaptized members of Congregational churches and even unbaptized ministers, and who frankly regard the sacraments, both Baptism and the Supper, as optional in the Church of Christ. This extreme view is not common amongst us, but many are confused and uncertain in this matter. No doubt there are those in other communions who hold very unspiritual views on the sacraments, but the repudiation of sacraments is not a sign of superior spirituality.

No man is saved because he has been subjected to the rite of Baptism nor lost because he is unbaptized. Our salvation rests upon the eternal promises of God, not upon a rite performed in church. That does not make the rite unimportant or generally unnecessary. Children born of Christian parents belong to the covenant of grace. The promise of God is to believing parents 'and to their seed after them.' Baptism is not a dedication service; it is the 'sealing,' as our fathers called it, of the promises of God. It is a church sacrament; it may not be isolated from its context in the church's life, from the promise of the parents that they will train the child in the admonition of the Lord and in the fellowship of the church. The idea that the ceremony alters God's attitide to the child or determines its eternal destiny is not far from superstition. The sacrament is given not to assist God but to comfort us. We parents dream dreams for our children desiring that their life may be crowned with honour and satisfaction and success. Such are our natural, human hopes. But, when we turn to prayer for them, our first prayer and our last is that they may love God and cleave to him; for then all our deepest longing for them will be satisfied, then we shall have no fear for them; then if it should please God to call them to suffer for his sake, we would not pray that such privilege be taken from them. Such is our prayer, and we lay hold upon the promises of God which are to us and to our children after us, knowing that he is able to keep that which we have committed to him. Then for the confirming of our faith the minister in Christ's name takes our children in his arms and seals the divine promise in their case. The slighting of Baptism is never found with those who understand its grace and meaning.

The Lord's Supper

No church in Christendom supposes that the Holy Communion is necessary to salvation, and the despising of sacraments is natural where, as sometimes, the Communion Sevice is so formless, hurried, unseemly, arid, with no great thanksgiving, no breaking of the bread, no invocation of the Holy Spirit, no expectation of the sacred elements being made to us the Body and Blood of Christ. But this is pitiful loss. The rite of the breaking of the bread takes us back to the very fountain-head of our religion. It is older that the New Testament; it was practised before there was a bishop in Rome, or even before St. Paul became a Christian. Never a Sunday has passed, perhaps never a single day, since the first Pentecost but Christians in a rite more intimate and eloquent than words have shown forth the Lord's death upon the cross for us, and they shall show it forth until he come. This rite proclaims in action the same Gospel that is declared in preaching; for it is the same Word of God, the same everlasting life, which is conveyed to us both in preaching and in sacrament. We come as poor, sick, hungry, sinful men, and our Saviour says to us, as he said to all our fathers and all the generations before us: 'Take eat: this is my body.'

The Church proclaims its good news by administering the sacraments no less than by preaching the Word. This, said Bernard Manning, 'is sound Congregational doctrine. Do not mistake it for the beginning of Roman Catholicism or other superstition. For notice, when I say that the Sacrament does this, I mean that it does this for those who receive it with faith. It is not a piece of magic which works of itself if you merely stay for the communion service. The man who receives the Sacrament needs faith in Christ if the benefits of Christ are to be found in it. And here is another guard against superstition: it is the Church which celebrates, not the minister. The minister presides at the celebration, but it is the Church, eating and drinking in faith, which celebrates. It is no magic worked by the word of one man. The Lord's Supper has sometimes been abused or thought of superstitiously, but that provides no reason for abandoning the chief of the means of grace. It is for us Congregationalists to draw from the Lord's Supper what the faithful have always drawn from it, and to think of it with true reverence but without superstition. Be sure of this: no Congregationalist knows what his church can do for him till he has learnt to value, as the church has always valued, Baptism and the Supper of the Lord.'

Should any church member be allowed to preside at the Lord's Table? There are some amongst us who in loud protest against sacerdotal claims would push laymen into that awesome place. In our churches, they say, anybody can occupy the pulpit, and it is 'priestcraft' to suggest that only the minister may preside at Communion. These enthusiasts are justified in so far as we are implacably opposed to 'sacerdotalism'; but to disparage the special responsibilities of the ministry is not Congregationalism. Any man may preach in our pulpits, if he have the requisite spiritual and intellectual gifts, and if the church commission him to do so – not otherwise. So, too, we reject the sacerdotalism which declares that the Lord's real presence, the validity of the sacrament, are only guaranteed when an ordained man officiates; but we have a ministry of the Word and Sacraments; our ministers have been called by God and prepared by the Church to exercise this office. It is their calling and duty to administer the sacraments in the church as the care of finances is the business of the deacons and pew-opening the business of the verger. Church, ministry and sacraments alike rest upon the Word of God, and the minister has no authority whatever except the authority of the Word which he has been commissioned to expound. The Congregational minister in his traditional and proper dress, cassock and gown and bands, is not aping the Roman priesthood but is the very symbol of the Reformed religion. He is called to rule the church by the authority of the Word of God committed to him. Yet he is no tyrant, for his people may only follow him so long as he follows Christ; they appointed him to be their minister, and in the last resort they must eject him if he seem to them to depart from Christ; but, while he holds his office, he is the minister of Christ to them, and it is his task and duty to preach the Word to them and administer its sacraments.

That ministers should preside at the Lord's Table is the rule. Can there be an exception to it? If, as may happen to any church, it should be through several months without a minister, is it to be deprived of the sacraments for all that time? Our Puritan fathers said Yes, but most of us would answer No. Under such circumstances it is usual for some neighbouring minister to visit the church and administer the sacrament; often, however, the duty is laid upon a theological student; he, no doubt, is a layman, but he is not any chance church member; he is one whose inward sense of call has been ratified officially by the fellowship of churches, and who is being trained and instructed in the duties of the ministry; what is essential is not ordination but spiritual calling and the commission of the church. The suggestion that no layman may under any circumstances perform that sacred office would seem to us false to spiritual realities, for it is the church that celebrates the sacrament, and the presence of Christ does not depend upon the presence of a minister. But no man may preach or administer the sacrament in church without the commission of the church. Commission is essential to order, and 'our God is a God of order' (I Cor. xiv 33). Therefore, just as we agree that our ministry should be recognised and commissioned by the whole communion, and we insist that a representative of the County Union be officially present at every recognised ordination, so for the sake of order it would be desirable that laymen who on occasion should be called to preach or celebrate the Lord's Supper should be commissioned by the wider fellowship.

Because in our claim that under special circumstances a layman may officiate we are going against the judgment of the vast majority of our fellow-Christians, and because we are under obligation to walk in fellowship and unity with all the churches of Christ so far as loyalty to him allows, we should be willing to go thus far to meet their scruples; but, to put an extreme case, we should never agree that a party of holy laymen wrecked on a desert island should be deprived of the Christian sacrament; it would be their duty, we say, as representing in their isolated spot the holy Catholic church, to set aside and commission one of their number for this office. But if we insist on this ultimate freedom, we must stress also the importance and obligation of a nomally binding rule.

Document IV.9

Methodist Views of the Atonement

(a) Vincent Taylor, *The Apostolic Gospel* (London: Epworth Press, 1953), pp. 11–12; (b) Frances M. Young, *Sacrifice and the Death of Christ* (London: SPCK, 1975), pp. 94, 97; (c) Frances M. Young, *Face to Face* (Edinburgh: T. & T. Clark, 1990), pp. 73–4.

The Atonement has traditionally been at the heart of nonconformist preaching. These three extracts reflect shifts in Methodist thinking in the mid-century. Dr Vincent Taylor, Principal of Wesley College, Leeds wrote a trilogy on the Atonement, and later a trilogy on the Person of Christ. The first extract is from a lecture given to the Pastoral Session of Conference in 1952. The other two come from books by Dr Frances Young, Professor of Theology in the University of Birmingham and Pro-Vice Chancellor, who was one of the leading scholars in Methodism at the end of the century.

(a)
What are we saying today about the Cross? We rightly preach Abelardian doctrine. The Cross truly reveals the love of God, and by its love kindles an answering flame within us. But I trust we do not stop there. Every theory of the Atonement expresses some aspect of the truth, and we cannot do without any of them. The so-called 'Classic theory', that Christ died to deliver men from sin, evil, and death, is especially relevant in our chaotic world. The Anselmic theory of satisfaction rises above merely feudal conceptions in affirming that the Son of God fully met all the moral conditions of righteousness; and the crudest theory of substitution preserves the truth that, although Christ was not the object of divine wrath, He shared the penal consequences of human sin. We shall always have our doctrinal preferences, for in her wisdom Holy Church has never authorized any theory of the Atonement. For myself, I believe that the most fruitful way of conceiving the nature of Christ's Passion is the view that, as the Son of Man, Christ identified Himself with sinners and offered in their name that supreme sacrifice of obedience, penitence, and love which we ourselves are unable to offer, but in which we can participate by faith union, sacramental devotion and sacrificial living. In these high matters we shall not all think alike. Nevertheless, and however the secret of the Cross is read, we are at one in believing that Christ has done all things needful for our deliverance from sin and our reconciliation with God, that, in Him, God was reconciling the world to Himself (2 Corinthians v, 19).

(b)
In a new history of the doctrine of atonement, then, justice must be done to the central importance of sacrificial imagery in the thinking of the early Church, and to the significance of the work of Athanasius in resolving the tensions inherent in early Christian thinking about atonement. As a consequence, one may hope that the persistent polarization of opinion about atonement may be mitigated. There is much

in the 'penal substitution' theory which comes near to the Athanasian picture, for it seeks to resolve the tension between God's justice and his mercy, his holiness and his love. We must begin to recognize that a simple clear-cut pattern fails to be sensitive to the ambiguous and elusive character of the relationship between God and the evil in his creation. Atonement means a conviction that God has somehow dealt with evil, with sin, with rebellion. Perhaps the nearest we can get to expressing this is to say that on the cross, God in Christ entered into the suffering, the evil, and the sin of his world; he entered the darkness and transformed it into light, into blazing glory. He took responsibility for the existence of evil in his creation; he bore the pain of it and the guilt of it; he accepted its consequences into himself, and in his love reconciled his holiness to a sinful and corrupt humanity, justifying the ungodly, accepting man just as he is: ...

Man cannot free himself from his follies and idols simply by wanting to or trying hard. We are justified by faith, not because Jesus Christ and his Father have patched up an agreement whereby our sins are to be ignored, but because by faith in Christ we are accepted, sinners as we are, and enabled to identify with his perfection, to share in his perfect sacrifice of praise and obedience. We are redeemed from corruption and re-created in newness of life. Worship, service and atonement are inseparable.

(c)
Jesus the light of the world is to be snuffed out, because the darkness could not grasp the light. And yet everything in this Gospel points to the cross as the hour of glory. In the end Jesus did not waft away the darkness of the world, all its sin and suffering and hurt and evil, with a magic wand. He entered right into it, took it upon himself, bore it, and in the process turned it into glory, transformed it. It is that transformation which the healing of the blind man foreshadows.

Seeing this story and indeed the whole drama of John's Gospel in these terms, gave me the clue, and the sermon. There could not be any philosophical answer to the problem of evil; not one is fully satisfactory. The only answer, the only thing that makes it possible to believe in God at all, is the cross. In fact I would now want to acknowledge that some of the traditional answers have a certain wisdom, and do provide partial solutions, aids to understanding. But I would still maintain that a properly Christian response to the problem of evil has to begin with the cross, with an understanding of atonement. We do not begin by explaining evil away, justifying God, excusing him for the mess he has made of his creation. We begin by contemplating the story which tells of God taking responsibility for the evil in his world, by entering it himself, taking it upon himself, in all its horror, cruelty and pain.

Document IV.10

Christianity and History

Herbert Butterfield, (a) *Christianity and History* (London: Bell, 1949), pp. 145–6; (b) Herbert Butterfield, 'The Obstruction to Belief' (1956), in C. T. McIntire (ed.), *Writings on Christianity and History* (Oxford: Oxford University Press, 1979), pp. 245–6.

Sir Herbert Butterfield, Regius Professor of Modern History at Cambridge and Master of Peterhouse, symbolised the new world of achievement open to nonconformists by the mid-twentieth century. A lifelong Methodist, he wrote on the relationship of Christianity and history to great effect, and his 1949 book was republished as a Fontana paperback in 1957.

The conclusion of the first extract has the character of a sermon, and has inspired many.

(a)
In regard to some of the most important things in life it is remarkable how little human beings know their liberty – how little they realize that the grand discoveries of the various inductive sciences still leave us free to range with the upper parts of our minds. In these days also when people are so much the prisoners of systems – especially the prisoners of those general ideas which mark the spirit of the age – it is not always realized that belief in God gives us greater elasticity of mind, rescuing us from too great subservience to intermediate principles, whether these are related to nationality or ideology or science. It even enables us to leave more play in our minds for the things that nature or history may still have to reveal to us in the near future. Similarly Christianity is not tied to regimes – not compelled to regard the existing order as the very end of life and the embodiment of all our values. Christians have too often tried to put the brake on things in the past, but at the critical turning-points in history they have less reason than others to be afraid that a new kind of society or civilization will leave them nothing to live for. We are told by many people that our new age needs a new mentality, but so often when one reads these writers further all that they say is that if we don't do now the things they have been continually telling us to do since 1919 we shall have the atomic bomb and presumably deserve it. I have nothing to say at the finish except that if one wants a permanent rock in life and goes deep enough for it, it is difficult for historical events to shake it. There are times when we can never meet the future with sufficient elasticity of mind, especially if we are locked in the contemporary systems of thought. We can do worse then remember a principle which both gives us a firm Rock and leaves us the maximum elasticity for our minds: the principle: Hold to Christ, and for the rest be totally uncommitted.

(b)
I think that Christians ought to show the world that they are prepared to renounce more of their history than they are usually prepared to do. We ourselves are very

slow to surrender our dream of a Christianity that is allied with power and privilege, though this is the one thing of which there is no sign or trace in the New Testament. Let us stop thinking that religion was in a better state in the old days, when certainly the great numbers came to Church but so often with the result that religion was debased and became less purely spiritual. It is better that Christians should be as they were in New Testament days – humble rather than proud, poor rather than privileged, claiming no rights against society, no rights in the world save that of worshipping the God in Whom they believe and preaching the faith they hold.

The fault of so many Christians in history was that they had not sufficient faith in the power of purely spiritual factors and forces – they wanted to help them out with the strong arm of the law. The same may be the fault of Christians today; yet the long-term results of history seem to me to vindicate the power of the spiritual more than anything else. The real victories of Christianity in history are the quiet ones – the victory of charity, for example, which works like a leaven in society until it leavens the whole lump, or the victory of the Christian martyrs who triumphed by virtue of their very defeat ...

Document IV.11

Unitarian Theology in Mid-Century

C. Gordon Bolam, 'Theological Liberalism: A Vindication', in K. Twinn (ed.), *Essays in Unitarian Theology* (London: The Lindsey Press, 1959), pp 127–30, 133–6.

Gordon Bolam was minister of High Pavement Chapel, Nottingham, and one of the leading scholars in mid-twentieth-century Unitarianism. The symposium, of which this essay is a part was intended to reflect on the challenges to theology in the post-war period; and Bolam's contribution sums up the problems of the contemporary context for liberal thought.

The contributors to this symposium met for discussion conscious of the inimical climate of opinion in which the modern theological liberal has to offer his apologia ... The factors producing the unfavourable contemporary situation are so frequently the topic of exploration and analysis that there is little need now to rehearse them; suffice to mention two as more particularly significant. There has been the *débâcle* of two world wars, with the consequent collapse of accepted patterns of thinking as well as confusion in the sphere of economics and society generally. One by-product has been the finding of a sense of spiritual defeatism, which has expressed itself in a tendency towards totalitarianism in thought and action. Liberalism in all its manifestations has become the scapegoat and a word of reproach. Independently of this, though not unconnected, liberal thought had reached a point at the close of the nineteenth century when it was being recognised that its horizons needed to be extended. On many frontiers of thought the new ideas which had illuminated men's minds for over three centuries had reached speculative deadlock, and it was obvious that a new era required re-examination of the seminal ideas if regeneration was to ensue. The pace of events in this century prevented any gradual re-assessment, and the forces of liberalism were forced into defensive positions before they could be redeployed. Not unnaturally, much of the criticism derogatory of liberal theology is thus directed against positions liberals themselves would have come to abandon...

By mid-century it is clear that we have to acknowledge we now live 'in a post-liberal, post-idealist, atomic age in theology'... It is now an illiberal world, marked by the repudiation of reason as a valid guide to truth; the dogmatic interpretation of history, whether from the particularity of traditional Christianity or Marxist materialism; and a fundamental disregard of the authentic value of human life. Facing this new situation the present writers are not concerned to advance arguments which are but weak alternatives to either traditionally accepted Christian formulations or the varieties of scientific humanism. There is a pressing need for a creative handling of human experience in such a manner as will be true to the initiative in the insight of Jesus which alone keeps the religious quest dynamic, experimental (that is, being put to the test in all ages) and a continuing discussion. Thus may religion be saved from becoming a formal recapitulation of the life of the Master merely as a rehearsal of historic happenings. It is not that the liberal theologian is engaged in trying to invent a Christianity without Jesus, but he takes the equipment which the modern world provides and seeks to expound a Christian truth as intelligible and significant in the situation in which men now find themselves. This is a very different attitude from assenting to doctrinal formulations as though this were the living core of religion. It is the attempt to harmonize the complementary nature of perceiving the truth in Christ and living that perceived truth as personal encounter where in the Johannine sense we must do the truth, be the truth...

For historical reasons the main stream of liberal theology has flowed in those churches now bearing the name of Unitarian, but it cannot be too strongly asserted that it would be a contradiction of the inner ethos of the movement if its adherents advocated a 'party line' or anything that could be called 'Unitarian' Christianity. Unitarianism is now honoured by its martyrs and by suffering, but it is no more than a name which describes those whose quest is ever determined by the unflagging search for truth. With all the equipment of scholarship and research the modern world provides, they seek not to preserve a religious position intact from criticism, but co-operatively would live out of their religious insights in a world where the old signposts have been destroyed for ever. 'What can men live by?' and 'What ought men to live by?' are questions to which they address themselves and they set no frontiers to the bounds of their search.

Such a quest may first be stated as the recognition of the need of an ideal for the individual. Response means a personal encounter. Religion to be vital must come out of a situation where I have existentially apprehended it. But since no two people live in exactly the same mental context this requires an expression of worship and theology which permits of diversity within unity of purpose. The ideal for the individual has its roots in the Old Testament, where the humanism of 'Son of Man, stand upon thy feet' becomes actualized in Jesus and henceforth presents the type-figure of Christian humanism.

Secondly, we recognize that religion must set forth a vision for society. In worship we meet as brethren of the Kingdom. In the church there is the practical awareness of knowledge which can only come to us by participation and not just as spiritual self-culture. Our response in this sphere is arrived at by our belonging to a definite group as participating in a particular experience or activity. To give significance to the concept of church as a fellowship of believers means returning to the clear differentiation Jesus himself made between 'neighbour' and 'brother'. What is commonly spoken of as the brotherhood of man ought more strictly to be regarded as the neighbourliness of man, where the moral basis of life requires of us at least a neighbourly responsibility. Brotherhood belongs to those who have voluntarily accepted the discipline and obligations of living in the context of the Kingdom of God. By neighbourliness we are lifted from self-interest (which a pure individualism would lead to) into the solidarity of common service. But a 'brother' has a dual function: he has a special relationship to the rest of the brethren and, secondly, has had to act as a catalyst in the world, transforming and transmuting. In the world it will be upon his shoulders that the burdens of the unthinking and the evil fall. Thus societal religion has to face the challenge that redemption is by the path of sacrifice.

Thirdly, we recognize that what has failed so tragically for modern man is the collapse of an imaginative awareness of God ... Karl Barth recoiled from what he termed the 'subjectivism' of liberal concepts of God. But it may be asked whether his 'objective' approach does not end in as great a difficulty where God is not merely remote but actually sundered from human communion. To speak of God breaking through to man is ultimately a counsel of despair, since revelation is subject to human interpretation and is not self-vindicating. God speaks to man though it may be that man mishears and cannot always rise up with certainty and exclaim: 'It is he'. Yet God speaks and will continue to do so; and this means that we hear through our subjectivity, the message is to us and we must learn to interpret it. And though Schleiermacher has been subjected to much severe criticism, his timely sentence is still directed against a narrow dogmatism which would shut up ideas of God instead of opening out new vistas of interpretation: 'You cannot believe in God arbitrarily, but only because you must'. The liberal is not projecting his subjectivism on to God, he responds with love to love.

Document IV.12

Religionless Christianity, 1962

Daniel Jenkins, *Beyond Religion* (London: SCM Press, 1962), pp. 78–80.

Daniel Jenkins was one of the leading Congregational theologians in the mid-twentieth century, and was first Chaplain at the new University of Sussex. This little book of 1962 raised many of the issues for theology which were to achieve wider circulation with John Robinson's *Honest to God* a year later, reflecting the (delayed) impact of contemporary German ideas in Britain.

... The Church as a visible institution alongside others in the world is essential. It is also sometimes necessary for the Church to express herself in elaborately organized forms. But these can quickly become a conspiracy against God unless the Church recognizes the insidiousness of her temptation to lead her members in a religious retreat from faith. Instead of thinking of itself as primarily an instrument of mission and ministry (in Kraemer's phrase), the Church easily becomes an end in itself. It no longer thinks of its function as subordinate to the divine purpose for mankind and is not prepared to lose its secular identity in service of its neighbour but concentrates on building its own worldly empire, which remains worldly even though it is adorned with all manner of religious symbols. The most striking proof of the ease with which the Church can succumb to temptation is provided by the prevalence within its midst of clericalism. Clericalism may be defined as the effort to mark out and establish a world of religion which is to be distinguished from the other areas of life, where decisive power lies in the hands of a self-perpetuating corporation of religious experts.

Clericalism is to be found in varying forms in all churches, and should be recognized as the characteristically ecclesiastical manifestation of false secularism, of conformity with this world which passes away. Catholicism, especially in its Roman form, provides the most fully articulated example of this, but even churches which try to resist the dangers of creating clerical castes do not escape its influence. The elaborate ecclesiastical apparatus of Protestant churches is designed to serve and sustain the members of the Christian community as they seek to fulfil their mission in service in the daily life of the world, but this apparatus often becomes an end in itself almost as readily as it does in Catholicism. It is one of the ironies of history that churches which proclaim their belief in the Fall and original sin and insist that the warfare against sin will continue while this earth remains, should frequently be less aware of the corrupting influence of power than states. The dangers of clericalism can be mitigated by devising church constitutions which define and limit the power of the clergy, but the only real safeguard is that clergy and people should recognize that the scattering of God's people in the world is as important as its gathering into church order if it is to fulfil its Christian obedience.

Here indeed is the only way in which the ideas lying behind the phrases 'religionless Christianity' and 'holy worldliness' are ever likely to find any significant expression. A religionless Christianity may strictly be impossible but a church which does not transcend its religion in the venture of faith is the abomination of desolation standing where it ought not, and therefore a sign of the imminence of the End. And that faith always works through love is as true for the institution as for the individual, even though the love may have sometimes to take more complex forms in the case of the institution. It follows that from this that true holiness in the world arises only when the members of the Church forget their corporate interest in themselves as participants in an earthly institution as they fulfil their common mission. That mission is fulfilled only in ministry, in identification with the Church's Lord as he identifies himself with men and gives them his redemptive power in their real lives on earth. The action of the Church is sheer unholy worldliness, however it may be dressed up in religious garb, unless it is covered with the holiness of Christ, and Christ is always found on this earth in the form of a servant. The element of separation which is always bound up with holiness is achieved only as the members of the Church exercise a self-forgetting ministry to their neighbours, as their neighbour's human need is seen in the light of Christ. This is the paradox of holy worldliness in the form of a servant (Phil. 2.7), that separation unto God is achieved only by identification with one's neighbour under God.

Document IV.13

Atonement and the Sacraments, 1988

Colin Gunton, *The Actuality of Atonement* (Edinburgh: T. & T. Clark, 1988), pp. 183–7, 188, 195–200.

Colin Gunton, whose academic career was spent at King's College, London, where he became Professor of Theology, proved that nonconformists could now attain the highest positions in a formerly Anglican foundation. If Forsyth was the greatest nonconformist theologian of the early century, Gunton was the greatest at the end, and his tragically early death in May 2003 deprived us of the systematic theology he had hoped to write in retirement. This extract illustrates the range and freshness of his approach to traditional themes.

[T]here is a real link between the way in which Jesus' victory is portrayed in the New Testament and his freedom to speak and be the truth. It was not intended to deny that the substance of his victory becomes real as the sacraments of baptism and the Lord's Supper speak their visible words. Like the preached word, the visible words have as their end the creation of space: or rather they are concerned with the realisation in the present of the achieved space of the atonement and the promised space of the new heaven and new earth. But the sacraments have, over and above proclamation, their own specific features. They are particular ways in which God the Spirit creates free human life. And just as victory was appropriated in terms of proclamation and truth, baptism's orientation ... is to judgement and forgiveness. To be baptised is to undergo judgement, by accepting the work of Christ in our stead.

To say that, however, is not to deny the double focus of baptism. Baptism also symbolises cleansing: the cleansing of human life from pollution through the atoning sacrifice. It therefore sets the baptised in a community of those who, by virtue of their reconciliation to God, live their lives under the promise that they will be presented perfect before the throne of grace. But although water is a symbol of cleansing, it can be argued that of equal, and perhaps greater, weight is the fact that water is the stuff that drowns. The baptism of Jesus was his undergoing the judgement of God proclaimed by John against Israel. Therefore to undergo baptism is to accept a sentence of death, metaphorical but real. Paul makes this clear in many passages: to have been baptised is to have died with Christ. John makes a similar point in the language of rebirth (Jn. 3). In what is perhaps his most radical assertion of the extent of Jesus' identification with the human race under judgement ('he made him to be sin who knew no sin'), Paul draws the conclusion that all have therefore died (2 Cor. 5.21, 15). The statement gains its force from the ontological universality of the humanity of Jesus. Because his is the humanity of the Word through whom all things exist, his death is the death of all.

The end of baptism is, therefore, the actuality, not simply the possibility, of a new form of existence. There is a 'new act of creation' (C. K. Barrett's translation of 2 Cor. 5.17). What is claimed is no more a magical transmogrification than it is literally the clinical death of the baptised. The judgement which is undergone in baptism is rather the means of entry into the living space created by the substitutionary death of Christ. Because he has undergone judgement for us and in our place, we may undergo it as a gift of life rather than as a sentence of death. But that means that it is, metaphorically but really a sentence of death on us ... Because the Son, through whom all things come to be, is among us in the way that he is – as a man who lives a certain life and dies a certain death – certain definite implications follow for our way of being on earth.

The heart of the significance of baptism is brought out by the fact that it is baptism for the forgiveness of sins ... The problem arises in the form traditionally given to baptism as the result of discussions in the Western church about sin and its relation to baptism. The doctrine of original sin developed in the West under the logic of the practice of baptising infants. Infants were baptised; baptism was for the remission of sin; therefore efforts must be made to show in what sense infants were sinful and underwent the remission of sins. As is well known, there came into prominence a doctrine that original sin was a kind of inherited stain or curse which was passed on from parent to child by means of sexual reproduction. Original sin then came to be distinguished from actual sin, so that the original was the inheritance, the actual the sinful acts performed thereafter.

While, however, the distinction between original and actual sin is an essential one, the way it was worked out was highly questionable. In the first place, sin was not treated relationally. Instead of seeing the heart of the matter in a relation between creature and creator, expressed metaphorically in terms of stain and the rest, theology tended to trace a train of historical causality back to Adam. The result was that the symptom was treated as the disease. The outcome was not only theologically problematic, but caused unnecessary difficulties for the concept of sin when historical critical scholars began to cast doubt on the existence of a historical Adam. Too much is made to hang on a chain of historical causality rather than on relations, or breach of them, with God. In the second place, the Western conception of original sin led to a tendency to operate with a dualism of inner and outer person. Original sin came to be seen as that which qualified the inner being, and was wiped away by baptism. Actual sin continued, and became the object of the disciplinary and legal structures of the church. Again, what is lost is an understanding of sin as a way of being – or failure to be – for the whole person in relation to God and the rest of creation.

The two weaknesses correspond to a weakness in the theology of baptism and of the church. In the first place, because original sin was conceived as an invisible taint of the individual, the sacrament came to be understood as a rite, in the control of the institution, in which that stain was wiped away. It was treated individualistically, and with minimal relational content, so that the primary function of baptism, relation with God through the mediation of Christ and in the context of a living community, became secondary. The familiar definition of a sacrament as an outward and visible sign of an inward and spiritual grace betrays all the worst aspects of the syndrome. It is not much of a parody to say that the sacrament was rather like a dose of religious medicine, administered by a priest, with little sense of its being institution into a living community of worship and life. It is small wonder that the baptism of infants has come into disrepute. But the chief point here is this: that the vital link between the atonement and a living community in which it becomes concrete is lost ...

In that sense, we cannot claim too much for the church, not as an institution dispensing grace, but as a community ordered to God through Christ and in the Spirit. The metaphor of the church as the body of Christ teaches that to be baptised is to be brought into relation with Christ through the community. That is something real: an ontic change, because to enter a new set of relationships – and particularly this one – is to be a new creation. Thus baptism is a way of making concrete the atonement achieved by God through Jesus. It is to enable participation in the justifying action of God. In turn, such a doctrine is definitive of the kind of community that the church is. It is the one called to live by the justice of God: accepting for itself the judgement of God on sin, borne on the cross by Jesus, so that it may in turn be the locus of transformed relationships ...

The doctrine of the Lord's Supper has, even more than that of baptism, been turned into a clerically controlled rite in which a sacrament is administered to individuals, as medicine by a physician. Indicative of the conceptual chaos which reigns is the development of expressions which fit the medical analogy, like 'receiving' communion. Can this be really what is meant by 'the medicine of immortality' or should we seek a more adequate construction of the metaphor? Such would stress the fact that communion is koinonia, community; and with that there comes a change of emphasis, from the individual's communion with God, which does not have to be denied in its proper place, to the community's participating in the wedding feast of the lamb.

The structure of much modern worship serves only to reinforce the individualistic interpretation. Despite the development of liturgies more expressive of communal celebration, many modern rites are in other ways inimical to communion. The trail to the altar rail accentuates both individual reception and the class division between active clergy and receptive laity; while in free church liturgy, despite many salutary developments, the manner of distribution maintains the tradition of nineteenth century individualism. What is lacking is a crucial link joining the atonement and the life of the community as a whole in the context of which the celebration takes place. The deficiency is ecclesiological: we lack a conception of the church as the space in which God gives community with himself and so between human people.

When we survey the depressing history of ecclesiological thought, the dimension of the problem become plainer. The background is to be found in the tendency to conceive salvation as something handed to the apostles – unhistorically seen as the first 'clergy' – which is then mediated to the people through an institutional élite. In place of a community, there developed a hierarchy. A similar point emerges in terms of the doctrine of the Holy Spirit. Rather than being conceived as God in his eschatological action of constituting the community of the age to come, the Spirit came to be depersonalised and treated as a force (causally) empowering an already given community: moving the institution into action. In place of this we need, as John Zizioulas has argued, a conception of the church as indeed *instituted* by Christ, but requiring *constitution* in every new present by the Spirit ... The time-honoured and sometimes time-worn emphasis on the church's relation to God in its past, mediated through the institutional structure, needs to be relativised by an emphasis on the present action of God the Spirit mediated through the life of the community as a whole.

We shall begin a reshaping of the conceptuality of communion by a return to the metaphor of sacrifice. It is, in the first place, clear that there is in the various New Testament accounts of the institution of the Lord's Supper a strong emphasis on sacrifice. Paul, Mark and Matthew alike link the cup with the covenant and with death, deliberately relating Jesus' death with an earlier covenantal sacrifice (1 Cor. 11.25f, Mk. 12.24, Mt. 26.28, cf Ex. 24.8); while Luke and almost certainly John make a direct link with the passover (Lk. 22.15, Jn. 19.14). Such differences as there are between the accounts are important in revealing the metaphorical character of the usages. They are not used in slavish dependence upon Old Testament meanings, but freely take up such aspects as enable the authors to draw out in different ways the redemptive significance of the event. It is one of the tragedies of church history that slavish use of categories, in the service of institutional ideology, insisted that the church's celebration of the event was literally a sacrifice. The point for us, however, is that the accounts of the institution of the sacrament do use sacrificial languuage but do so in the context of the other metaphors of atonement. Thus Paul links sacrifice with judgement and so, we might say, the eucharist with a renewal of baptism. In his somewhat obscure pastoral application of the words of institution he clearly implies a relation between celebration and judgement and, when it is duly celebrated, with salutary (transformative) judgement: 'when we are judged by the Lord we are chastened...' (1 Cor. 11.32). Similarly, Luke's use of passover rather than covenantal language links the supper with liberation, thus forming the obverse of his concern to show that the encounter with the demonic comes to a head in the passion of Jesus (see 22.40. 23.35–7).

In following up the implications of the narratives of institution, we must remember that the metaphor of sacrifice is at once the richest and the most difficult to handle conceptually – as the vagaries of church history again indicate – because, of all the language, it brings us closest not only to the historical action of God in Christ, but to the heart of his very being. Such a claim indeed justifies the concern that the church has always had for the integrity and centrality of the Lord's Supper (even though it has not always maintained them in the right way). It is not only, as is often pointed out – though the irony should be noted – the sacrament of unity; it is also the place where its community, in the image of the community that God is, is constituted by the Spirit who realises the presence of Christ anew in his world. When all this is said, however, the caveat already made in this section should be repeated. The actual shape the church's life and worship have taken is often a practical denial of such claims, making them appear the product of false consciousness. The challenge therefore recurs. Can the central conceptuality be reshaped under the impact of the historic sacrifice in such a way that the claims appear less hollow?

The sacrifice of Jesus, as we saw, must be understood on two levels. It is, on the one hand, the concentrated self-giving of God through the birth, life, death and resurrection of his incarnate Son. The Son, by a complete identification of himself with the world, even to death, does the work of the Father, and so mediates his eternal love for the world in the face of and in order to heal the world's evil. It is in that sense that it is necessary to speak of the lamb slain from the foundation of the world. However, in so speaking we do not peddle some mythology of a suffering God, but a theology of the (concentrated) taking place in time of the eternal loving world-directness of God the Son, taking form as the expression of the freedom of God to be both himself and incarnate for us. In that sense, all that Jesus does is the concentrated action of God: the taking place of the life of God, as love and judgement, in, with and for the world. On the other hand, at another level Jesus' self-sacrifice is, through the action of the Spirit, the concentrated offering of human life to the Father. To say that it is the Son's life is to say that is is representative of all life. The incarnate Son pours out his life so that the Spirit may lift unredeemed life into communion with God. Jesus is thus at once the realisation of the communion of creator with creature and of creature with creator.

The ecclesiological outcome, so to speak, is that the work of Christ and the Spirit is to create, in time and space, a living echo of the communion that God is in eternity. There emerges a notion of the church as the community that is created and called to be the finite embodiment of the eternal communion of Father, Son and Spirit. This conception is one that has been more influential in the thought of Eastern Orthodoxy than in the various strains of Western Christianity, for a number of reasons, among them the greater stress laid by the East on the doctrine of the Trinity and that by the West on the legal-institutional aspects of ecclesiology. The latter in its turn has helped to shape the dominance in Western liturgies of notions of sin and forgiveness, at the expense of a stress on both community and the wider dimensions of life in the world. Here we take up the theme promised at the end of the previous section, where it was recalled that the justifying work of God is directed not to human life alone, but to that in the context of God's loyalty to the whole creation. That dimension is taken up in a notion of communion which bursts the limits of human community, and spills over into the rest of the world. 'The eucharist is the great sacrifice of the whole creation ... (it) opens up the vision of the divine rule which has been promised as the final renewal of creation' (*Baptism, Eucharist and Ministry* 1982, 4.22).

Again we can only adumbrate the implications for the life of a community gathered around the Lord's Table. It has already been argued that the first calling of the church is the creation of reconciled forms of community, both for their own sake and for the sake of human community in general, as reflections of God's movement into the world in the incarnation. Human community is the gift of the God who is himself communion. The church is called to be the echo of the very being of God, and is enabled to be so as it is taken up in worship into the life of the Trinity.

PART V

NONCONFORMITY AND POLITICS

Introduction

The classic political issue for nonconformity in the nineteenth century had been the removal of nonconformist 'grievances' dating from the Act of Uniformity. The last step towards this was taken in 1898 when registered nonconformist chapels could appoint 'authorised persons' for the registration of marriages, removing the necessity for the civil registrar to attend a marriage in a nonconformist church. Under the influence of Edward Miall this piecemeal approach to particular issues had been supplemented in mid-century with the development of a campaign for the disestablishment of the Church of England – and also the Church of Scotland, though this never figured so largely in public discussion.

The campaign was not successful: the disestablishment of the Church of Ireland in 1869 was a political initiative by Gladstone, intended to outflank nonconformist elements in the Liberal party by presenting a proposal which they could not oppose but which did not go so far as they wished. In the 1890s the disestablishment of the Church of England in Wales was accepted by the Liberals as party policy; but this reflected a nationalist agenda which had nothing to do with nonconformity. Moreover the separation of the part of the Church of England, where it was most probably a minority, was likely to strengthen the rest of the Church.

In the last third of the century, however, a different issue came to the fore – education. The 1870 Education Act made possible the establishment of School Boards in those parts of England and Wales where there were not enough places for children under 14, elected by ratepayers and with the power to levy a rate for their support. By the Cowper-Temple clause the religious education in such schools was not to include any 'religious catechism or formulary distinctive of a particular denomination'. However, under clause 25 (which was never debated at the time) it was possible for church schools in School Board areas to seek rate-support, and from the early 1870s an increasing number did so. This enraged nonconformists, but their attempts to change the law were unsuccessful. Nevertheless the financial position of many church schools remained shaky. Education Office officials did not feel that it was affordable (or sensible) to develop a rate-funded education system which ignored existing church schools, and Balfour brought forward an Education Bill in 1902 to replace School Boards with Local Education Authorities on a county or county borough basis, which would support all schools in their area from the rates, with certain conditions for the rate support of church schools. Discussion of this bill occupied more parliamentary time than any previous non-Irish measure (this was before use of the guillotine had become normal for government legislation) and provoked keen nonconformist opposition. In particular, it did not address the problem of the 'single school area' – those rural areas where the parish school had sufficient accommodation for all children and it was therefore not possible to establish a School Board; indeed the provision of rate aid to such schools seemed to guarantee their perpetuation.

Even the Wesleyan Conference, the most conservative of Free Church bodies on political questions, opposed the lack of provision for nonconformist parents to avoid being driven to send their children to church (or 'denominational') schools (**V.1**). This was also significant because the Wesleyans had more elementary schools than any other Free Church; a large proportion of British and Foreign Schools Society schools (representing the older Free Churches) had been handed over to School Boards after 1870. At its most extreme local Free Church opposition to the 1902 Education Act took the form of 'passive resistance' – that is, refusal to pay the education rate, a self-conscious reminder of the refusal by many nonconformists to pay church rates in the mid-nineteenth century. The Revd Dr John Clifford of Westbourne Park Baptist Church, London, was probably the most famous passive resister.

The Education controversy helped to ensure a high nonconformist turnout in the 1906 General Election, when the Liberals secured a landslide victory. This marked the highest number of nonconformist MPs ever elected to the House of Commons – more than the total number of Conservatives. The Revd Sylvester Horne, a Congregational minister, wrote an article for the *Christian World* expressing nonconformist hopes for the new government (**V.2**). It reflected very clearly the belief that education had been a fundamental issue, with only a glancing reference to the Licensing Act of 1904, which also aroused opposition from temperance supporters. The government's attempts to reverse the Education Act took up a considerable amount of time between 1906 and 1908, and all resulted in failure in the House of Lords. The Wesleyan, John Scott Lidgett, commented on these problems as illustrated by the 1906 Bill (**V.3**). Eventually the House of Lords' rejection of the 'People's Budget' of 1909 precipitated the Parliament Act of 1910 to curb their power to veto legislation approved by the House of Commons, albeit after a second General Election in 1910 to meet the anxieties of the King. However, it is significant that the Congregational Union Assembly's resolution of 1909 (**V.4**) that supported some measure to curb the power of the House of Lords was still based entirely upon the Education question. In fact, nonconformist grievances in this area never were remedied by legislation: the Education Acts of 1918 and 1936 were concerned with other matters, and even the Education Act of 1944 did not directly deal with single school areas; but in the inter-war period the number of LEA county primary schools in rural areas increased, replacing church schools in several parishes and lessening their significance. Moreover by 1944 the decline of nonconformity, particularly in rural areas, had begun to take hold.

The dominance of the Education issue in nonconformity in these years did provoke some reaction. The anonymous book, *Nonconformity and Politics* (1909), summarised the essential argument (**V.5**). The Church, its author argued, had no role in politics; its primary task lay in the moral reformation of people. He did not condemn the activities of the 'institutional churches' in their neighbourhoods; but he did suggest that they too easily led to an assumption that political activity by the churches was inevitable and right. Interestingly the Conclusion suggested that there would be a place for a party of Right, which was solely devoted to the political achievement of Christian goals, though he thought that such a party would not be exclusively nonconformist in composition. It is impossible to judge how typical the views represented in the book were – the anonymity of the author suggests a belief that they would be unpopular; their primary interest lies in the fact that they were voiced. Moreover, other internal evidence suggests that the book came from the older Free Churches rather than Methodism, probably Congregationalism.

The Liberal government of 1906 had to deal with the disestablishment of the Welsh Church. The only immediate action was the appointment of a Royal Commission to investigate the state of the Welsh Church, which reported in 1909. The reduced Liberal majority in the 1910 elections meant that primary attention once more was focussed upon Irish Home Rule, because of the need for the support of Irish members. Nevertheless legislation to disestablish the Church of England in Wales was introduced in 1912, but defeated in the House of Lords. The Congregational Union Assembly in 1913 supported the reintroduction of the Bill under the Parliament Act (**V.6**). It was necessary to do this again in 1914, and the Bill was one of those passed under the Act at the outbreak of war to come into force when hostilities were concluded. In fact, when disestablishment did come in 1920, the precise terms were modified slightly from those approved in the 1914 Act without comment from the nonconformist churches. Densil Morgan suggests that for the majority of Welsh people 'disestablishment had become something of an anachronism if not an irrelevance'.[1]

At the end of the war a procedure was approved – somewhat unexpectedly – whereby the Church Assembly could legislate for the Church of England, without having to go through the time-consuming process of normal legislation. From 1919 Measures approved by the Church Assembly became law as a result of a single vote in each House of Parliament, after a preliminary review by a Joint Committee of both Houses. The Congregational Union Assembly in November 1919, expressed concern (**V.8**) at this delegation of parliamentary power, but without success.

The First World War changed the political scene decisively. The division of the Liberal Party in 1916, and more significantly the failure to heal it, made the extension of Lloyd George's ministry after the General Election of 1918 dependent on Conservative support. This accelerated the replacement of the Liberals by Labour on the left of British politics. The Labour Party also drew on significant reservoirs of nonconformist support, though there always had been some nonconformist support for the Conservatives which did not disappear.

The Labour support often came from Methodism. Jack Lawson, a member of the first Labour Government in 1924, represented the mining tradition from the north of England (**V.7**); George Thomas, a minister and Speaker of the House of Commons a generation later, represented the mining traditions of South Wales (**V.9**). For Lawson the die was cast before the First World War; for Thomas the critical period was the early 1920s. The shift to Labour took a generation to work through. Thus the formation of the Labour Representation Committee from Trade Unionist MPs and the Independent Labour Party in 1906, was probably as significant in the long run as the Liberal Landslide. This support for Labour lay behind the oft-quoted remark of Morgan Phillips, General Secretary of the Labour Party, in 1951 that 'the Labour Party owes as much to Methodism as to Marx'.

George Thomas referred to 'the agony of the General Strike'. That caused the cancellation of the 'May meetings' of the Baptist and Congregational Unions, but not the General Assembly of the Presbyterian Church of England. Its resolution on the matter (**V.10**) showed an underlying sympathy for the position of the miners and a feeling that the employers had been unreasonable, whilst characteristically appealing to everyone not to shut the doors on further negotiations. William Temple in the Church of England represented those bishops who were also critical of the employers, and Randall Davidson, as Archbishop of Canterbury, sought (unsuccessfully) to persuade the Government to steer a moderate course in the House of Lords. Since the Strike was called off after eight days, one can only speculate on what the churches' attitude might have been if the crisis had been prolonged further. However, they remained unsympathetic to the employers in the months following. The crisis did pose a question for the Churches, which perhaps had not been as sharp since the campaign to repeal the Corn Laws in the nineteenth century, namely how far they could comment effectively on issues which were technically concerned with economics – an issue which remained significant in the second half of the century. The General Strike raised in a new way the question of when economic pressure on the community becomes in effect a concerted challenge to the authority of government. That issue was only indirectly addressed in the Presbyterian resolutions.

The Church of England's programme of internal reform after the Enabling Act ran into a crisis when the Revised Prayer Book of 1927 failed to secure parliamentary approval. The discussion in the General Assembly of the Presbyterian Church of England illustrated the division of opinion over the matter (**V.11**); the resolution eventually adopted declined to condemn the Book, but called upon the bishops to make sure that usages outside its scope were suppressed. The Congregational Union by contrast passed a resolution of unqualified disapproval. This was the last occasion when the internal affairs of the Church of England were the subject of debate within nonconformist assemblies.

Nonconformists were also discovering that they needed parliamentary legislation for some of their internal affairs. This first became clear in the opening years of the century when the attempt of the Free Church of Scotland and the United Presbyterian Church to unite without supporting parliamentary legislation exposed the United Free Church to a successful legal challenge from the Free Church minority. The Churches (Scotland) Act of 1905 was necessary to set things right. Consequently when the three smaller Methodist bodies came together in 1907 to form the United Methodist Church, parliamentary legislation was used to settle many of the details. A crisis developed in the late 1920s in the Salvation Army.[2] William Booth had placed succession to the office of General in the gift of the current General. He nominated his son, Bramwell Booth, who succeeded in 1912. In 1928 Bramwell became ill, and the question of the succession became increasingly urgent. There were already those who wished to change the system of nomination by the General; Bramwell resisted these suggestions. In 1929 a meeting of the Army High Council was convened which, after various legal proceedings, decided to remove the General on grounds of ill health and elect a successor in

February. Bramwell died in June 1929. But this exposed the fact that his three executors became trustees of all the Salvation Army's assets vested in his name. It was clear that a new structure was required which substituted election of the General by the High Council for nomination by the previous General, fixed a retirement age for the General, and set up a Trustee Company to hold the assets of the Army. These were the purposes of the Salvation Army Act of 1931, which went through parliament as a Private Bill (**V.12**).

The affairs of the European churches rarely figured in nonconformist discussions until the inter-war period. The Presbyterian Church of England had been one of the churches most aware of the European dimension of church life, partly because of long-standing links with the Waldensian Church in Italy. It was characteristic therefore that it was that Church which first registered concern about the effects of Hitler's coming to power in 1933 on the German churches. Their resolution of 1933 (**V.13**) also reflected the abiding interest of W. T. Elmslie in the European Churches. However, their resolutions on the Jews five years later (**V.14**) neatly illustrated the difficulties the churches had in coming to terms with anti-Semitism in practice as well as in principle. It was easy to deplore anti-Semitism, and this resolution was passed before the 'Kristallnacht' attacks on synagogues in November 1938. But the Presbyterians also had a long-standing Fund and Committee for evangelism among the Jews; so the second resolution was passed, even though seventy years later the combination of the two seems incongruous. Several other Free Churches were expressing concern by 1938–39. After the war the churches took a more direct part in the process of reconciliation. In 1957 the International Congregational Council established a link with the Church of the Palatinate in Germany, which united Lutheran and Reformed (**V.17**). This was carried forward by the Congregational Union, and continued through the United Reformed Church.

The structural resolution of the main matters in the Education controversy, unresolved in the first decade of the century, was achieved by R. A. Butler's Education Act of 1944. The provision of compulsory religious worship and education in schools, subject to parental rights of withdrawal, largely ended the controversy that had characterised the earlier period. The Agreed Syllabuses for Religious Education, beginning with Cambridgeshire in 1924, showed that it was possible for Anglicans and nonconformists to reach agreement. But not all was sweetness and light at the time, as Albert Peel's editorial paragraph in the *Congregational Quarterly* (**V.15**) shows. There were equally discontented Anglican voices.

Attitudes to the state were changing, however. A third Anglican Commission on Church and State reported in 1949, though nothing substantial was done to implement its recommendations. It did provoke a Report from the Free Church Federal Council on *The Free Churches and the State* (1953). This showed that fears that simple disestablishment of the Church of England would involve a secularisation of the state were starting to worry Free Church thinkers as well (**V.16**). The Church of England had used this argument rhetorically for more than half a century, with the example of France prominent in people's minds. Now the

Free Churches began to wrestle with the question of how England could remain an identifiably Christian country without a public Christian presence. No solutions were offered.

The 1950s were also a period of transition in colonial affairs. The missionary involvement of the churches led to a concern about developments in Africa, and the twin issues of apartheid in South Africa and the independence of British colonies provoked comment. The Congregational Union resolutions on South Africa and the Central African Federation of 1960 (**V.18**) were typical of many, and the concern over South Africa was accentuated after the Sharpeville massacre in 1961.

Almost inevitably the tercentenary of the Act of Uniformity in 1962 provided the opportunity for rethinking or re-presenting some of the issues involved in a later twentieth-century context. The Affirmation of the Congregational Union Assembly in 1962 (**V.19**) illustrated both the movement, and the limits to movement, that ecumenical developments had brought. These are considered more fully in Part VIII. The inevitability of parliamentary legislation for any church union, and indeed for other matters connected with church property, was accepted. The Baptist and Congregational Trusts Act of 1951 and the Sharing of Church Buildings Act of 1969 are examples of the latter.

In 1976, when Anglican–Methodist union was no longer an immediate possibility, the Methodist Church secured an Act of Parliament to empower the Conference to make certain changes which the original Methodist Church Act of 1929 had not allowed (**V.20**). This gave the Methodist Conference control over its own doctrine – or rather made it impossible for any future dissentient group to claim property from the Methodist Church on the ground that the doctrinal standards of the Church no longer corresponded to the Deed of Union; and it also made possible a restructuring of the government of the Church.[3] By contrast the only doctrinal reference in the United Reformed Church Acts of 1972 and 1981 came in the first purpose for which trustees hold places used for religious worship: 'The public worship of God according to the principles and usages for the time being of the United Reformed Church.'

By the end of the twentieth century, therefore, relations between church and state had changed significantly. The privileged position of the Church of England consisted more in matters of social precedence and the position of bishops in the House of Lords than in substantial political influence. The issue of disestablishment had virtually disappeared from Free Church life, although the Free Churches continued to affirm the distinction between the powers of government in church and state. With the development of indigenous Islam, Hinduism, Sikhism and Buddhism as a result of Commonwealth immigration to Britain, the key issue became whether Christianity as such, rather than any particular church, should have a privileged position in British society.

The two nonconformist Labour Prime Ministers of the second half of the century came from interestingly different backgrounds: Harold Wilson was an academic economist; Jim Callaghan was a Trade Unionist. Both of them also came from the older Free Churches. Wilson was a Congregationalist (**V.21**) and Jim Callaghan began as a Baptist (**V.22**). Both their wives came from similar backgrounds.

Wilson's experience at Oxford illustrated the significance of nonconformist student societies (**I.13**) in holding people together who were away from home for the first time. Callaghan went into the Inland Revenue, another example of nonconformist upward social mobility. Baptist church contacts facilitated his settlement in Maidstone, again a move away from home; but Callaghan did not retain Wilson's active commitment. What is perhaps most unexpected, but also significant, is that Callaghan's successor as Prime Minister, Margaret Thatcher, also had a nonconformist background (**V.23**). Thatcher's background was Methodist and her father was a shopkeeper. Her memoirs show that their family stood out because of its staunch Conservatism even when she was a child. However, she too valued the Methodist Society at Oxford as a home from home. Like Callaghan, she moved away from her church background in later life. This period sequence of Prime Ministers with nonconformist origins may even have facilitated the approval at the highest level of new ways of freeing the Church of England from effective government control – for example, in the method for the nomination of bishops by the Prime Minister introduced by Callaghan in 1978.

The position of Wilson, Callaghan and Thatcher (and other leading political figures such as Selwyn Lloyd or David Blunkett) illustrated the 'generational lag' in nonconformist history in the later twentieth century. Their formative period was before the Second World War, before nonconformist decline intensified. At the end of the century it is not easy to see possible successors. The period after the Second World War reflected the increasing marginalisation of nonconformity in politics. This was partly a result of decline and partly a consequence of the difficulty of mobilising 'the nonconformist conscience' in late twentieth-century politics. Nonconformity was not all 'on the same side'. In the nineteenth century, nonconformist political involvement was primarily driven by the determination to eliminate discrimination against them; when that goal was achieved, no other single one could command such comprehensive political allegiance.

Notes

1. Sell & Cross (2003), p. 79; D. D. Morgan (1999), pp. 30–37, 78–81.
2. F. Coutts (1973), pp. 79–101.
3. G. W. Dolbey (1978).

Document V.1

The Education Act, 1902

Minutes of the Wesleyan Methodist Conference, 1902.

Methodism had its stake in Primary Education with 900 schools in 1875, most of which were absorbed into the state system after 1902. The Government's alienation of Wesleyan Methodism by its legislation of 1902 indicates how deep the rift with nonconformity was, particularly because of its failure to tackle the 'single school area' problem, those places where there was no alternative to a Church of England school.

Education Bill. 1902

The Conference once more declares that the primary object of Methodist policy in the matter of Elementary Education is the establishment of School Boards everywhere, acting in districts of sufficient area, and the placing of a Christian unsectarian school within reasonable distance of every family. The Conference, therefore, deeply regrets that the present Education Bill is intended to destroy the School Board system, and to make no adequate provision for the just claims of those parents who do not desire their children to be driven into denominational schools. The Conference has no wish to abolish the denominational schools, or to prevent them from being used, with equitable restrictions, for the purpose of giving denominational education to those children whose parents desire it. But the Conference expresses once more its deep conviction that no increased grant from public funds is accompanied by adequate and representative public management. If, however, denominational schools are to be almost wholly maintained from imperial taxes and local rates, the irreducible minimum of the right of conscience and of public justice demands that at least a majority of the local education authority and of the governing Committee of every school shall consist of publicly elected persons.

Document V.2

Nonconformists and the Liberal Landslide, 1906

C. Sylvester Horne, 'A Free Church Parliament', *The Christian World*, 1 February, 1906.

C. Sylvester Horne was a Congregational minister, who later became MP for Ipswich, 1910–14. The significance attached to the Education Act in explaining the result is striking.

The Education Act, according to the late Cardinal Vaughan, was the triumph of the Conservative Government over the Nonconformists. The General Election is the triumph of the Nonconformists over the late Conservative Government. The great fact about the new political situation is that more English and Welsh Free Churchman have been returned to Parliament than members of the Tory party. If we add the Scotch Free Churchmen the numbers are still more impressive. It is a marvellous result, and emphasizes anew our indebtedness to the Education Acts. They were designed to destroy us, and they consolidated our ranks and taught us strategy into the bargain. We had not realised that we could compete with our adversaries in the battle for the Parliamentary machine. We have never lacked spokesmen in the House of Commons for many a long year, and men of distinction to boot. But for the first time we are adequately represented, and our influence in the national life is reflected in our preponderance in the political counsels of the nation. I have been lately pointing out to the electors that if we had the Church test in the highest branch of our civil service which we have reintroduced into the teaching profession, we should be in a strange predicament. For 'C-B' could not be Premier, nor Mr Asquith Chancellor of the Exchequer, nor Sir Robert Reid Lord Chancellor, nor Mr Bryce Minister for Ireland, nor Lloyd-George at the Board of Trade, nor John Burns at the Local Government Board, nor Augustine Birrell at the Board of Education, nor Mr Haldane at the War Office, nor John Morley at the India Office. In fact, it is a Government of Nonconformists from the Episcopal Church. And it has been acclaimed in all sorts of circles as the strongest of modern Ministries. A sectarian test would have tariffed out the men of the best brain and character among our statesmen. We shall not be satisfied until all the branches of our civil service are as free and open to men of merit as the highest positions are.

It was inevitable that our Nonconformist M.P.s at this time should be found in the ranks of Liberalism. Indeed, the one or two Nonconformists who supported the late Government have paid the penalty. All his personal popularity and local influence could not save Colonel Pilkington, while his mercantile interest in Workington could not avail Sir John Randles. Never has Nonconformity been so deeply moved, and never so splendidly united. There were, of course, exceptional cases. Sparkhill Free Churchmen did not desert Mr Austen Chamberlain, who has made much of the fact that he is a Nonconformist. But such a case is the nature of the exception that proves the rule. *The Times* was careful to explain that even Mr Chaplin had 'fallen a victim to Nonconformist animosity.' This is good news, for it means that education counted in the struggle even more than Free Trade. We could not help noting also that the most outspoken and determined Nonconformists won the greatest victories. Mr George White's feat was phenomenal. In an agricultural constituency he raised a majority of 450 to one of 2,800. George White was the Parliamentary leader of passive resistance. He preached the doctrine through the Eastern Counties with the greatest determination. We used to be told that the average elector had no sympathy with these extremists. The answer is that something like thirty prominent passive resisters have been returned to the new Parliament; that Wales, the 'nation of passive resisters,' has beaten all political records by sending an unbroken phalanx of staunch Liberals to represent her in the National Assembly; and that such conspicuous leaders as Lloyd-George and George White have received unparalleled majorities. Evidently the people want a final settlement of the lines of educational progress; and they realise that the reform must be drastic if it is to be final. The more their candidates hated the Education Acts, the more enthusiastic the constituencies generally were for their candidates. All this is a phenomenon which cannot be lost upon the new Administration. There are men among them who have never shown any real appreciation of the plea for religious liberty. But we believe the verdict of the constituencies will give them food for thought.

THE CHRISTIAN WORLD was good enough to allow me to appeal, some two years back, for a larger representation of Nonconformity in the next Parliament. My letters at that time were misunderstood by some to be a plea for an independent Nonconformist party. That was never contemplated. But one result was that many more leading Free Churchmen did come forward, and undertook to fight constituencies. At that time we feared that all the promising constituencies were pre-engaged; but events have proved the truth of what was so freely said at the time, that to a good fighting candidate nothing was impossible. We could quote the tribute of a Liberal in a high position that of all candidates young Free Churchmen were the most welcome. The constituencies trust them. They know that they will not try to plunder the public purse to subsidise Nonconformist institutions. They recognise in most of them the true Puritan fibre, and the fearless democratic principle. They are men who can be relied upon to go straight, and do their duty. Moreover they are not Whigs; their place is rather left than right. They are among the advanced Radicals for the most part; and they will seek in Parliament to take the straightest line to the positions indicated in their campaign.

Well, once again in English story, we have an organised army of Puritans; well equipped, and animated by a resolute spirit. It has been called into being by the same motive as of old; the sense of liberty in danger, and the imperative need to reform the Commonwealth. We cannot forget, today, how Cromwell's men saved the Parliamentary side from betrayal by the laodiceans. There are always some faint-hearted souls among us whose aim is not the triumph of a cause, but a weak accommodation. In Cromwell's day, these trimmers would have sacrificed all the fruits of victory by an inglorious compromise. Their heart was not in the business on which they were ostensibly bent. The nation got its way nevertheless, thanks to the Independents. It is just possible that the Free Church rank and file will have to play a similar part in the new epoch. We shall not allow ourselves to be robbed of the fruits of victory by faint-hearted Whigs, who are all for a quiet life. We do not want to have to continue the struggle, but we are prepared for it if need be sooner than betray the democratic cause. And we may not forget that this wonderful parliament has a large mandate; and that living problems confront it. In Cromwell's day there was an English yeomanry on the soil, 'men of a spirit,' among whom he found the ablest lieutenants for the national cause. We want a new English yeomanry and a more independent peasantry, and this means a measure of Land Reform that will inaugurate a new era in social England. For this we shall need courage, patience, and wisdom; and we have faith that we shall find these qualities in our Free Church members. We expect great things from our Liberal leaders, but even greater things from the rank and file. Within a few months we hope to see rural Nonconformity effectually safeguarded from some of its strongest persecutions; and new security of tenure guaranteed to our Free Church peasants and yeomen in whom the hope of England lies.

Document V.3

Scott Lidgett and the Education Bill of 1906

John Scott Lidgett, *My Guided Life* (London: Methuen, 1936), pp. 187–90.

John Scott Lidgett, Wesleyan minister at the Bermondsey Settlement in London, played an important mediating role between the Church of England and the Free Churches on educational matters between 1902 and 1944, so far as party politics made it possible. His account of the problems faced by the new Liberal Government in 1906 is revealing, not least in identifying the problem of Roman Catholic schools and the Liberal need to secure their support.

The Government was pledged to bring in an Education Bill to establish complete popular control over all forms of education as its first legislative measure. Mr Birrell was President of the Board of Education, and the Cabinet at once appointed a sub-committee to prepare the Bill. Mr Lloyd George was a member of this sub-committee, and was deputed to keep in special touch with certain Free Church leaders, among whom, of course, Dr Clifford was prominent ... So far as the House of Commons was concerned, the crucial difficulty lay with the treatment of the Roman Catholic Schools, in view of the necessity of, at least, disarming the opposition, and, if possible, securing the support of the Irish Parliamentary Party. In order to accomplish this feat, the at that time famous Clause 4 of the Bill was devised, which, under cover of complete popular control, sought to give, by indirect means, some sort of guarantee to the Roman Catholics that the denominational character of the teaching staff and the special atmosphere of their schools would be, for the most part, preserved. Another difficulty that was immediately encountered by the Government was the unwillingness of the ordinary Englishman to proceed to extremes. I remember Mr Birrell telling me soon after the introduction of the Bill that an official at a country railway-station had said to him, 'I voted Liberal at the Election, but now I think you are going too far.' And beyond all these difficulties stood the House of Lords! ...

In these circumstances it was no easy task to pilot the ship of the National Free Church Council. The task became the more difficult when the late Mr J. Hirst Hollowell formed a special fighting organization to resist all concessions, and, in particular, to defeat the obnoxious Clause 4. Mr Hollowell had been a Congregational minister at Nottingham, and a member of its School Board. He had subsequently given up his ministry to form the Northern Education League, and his ideals for English education were entirely based upon the model of the United States. It is literally true that Clause 4 killed him, for its defeat was a matter of life and death to him. I remember meeting him in the street during that spring, looking haggard and distraught. I enquired, 'What is the matter?' 'I am not sleeping', was his reply. 'Clause 4?' I asked. 'Yes', he answered. Shortly after that he had a stroke, and, this being followed by another, he died before the conflict was over. Dr Clifford was another source of difficulty; for while his usual answer, when sounded as to some concession, was, 'If it be put upon us, we must submit to it, for we cannot expect to get everything at once,' this attitude, in private, did not prevent him from taking immediate and public action to prevent it from being 'put upon us'.

So the swaying battle went on throughout the spring and summer and autumn, the Government being forced into concession after concession, first in the Commons and then in the Lords, in order to convert the illusive Clause 4 into something that could be accepted as a practical guarantee by the Roman Catholics. The process continuously undermined the support of the political Nonconformists, while it did not allay the opposition of the Conservative Party, then entrenched in the House of Lords. So the situation was almost hopeless when the Bill went to the Upper House in the late autumn. The Archbishop of Canterbury took full advantage of the situation with astute statesmanship, directed, in part, to making the Bill tolerable to denominationalists, and, in part, to securing for the schools of the National Society conditions at least as advantageous as those to be tacitly accorded to the Roman Catholics. Thus Lord Crewe, the Liberal leader in the House of Lords, was placed in an impossible position. A conflict between the two Houses over the mutilated Bill took place, and on the eve of Christmas 1906 the Government withdrew the measure.

Document V.4

Congregationalists and Education, 1909

Congregational Year Book, 1910, p. 28.

The successive failures of the Government to carry its Education Bills in 1906, 1907 and 1908 led to this resolution at the Congregational Union Assembly on 12 May 1909, which was carried unanimously. The House of Lords was identified as the crucial problem.

That this Assembly, profoundly and justifiably disappointed that the most powerful Liberal Parliamentary majority of modern times has not secured the fulfilment of its pledges to solve the education problem on democratic lines of efficient public control, freedom for the teachers from ecclesiastical and theological tests, and removal of all statutory foothold for sectarianism in the schools, is nevertheless satisfied that the chief hindrance to such a solution is the irresponsible veto of the House of Lords, and earnestly assures the Government of its unwavering support in their determination to break down this barrier to educational and other progress, and to make the will of the people supreme.

Document V.5

Another View of Nonconformity and Politics, 1909

A Nonconformist Minister, *Nonconformity and Politics* (London: Sir Isaac Pitman & Sons Ltd, 1909), pp. 192–223.

The extent to which nonconformists were involved in the education controversy, which Scott Lidgett noted as being damaging to the Free Church Council, produced its reaction, though the author of this book significantly felt it wise to remain anonymous. This extract from the final chapter is interesting in reaffirming the central contention that the Church had no concern with politics and also suggesting that there might be a place for a party of Right, which would seek to pursue Christian goals in politics.

(1)

The change for which the writer would plead has been already more than once suggested or implied. The Nonconformist Churches need to realise afresh their own constitutive idea – to realise afresh that the Church exists solely for the sake of spiritual ideals, for the sake of making character, for the sake of inspiring and creating goodness, for the sake of persuading to those exercises and cultures of the soul by means of which goodness can be obtained. And in saying this, it is necessary to insist once more on a distinction made at the outset of this book – a distinction between the activity of the Church as such and the activity of individual Christian men ...

The particular application of the general principle in regard to the subject with which we are dealing, the fundamental fact to be ceaselessly remembered, is that the Church, as such, has no concern with political affairs ... This is not to say (and one needs, at some risk of monotony, to re-emphasise this, because the present contention is so often misrepresented, and, having been misrepresented, answered by a sneer) this is not to say that the *individual church-member* has not, or may not have, any concern with politics. But it is as a citizen, not as a church-member, that his political functions devolve upon him. Care was taken at the outset to guard against the conception of the large world as a sphere of evil from which the true man must stand aloof. This is the conception of Plymouth Brethrenism and of some kindred types of religious life and thought; but there is nothing in the contentions of this book that points that way. On the contrary, it is held that the individual church-member, having given himself up to, and profited by, the spiritual ministries of his Church, will be all the better equipped for the tasks of citizenship, and will throw himself into political affairs (if it be on political lines he elects to serve his day and generation) with all the greater wisdom, with all the worthier motive, and with all the purer and more unselfish aspirations for the general social good. Also – as there will presently be occasion to insist from another point of view – in the contention that direct interference of the Church with political affairs lies outside the Church's constitutive idea, there is no depreciation of zeal for the poor and oppressed, no denial of the fact that the service of man is an essential part of the service of God. It is by confusing the issue on this point, though, of course, it is not deliberately done, that the fiery advocates of political activity on the Church's part often seek to maintain their case. Religious people have thought too much about the mere saving of their own souls – so runs the conventional cry of the day – and by way of putting this right, it is the Church's duty to take up the mission of influencing the political life of the nation for good and to determine legislation in the direction of elevating the masses of men. The premise may be admitted; but the conclusion does not follow. Religious people may have forgotten their duty to their fellow-men – but the inference is simply this, that *they* must now remember it in the sphere where it ought to be remembered, not that *the Church* as such, must remember it. It is part of the Church's task to teach the duty of mutual service, inasmuch as the service of man is an essential part of goodness itself...

(2)

It is impossible, however, not to see that in discussing the matter on these lines, one is brought into contact with another topic – a topic more closely related, indeed, to the main topic of these pages than may at first sight appear, and yet a topic not quite the same. In insisting that the Church's one mission is to make men and women good, and that all other enterprises are outside its formative idea, is one not condemning a good many things besides that political absorption which has through this book been the principal matter in hand? The Church in its collective and corporate capacity bends itself to a good many tasks now. It frequently enters, for instance, upon a definite social mission, supplies itself with a whole apparatus for such a mission, takes up those thousand lines of activity which 'institutional Churches' have made so familiar in our time. Nonconformist Churches, in many instances, become not only Churches, but clubs, friendly societies, recreation rooms, employment bureaux, and much else, touching at countless points the lives and fortunes of those who worship there. Are all these things also outside the Church's constitutive idea? If they are, are they to be condemned? If they are not to be condemned, on what ground can they be consistently spared from condemnation?

There is no irrelevance in turning aside for a brief dealing with the point. As a matter of fact, it is the social mission which the Nonconformist Churches are taking up that not seldom drives them further; and political activity is added to social activity under the pressure of motives not at all difficult to comprehend. Undoubtedly Nonconformity's adoption of the 'institutional Church' has accentuated Nonconformity's political tendency; and it is only natural that this should be the case. In the Church's endeavours to ameliorate the lot of those whom its 'social' agencies touch with a helping and healing hand, the Church necessarily comes close to many evils that call aloud to heaven, and evils which it appears that only drastic legislation can cure. It is small wonder that the Churches which carry on their 'social' work under conditions such as these and in sight of the many glaring iniquities of the social order should pass on, having done what in them lies to assist the suffering ones, to make their power felt in the political sphere for the carrying out of what so many of their members consider needed political reforms. That political action of the kind is to be the concern of individuals, not of the corporate religious associations, has already been insisted on, and reasons for the contention have been given. It has to be said now that there is no *inevitable* step from the 'social' activities of the Churches to the political activities into which the Churches so often allow themselves to be borne. The reason why the step from the first to the second very frequently follows lies in this – that the Churches fail to realise wherein the only justification for their 'social' activity lies. The social work of the Church, just as much as its political work, is, as a matter of fact, outside the Church's constitutive idea; but for the social work excuse and justification can be pleaded which are not available to give the political work any legitimate status; and it is in an apprehension of this fact that the safeguard lies ...

The Church, then, is not primarily an agency for dealing with the problems of the social order or of social life. But the Christian – the individual Christian man – remains under an immediate and pressing duty to do all that lies in his power for the welfare of his fellows ...

(3)

... The fact that Christian men have not played their due part, throws back upon the Church the duty of stepping into the breach. For the problem *must* be attended to, if the mind and intention of Christ are to be worked out, if the implications of Christ's gospel are to be realised ; and if they who should be eager volunteers in this service hang back, the Church must press to the front. It may not be – according to the fundamental contention of this book, it is not – any part of the Church's original and constitutive idea to put her hand directly to the task of social reform; but in face of clamant necessity, there is assuredly no wrong in her doing so – the wrong would be rather perpetrated if she still refused. She can find ample warrant for adaptability to the new conditions in the general implications of the spirit of Christ, if not in any particular clause of the charter on which she founds. Moreover, in the special matter just now under discussion, the Church cannot be faithful to her own constitutive idea unless she steps beyond its immediate requirements (a point which, like the other, does not hold good in regard to the Church's intrusion into the political realm): she cannot save the souls of men unless she ministers also to other parts of human nature; and she may, besides, be the more urgently impelled to the additional task by the thought that somehow she has failed to imbue her members with a true spirit, and must make her own failure good. She has not made nor inspired the workmen, and must consequently put her own hand to the plough. If there be any risks in thus widening her scope, she must take them, guarding against them by added watchfulness and prayer. The justification for the Church's interference in social matters – for the Church's devoting herself to activities of the social or 'institutional' kind – lies in the fact that if she holds her hand, there is no other power in the field by which the ministries so sadly neglected will in the worthiest spirit be performed. It is possible, as hinted earlier, that all this may be looked upon as having comparatively little practical bearing after all. Since it is the Church's task now – since it has become the Church's task – to take up and solve the problem of social service, it matters little, it may be said, how the task has come into the Church's hands. The present writer believes that it matters a great deal.

For one thing, if it be realised that this attacking of the social problem is, as it were, an extra task, there will be no reproach for him who feels that his call is not along that particular line, and that it is in more directly spiritual ways that he is to expend his strength. Reference has been previously made to the fact that non-political ministers are looked upon askance. The same thing is true as to ministers who do not give themselves to the 'institutional' activities of modern Nonconformity. It cannot be denied that there is a sort of bigotry of social service abroad in a good many quarters, and that the social side of the Church's enterprises is at times exalted as if it were the only thing worthy of care. A realisation of the true position will bring about a ready acknowledgment of the usefulness, nay, of the absolute necessity, of the men who remain upon what are too slightingly called the old ways.

But more important still – and this is the point to which all that has been said concerning the Church's social service is meant to lead up – by realising the true facts of the situation the Church will be saved from passing over to that political activity which too often follows when social activity has been taken up. It was said that the social mission in which the Nonconformist Churches are so earnestly engaging not seldom drives them further; and by the adoption of the 'institutional' idea Nonconformity's political tendencies have been strengthened to a very great degree. This is in a manner natural, and yet it need not occur. The 'institutional' idea can be saved, without being allowed to become a force thrusting the Church into the political field ... But even amid the new enthusiasms, the Church, remembering its first and greatest call, will keep the old enthusiasm too, and, if it become all things to all men, will do so only in order that it may save (in that sense of the word which in these days the word is nearly losing) that it may save some. And then, with the first downward step avoided, the second will in all probability be avoided too. At any rate, if the Church accept her social mission simply as the extra task which in truth it is, she will in the discharge of it refuse to let herself be taken yet further away from her own constitutive idea ...

(4)

The fundamental assertion, then, may be made once more. The Nonconformist Churches need to come back to a realisation of their own fundamental idea. And, according to that fundamental idea, the Church and politics belong to different spheres.

There is, indeed, one way in which a nation's activities and religion might be brought into a relation of a direct and positive kind. It was said some time since that if the 'kingdom' really did signify a perfect social and political ordering of things, then not only would there be a distinctive political and social mission allowed to the Church as such, but it would become the Church's binding duty to take it up. Even then, however – it must be added, – it would not be by the identification of any

Church, or any number of Churches, with any of the present political parties that the thing could be done. It would be done only by the formation of a party of conscience, a religious party in the wide signification of the term. And, though the 'kingdom' does *not* mean a perfect social and political order, and the matter cannot therefore be urged from that particular point of view, yet it is for some element of the indicated kind in the national life that a good many wait and hope ...

For in all that has been said concerning the mistake of Nonconformity's political absorption, there has been no implication that religion and a nation's activities must be always things apart. The Church, in its corporate capacity, has no concern with politics as the parties of the day understand and pursue them. That remains. The individual church-member may, if he feel himself called, take a share in the party political energies of his time. That remains. And in this latter way some connection between religion and politics is made – at any rate, the presence of religious men in the political parties, to the purifying and ennobling of the parties themselves, is secured. But it were better still if the nation had in its midst a party of Right – a party to which the best men in all parties might gradually be drawn. And thus would be made a connection between religion and politics – or rather, between religion and the activities of the nation, so far as the party of Right swayed and moulded them – that would be vital and fraught with measureless good.

For, indeed, one of the saddest things in the national life is the absolute rule allowed to the idea of expediency; and one of the lessons most needful to be learnt is that it is a nation's first business, in all its greater affairs, to seek for the one entirely right course, as distinct from the course that is safer, or most profitable, or directed along the line of least resistance ... There is, therefore, no important question of national action on which the conscience should not have the final and decisive word. Such a connection between politics and religion as is implied in a party of Right – a party devoted before all else to the emphasising of this truth – would be a connection of mightiest power in the nation's life. It would be the relating, not of the Church as such, but of Christian men, with the nation's affairs; and it would be by so much better a thing than the participation of Christian men in the present party strife as religion as a regnant and dominant force is better than religion as a mere flavouring in something stronger than itself. If politics and religion are to be vitally related to all, it can only be through the existence and working of a party of Right.

It would not be a Nonconformist party, of course. But surely not even the most political Nonconformist would contend for that, or would regret finding at his side, as he strove for the Right's victory in national affairs, men of a Church not his own. Such a party would draw into its ranks all the best men of all the Church organisations, and the best of many organisations that are not Churches at all in the common acceptation of the term. It would be the visible assertion of the rightful supremacy of conscience in the affairs of the world ... The present writer, at any rate, does not think that the formation of a definitely Christian party in the State is altogether the visionary thing that some hold it to be. He believes that such a party would unite many of the differences which now prevail. And if there were any sign of the establishment of such a party, he would hail the day as the beginning of a new era in which progress and religion would be really one. The taking up of politics into religion he holds to be in this sense a quite possible thing.

(5)

And yet he does not know. It may be a vain dream. It will be no more than a dream, certainly, so long as Nonconformity keeps those scales upon its eyes which blind it to the dangers of that political course on which it runs with feet so willing and swift. ... No one is able, or needs, to prophesy what the result would be. It may be that the party of Right would be born: it may be that it would not. One cannot tell.

But if not a single Nonconformist changed his political views, the gain to corporate Nonconformity would nevertheless be incalculable. For once more Nonconformity would be what it set out to be – the clear-voiced witness to goodness and to God, with no message to deliver save the message which bids men be worthy children of their Father in Heaven. Once again its atmosphere would be that of the Temple rather than that of the committee-room and the hustings. Once again it would make saints. Surely they who love it will see to it. Nonconformity in its political absorption has wandered far, and must come home ...

Document V.6

Welsh Disestablishment, 1913

Congregational Year Book, 1914, p. 6.

The Parliament Act became law in 1910, but ironically no education measure was introduced under it. Instead priority was given to Irish Home Rule and the disestablishment of the Church in Wales. This resolution of the Congregational Union Assembly on 8 May 1913 was carried unanimously, and marks the first reintroduction of the Welsh Church Bill after its failure in 1912.

The Assembly of the Congregational Union of England and Wales thanks the Government for reintroducing under the Parliament Act the Bill for the Disestablishment and Disendowment of the State Church in Wales. The Assembly urges the Government to secure the passage of the Bill into law at the earliest date possible, and further urges upon the Government to resist in justice to the demands of the Welsh people any further change or concession in the provisions of the Bill, believing as it does that its passage into law will bring peace where too long there has been religious strife, and will liberate the disestablished Church for more fruitful service in the Kingdom of Christ.

Document V.7

Methodism and the Early Labour Party

Jack Lawson, *A Man's Life* (London: Hodder & Stoughton, 1932), pp. 111–13.

Jack Lawson began his working life as a miner; he attended Ruskin College, Oxford, and was urged to enter the University and take a degree. But he returned to the pits and later became an MP, holding office in the first Labour Government of 1924. Here he paints a picture of Methodism in the northern coalfields.

Their hymns and sermons may have been of another world, but the first fighters and speakers for unions, Co-op. Societies, political freedom, and improved conditions, were Methodist preachers. That is beyond argument. And the gospel expressed in social terms has been more of a driving-power in northern mining circles than all the economic teaching put together. Room for criticism there may be, but that the eighteenth century Revival has been a motive power in the personal, domestic, and social life in the Kingdom of Collieries is beyond doubt. And here and now I wish to pay my tribute to that movement, and to the humble people who composed the Society of Methodists, which I joined in my youth, and of which I remain a loyal member to this day. It was composed of men and women who in many cases had received no education worth speaking of, but who had become really cultured, though their reading was limited to certain schools of thought.

One there was who would sing you a 'spiritual' or equally a comic song in fine style, or he would preach a sermon. Others would lead a choir, play the organ or piano, or preach a sermon. One, who had only been taught by his wife to read when he was in his thirties, used to wait for me when I was putting and he was hewing at the same flat. As we went 'out bye', my pony trotting before, we would talk books while we walked, bent double in the dark roadway. I remember well when this elderly man first struck Nietzsche. That was a 'find' – and I also remember how the man turned me upside down mentally. Which was all to my good.

This man read the New Testament in Greek, and oratorios were as easy to him as the latest song is to the man in the street. Many of the members of course were illiterate, but they were fine types of men and women, and had individuality – and that is not a common thing. All, even the most ordinary – or, if you like, ignorant as far as education goes – all of them were 'something'. Methodism took the 'nobodies', and made the most humble and hopeless 'somebody'. They set aside the things that are not good for a man; they had some little pride in their dress; they made their homes to be things of beauty, and aspired and worked to give their children a better life and opportunity than themselves. They are as a whole among the best men and women I have ever known …

Document V.8

The Enabling Bill, 1919

Congregational Year Book, 1920, pp. 63–4.

The Autumnal Assembly of the Congregational Union on 20 November 1919 passed the following resolution on the Church of England Assembly (Powers) Bill, which gave the Church Assembly power to legislate for the Church of England under specified conditions. The reference to 'life and liberty' in the final clause was probably intended to allude to the Life and Liberty Movement within the Church of England which had campaigned for the bill.

That this meeting of the Congregational Union of England and Wales, while rejoicing in the desire of the Established Church for fuller spiritual development assisted by more self-government, is strongly opposed to the Enabling Bill, the provisions of which, while leaving undisturbed the Church's establishment by law, involve the 'surrender by Parliament of the authority which it has exercised since the Papal supremacy was abrogated.' This meeting records its conviction that, so long as the Church retains the privileges and dignities of establishment and is maintained by vast national funds, the proposed abolition of Parliamentary control is unjust; and urges that the fullest life and liberty for the Church can only with propriety be obtained by complete severance from the State.

Document V.9

Methodism and Labour in Wales in the 1920s

George Thomas, Mr Speaker: The Memoirs of The Viscount Tonypandy (London: Century Publishing, 1985), pp. 28–9.

Working-class nonconformists growing up in the 1920s were more likely to join the Labour Party. George Thomas became an MP, held office in the first Wilson government, and was eventually Speaker of the House of Commons, receiving a peerage on his retirement.

Two other decisions were made that year that were to determine the course of the rest of my life. The first was to join the Labour Party.

As well as being president of the local Co-operative Women's Guild, Mam was elected chairman of the Tonypandy Labour Ward, and I used to go to meetings with her. She was a very eloquent speaker, even though she had once been tremendously shy, so much so that when there were visitors at her parents' house, she would sometimes wait outside to avoid meeting them. She and I both believed that having to fight to bring up her children changed her, so by the time I remember her, she could stand and face large crowds calmly, even when her speeches were interrupted by noisy Communist hecklers. Even then the Labour Party had difficulties with the hard left.

I made another decision that year one Sunday at a special youth service when the minister, the Reverend W. G. Hughes, appealed to all of us there to commit our lives to Christ. Those who were prepared to accept the call were asked to give public proof of their commitment by walking up to the platform where he stood. I felt myself go hot and cold. The challenge seemed directed straight at me. I said a silent prayer, and stepped forward. It was the watershed of my life and ever since then I have started each day with a moment of silent prayer.

So the pattern of my life began to form. At the same time the pattern for the country began to change. The reforms many of us were dreaming about were not so far away but first we had to suffer the agony of the General Strike.

Shortly before it began the Reverend R. J. Barker was appointed minister of Tonypandy Central Hall. His sermons were never less than forty-five minutes long, yet people would queue for an hour before the service to get in and there were seldom less than a thousand to listen to him. He was typical of those English middle class who are in a state of rebellion against the conditions of the poor compared with the comfort of their own people. And he was an essential part of the very radical atmosphere in which I grew up, when we all talked of revolution and of changing the system.

He was also an ardent fighter against Communism and taught me the importance of the individual and individual conscience, the basis of our democracy, which guarantees the rights of the individual at the same time as it depends on individual responsibility being accepted.

Document V.10

The General Strike, 1926

PCE, *Record of General Assembly*, 1926, pp. 433–4.

The Presbyterian Church of England did not have to cancel its General Assembly because of the General Strike (4–12 May 1926) and began its meeting just before it in Liverpool. The resolutions moved by the Revd Dr Carnegie Simpson and approved unanimously on 5 May recognised the complexity of the situation, but significantly put first the principle that the workers should not be expected to bear the burden of the broader economic problems of the coal industry.

1. The Assembly, met as it is under the shadow of an industrial crisis of unprecedented gravity, issues to its faithful people, and to others whom it may concern, the following statement on the situation:–
2. The Assembly is sensible of the complexity of the issues involved (on some of which the public is presently imperfectly informed), and recognises that, on the strictly economic aspects of the problem, it is not qualified to speak. It therefore

disclaims any desire that the Church should be a judge or divider on matters outside its spiritual province. But this grave crisis raises also moral and personal issues with which the Church is deeply concerned, and on which it should not be silent.

3   In particular, the Assembly, maintaining as it does that in any Christian view of industry the first charge on its fruits should be the provision of a living wage for all workers, is in full accord with the effort to maintain the standard of livelihood, and therefore the standard of wages – in many cases far from adequate – of the workers, and not least of those engaged in the vital and perilous occupation of the miner. It feels that, if it be the fact that the economic situation of the mining industry at present makes the continuance of the existing rate of wages impossible – an economic question on which the Assembly does not pronounce – the burden of meeting this should not fall solely, or even primarily, on the worker.

4   With regard to the present grave situation which has arisen and which menaces the life of the nation, the Assembly, without in the present urgency entering in to any question of the degree of blame to be attributed to any of the parties in the matter in dispute, earnestly calls on the Government even yet to open the door for further negotiation – without conditions on either side, or, alternatively, by requiring the withdrawal of the lock-out notices and of the strike notice – believing that the sense of gravity of the position, and the desire of responsible men of all parties to find a solution, will yet, with the blessing of God, save the country from a great disaster, which will entail suffering on thousands of men and women and children, and from the incalculable bitterness which would inevitably follow.

5   Meanwhile the Assembly enjoins its people to do all in their power to preserve the public order, to refrain from bitterness of speech, to alleviate suffering, and to continue in prayer that God may show the way to a righteous peace and give the will to pursue it.

It was further resolved that copies be sent to the Prime Minister, the Earl of Oxford and Asquith and Mr. J. Ramsay MacDonald.

Document V.11

The Revised Prayer Book, 1927

PCE, *Record of General Assembly*, 1927, p. 861.

The Revised Prayer Book of the Church of England received hostile comments from nonconformists in advance of its rejection by Parliament. The record of the discussion in the Presbyterian Church of England reflects greater variety of opinion, with the successful resolution being that moved by Dr Carnegie Simpson, who had played a significant role in the Free Church discussions with the Church of England after the Lambeth Conference of 1920.

Major Fraser submitted the motion of which he had given notice:–

The Assembly regrets that the National Church in its Deposited Prayer Book should have departed to such an extent from Reformation principles as to render it desirable, on the whole, that its passage through Parliament should be resisted.

This was seconded by Mr C. C. Brown Douglas.

The Rev. Dr. Carnegie Simpson, seconded by the Rev. W. Lewis Robertson, then moved as follows:–

The Assembly desires to be allowed to express its sincere good will towards the Church of England in the important task of the revision of the Prayer Book of the National Church; and to disclaim any wish to interfere with or embarrass that task in so far as this is a domestic concern of another Church. Inasmuch, however, as issues arise in this matter which are of wide public and of distinctly religious concern, in which the Nation and the Churches, especially those which value the maintenance of evangelical and reformed truth in the land, have a legitimate and responsible interest, the Assembly, having had the subject formally brought before it, declares as follows:–

The Assembly, while not called on to express approval of the book, declines to give its support to the movement for the rejection of the book by Parliament, believing that such a result would be a grave injury to the peace and efficiency of a sister Church, and that it would not check but would rather perpetuate practices within the Church which are inimical to the principles of the evangelical and reformed faith. The Assembly, however, expresses its conviction, that it is due to the Nation that the episcopate, in seeking national sanction for the measure, should give unambiguous and adequate guarantees that the book, if its adoption be authorised by Parliament, will be administered in what it inhibits as well as what it sanctions, and will set a limit as to what is permitted within the Church of England as by law established.

On a division being taken, the motion of Professor Simpson received 185 votes and the motion of Major Fraser 138. On being put as a substantive motion, Dr J. K. Fotheringham moved the following amendment, which was seconded by the Rev. Joseph Rorke:–

The General Assembly of the Presbyterian Church of England Ministers and Representative Elders now met in Newcastle-on-Tyne, sends its fraternal greetings to the National Assembly of the Church of England. This Assembly notes with interest the long and prayerful attention which the Church of England has devoted to the revision of the Book of Common Prayer, and, believing that the work is of importance to the whole Church of God in this Kingdom, desires to associate itself with the National Assembly of the Church of England in the prayer that the deliberations of that Assembly may be guided by the Holy Spirit and that it may be led to such a decision as will most redound to the glory of God and will best promote the purity, peace and increase of His Church.

This amendment was lost on a division.

The motion of Dr. Carnegie Simpson being put as a substantive motion, was carried by a very large majority, and became the Resolution of the Assembly.

From this decision the following members dissented:– The Revs. David Anderson, J. H. Wishart, J.Gordon MacLeod, John Reid, Mr A. Milne, Dr. S. W. Carruthers. The Rev. David Anderson submitted in writing reasons for his dissent. They were ordered to be kept *in retentis*.

Document V.12

The Salvation Army Act, 1931

21 & 22 Geo. 5, Ch. xciv.

After the problems experienced in the succession of Bramwell Booth as General of the Salvation Army, an Act of Parliament was secured to replace deed polls enrolled in the Chancery Division of the High Court. This illustrates the difficulties the Free Churches had in making changes in their constitutions without parliamentary intervention.

An Act to provide for the better organisation of the Salvation Army and for the custody of real and personal property held upon charitable trusts by or the administration whereof devolves upon the general of the Salvation Army and for other purposes [31 July 1931].

Whereas by a deed poll (hereinafter called 'the deed of constitution') dated the seventh day of August one thousand eight hundred and seventy-eight and under the hand and seal of William Booth (the founder and general superintendent of a religious society or organisation known as 'the Christian Mission') and afterwards enrolled in the Chancery Division of the High Court of Justice the origin name and doctrines of the said Christian Mission were recited and stated:

And whereas it was by the deed of constitution amongst other things provided –

… (Clause 5) that the said William Booth and every general superintendent who should succeed him should have power to appoint his successor to the office of general superintendent and all the rights powers and authorities of the office should vest in the person so appointed upon the decease of the said William Booth or other general superintendent appointing him or at such other period as might be named in the document appointing him. …

And whereas as well for the better organisation of the Salvation Army as for the furtherance of the work carried on by it it is expedient that such provisions should be enacted as are in this Act contained with respect to the mode of appointment of the general of the Salvation Army and the vacation of that office …

And whereas it is expedient that the custody of certain of the property subject to the several trusts aforesaid in this Act described or referred to should be transferred to a company to be incorporated as in this Act set forth;

And whereas it is expedient that the other provisions contained in this Act should be made:

And whereas the purposes of this Act cannot be effected without the authority of Parliament:

May it therefore please Your Majesty that it may be enacted and be it enacted by the King's most Excellent Majesty by and with the advice and consent of the Lords Spiritual and Temporal and Commons in this present Parliament assembled and by the authority of the same as follows –

...

3 – (1) From and after the passing of this Act the general shall cease to have the power or duty of appointing his successor to the office of general of the Salvation Army or to make any statement as to the means which are to be taken for the appointment of such successor and every statement made by the existing holder of the office of general in pursuance of clause 6 of the deed of constitution or of clause 1 of the supplemental deed of constitution shall forthwith upon the passing of this Act be destroyed unopened.

(2) Not more than four months nor less that three months and three weeks before the date of retirement of the general the high council shall (if not already convened) be convened for the purpose of appointing a successor to the office and immediately after the constitution thereof proceed to the election of a general of the Salvation Army who shall succeed to that office upon the date of retirement of the general or upon the sooner happening of any event by which the office of general shall be vacated...

(3) Upon the vacation of the office of general of the Salvation Army from any cause and unless a successor has been elected under subsection (2) or subsection (5) of this section the high council shall (if not already convened) be convened for the purpose of appointing a successor to the office and immediately after the constitution thereof proceed to the election of a general who shall thereupon succeed to that office in succession to the one who has vacated office. ...

(4) If –

(a) upon the vacation of the office of general of the Salvation Army from any cause; or

(b) four months before the date of the retirement of the general;

the high council shall already have been convened for a purpose other than that of appointing a successor to the office the high council so convened shall be deemed also to have been convened for the purpose of appointing a successor to the office and shall accordingly proceed (after the business pertaining to any such other purpose shall have been disposed of) to the election of a general of the Salvation Army who shall succeed to that office upon the date of the retirement of the general or the sooner happening of any event by which the office of general shall be vacated.

(5) If a person elected under this section as successor to the office of general as from a date or even subsequent to the date of such election shall prior to such subsequent date or event die or intimate in writing to the chief of the staff his inability or unwillingness to perform the duties of such office the high council shall be convened for the purpose of appointing another person as such successor in his place and immediately after the constitution thereof proceed to the election of a general of the Salvation Army who shall succeed to that office upon the date of the

retirement of the general or upon the sooner happening of any event by which the office of general shall be vacated....

(6) The provisions of the schedule to the supplemental deed of constitution shall (mutatis mutandis) extend and apply in the case of the election of a general under this section in the same manner as they would have applied if the election had taken place upon the happening of any of the events mentioned in clause 4 of the supplemental deed of constitution.

(7) So much of the deed of constitution and the supplemental deed of constitution as is inconsistent with the provisions of this section shall be and the same is hereby annulled without prejudice to anything done or suffered thereunder.

4 – [Provision for the general to retire]

5 – (1) The general shall as soon as may be after the passing of this Act cause a company to be formed and duly incorporated under the Companies Act 1929 (in this section called 'the Act of 1929') as a company limited by guarantee and registered with a memorandum and articles of association in the form set forth in the Fourth Schedule to this Act or in such other form as may be approved by the Board of Trade and such company shall not (unless by order of a court of competent jurisdiction) be wound up unless and until its custodian trusteeship shall have been terminated in accordance with section 8 of this Act.

(2) The conditions contained in the said memorandum shall not be altered except in the cases in the mode and to the extent for which express provision is made in the Act of 1929.

(3) Nothing in this Act shall be deemed to prevent the trustee company from altering the provisions of its memorandum or altering or adding to its articles subject to and in accordance with the provisions of the Act of 1929 ...

Document V.13

The Problems of the German Churches, 1933

PCE, *Record of General Assembly*, 1933, pp. cxlvii–cxlviii.

The Presbyterian Church of England was one of the first churches to take note of the developments in Germany after January 1933, largely because of the interest of W. T. Elmslie, Convener of the Committee on Intercourse with other Churches at Home and Abroad. This resolution was carried by a large majority in May 1933.

5. The Assembly resolves to send a letter to the President and Vice-President of the Deutsche Evangelische Kirchenausschuss, in the following terms:–

'We are instructed by the General Assembly of the Presbyterian Church of England, now in Session in the city of Newcastle-upon-Tyne, to send to you, and through you to the Churches which you represent, the most cordial Christian greetings.

'The Assembly is well aware of the difficult and critical times through which the people and Churches of Germany have been passing for many years, and of the great anxieties which have been yours. We admire the way in which your Churches are meeting grave difficulties in a time of unemployment and depression, and the courage with which you have stood for Christian principles in the face of indifference and aggressive atheism.

'We are aware that the future relationship of Church and State is at stake, and that the leaders of the Church have as a pressing duty to secure for her the freedom which is essential to the discharge of her own divine ministry.

'The Assembly is gravely concerned, in common with Christian people everywhere, at the recent discrimination against Jewish people in Germany, and at the anti-Semitic views expressed by certain German Christians in positions of influence.

'The Assembly is further concerned at the position in which Christian people, who do not share the views of the present Government, may find themselves; and believes that the German Churches share its abhorrence of any attempt to suppress the spirit of Christian understanding and good will between people belonging to different nations and races.

'The Assembly gladly recognises the restraint observed in this connection by the great body of Christian people in your country, and, aware of the difficulties which may have prevented you from publicly expressing your views, and believing that you are seeking an early opportunity of declaring your mind on these matters unequivocally, desires us to assure you of its confidence; and to promise to you full support of its sympathy and prayers in every stand you take for Christian principles and for the inherent liberties of Christian men.

'We are in the name of the General Assembly, in Christian love ...'

(To be signed by the Moderator and Clerk.)

Document V.14

Attitudes to the Jews, 1938

PCE, *Record of General Assembly*, 1938, p. 657.

The Presbyterian Church of England was unique in having a Committee for Jewish Missions. These Committee resolutions of May 1938 illustrate the tension between concern over anti-Semitism and the missionary impulse; the incongruity of the two was not apparently perceived.

1. The Assembly hears with satisfaction that evidences of approach between Jews and Christians are increasing and urges its faithful people to encourage every effort to overcome the evil spirit of anti-Semitism, which is hateful to every thoughtful Christian.

2. The Assembly calls to the attention of Presbyteries and Congregations which find themselves with Jews as their neighbours to take advantage of this missionary opportunity for evangelism.

Document V.15

The Education Act, 1944

Congregational Quarterly, vol. xxii, no. 2, April 1944, pp. 100–102.

The Education controversy was finally solved by R. A. Butler's Education Act of 1944. Unlike previous attempts at a solution there were negotiations with representatives of the churches, including the Free Churches, before the bill was introduced. Scott Lidgett and Dr Archibald Harrison (1882–1946), Principal of Westminster College, Oxford, were actively involved. This editorial in the *Congregational Quarterly* illustrates that there were still concerns about what was proposed.

At the time of writing the Education Bill is making its slow progress through the House of Commons. From all sides there have been expressions of approval, even if there has often been a 'But', and the chances are that the Bill will go through substantially unaltered. For the advances it proposes we have nothing but praise, though we wish that there had been more definite commitments about raising the school leaving age, nursery and continuation schools, and so forth. With the war still on and the future uncertain, perhaps Mr Butler has done the best that can be done; it will be for all who believe in education to strengthen his hands, and secure that the Bill's proposals be implemented and improved upon at the earliest possible moment.

The Churches have not, we fear, come well out of the discussions; they have given the impression that they were more concerned with their own interests than with those of the children of the land. The Roman Catholics have been out to get as much financial help from the State as possible, and it is plain that Anglicans have felt their own schools would be safeguarded by Roman activity. To the denominationalists it never seems to occur that if parents believe that the education by the State is incomplete and unsatisfactory, they themselves should be prepared to pay for their extra requirements. It is not the business of the State to make children into good Catholics, Anglicans, or Baptists: that is the business of the parents themselves and of the Churches to which they belong. That clergy, ministers, and parents are ill-equipped, and all branches of Christians unwilling to make the sacrifices necessary to enable the Churches to give distinctive teaching is no justification for demanding that the State should provide it. If the Churches were to devote the money now spent on obsolete and superfluous buildings, over-large salaries, and elaborate machinery, and if they were to make use of 'voluntary clergy', they would have ample resources for the teaching of the form of Christianity they favoured.

It looks as if verbal acknowledgment of the injustices suffered by Free Churchmen in single-school areas and a few kind words from the Archbishop of Canterbury will be all that happens, and that the policy of a public school within the reach of every child will be brought only a little nearer by the Bill.

We are not among those who believe that the Anglican leaders have played an astute game and outmanoeuvred the Free Churches, though on the surface there is much to be said for the contentions of those who take this view. Fifteen years ago many Anglicans would admit in private, 'Our Schools are done for'; ten years ago they would suggest that if agreed syllabuses were accepted in all schools they were prepared to see the end of the dual system. Then suddenly they are given 'a glorious opportunity' to save many of their schools; they take advantage of Catholic activity on the one side and the Free Church desire for peace on the other, and hope that the teachers in war-time are so sick to death of religious strife that they will fall in with proposals incorporated in a Bill which makes for general educational progress. That is accurate history, we believe, though we need not assume that Anglicans have been guilty of supreme Jesuitry. But the recrudescence of talk of Nonconformists getting all they want in 'simple Bible teaching' or 'agreed syllabuses', and being unwilling to recognize the huge sacrifices made by the supporters of non-provided schools (the total figures of initial outlay and of amounts received from local educational authorities would be revealing) serves to arouse suspicion.

It is worth following up the dissatisfaction of some Anglicans with 'simple Bible teaching' and 'agreed syllabuses'. What is wanted in addition? 'Church teaching', they say, generally with the reminder that it has long been declared legal to teach the Apostles' Creed in provided schools. And when it is pressed as to what is 'Church teaching', it is found to include not merely the Creed, but the teaching that the Church is a continuation of the Incarnation, that the threefold ministry based on Apostolical Succession is a *sine qua non*, and that Sacraments are obligatory and are invalid except when administered by the episcopally ordained. We shall watch the evolution of the 'agreed syllabus' with interest. The kind of development many Anglicans desire is stated without any camouflage in the Rev. R. Lumb's 'Evangelistic Programme for Education', *Beyond the White Paper* (Dacre Press, 3s. 6d.), which argues that 'agreed' syllabuses do not give 'Church teaching' about the Bible and have no authority from the Church, and that 'our long-term policy should aim at denominational teaching in all State schools'. Meanwhile we believe that the reaction of the non-religious to the insistent claims of the denominationalists will be increased indifference to organized Christianity; it is a pity the leaders of the Churches are so aloof from ordinary folk that the cynical comments heard on every side never reach them.

Imagine how different would have been the impression if the Bishops had announced that, as the Church of England was financially interested in the proposals, they would take no part in the Lords' discussion of the relevant clauses of the Bill; and further, that they were willing to make any sacrifices in single-school areas so that the injustice to Nonconformists might be removed.

Let it not be thought that in saying this we are contending that the Free Churches are superior to the Church of England. In this instance Free Churchmen are claiming nothing for themselves, but we do not see in any branch of organized Christianity any willingness to renounce an iota of power, prestige, or the advantages money secures. Bishops, Moderators, ministers, deacons, cling to pomp, dignity, authority, office, in a way they would scorn to do in their private capacities. Dr. Reinhold Niebuhr has written about moral man in an immoral society, and it often seems to us that the ethical standards of Churches as now organized are below those of the individuals composing them. Men and women who in their personal lives are making heroic sacrifices and apparently never thinking of self, when banded together become avid of power, acquisitive and intolerant, and will give up nothing. 'We must keep what we have', or '*Our* church must be rebuilt' – it almost seems as if the injunctions about self-denial, taking up one's cross, walking the second mile, are held to have no application except to the individual.

Document V.16

The Free Churches and the State, 1953

The Free Churches and the State (London: Free Church Federal Council, 1953), pp. 52–65.

The Free Church Federal Council appointed a Commission to consider questions of church and state in the contemporary context in 1949, about the same time as the Church Assembly appointed its third Commission on the same subject, which reported in 1952. The final chapter stated 'Free Church Principles and Future Policy', illustrating a shift from the simple calls for disestablishment of the nineteenth century.

… The purpose of this chapter is to restate positively the basic principles of the Free Churches in England and to offer, in the light of them, some comments on the recent Anglican Report on Church and State …

In some places, especially in rural areas, it is still not unknown for the vicar to exercise a petty persecution of Free Churchmen and for some of his flock to abet him in a social ostracism of dissenters. But such behaviour is now happily rare, and in the country generally a much more friendly spirit is abroad and there is cordial co-operation in many ways. This is greatly to be welcomed. Yet it is not unnecessary to say that if Nonconformists have largely won civic and religious freedom they have had to fight for it. The Dissenting Deputies had to wage a long and stern fight against the iniquities of the Test and Corporation Acts. We cannot forget that civic office and the universities were long closed to all but real or pretending members of the Church of England; indeed it was not until 1877 that the doors of the universities of Oxford and Cambridge were reopened. In the discussions which preceded the Education Acts of 1936 to 1944 disturbing evidence was afforded of the irregularities and injustice from which Free-churchmen and their children suffered in single school areas where only Church of England day schools existed. This grievance, though recognised, has not yet been completely removed. If Anglicans remembered more than most of them do the severe disabilities imposed upon the Free Churches and the long struggle they had for elementary rights, it would help them to understand the suspicions and hesitations still cherished by some among us. In saying this we do not forget that the spiritual ancestors of some of the present day Free Churchmen were themselves guilty of persecution and of overriding the consciences of others. We all have much of which to repent and much to forgive and forget. We do not wish to revive memories of 'old unhappy far off things and battles long ago', but no serious discussion of the present situation can ignore that they are there in the not far distant background.

Happily we no longer think of the Church of England as an oppressor to be resisted, but rather as an ally in Christian service. Free Churchmen rejoice in the growth of fellowship and co-operation and in our mutually acknowledged agreement on the fundamental doctrines of our faith ... We sincerely wish for the peace and prosperity of the Church of England, and if we must offer criticisms of her present attitude and policy in this field of Church and State it is in no spirit of bitterness or antagonism. Even here we are happy to note a growing approximation of view, as will be demonstrated later in this chapter.

1. Free Church Principles

Though, like Anglicans, Free Churchmen are not all of one opinion on this subject, certain principles are generally accepted among us today, and these, though often stated negatively in relation to existing institutions, are not in themselves negative but positive.

To the Free Churchman the Church is essentially, in the phrase of his fathers, 'a gathered Church,' that is, a community composed of Christian believers gathered 'out of the world' by God for His worship and service; not a man-made association of likeminded people, as those outside our ranks are apt to interpret it. It has seemed to us that the Anglican emphasis lay, at least until recently, upon what may be called the 'geographical' Church, composed of all the baptised residents in the land. Quotations to illustrate this could be multiplied from Hooker and Laud down to quite recent days ... We cannot think of Church and State as obverse and reverse of a coin.

... The recent creation of the Parochial Roll by the Church of England is at least a partial recognition of the Free Church assertion that the Church is not a nation, nor yet the baptised citizens, but the committed disciples. The Church of England was not prepared to limit the Roll to communicants, but at least the Enabling Act has 'made it plain that citizenship is not the same as churchmanship' [Garbett, *Church and State in England*, p. 117].

It was primarily because of our conception of the Church and churchmanship, in protest against what we held to be the defective standards of the Anglicans at that time, that we left or were turned out of the national Church.

It follows for us that this Church of avowed disciples must be free from all external control in spiritual matters. Precisely how the gathered Church governs itself, under Christ, is to the Free Churchman a secondary question; but the need for its spiritual freedom admits of no argument. Christ is the only King and Head of His Church. In its government, authority in spiritual matters is derived only from Him. This does not, of course, mean that the Free Churches claim to stand above the law of the land. In some aspects of its life, as in its ownership of property, the Church is a legal body and its trust deeds are properly subject to legal interpretation. But it is not for the State to draw up our trust deeds, control our forms of worship, or nominate our Superintendents or Moderators. For the ministry of the Word and Sacraments to be under the direction or censorship of any outside body whatever is for us unthinkable. We yield to none in our love of our country and our loyalty to its Sovereign, but within the Church 'the Crown Rights of the Redeemer', in our ancient phrase, are for us supreme.

Yet we do not regard the State as a merely secular body; it too may be an organ of the Kingdom of God and the 'magistrate' can be His officer. Free Churchmen have from the first taken a steady, and at times vigorous, part in political life. By consent of the historians they can claim to have taken a major share in the development of the institutions of modern democracy. For us, Church and State are two 'orders' set up by God for the good of men. If it is not the business of the State to urge men to love God, it is certainly concerned with the love of one's neighbour, the ethical expression of religion. 'The powers that be are ordained of God,' and so long as they command no contravention of His laws the citizen must in conscience obey. But the State must not make transcendent claims: it has no absolute and ultimate authority. The State exists under God to promote the good life for its citizens: its citizens do not exist for the sake of the State. Both Church and State stand under His authority and their service of Him should be complementary, not antithetical ...

Many Anglicans would now assert the spiritual freedom of the Church as vehemently as any Free Churchman. They admit that the present position of the Church of England in relation to the State is not compatible with that claim. Yet it seems to us that as a body they acquiesce, and seek only palliatives in what one of their own Archbishops, Dr. Temple, then Archbishop of York, described as 'an intolerable situation.' ... The increasing claims made on behalf of the State and its invasion of many realms hitherto left to voluntary responsibility, together with the development of modern means of propaganda with their power of moulding men's minds, make it more and not less necessary to stand for the freedom of the spirit. The extreme form taken by State control in many other countries in recent years and the still continuing persecution in many lands, make the issue obvious. Though no such stark challenge confronts us in present day England, the Church cannot relax its vigilance.

2. The Present Position of the Church of England

We turn now, in the light of this statement of Free Church principles, to consider the present position of the Church of England, particularly as revealed in the Report of the Commission on Church and State, appointed by the Church Assembly in 1949, following two others in 1916 and 1935. The resolution appointing it significantly said: 'That the (Church) Assembly while valuing the Establishment of the Church of England as an expression of the nation's recognition of religion, nevertheless is of opinion that the present form of it impedes the fulfilment of the responsibilities of the Church as a spiritual society.' In the Church of England today we have 'a church whose chief pastors are nominated by a Prime Minister who need not belong to it; whose corporate worship cannot be enriched or changed without the approval of an assembly whose members need not be Christian; whose rules for the better government of its affairs cannot be made without the licence of the Crown; and whose doctrine and worship are interpreted in cases of dispute by a State Court.' These words are not taken from a manifesto of the Liberation Society. They occur in *Church and State in England* by Cyril Garbett, Archbishop of York ...

There is indeed acute concern in many Anglican circles. It might fairly be said that the leaders of the Church of England are both worried and puzzled, and find it hard to make up their minds just what course to pursue. The members of the Commission are learned and able men trying to find the Christian way and as concerned as any of us to secure the spiritual freedom of the Church. They have presented the most alert and constructive of the series of Reports and reveal incidentally an increased understanding of the Free Church point of view. Yet they show an intelligible reluctance to disturb a relationship so deeply rooted in the life of the nation, and a readiness to accept anomalies, or worse, on the ground that on the whole they work pretty well. They come definitely and unanimously to the conclusion that disestablishment would be a mistake and that any gains would be far outweighed by losses.

There is much in the Report that might be further discussed. The Commission, for example, do not really understand the principle of 'the gathered Church'; indeed their description is not far short of a caricature. They also imply, if they do not actually say, that Free Churchmen believe in going into a spiritual huddle and leaving the State to go its own way, a misunderstanding with which we have already dealt. They seem to think it an effective retort to say that after all we also are subject to the Law Courts. We have, of course, as explained above, never sought to be free from the State in legal affairs; but it is not really true to say that a Free Church must seek from the State 'leave to reformulate its doctrine' ... Again, the Report says that the Church of England has never been 'established' by Parliament (p. 7). Perhaps; but it holds its present position of privilege by virtue of Acts of Parliament, notably the Act of Uniformity of 1662, which incorporated the Prayer Book. It is on that basis that it holds the property of the pre-Reformation Church and that the rest of us have been disinherited. We confine detailed comment to two fundamental issues: the control of worship and the appointment of bishops.

The rejection by Parliament of the revised Prayer Book in 1927 and 1928 made it clear that worship in the Church of England is controlled not by the worshippers themselves but by the votes of members of all churches and of none. Parliament was entitled to debate and reject proposals based upon many years' work by the authorities of the Anglican Communion. The Commission, however, maintain that second thoughts should mitigate the dismay felt by the Church. There were strong minorities in the Church itself which opposed the changes in the Communion Service and Parliament was right in not letting them be overridden. Parliament is justified in imposing delay if it feels that proposals are in advance of the general body of opinion in the Church, though 'any claim by Parliament to override the mind of the Church when that mind had been indubitably formed would be intolerable' (p. 23). Yet the situation is unsatisfactory; all the more so, as the Commission points out, because in spite of the law there are many deviations in use from the Book of Common Prayer, some completely unauthorised, and some acquiesced in, with very doubtful legality, by the bishops. Priests and bishops solemnly undertake to carry out a law which in fact nobody observes, and which indeed it is practically impossible to observe … There is no question that the Prayer Book needs revising. But the scandal is not really that Parliament rejected a proposal for its revision; the scandal is that it should have been necessary to ask its permission at all. The order of worship of a Christian Church is under the control of a body composed of men and women who need not even be Christians! Yet the action of Parliament was entirely constitutional, and if the Church is to be established the State must have some say in its conduct and principles.

The same kind of dilemma is raised by the appointment of bishops. To Free Churchmen it is axiomatically wrong that those appointing spiritual leaders may profess any religion or none. Part of the reply of the Commission is that in practice the method works well. This may be admitted. The Bench of Bishops as a whole justly commands respect, and popular election might sometimes produce less satisfactory results. But the system is fundamentally wrong in principle and potentially disastrous in practice...

3. The Next Step

The trouble is that the Commission is trying to reconcile two irreconcilables: the spiritual freedom of the Church and the preservation of the existing establishment. Nevertheless, to urge that the Gordian knot be severed by the sword of disestablishment is not so simple and obvious a solution as might at first be thought. It is an open question whether any practicable alternative in the present situation would not be worse than the existing order with all its anomalies. This no doubt explains the fact that while Free Churchmen do not believe any less than they did in the spiritual freedom of the Church, and while a growing number in the Anglican Church are alive to the dangers inherent in the State connection and profess readiness to pay the price of disestablishment if freedom cannot otherwise be obtained, there is yet no sign of a campaign for disestablishment. Few Free Churchmen are prepared to assert dogmatically that they have a clear policy to put forward in view of the complexities of the situation.

For example, there is much force in the contention of the Commission that disestablishment now would be a further large stride towards a completely secularised State, and would be interpreted throughout the world 'as the British People's deliberate repudiation of a continuous Christian tradition' (p. 10). This would be true even if the motive behind the severance was the conviction that the Church would be the stronger for it … It may be argued that if there were a United Church of England, comprising the Anglican Communion and the main Free Churches, some new form of concordat with the State could be secured. That may be so; but any such United Church seems far from probable in the immediate future. If what may be called the Scottish type of solution is not practicable in England, it does not follow that the right alternative is disestablishment and the probable effective separation of Church and State. This is the American position, which some Free Churchmen find attractive. In the United States there is strict separation of Church and State and few Americans would wish it otherwise. But it involves the absence from State schools of religious observances or teaching, and has prevented the giving of State aid to the churches in forms which even to Free Churchmen seem innocuous in this country.

For though Free Churchmen reject the State *control* of religion they welcome State *recognition* of religion. We do not desire to see a secular State in England. We hold it right, for example, that public education should be on a Christian basis, and that there should be chaplains in our hospitals and in the armed forces. It is right that on great national occasions, such as a Coronation, there should be solemn acknowledgment by the State of the ultimate sovereignty of God ... It would be easy by ill-considered proposals for disestablishment to jeopardise the existing valuable co-operation between Church and State, in which the Free Churches have come increasingly to share. As Dr. Payne points out, the Free Churches have in recent years accepted forms of State aid and recognition at which earlier generations of Free Churchmen might have looked askance. They have, for example, shared in tax exemptions and in preferential terms for churches in respect of War Damage. They have not only claimed the right to State-paid chaplaincies, they also receive State grants for their educational and social work ...

Yet so long as there is an established Church with State recognition and privileges, the State must inevitably have some say in its conduct ... It is inevitable, as things are, that any proposals put forward by the Church of England should be scrutinised by the nation, and the Free Churches have every right to express a judgment along with others ... While, therefore, the proposals contained in the Report fall far short of securing that full freedom which in our judgment any Church should possess, yet they do constitute a real step forward and Free Churchmen might well feel that they ought not to be resisted ... If the State refused to give such a measure of freedom the Free Churches would have every sympathy if the Church of England insisted upon disestablishment.

If, however, the Free Churches in the present total situation feel it right to regard sympathetically the desire of the Church of England for a larger measure of freedom, there is something we on our part may reasonably expect from that Church. It ought to be recognised that the present position of exclusive privilege in many fields of the Church of England is anomalous, now that it is in fact one denomination among others, and represents no more than perhaps half of the Christian communicants in England ...

The future will see, we hope, a growing partnership and fellowship between the Church of England and the Free Churches, and a recognition that we stand together as allies and as fellow servants of our Lord Jesus Christ ... We would, therefore, emphasise in conclusion two concerns: that there should be a more realistic recognition, both by the Established Church and by the State, of the true balance and strength of the Christian forces in the nation, so that there might be more equity in relative privilege than at present obtains; and that there should be no misunderstanding as to the continued and convinced Free Church adherence to the essential principles of the Reformation and of Protestantism. While not cavilling at certain uses of the word 'Catholic', co-operation between the Free Churches and the Church of England would be gravely prejudiced if the essential and constitutional Protestantism of the Church of England became a dead letter.

Document V.17

Post-War Relations with Germany

Congregational Quarterly, vol. xxv, no. 3, July 1957, pp. 199–200.

As a result of relief work done in Germany after the war a relationship developed between the Church of the Palatinate and the International Congregational Council, which was formally inaugurated in 1957. It was essentially maintained by the Congregational Union and after 1972 by the United Reformed Church.

A representative party of British Congregationalists headed by the Moderator of the International Congregational Council, Dr Maurice Watts, and the Minister and Secretary, Rev. Ralph Calder, visited the Palatinate in April to take part in services held in Speyer to mark the formal association of the United Protestant Church of the Palatinate with the Council.

Sunday, April 28th, will long be remembered by those who were present at the Communion service in the splendid Memorial Church, built by the Protestants of the world to commemorate the Reformation whose beginnings were closely associated with Speyer. The minister conducted the service at which Dr. Watts preached the sermon, after which Dr. Hans Stempel led us in a great united celebration of Communion. In the afternoon we gathered again in the Church of the Holy Trinity, rightly described as 'one of the most beautiful and joyful churches of baroque style in Germany.' Here we joined a number of representatives bringing greetings, including Dr. Niemoller, and Dr. Howard Schomer of the World Council. In the evening, in the German style rather than the British, we were entertained at a civic banquet at which the deputy Burgomeister, himself a Roman Catholic, welcomed us to Speyer in the most hospitable spirit.

The United Protestant Church of the Palatinate is a union, founded in 1821, of Lutheran and Reformed churches for which each, as Dr. Schneider has written, 'gave up her special confession, celebrating the Lord's Supper in Biblical form and declaring the holy scriptures to be the only rule and norm of the Church.' It is on that same basis that this new association with the International Congregational Council is possible. It is a situation which deserves more consideration than it has yet received. A visitor to the Palatinate is bound to be deeply impressed by the vigour of the spiritual, social and educational work of the United Church. In an article in this journal of April, 1953, to which we refer our reader for a full account of the Church and its history, Dr. Carl Schneider wrote, 'the spirit of the love of Christ, which really was the main factor in the origin of this Union Church, created a spiritual unity which did not need any more the confessional crutches. There was, and still is, no unity of form. You will find in the Palatinate liturgical and non-liturgical services. You will hear orthodox and liberal sermons, but there is one spirit. This is seen and proved by the astonishing extent of the works of love which, as a real result of union, is not surpassed by any other Church. The Church has a highly developed system of schools of all kinds, hospitals, homes of all kinds, asylums, hostels, kindergartens, and youth homes, deaconesses, parochial workers, city missions, inner missions, station missions, and the like. But there is more: there was and is, as in Reformation times, a constant free discussion of all the problems of faith, and therefore a unity underlying the manifold opinions and works: it is one Church.'

So long as in this country reunion with the Anglican Church tarries, and apparently will tarry until the Free Churches accept episcopacy, the most hopeful way of advance is the union of the Free Churches. The union of the Lutheran and Reformed Churches in the Palatinate called for great courage, but it is no longer an experiment. It has long since been justified by its fruits.

Document V.18

Concern about Africa, 1960

Congregational Year Book, 1961, pp. 81–2.

In the late 1950s concern was mounting in the British churches both about apartheid in South Africa and about the government's policy over the Central African Federation. These resolutions of the Congregational Union Assembly in May 1960 represented a new development in the kind of business discussed.

(2) *On South Africa ...*
The Second Assembly of the World Council of Churches made the following declaration,

'Segregation in all its forms is contrary to the Gospel, and is incompatible with the Christian doctrine of man with the nature of the Church of Christ. The Assembly urges the Churches within its membership to renounce all forms of segregation or discrimination and to work for their abolition within their own life and within society.'

The Congregational Union of England and Wales adheres still to these convictions and

Affirms in unison with the Christian Council of South Africa that the recent shootings of African men, women, and children are a shock to the Christian conscience, and it

Identifies itself with the position taken by the Congregational Union of South

Africa in its opposition to the policy of Apartheid and in its stand for those human rights subscribed to in the Charter of the United Nations, and it

Associates itself in intercession with all the churches in South Africa, praying that they may be faithful in their witness to justice and may fulfil the ministry of reconciliation between the races, and

Calls upon Christian people in Britain to recognize their responsibilities in the field of inter-racial relations within our own country, and it

Commends to the generosity of our churches the Christian agencies which are seeking to relieve the plight of those at present suffering in consequence of the policies being operated in South Africa.

(3) *On Central Africa ...*
This Assembly of the Congregational Union of England and Wales welcomes the assurance of the Prime Minister that the protection of the British Government will not be removed from either Northern Rhodesia or Nyasaland until it is the expressed wish of these peoples to enter into a free and independent federation and urges that bold steps in constitutional progress for Africans in both these territories should be taken as soon as possible following the present consultations.

Document V.19

The Tercentenary of 1662

Congregational Year Book, 1962, p. 87.

It is a measure of the improvement in Anglican/Free Church relations that the tercentenary of the Act of Uniformity in 1962 was not marked with the kind of bitterness that marked the bicentenary a century earlier. This Affirmation, unanimously agreed by the Congregational Union Assembly on 15 May 1962 at a session addressed by Dr Ernest Payne, General Secretary of the Baptist Union, combines a firm insistence on the original principles with a more conciliatory tone.

We, the members of the Congregational Union of England and Wales, meeting at Westminster Chapel, London, in the year of the Tercentenary of the Great Ejectment of 1662, desire to express our gratitude to Almighty God for all He has wrought in the witness of our forefathers, and for all that He has done for us during three centuries.

We rejoice that we ourselves are no longer bound by the Act of Uniformity, that the Church of England itself has modified some of its provisions in directions that our forefathers would have desired, and that there now exists among the churches of our land so large measure of tolerance, goodwill and co-operation.

In the hope that we ourselves may make a contribution out of our past history to such better understanding we record, for our help and for our brethren in other churches, the things we believe that we have been taught of God during our separation.

(1) That the authority of the visible church in matters concerning its Faith and Order is distinct from, and not subordinate to, the civil authority.

(2) That the revelation of God recorded in the Scriptures is the supreme standard within the church in matters of Faith and Order.

(3) That the historic episcopate is not a divinely required constituent of the visible church and the validity of the spiritual oversight and ministry of the Word and Sacraments exercised by ministers duly ordained, in harmony with the word of God as recorded in the Scriptures, should be recognised.

(4) That the orderly public worship of God should not be required exclusively to follow the patterns laid down by a particular book.

We deeply regret the long period of bitter controversy which followed the Ejectment of 1662. Our hope is that this commemoration will not lead to any such controversy but rather to better mutual understanding between all the churches in this country.

We acknowledge with many of our brethren in other churches that God is calling all His people to seek such unity of spirit and purpose that together they may bring the people of this country and of the whole world into a new unity in the Church in acknowledging Jesus Christ as the Saviour and Lord of all men.

Document V.20

Methodist Church Act, 1976

Elizabeth II 1976 c. xxx.

When it was clear that the Anglican/Methodist unity scheme had failed, the Methodist Church decided to address various questions relating to the power of the Methodist Conference to amend its doctrinal standards and change its constitution. As this could only be done by Act of Parliament, an Act was secured in 1976.

WHEREAS under and by virtue of the enactments in that behalf contained in the Methodist Church Union Act 1929 (hereinafter referred to as 'the Act of 1929') and a deed of union executed in pursuance thereof on the 20th September 1932 (hereinafter referred to as 'the date of union') the Wesleyan Methodist Church, the Primitive Methodist Church and the United Methodist Church became as from that date of union a united church or denomination under the name of the Methodist Church:

And whereas pursuant to the powers contained in section 8 (Power of Uniting Conference to adopt Deed of Union) of the Act of 1929 the Conference of the Methodist Church had from time to time subsequent to the date of union amended the said deed of union (hereinafter as so amended referred to as 'the Deed of Union'):

And whereas the constitution and doctrinal standards of the Methodist Church are declared and defined in the Deed of Union and under and by virtue of the proviso to subsection (2) of the said section 8 (and of clause 31 (a) of the Deed of Union) the Conference of the Methodist Church has no power to alter or vary in any manner whatsoever the clauses contained in the Deed of Union which define the said doctrinal standards:

... And whereas the Sharing of Church Buildings Act of 1969, which applies to the Methodist Church, makes provision for the sharing and using of church buildings in England and Wales by different churches in manner inconsistent with the trusts of the model deeds relating to the doctrinal standards of the Methodist Church:

And whereas under and by virtue of subsection (4) of section 15 (Power to alter new model deed) of the Act of 1929 (and clause 32 of the Deed of Union) the Conference of the Methodist Church has no power to alter or to vary in the Model Deed the clause therein contained relating to the doctrinal standards of the Methodist Church:

And whereas no provision was made in the Act of 1929 for the definition of purposes of the Methodist Church and it is expedient in the circumstances now prevailing that such provision as is made in this Act should be made for the definition of such purposes:

And whereas it is expedient that the Conference of the Methodist Church should be empowered to alter any provision of the Deed of Union, including any such provision relating to the doctrinal standards of the Methodist Church ...

And whereas the purpose of this Act cannot be effected without the authority of Parliament:

May it please Your Majesty that it may be enacted, and be it enacted, by the Queen's most Excellent Majesty, by and with the advice and consent of the Lords Spiritual and Temporal, and Commons, in this present Parliament assembled, and by the authority of the same, as follows:–

...

3 – (1) Subject to the following provisions of this section and to section 4 (Purposes), section 5 (Amendment of the Deed of Union) and section 6 (Power to unite with other churches) of this Act, the constitution of the Methodist Church and the doctrinal standards shall be as declared and defined in the Deed of Union:

Provided that in the event of any conflict between any provision of this Act and any provision of the Deed of Union the provision of this Act shall prevail.

(2) The Conference shall be the final authority within the Methodist Church with regard to all questions concerning the interpretation of its doctrines.

...

5 – (1) Notwithstanding any provision of the Deed of Union to the contrary, the Conference may amend the Deed of Union by such variation or revocation of any provision thereof or by such addition of any new provision thereto as the Conference may from time to time consider to be expedient.

(2) Subject to the provisions of the next following subsection, the Conference shall make any amendment of the Deed of Union by deferred special resolution if the doctrinal standards are thereby affected but otherwise by special resolution.

(3) So long as the Conference shall consist of both the Representative and Ministerial Sessions the Conference shall make any amendment of the Deed of Union by the special resolution of both the Representative and Ministerial Sessions if such amendment shall affect the continuance as a separate body of the Ministerial Session as provided by the Deed of Union, or shall affect the definition, by virtue of that Deed, of the relative duties and privileges of the Representative and Ministerial Sessions respectively.

(4) After any amendment of the Deed of Union any reference to that Deed in this Act or in any written instrument, whenever executed, shall be deemed to be a reference to the Deed of Union as so amended.

Document V.21

Harold Wilson

Harold Wilson, *Memoirs: The Making of a Prime Minister, 1916–64* (London: Weidenfeld & Nicolson and Michael Joseph, 1986), pp. 16–17, 33–4.

Three of the four Prime Ministers in the quarter-century after 1964 came from a nonconformist background. Harold Wilson was a Congregationalist, who married the daughter of a Congregational minister in Mansfield College Chapel. His church links remained strong throughout his life.

The Wilsons attended church regularly. Both my parents were Congregationalists, but there was no church near enough, so at 10.30 every Sunday morning Marjorie and I were taken by them to the local Baptist church, where the minister, the Rev. W. H. ('Pa') Potter, enjoyed a great local influence. Marjorie and I also went to his Sunday School in the afternoon. I would not say there was an atmosphere of religious fervour at home, but this practice was a normal and accepted part of our lives.

My father was very busy on the social side, always organizing parties and get-togethers, and there was a very strong Scout Group which Mr Potter ran as a constituent branch of his church. My father was a Rover Leader, my mother a Guide Captain and Marjorie a Guide. I became a Cub at a very early age and in due course a Patrol Leader in what was the biggest Scout Group in Yorkshire, the 3rd Colne Valley Milnsbridge Baptist Scouts, which was in due course merged to become the 20th Huddersfield. We went camping, organized debates and I even joined the band, playing first the triangle and later the side drum. I happily acknowledge my membership as one of the main elements in my formative years ...

> Have been to see the chaplain of Mansfield, a really nice fellow named Micklem. He gave me coffee and seemed glad to see me ... I am going to Mansfield tomorrow and then he is going to put me in touch with the Oxford Undergrad. Congregational Society and Discussion Group with a view to joining, as I probably shall.

That needs some elucidation. Mansfield was the Congregational theological college in those days, and the Principal, Dr Nathaniel Micklem, was a substantial figure with whom I maintained close contact. In due course, Mary and I were married by him and her father in the chapel there. It was the one firm link in my upbringing that I never broke and it governed many of my attitudes. I see that in my first letter to my sister Marjorie, dated early in that October, I said:

> I went to a Coll. Discussion Group of the Anti-war Movement and soon made my presence felt. I tried to counteract the Labour element with the Christian lines of argument so to speak, advocating closer co-operation with the churches etc. I thoroughly enjoyed the services at Mansfield College and intend to go there every Sunday.

And so I did. It has often been said that Gladstone was a High Church radical, Attlee a Church of England radical and that I was the first Nonconformist radical Prime Minister. The tradition was very strong in Yorkshire and Lancashire and formed the basis of a substantial body of political opinion. My father had one catch-phrase that he often used to quote: 'What is morally wrong can never be politically right.' It was Morgan Phillips who said that the Labour Party owed more to Methodism than to Marx.

Document V.22

James Callaghan

James Callaghan, *Time and Chance* (London: Collins, 1987), pp. 34–6, 39–40.

Jim Callaghan came from a Baptist background and he acknowledges in his memoirs how important this was. Nevertheless he moved away from regular church commitment.

There were many voluntary organisations with the aim of relieving poverty. The chapels too did their best. I remember that on the Sunday before each Christmas, one of the deacons at the Baptist Chapel would load up a handcart with groceries which we pushed round the streets, calling at homes we knew were in need to leave a pound of sugar, a pound of sultanas and margarine to help towards the Christmas pudding. We knew families in deep poverty and there was a sense of sharing ...

The fever van was a familiar sight in the street, calling to take children to the fever hospital. I do not recall any vaccinations other than those against smallpox. My sister used to argue that we were brought up in Sunday School to accept that child mortality was a natural event, and that we should look forward to going to Heaven as a reward ...

I cannot say I was thrilled by the notion. My mother was deeply religious and fundamentalist and she looked forward to the Second Coming of the Lord when all who had been saved would be taken up to Heaven. This would be for her a joyful day, one to which she looked forward, and the expectation enabled her to bear her present troubles. As a child I imbibed this same belief, but to me it was a dread prospect. Only God and I knew what terrible sins I had committed: *I* knew that I was unworthy to be taken up to Heaven with all those who were saved; and what shame my mother would feel when she ascended to Heaven but I was left on earth as unworthy. To a seven-year-old the fear was real and tangible. I came home one day from school to find the house empty and silent and I knew at once that it had happened. The Second Coming had taken place, my mother had been taken up to Heaven and I had, as I had always feared, been rejected. For a moment near-panic set in and then, with a relief almost too great to describe, I heard the sound of my mother's voice. My sense of shame was so great that I was never able to tell her how I felt, but it left its mark and even in adult life I have never been able wholly to shake off a sense of guilt.

Our Sunday School was typical in having over six hundred 'scholars' and one hundred teachers. We lived up to our name of scholars. When we were young we learned by heart long passages from the Bible. As we grew older, our Sunday School teachers set us written examinations and, if we passed well, we were allowed to choose a book as a prize ...

The chapels were much more centres of the community than they are today. Almost every night of the week there were different activities: Monday, Band of Hope; Tuesday, Christian Endeavour; Thursday, prayer meeting; Friday, juvenile choir practice. Our Sundays were spent at chapel. Sunday School started at 9.30 in the morning. From there we went into chapel at 11 o'clock. Home to Sunday dinner, which was usually cold ham and mashed potatoes, and at 2.30 we returned to afternoon Sunday School. Finally to Chapel at 6.30 in the evening with sometimes a Sunday School tea in between. We were not permitted to have playing cards in the house and we did not read newspapers on Sundays. I was allowed the *Children's Encyclopaedia* but nothing else secular. At home we began each day with a short Bible reading before leaving for school, and of course we never omitted to say Grace before meals, a practice that has fallen into disuse in most homes. ...

My mother's joy at my success in the Civil Service examination was dampened when I received a letter from the Civil Service Commission instructing me to report to the Inland Revenue Tax Office at Maidstone, Kent ... We knew no one in Maidstone, but the Baptist Chapel rallied round and I was found lodgings. As a leaving present I was presented with a large Bible signed by the Pastor and Sunday School Superintendent and inscribed with the text 'The steps of a good man are ordered by the Lord.' I still have it. As my mother and I stood waiting for the coach that would bear us to London on the first leg of my journey to Maidstone the Sunday School Superintendent, a jobbing builder, cycled up bearing a huge bag of ripe pears which he presented to me and, clutching this kind gift, I set off to an entirely new life, different from anything that had gone before. I was about to earn my own living ...

I became a Sunday School teacher and it was in Sunday School that I met Audrey Moulton. She was a tall, slim sixteen-year-old, in the first year of the sixth form at the local grammar school ... Her father, Frank Moulton, was both Superintendent of the Sunday School and also a Deacon of the Church ... Audrey's family were very kind and invited me to table on Sundays, to picnics and to visits to the seaside, all of which I eagerly accepted. I benefited very much from being allowed to become so much a part of the home and family, and from joining in their activities ...

It was at Maidstone that I began a voyage of political discovery as a consequence of one of my seniors in the tax office introducing me to new books ... I read all I could find of Bernard Shaw, H. G. Wells, H. N. Brailsford, G. D. H. Cole, Harold Laski and many others, and ... endeavoured to overcome the great gaps in my education by joining WEA evening classes in social history and economics, in which our tutor, an Oxford graduate by the name of de Vere, even dipped a toe into *Das Kapital*.

... This new experience that I was living through seemed much more real and true than the fundamentalist religion in which I had been brought up, and I impetuously dashed off a letter of resignation to the Secretary of the Maidstone Baptist Chapel. This created something of a stir. It was apparently acceptable for someone unostentatiously to stop going to church services and gradually drift away, but it was practically unheard of formally to resign membership. So it was arranged that one of the Senior Deacons should have a conversation with me. He was a wise man who argued that although he disagreed with my new-found socialist beliefs, there need be no conflict between them and Church membership. Many tenets of the Christian faith were reconcilable with socialism ... So I stayed, but from then on, my activities in the Labour Party and Trade Union Movement increasingly had the first charge on my energies, although I never forget the immense debt I owe to a Christian upbringing, nor have I ever escaped its influence.

Document V.23

Margaret Thatcher

Margaret Thatcher, *The Path to Power* (London: Harper Collins, 1995), pp. 5–6, 8–9, 10–11, 39–40.

Lady Thatcher, Prime Minister 1979–90, writes of her debt to Methodism. The Robertses had been shoemakers; Alfred Roberts, her father, was a grocer and councillor and her mother was a dressmaker. They lived 'over the shop' in Grantham, and are examples of Methodists who had always been Conservatives.

I was born into a home which was practical, serious and intensely religious. My father and mother were both staunch Methodists; indeed, my father was much in demand as a lay preacher in and around Grantham. He was a powerful preacher whose sermons contained a good deal of intellectual substance. But he was taken aback one day when I asked him why he put on a 'sermon voice' on these occasions. I don't think he realized that he did this. It was an unconscious homage to the biblical message, and quite different to the more prosaic tones in which he dispatched council business and current affairs.

Our lives revolved around Methodism. The family went to Sunday Morning Service at 11 o'clock, but before that I would have gone to morning Sunday School. There was Sunday School again in the afternoons; later, from about the age of twelve, I played the piano for the smaller children to sing the hymns. Then my parents would usually go out again to Sunday Evening Service.

This I found somewhat too much of a good thing, and on a few occasions I remember trying to get out of going. But when I said to my father that my friends were able to go out for a walk instead and I would like to join them, he would reply: 'Never do things just because other people do them.' In fact, this was one of his favourite expressions – used when I wanted to learn dancing, or sometimes when I wanted to go to the cinema, or out for the day somewhere. Whatever I felt at the time, the sentiment stood me in good stead, as it did my father ...

Religious life in Grantham was very active and, in the days before Christian ecumenism, competitive and fuelled by a spirit of rivalry. There were three Methodist chapels, St Wulfram's Anglican Church – the sixth-highest steeple in England, according to local legend – and a Roman Catholic church just opposite our house. From a child's standpoint, the Catholics seemed to have the most light-hearted time of all. I used to envy the young Catholic girls making their first communion, dressed in white party dresses with bright ribbons, and carrying baskets of flowers. The Methodist style was much plainer, and if you wore a ribboned dress an older chapel-goer would shake his head and warn against 'the first step to Rome'.

Even without ribbons, however, Methodism was far from dour, as people are inclined to imagine today. It placed great emphasis on the social side of religion and on music, both of which gave me plenty of opportunities to enjoy life, even if it was in what might seem a rather solemn way. Our friends from church would often come in to cold supper on Sunday evenings, or we would go to them. I always enjoyed the adults' conversation, which ranged far wider than religion or happenings in Grantham to include national and international politics. And one of the unintended consequences of the temperance side of Methodism was that Methodists tended to devote more time and attention to eating. 'Keeping a good table' was a common phrase, and many of the social occasions were built around tea parties and suppers. There was also a constant round of church events, organized either to keep the young people happy or to raise funds for one purpose or other ...

Our religion was not only musical and sociable – it was also intellectually stimulating. The ministers were powerful characters with strong views. The general political tendency among Methodists and other Nonconformists in our town was somewhat to the left wing and even pacifist. Methodists in Grantham were prominent in organizing the 'Peace Ballot' of 1935, circulating a loaded questionnaire to the electorate, which was then declared overwhelmingly to have 'voted for peace'. It is not recorded how far Hitler and Mussolini were moved by this result; we had our own views about that in the Roberts household. The Peace Ballot was a foolish idea which must take some of the blame nationally for delaying the rearmament necessary to deter and ultimately defeat the dictators. On this question and others, being staunchly Conservative, we were the odd family out. Our friend the Rev Skinner was an enthusiast for the Peace Ballot. He was the kindest and holiest man, and he married Denis and me at Wesley's Chapel in London many years later. But personal virtue is no substitute for political hard-headedness …

… Religion also figured large in my Oxford life. There are many tales of young people entering university and, partly through coming into contact with scepticism and partly for less wholesome reasons, losing their faith. I never felt in any danger of that. Methodism provided me with an anchor of stability and, of course, contacts and friends who looked at the world as I did. I usually attended the Wesley Memorial Church on Sundays. There was, as in Grantham, a warmth and a sober but cheerful social life which I found all the more valuable in my initially somewhat strange surroundings. The church had a very vigorous Students' Fellowship. After Sunday Evening Service there was usually a large gathering over coffee in the minister's house, where there would be stimulating discussion of religious and other matters. Occasionally I would go to the University Church of St Mary the Virgin to listen to a particularly interesting university sermon – though that church has about it a certain 'official' formality, which makes it a somewhat cold place of worship. Sometimes I would go to the college chapel, especially when I knew that Miss Helen Darbishire, who was Principal and a distinguished scholar of Milton and Wordsworth when I first went up to Somerville, was preaching.

PART VI

PEACE AND WAR

Introduction

One of the greatest challenges for Nonconformist attitudes in the twentieth century was war. The new scale of war posed new questions; but what is more striking is the shift in the balance between an instinctive reluctance towards a greater readiness to support war in certain circumstances. Keith Robbins suggests that 'Nonconformity did not as a whole stand out for the belief that war was always wrong'.[1] This is demonstrated by the attitudes to the Boer War. Hugh Price Hughes did not want it discussed at the Free Church Council meeting, precisely because it was divisive (**VI.1**), whereas John Clifford was keenly against the war (**VI.2**). Both Hughes and Clifford were Liberals: this was a division within party not between parties, and it was never likely there that the pacifist line would ever dominate.

However, there were protests against increasing armaments and support for disarmament conferences, such as that at The Hague in 1907. Thus the argument that the German invasion of Belgium made it impossible for Britain to stand by and do nothing in 1914 was extremely important for nonconformists. The two extracts from the Sir Arthur Howarth's Addresses as Chairman of the Congregational Union Assemblies in 1915 (**VI.3**) make this clear. The resolutions of the Primitive Methodist Conference in 1915 and 1918 (**VI.4**) illustrate the way in which opinion hardened, even in what was probably the largest nonconformist denomination likely to include pacifist voices.

Howarth still hoped in the autumn of 1915 that conscription could be avoided. Nonconformists won a concession in the principle of conscientious objection (borrowed from nonconformist objections to compulsory vaccination in the late nineteenth century); but conscription proved inevitable.[2] It brought further division within the nonconformist ranks. Among Churches of Christ, for example, this was one of the issues which led some conservative churches eventually to leave the Association between the wars. The resolution of the Churches of Christ Annual Conference of 1916 (**VI.6**) balanced concern for those away at the Front or already bereaved, with concern for those who were suffering from the way in which conscientious objectors were being treated in many places.

There had been Roman Catholic and Wesleyan (and Church of Scotland) chaplains to the Army since the Crimean War; provision was made for chaplains from the smaller denominations from May 1915,[3] but the Church of England chaplains were separated from the rest under their own Deputy Chaplain-General from July 1915. Many chaplains did heroic work (**VI.5**).

In 1917–18 the Society of Friends was involved in conflict with the government over the new censorship rules introduced in 1917. Because a pamphlet entitled 'A Challenge to Militarism' was not submitted to the censor, those concerned were prosecuted, and subsequently imprisoned. By chance the Yearly Meeting of 1918 was taking place at the time of the trial, and its Minute 11 (**VI.8**) reflected the support of the meeting for those charged. Other Friends protested against the action of Yearly Meeting, since not all Friends were conscientious objectors.[4] This was the most direct conflict between an official nonconformist body and the government during the First World War.

The majority in most denominations supported the war, particularly by 1917–18, as the Baptist letter to their counterparts in the USA indicated (**VI.7**). But the official celebrations to mark the end of the war were not interdenominational; and John Clifford's diary note in 1918 (**VI.9**) reflects satisfaction that at least the King and Queen had officially recognised the place of the Free Churches by attending their service in the Royal Albert Hall to mark the end of the war.

The Congregational Union's special commission to consider the position of Chaplains to the Forces, which reported in 1933, illustrated the way in which opinion was still divided (**VI.10**). The Commission, while recommending no change in the position of Congregational Chaplains to the Forces, affirmed that this was not incompatible with continued opposition to war as a means of resolving international disputes. The date of this discussion was ironical in view of Hitler's accession to power, and the churches found themselves on the horns of a dilemma, as the problems for the German Churches became more apparent and the possibility of a peaceful resolution of the issues became steadily less plausible.

The Free Church continued to oppose the build up of armaments. One reason was the changing nature of warfare, and particularly the likely impact of bombing. Stanley Baldwin's gloomy prediction in November 1932 that 'the bomber will always get through' heightened criticism of this as a strategy.[5] The resolution of the Presbyterian Church of England in 1937 condemning bombing as terrorism (**VI.11**) is a reminder that different generations use the same word to describe different situations.

As the 1930s debate had predicted, the Second World War involved civilians on an unprecedented scale. The bombing of cities took a heavy toll of church buildings and raised a series of questions about whether and how they should be replaced. The Baptist Union produced a survey of bombed churches as part of its post-war appeal for funds (**VI.13**). The London headquarters of the Presbyterian Church of England in Tavistock Place suffered a direct hit from a V2 bomb on 9 February 1945, and several senior staff were killed, including the Revd W. T. Elmslie, the General Secretary. The letter found in his secretary's typewriter (**VI.12**) illustrates the Church's help for refugee ministers from Europe in their various situations.

The V2 was only one form of new military technology in use by 1945; the atomic bomb was another, soon to be followed in the 1950s by the hydrogen bomb. The destructive power in the hands of the major powers had become so great as to relativise much previous thinking on war and peace. The churches made many critical comments as the arms race developed in the post-war period. The Methodist Church's Declaration on Peace and War, adopted by Conference in 1957 (**VI.14**), was a good illustration of the different context in which the issues of pacifism and non-pacifism, just war and unjust war now had to be discussed. The same kinds of division reflected in the Boer War and the First World War were still there; but the Statement's public recognition of differences of view was new. One interpretation would be that the Church wished to sit on the fence; another is that it reflected a new kind of realism and honesty in the discussion of such matters. More complicated issues were raised by the development of guerilla warfare; and this became acute after the Unilateral Declaration of Independence by Southern Rhodesia in 1965. Methodists such as Colin Morris (**VI.15**) were prepared to support those fighting for majority rule.

In fact, there was no nuclear war in the latter part of the twentieth century, but the actions of the USA in Vietnam demonstrated that 'conventional war' could still be much more horrific than in 1939–45, and the development of guided missiles and high-flying, heavy bombers considerably increased the destructive capacity which the Western powers were prepared to use. By the end of the century the Churches were more unitedly critical of wars such as those in the Falklands (1982) and in the Gulf (1991) (**VI.16**).

Notes

1. Sell & Cross (2003), pp. 221–2.
2. Rae (1970), pp. 43–8.
3. Smyth (1968), pp.162–3.
4. Kennedy (2001), pp. 357–420; Hirst (1923), pp. 492–525, 538.
5. Middlemas & Barnes (1969), p. 735.

Document VI.1

Hugh Price Hughes and the Boer War

Dorothea Price Hughes, *The Life of Hugh Price Hughes* (London: Hodder & Stoughton, 1904), pp. 550, 557, 573–4.

The Boer War split nonconformists. The Wesleyan minister, Hugh Price Hughes, was one of the most fervent Liberal Imperialists, as these extracts reveal. The final quotation is from a letter to Henry Lunn written from SS *Argonaut*, dated 12 February 1900. By the end of the Boer War, Hughes had died. The Free Church Council discussed the War at Cardiff in 1901, passing an innocuous resolution superceded by a six-point peace plan in July put forward by John Clifford, which formed the basis of a subsequent Memorandum.

On returning from his tour in the Eastern Mediterranean in 1900, he said, 'I have seen many fair and wonderful sights, but the fairest and most wonderful of all was a grinning Tommy Atkins at Alexandria. I sighted him as our vessel was approaching the shore – grinning for all he was worth, and my heart leapt up at him. Oh, my God, the wretched Egyptians have at last attained something approaching happiness in this world! Everywhere, justice and the Pax Britannica. The very donkey boys were full of it. They said to me, "Wonderful! Wonderful! A donkey boy and a cadi equal before the law! Wonderful, wonderful!" The Englishman, you see, in spite of his slowness, has grasped something of justice, and, being a bull-dog, does not let it go. Oh! It is marvellous – look at India and all these fellows. Peace at last after centuries, and the princes and potentates stopped from cutting each other's throats, and something like decent civilisation.' ... If the British also did not assert themselves in Africa, the Dutch or somebody else would do so, introducing their imperfect ideas of justice and government ...

In the notes of the *Methodist Times* he made clear that he supported the British on the following issues:– Firstly, that he believed the regime of Kruger to be reactionary, and opposed to those principles of liberal self-government, which all the Anglo-Saxon nations had adopted. Secondly, he was convinced that the rule of the Boer meant licence for the drink traffic. Thirdly, he held that under the Boer the natives were in a condition of practical slavery, having no right to own land ... 'I am very sorry the South African War is to be discussed at Sheffield. Excellent Free Churchmen differ so deeply about that, that if I had been at the Committee I should have done my utmost to induce them to leave the subject severely alone. The War, Home Rule, and all topics on which we are not agreed, should never be touched. The one great peril of the moment is the perpetual attempt to drag such burning questions into our midst. Our business is to keep to the deep theological and ecclesiastical issues on which we are agreed.

'So far as the war is concerned, I wish you and all who agree with you could see the blissful results of British rule in Egypt, and could realise the effect abroad of the incessant nagging at your own great country, and the even more pestiferous whitewashing of one of the most cruel and mendacious military oligarchies that ever enslaved black men and outraged white men.'

Peace and War

Document VI.2

John Clifford on the Boer War

J. Marchant, *Dr John Clifford* (London: Cassell, 1924), pp. 150–51.

Dr John Clifford, a leading Baptist minister, was President of the General Committee in favour of stopping the war; he had the police at his Westbourne Park chapel for three nights in 1900, because of an attack on the building threatened by 'rowdies'. In this extract he expresses his views in an undated letter to a friend.

I am boiling over with indignation against the iniquity of the Concentration Camps. I have again and again referred to them, denounced them and formulated protests against them; and shall go on doing it as far as I can. But I wish to aid in the emancipation of my people from the tyranny of those blinding delusions which have played so large a part in this horrible war, and one of them, perhaps the most fatal of all the delusions, is the notion that we can really abate the mass of evil whilst the declared and operative policy of the Government is supremacy over, and not the blending of the British race with the Boers. We may shift part of the evil trade from one place to another, but the mass itself will go on increasing. I said so more than a year ago, and the proofs of the truth of my forecast have accumulated with appalling strength. Mr Brodrick's promise is a delusion. Improve the condition in the camps, may be his mandate, but the policy of his Government involves the destruction of the children in the camps, and, as I say in my letter, I shall be surprised if the death-rate is not higher for October than it was for September. I am for mitigating the evil of the war, whatever it can be done, to the uttermost; but till we give up our false pride of race and our blind hatred of the Boer, and we are ready to offer him definite and clearly expressed terms of peace, we shall have executions like that reported this morning: deputations of those who go to alleviate the miseries of women and children and to reduce the death-rate, like that of Miss Hobhouse, and still worse evils of which the censor will not let us hear! Alas! alas! for England.

Document VI.3

The Congregational Union and the First World War

Congregational Year Book, 1916, (a) pp. 49, 51; (b) p. 63.

The Chairman of the Congregational Union in 1915 was Sir Arthur A. Howarth. His Spring Chairman's Address on 10 May (a) set out clearly why so many nonconformists changed their minds and supported the war. His Autumn Address on 4 October (b) reflected increased anxiety about the way things were going, and was clearly against conscription, provided there were sufficient volunteers. There were not, and conscription was introduced a few months later.

(a)

... The situation at the beginning of August was extraordinarily simple and clear. We as a nation had guaranteed the integrity of Belgium, in conjunction with Germany and other nations, and when Germany had perfidiously departed from her undertaking and invaded Belgium in violation of the treaty, for her own ends, it seems to me – and I am glad to think the Christian feeling of Britain agrees – that if we had refused to assert our powers, physical and moral, to maintain our pledged word, we should have shown ourselves false to the spirit of honour imposed upon us by the teaching of Jesus Christ, Whom we profess. As a business man, I know what great harm is not infrequently done to the religion of Christ by prominent church members and teachers who fail to carry out their bond, or who indulge in subterfuges to save their financial skins; and perhaps I may be allowed to add, in parenthesis, that sometimes it happens that those who are loudest in their profession of religion are the least reliable in business. It would be invidious to distinguish between sects; but as one who has the blood in his veins of the Society of Friends, I may be further allowed to say that 'Deeds speak louder than words' – 'By their fruits shall ye know them'.

So far the position of the Christian Church in Great Britain with regard to the war is quite clear; but I do not feel that, if Germany had not invaded Belgium, our position would have been quite so obvious ...

One of the ablest Christian Pacifists I know has recently taught me that the only justification for Christians going to war is if that war is redemptive in its aims. England strove splendidly for peace, but failed in her efforts, and certainly had not prepared for anything but a war of defence. Germany felt that the hour had come for which she had long and carefully prepared, and we were surely called upon then to help to redeem the peoples of the world, by every means in our power, from the spirit of self-aggrandisement and tyranny which is so absolutely opposed to the teaching of Christ. We seek no material gain, but are proving ourselves able to rise to the heights of great sacrifice. May we be purified by its fires and become more worthy to bear the name of our great Redeemer?

(b)

I do not want this evening to say anything about the war; but we could not possibly have forgotten it at this time, even if my subject had not thus inevitably led our thoughts to it. We pledged ourselves, as a Union, last May, to support the Government in their endeavours to bring the war to a successful conclusion, because we felt it right for Christian men and women to strive to the uttermost, laying down their lives if necessary, to preserve the human freedom of the world. The response to the call of Duty has been splendid from the young men of our Churches; but I must frankly confess that I should like to have been able to feel that we ourselves, because we had more clearly grasped the fact that our dearest principles were at stake, had been so busy in carrying out our resolution of last May, in our hundred-and-one different ways, as to be unable to spare time for these present meetings.

We have been for the past fortnight living in a state of excitement caused by the consideration of the question of State Compulsion of military service. Conscription has for long been viewed with the greatest suspicion and abhorrence by the majority of the people of this country, and rightly so. To compel a man to fight, and possibly lay down his life, for his country, is the greatest infringement of liberty, and ought to be strenuously resisted as such. Only on one consideration can we acquiesce in compulsory military service. Voluntaryism, of course, carries with it the corollary that you must have volunteers; and if, after a clearly proved official statement that, magnificent though it has been, the voluntary system has been found inadequate to the present needs, our ideas of liberty can no longer be maintained without being harmful to others, and must be temporarily surrendered in this case also to the common good. Such a statement has not been made, and I trust will never be possible. With a clear knowledge of what is wanted, I believe the voluntary system will still prove adequate.

Document VI.4

Primitive Methodists and the First World War

(a) *Minutes of Primitive Methodist Conference*, 1915, p. 244; (b) *Minutes of Primitive Methodist Conference*, 1918, pp. 3–4.

Within Methodism the Primitive Methodists were those with the strongest anti-war tradition. These two resolutions, both in content and tone, illustrate the way in which pro-war feeling hardened as the war went on.

(a)
That this Annual Conference of the Primitive Methodist Church views with grief and horror the European War and regards as guilty of treason to Christian civilisation those who have provoked this awful conflict. We believe in the sanctity of peace and should strive to enthrone the will of the Son of Man among the nations. We acknowledge the effort made for peace by our King, his government and especially by the Secretary of State for Foreign Affairs. This hideous calamity has been forced upon us by the brutal arrogance and lawless ambition of a military caste and a materialistic philosophy which would, if triumphant, fling the world back into the most piteous savagery. We have been called to resistance by sacred claims of honour by the impulse of fidelity to international relations and by the urgent need of small nations. We support His Majesty's government in its call to Britain to spare neither blood nor treasure to crush the German conspiracy against the freedom and peace of the world.

(b)
The Conference places on record its admiration for the heroic sons of our church who are engaged in deadly combat with a ruthless enemy and expresses its deep sympathy with all our beloved people who have been called upon to share in the poignant sorrows and crucial sacrifices of the nation.

No less than 150,000 Primitive Methodists have joined the Army and Navy including upwards of 4,000 local preachers. Forty-three ministers have served as chaplains and nearly 200 as officiating clergymen. In the various philanthropic and beneficent ministries of the war, our people have nobly borne their part. A solemn and impressive Conference service was held in memory of 15,000 brave sons of our church, who in this great hour of Destiny have given themselves for England and humanity and who, having made the supreme sacrifice are now assembled as God's happy warriors on the Plains of Peace clothed in the white robes of immortality. The truths taught them in the Sabbath School enabled them to meet death with calm assurance. They shared the faith of Rupert Brooke, the poet who just before he fell mortally wounded at Lemnos wrote on a piece of paper:

> 'Safe where no safety is
> Safe though I fall
> But if these poor limbs die
> Safest of all'.

Document VI.5

A Wesleyan Military Chaplain

John Smyth, *In This Sign Conquer: The Story of Army Chaplains* (London: Mowbray, 1968), p. 161. © Sir John Smyth, reprinted with the permission of the publisher, The Continuum International Publishing Group.

The provision of nonconformist Chaplains to the Forces was extended to the smaller Free Churches in the First World War. The Revd Owen Spencer Watkins (1873–1957) was the Senior Wesleyan Methodist Chaplain to the Forces and Hon. Chaplain to the King. After the War he became Assistant, later Deputy, Chaplain General, and a leading figure in Toc H. This is part of his description of the retreat from Mons.

We could hold no Services but none the less the chaplains were busy about their Master's business. To them no service was too menial, no task ever came amiss. They washed the swollen, filthy feet of the footsore infantry; the white-haired Bickerstaff-Drew (the Roman Catholic Chaplain), on bended knees, swabbed up the blood-stained floor of a dressing station; they helped the doctors with the wounded, lent a hand to carry a stretcher, rode ahead to choose bivouac or billets, and then guided the unit to its place of rest. These were the things which brought us close to our men and opened their hearts to us so that we could minister to their spiritual needs. But most precious and most sacred was the service rendered to the dying and when the end came, the last sad office to the dead. ... I declare that never before have men been so tested as these were during the fortnight of the retreat from Mons ... It was a triumph of mind and spirit over physical weakness, and it impressed our comrades of the fighting services far more than our preaching has ever done or is likely to do.

Peace and War

Document VI.6

Churches of Christ and the First World War

Churches of Christ Year Book, 1916, pp. 148–9.

The Churches of Christ probably had a larger pacifist minority than some of the larger Free Churches. Nevertheless the majority view in the Conference supported the War. The resolution of the 1916 Conference, after conscription had been introduced is more balanced than that of 1915, which referred only to those who had suffered or died in battle or had been bereaved.

That this Conference, after another year of intense and ever-increasing strain consequent upon the great world-struggle still unfortunately continuing, re-affirms its expressions of heartfelt sympathy with the largely augmented number of those who are more immediately affected in this great crisis.

It remembers with deepest solicitude the many hundreds of young men, members of our Churches and families, who have gone forth at the call of duty to take their part in the defence of principles held supremely dear, and who, on land and sea, in camp, or on the stricken field, are facing temptation, danger, and death; the many who are lying wounded, maimed, and sick in hospital; those who have been made prisoners of war; the multitudes of those whose hearts are filled with anxious forebodings for dear ones far away, and especially those whose hearts and homes have been devastated on account of the many who will never return.

It remembers also with deepest solicitude those who, for conscience sake, are suffering imprisonment and other disabilities, and calls upon the government to release them for work of national importance not under the control of the military authorities; and extends deepest sympathy to all who in body, mind, or estate are partakers in the world-fellowship of suffering.

It bears up at the throne of grace all such, praying that all needful courage, consolation, and endurance may be vouchsafed in this time of need, and anticipates with profoundest longing the day when righteousness and peace shall reign upon earth.

Document VI.7

British Baptist Message to American Baptists, 1917

Message from the Baptist Union of Great Britain and Ireland to the Baptists of the USA, 1917, pp. 4, 5, 6–12.

This Message sent in May 1917 when the USA was on the point of entering the war, offers the justification which had become characteristic by this time. It is significant that the signatories included John Clifford as Ex-President of the Baptist World Alliance.

Through all our history there shines clear and strong our common devotion to peace. Although we never accepted the absolute 'non-resistance' theory of the teaching of Christ, we have always been advocates of peace ...

Like you, we British Baptists hate and loathe all war. ... Many of us, at great cost, opposed the Boer War. Indeed, we have never unsheathed the sword whilst it was possible to keep it in its scabbard; and if any other way had been possible for us we should not have taken it out in August 1914. But there was no other way. As your President says, 'We could do no other.'

It is indisputable that not only was Germany preparing for this world war in her own boundaries, but was always endeavoring to create occasions of war, with a persistence and a subtlety that filled all lovers of peace with apprehension and despondency.

The story of the provocation of France is one of the most pathetic chapters in the history of that brave people. The more pacific they became, the more Germany thrust in its goads ... For over forty years the policy of provocation was carried on ...

All through these years our Government was doing whatever it could to avoid war. At the Hague Conference England laboured most strenuously to secure a limitation of armaments. We saw the peril of the increase that was going on from year to year, and our people backed the appeal in every way they could. But no, Germany would have none of it. On the contrary, the appeals for reduction were met by an enormous extension of shipbuilding on the one hand and a vast increase of the land forces on the other.

In defence of her action Germany complained that she wanted 'a place in the sun' and that the 'Powers' were setting up barriers against her advance, and yet from 1884 she had acquired 1,800,000 square miles of territory, *i.e.* an area larger than Germany and France, Austria and Hungary, Italy and Serbia, Portugal and Bulgaria, and had done so with the consent of the Powers alleged to be thwarting her. The real situation was summed up by the German Staff in 1914 in the words, 'We shall smash France in three weeks; then wheel about and deliver a knockdown blow to Russia before she has time to complete her mobilisation. Belgium will offer only the resistance of sullenness. England will not come in at all.' Thus they planned to subjugate Europe to the German sceptre. It was with that temper that our Government had to deal, and it is undeniably certain that Viscount Grey strove with the utmost sincerity and with persistent energy for the pacification of Europe. He strained every fibre to keep the peace ...

But the German Government had made up its mind, and the neutrality of Belgium was deliberately violated in the face of the treaty of London made on April 19, 1839, between England, Austria, France, Russia and Prussia on the one hand and the Netherlands on the other.

That action swept us at once over the barriers between peace and war. It was a flagrant violation of law. It was a wrong done to the soul and to the homes of a small nation, a scornful and contemptuous tearing up of a solemn compact in the face of Europe, cynically described by the German Chancellor as 'a scrap of paper.' Like the shot that rang round the world, and roused the farmers of New England to the defense of their rights, so this calculated and deliberate defiance of an international compact stirred the spirit of Britain to rise and defend the Belgian people. A wave of moral indignation spread through the land. We were compelled to act, and to act in one way. It was the one duty. It was the will of God ...

Immediately we were a united people as we rarely have been in our long history. There has been nothing like it in the churches; certainly not among our own people. Thousands of the young men of our churches rose with spontaneity and resolute daring to offer the great sacrifice of their lives to the cause. Our workers, Sunday-school superintendents and teachers, deacons and leaders rallied to the flag as to a most holy task. Many of our ministers volunteered as chaplains and are acting as such. Our Young Men's Christian Associations rendered a magnificent service. The women of our churches were as keen and eager as the men. In short, the nation is one. Five million and forty-one thousand men voluntarily enrolled themselves in the Army before conscription. They could not hold back, the call was of God, and they must respond. It was a question of conscience. We are fighting for Christianity against Paganism, for right against cruel might, for liberty against tyranny, for humanity against the work of the devil ...

Germany ... began by trampling law and treaty under foot in the violation of the soil of Belgium; then staggered humanity in the destruction of Louvain and Rheims; aroused indignation by slaying non-combatants, women and children, at Scarborough; sent out a cold-blooded decree that made the killing of non-combatants not an incident of heated warfare, not an accident, no, but a regular method of obtaining military advantage, and sent a thousand innocent people to death in the 'Lusitania.' Lord Bryce's report consists of sifted evidence. We had difficulty in believing what is found in our papers. We said there must be exaggeration. This and that could not be true, but here you have the proofs set out by one of the most important and most responsible committees that ever sat on any international question. That committee says:

'It is proved –

'1. That there were in many parts of Belgium deliberate and systematically organized massacres of the civil population, accompanied "by many isolated murders and other outrages."

'2. That in the conduct of war generally, innocent civilians, both men and women, were murdered in large numbers, women violated, and children murdered.

'3. That looting, house-burning, and wanton destruction of property were ordered and countenanced by the officers of the German Army. That elaborate provision had been made for systematic incendiarism at the very outbreak of the war, and that the burnings and destruction were frequent where no military necessity could be alleged, being indeed, part of a system of general terrorisation.

'4. That the rules and usages of war were frequently broken, particularly by the using of civilians, including women and children, as a shield for advancing forces exposed to fire, to a less degree by the killing and wounding of prisoners, and in the frequent abuse of the Red Cross and the White Flag.'

... Now, it is because we are seeking to bring this calamitous reign of barbarism and savagery to an immediate end that we hail with profound thankfulness and boundless hope the entrance of America into this European war. It is a mighty event for you and for us ...

As our Prime Minister, Mr Lloyd George, said: 'The Americans coming into the war give the final stamp and seal to the character of the conflict as a struggle against military autocracy through the world'.
London, May 2, 1917.

Document VI.8

Friends and Censorship in the First World War

Extracts from the Minutes and Proceedings of the London Yearly Meeting of Friends 1918 (London, 1918), pp. 8–10.

Despite their traditional pacifism the Society of Friends was as divided over the First World War as other nonconformists were, the difference being that in their case the majority were pacifist. The clash with government came over Regulation 27C of the Defence of the Realm Act, issued in November 1917, which required all pamphlets concerning the war to be submitted to the censor before publication. Meeting for Sufferings declined to comply with this and publicised the fact. The leaflet which was the basis for the prosecution stated the principles for which conscientious objectors had gone to prison. Proceedings were taken against the three executives of the Friends' Service Committee. The trial was held while the Yearly Meeting was in session in May, the two men being sentenced to six months' imprisonment and the woman was fined £100; the sentences were upheld on appeal. Some members of the Society published their dissent from Yearly Meeting. The government did not, however, bring any further cases against the Society.

22nd of Fifth Month, 4th Day Morning 1918

11   Our friend, Harrison Barrow, has made a statement on behalf of the Service Committee regarding the prosecution of three of their number, Edith M. Ellis, Harrison Barrow and Arthur Watts, under the Defence of the Realm Act, for engaging a printer to print a leaflet entitled 'A Challenge to Militarism' and for having in their possession copies of the same, without first submitting it to the Censor, and also because the leaflet bore the name of the Committee as author and not the individual names of the Members of the Committee, in the way required by the regulation.

The question of principle involved in this prosecution received prolonged and careful consideration by the Meeting for Sufferings immediately after the issue of the regulation '27C' under which this prosecution is taken, and the following Minute was adopted by the Meeting for Sufferings and communicated to the Government and to the Press:–

> The Executive body of the Society of Friends, after serious consideration, desires to place on record its conviction that the portion of the recent regulation requiring the

submission to the Censor of all leaflets dealing with the present war and the making of peace is a grave danger to the national welfare. The duty of every good citizen to express his thoughts on the affairs of his country is hereby endangered, and further, we believe that Christianity requires the toleration of opinions not our own, lest we should unwittingly hinder the workings of the Spirit of God.

Beyond this there is a deeper issue involved. It is for Christians a paramount duty to be free to obey, and to act and speak in accord with the law of God, a law higher than that of any State, and no Government official can release men from this duty.

We realise the rarity of the occasions on which a body of citizens find their sense of duty to be in conflict with the law, and it is with a sense of the gravity of the decision, that the Society of Friends must on this occasion act contrary to the regulation and continue to issue literature on war and peace, without submitting it to the Censor. It is convinced that in thus standing for spiritual liberty it is acting in the best interests of the nation.

After earnest consideration this Meeting unites in this Minute. As the action of the Service Committee is in full conformity with the Minute of the Meeting for Sufferings we appoint the following Friends to attend at the trial (tomorrow at 12 o'clock at the Guildhall) and to read the Minute if way opens. They are asked to state to the Court that the Yearly Meeting now in session endorses this Minute, and desires to share responsibility for the action of its three members now charged under the Defence of the Realm Act: – John Henry Barlow, J. Thompson Eliott, Gulielma Crosfield, Edith J. Wilson, William A. Albright, T. Edmund Harvey.

Document VI.9

John Clifford on the End of the War, 1918

J. Marchant, *Dr John Clifford* (London: Cassell, 1924), p. 235.

The Free Churches were excluded from the National Thanksgiving Services for the End of the War in Westminster Abbey. This entry from John Clifford's diary for 1918 reflects the hope that a new era had begun.

Saturday, November 16th – Thanksgiving Service of the Free Churches in the Albert Hall. King and Queen present. It was a great and most impressive gathering. It is the beginning of a new day in the relations of the State to 'Dissent'. It is the lifting to a slight extent of the social stigma. Of course it will not go far, but so far as it goes it is in the direction of greater freedom in religious thought and life, and may be regarded as a movement toward reality. The Free Churches are glad; but they must not forget that their strength is in their inward simplicity and faith.

Document VI.10

The Congregational Union and Chaplains to the Forces, 1932

Congregational Year Book, 1933, pp. 64–5.

The question of Chaplains to the Forces continued to cause controversy after the First World War was over. The Congregational Union Assembly approved this Report of the Commission on Chaplains to the Forces in May 1932 with one dissentient.

The Commission was appointed as the result of a discussion in the Assembly in May 1931 on a Resolution moved by Dr Norwood and seconded by the Rev. A. D. Belden as follows:–

'Whereas it is the common Christian conviction that War is incompatible with our Lord Jesus Christ, and whereas the Nations of the World have covenanted to renounce its use as an instrument of Policy, and whereas a Chaplaincy in the Army involves taking rank as an Officer, implies in peace time general consent to the War system, and in War time prevents freedom of opinion concerning the struggle engaged upon, and whereas the holding of Official rank gives to War the appearance of its sanction by the Church,

Be it now resolved that the Congregational Union of England & Wales will henceforth refrain from nominating Chaplains to the Forces unless upon an entirely voluntary basis subject only to the discipline of the Church.'

On a vote being taken, the Chairman declared that it was impossible to state whether the Resolution was carried or not, and in the result it was decided to remit the matter to the General Purposes Committee with a view to the appointment of a small Commission to consider the question and report to the Assembly in May 1932...

The Commission was faced with the fact that there were Congregationalists in the Services who have a right to all the help and guidance the denomination can give. It endeavoured to find some way by which such help could be given without chaplains being under military authority, and it directed its enquiries mainly to the consideration of the question whether it were possible for chaplains to be appointed and to do their work subject only to the discipline of denominational authorities.

The precedent for unofficial chaplains, pleaded in support of the proposal for voluntary chaplains, was thoroughly investigated. Prior to 1914 certain denominations for a time appointed 'Acting Chaplains' who were not commissioned. They were paid either by capitation grant estimated on the number of their men, or by a fixed annual payment arranged with the War Office. They were, however, subject in all respects as regards their ministrations to the same Army Regulations as the Regular Chaplains, but were denied some of the privileges given to commissioned officers. The system had many disadvantages, as was proved by the evidence of those who had worked under both systems, and as the result of this experience these denominations have accepted the system of Regular Chaplains. At the present time voluntary workers appointed by two religious organizations are in practice under the control of the Army Chaplains Department and are subject to military discipline. All the evidence received by the Commission went on to show that direct control of the work of the chaplains by denominational authorities was unworkable in practice.

As the discussion proceeded a division of opinion became evident. Some of the members of the Commission not only argued that the present was the only practicable method of ministering to the religious needs of the men of our denomination in the Forces, but that such ministrations had nothing whatever to do with our views as to the ethics of war. So long as the Navy, Army and Air Force exist, they believed that it was our bounden duty to take our share along with the other Churches in seeing that the men in the Forces have adequate opportunities of attending divine worship and of receiving such help and guidance as chaplains can give.

Others maintained that the appointment of chaplains and the participation of the denomination in the Navy, Army and Air Force Board was liable in the public mind to associate the Union with the approval of war and to compromise its peace witness.

In exploring these differences it became clear that the association of the Union with the United Navy, Army and Air Force Board was for purposes mainly of guaranteeing the character and status of chaplains who are considered to be devoted solely to the spiritual interests of the men, and that this association ought not to be interpreted in any sense as an endorsement of the war-system. Hence the Commission unanimously recommends that while continuing the present policy the Union place on record the most emphatic declaration that it regards this association as consistent with the absolute repudiation of war and the war-system, which it believes incompatible with the teaching and example of Jesus Christ, and which it is determined by every means in its power to abolish.

Document VI.11

Indiscriminate Bombing, 1937

PCE, *Record of Assembly*, 1937, pp. 324–5.

Stanley Baldwin's comment that 'the bomber will always get through' summed up the helplessness which was felt in the face of the development of aerial warfare. This resolution was brought by the Committee on the State of Religion and Public Morals to the Presbyterian General Assembly in May 1937 and adopted. Its use of the term 'terrorism' is interesting in the light of subsequent developments.

That the Government be urged to protest against the use of terrorism as a method of warfare by the indiscriminate bombing and burning of open towns and the slaughter by machine guns of the fleeing inhabitants.

Immediate steps should also be taken to invite all other civilised Governments to join in this protest and in addition the question should be raised as soon as possible at the Council of the League.

The Assembly, in view of the inordinate military preparations and the apparent reliance on military force throughout the whole world, convinced that the faithful propagation of its evangelic faith involves removal of the causes of war, the attainment of economic justice and the cultivation of mutual understanding, appeals to H.M. Government to take the initiative in calling an inclusive Conference of the Nations with a view to achieving such adjustments as will promote general agreement and the reduction of armaments.

Document VI.12

Assistance to Continental Pastors, 1945

Revd W. T. Elmslie to the Revd Dr W. M. Rochester, 9 February 1945, United Reformed Church Archives.

This letter was written by the Revd W. T. Elmslie, General Secretary of the Presbyterian Church of England to the Revd Dr W. M. Rochester of the Presbyterian Church in Canada. It was rescued from his secretary's typewriter, which survived the V2 bomb that destroyed Presbyterian Church House and killed several staff, including Elmslie, on the day it was written, 9 February 1945.

I have now been able to distribute the whole of the most generous gift sent to me by you from an anonymous donor in the Presbyterian Church in Canada. You will remember that the gift amounted in our currency to £223.11.9d, and that, according to your letter of November 1st, it was to be used –
(1) 'Partly for Continental pastors who have congregations in this country, for use at their discretion from time to time to assist needy people in their flocks'.
(2) 'For the purpose of assisting theological students of the Continental Churches who are, or will be, studying here owing to the destruction of the theological colleges in their own countries'.

I duly approached all the continental pastors mentioned in my letter of 21st September, namely; 'Swiss, French, German, Norwegian, and perhaps Swedish and Finnish chaplains'. The Dutch, as I knew, were not in need of such help, and I found on enquiry that the same was true of the Swiss, Norwegians and Swedes.

Eventually I distributed the following sums:–

Rev. F. Christol (French) for distribution		£20
" H. Migot (French) for two ladies		£10
" " his own use		£ 5
" T. Harjuan (Finnish) for his own use		£20
" V. Jenssen (Danish) for distribution		£10
" his own use		£10
" Dr J. Rieger (German) for distribution		£45
		£120

You will readily understand how it comes to be that the Germans, though anti-Nazi, are in greatest need. In regard to the gifts to pastors for their own use, perhaps I should say that I found them very hesitant about accepting these gifts, but very grateful for them. In some cases they had ample funds for assisting their compatriots, but they themselves had been overlooked. I made very careful enquiries in various quarters in regard to this matter.

The balance of the gift, viz: £103.11.9d, I have handed over to a fund that is under the supervision of our own Assembly's Committee on Intercourse with Other Churches at Home and Abroad for the purpose of assisting continental theological students to take theological courses in this country. We have been gradually accumulating a sum (which is still all too small) for this purpose during the war, as we know that there will be many who will desire to avail themselves of it. I may add that I and others have been trying to stimulate all denominations in this country to make similar provision, and there is good hope that we may be able to do something substantial altogether, providing that our own colleges can find accommodation during the somewhat congested period that we expect after demobilization.

I hope that the donor, to whom we are all most grateful, will feel that the money has been distributed on lines that he would approve, and I enclose a number of letters of information and of thanks.

All kind regards and good wishes.
Yours very sincerely,
Wm. T. Elmslie

Document VI.13

Bombed Churches

Our Bombed Churches (London: Baptist Union, n.d.), pp. 2, 3, 41.

The effects of bombing on nonconformist churches in the Second World War were considerable. and incidentally raised questions about whether it was sensible to rebuild in the same places. This leaflet from the Baptist Union paints a picture of many buildings that were destroyed and appeals for money for their rebuilding.

The pages that follow tell a little of the grim story of the havoc of war in some of our Baptist churches. Only a few of these can be named. There are many others. Lives were lost as well as buildings and these nothing can replace. The work of some churches came to a full stop. In others, the results of generations of service and sacrifice were swept away in a few dread seconds and the garden of the Lord was turned into a desert.

But the desert may 'rejoice and blossom as the rose.' The writer has not missed the 'many-coloured splendour' of Christian heroism and devotion, of men and women who never gave up. They are our hope and glory and now they look to us for help.

The total of claims for damage to Baptist church property comes to over £6,000,000. The task before us is enormous. The Government is pledged to give us 'plain substitute buildings' or 'plain repairs' when material and labour can be spared. No embellishments can be expected unless we pay for them. The contents, even if reasonably insured at pre-war values, must be replaced at post-war cost.

Depleted churches must be helped to meet the charges of their work, to secure ministers, to revive Sunday schools. Those who have suffered are doing much. Those who did not suffer ought to do far more in gratitude and brotherly love.

Our Thanksgiving Fund aims to get £150,000 at any rate to begin with, and a third of that amount will go to those on the Continent whose need is great. It seems little enough but it will mean a great deal ...

The story of our churches under war conditions is a proud page in our Baptist history. It is a story of the wail of the siren, the crashing of the bombs, the glare of the fires and then of brave hearts meeting on the ruins the next morning and determining, somehow or somewhere, to carry on the life of the churches, but any way to carry on.

There was this to encourage them. Offers of assistance came from all quarters. Never did denominational boundaries seem more unreal. Anglicans, Methodists, Congregationalists, Presbyterians, offered the use of their church premises to the Baptists. Educational authorities threw away their restrictive rules and opened their school buildings. In their turn, the Baptist churches became the refuge for churches from many other denominations.

But this is only part of the story. Those same bombs brought death and injury to people young and old, and destruction to their homes. Church halls of all denominations were opened to give temporary shelter to the homeless. Comfort and courage were brought to many by a visit from the minister while the 'alert' was still in operation. Services were held at night in shelters to the crashing of bombs.

One vivid impression left by the war was the part played by the churches in keeping the nerves of the people steady in danger, and in focussing the desire to help into practical channels.

A less spectacular, but no less real, service was that performed by church members who, as voluntary fire-watchers, in turns watched during the lonely nights over the safety of their beloved churches, and by their own efforts with the humble stirrup-pump, or by their early call to the Fire Service for aid, saved many a church.

Seven hundred of our Baptist churches were damaged, of which sixty-six were totally destroyed. London, Coventry, Birmingham, Norwich, Portsmouth, Southampton, Plymouth, Bristol, and many other places have each their stories of destruction and great-hearted devotion ...

These pages are a record of the destruction of churches. And be it remembered that these pages only record a few of the churches which have been destroyed or badly damaged.

Nevertheless it is not a depressing story, for it tells of brave-hearted congregations facing the future with courage.

Destruction has become a challenge to reconstruction. Throughout these pages will be found examples of churches which have sought to use the opportunity for development on new lines, sometimes in new areas. An opportunity of fresh vision has been given, a vision which may entail a break with the hallowed traditions of past services on the old sites, and a call to fresh endeavours in new surroundings. It is a vision also of every church in the denomination joyfully stretching out a helping hand to those who have suffered, and so showing to all that Christians in these days, as in days of old, stand together in times of need.

Document VI.14

Methodism on Peace and War, 1957

D. Deeks (ed.), *Methodist Church Statements on Social Responsibility 1946–1999* (London: Methodist Church Division of Social Responsibility, 1992), pp. 94–8.

The development of nuclear weapons in the latter part of the Second World War and subsequently raised new issues and accentuated old ones for the churches. This declaration of the Methodist Church on Peace and War was adopted by Conference in 1957: it has not been replaced.

The Responsibility of the Church
The Conference of the Methodist Church in Great Britain shares with its sister communions of the Christian Church throughout the world, and with Christian people everywhere, a deep and passionate desire to see the establishment of a world order based upon righteousness, abiding goodwill and peace. We accept, as an essential part of the redemptive mission of the Church, the duty to promote peace and to prevent war ...

The Mind of Our Lord
We acknowledge that war is contrary to the spirit, teaching and purpose of our Lord. The simple, yet all-comprehending, command He laid upon those who follow Him, that they should love God and should love their neighbour, shattered all narrower limitations and extended the obligation of love and charity to include the stranger and the enemy. He Himself met evil with good, hatred with love, and persistent injury with persistent readiness to forgive. He faced the world with unfailing and unyielding goodness, teaching men, both by precept and example, to love their enemies. He forgave those who wronged Him even unto death.

We believe that His teaching and example were intended to apply not only to individual relations, but to the social and corporate affairs of men, and to the intercourse of nations. If the prayer, 'Thy kingdom come', is ever to be finally and fully realized on earth it can only be in a world-embracing brotherhood of righteousness, love and peace. Since the causes of war are ultimately to be found in the unregenerate hearts and uncontrolled passions of mankind, the Conference calls the Methodist people, in their service for peace, to unwearied devotion in witness to the redemptive power of Christ, and to a life of love and charity with their neighbours, rendering to no man evil for evil, but striving to overcome evil with good.

The Christian Attitudes to War
We must, however, face the fact that there is division of judgement among earnest and convinced Christians concerning the application of these generally accepted principles to the harsh realities of the present situation. All Christians agree that war is evil. Some believe that it is, therefore, in every circumstance to be rejected by the follower of Christ. Others believe that there are situations in which the waging of war is inevitable as the choice of the lesser of two admitted evils.

(i) **Christian Pacifism**
The Christian pacifist case is rooted in a theological interpretation of the Cross, and an acceptance of the practical obligations to act on that belief. It is a faith in the power of God to achieve His purpose through human obedience to the Cross of Jesus Christ as the instrument of salvation. Jesus taught that we must love our enemies. He Himself loved his enemies with such complete dedication that for their sakes He deliberately laid down His life. His teaching, exemplified in His life and supremely validated by His death on the Cross, was that the way of God is the way of love, conversion and reconciliation. This He practised, no matter what the cost to Himself or to others. Those who have become reconciled to God through Christ are called to follow this way.

It is of the essence of war that it involves the deliberate and intentional killing of other human beings. The pacifist does not condemn the use of any and every kind of force. Any penal action requires force of some kind, and force can be used in many ways that are entirely beneficent. A restraining force used against a criminal, which still leaves open the way towards his reform is an acceptable use of force. But to employ it of set intention for the destruction of others is altogether unacceptable. It is true that war lays upon the participants the readiness to die, but it is not, therefore, necessarily to be equated with sacrifice. For these reasons the Christian pacifist believes that participation in war is incompatible with his obedience.

The appalling developments of modern warfare – mass destruction, bacteriological warfare, indiscriminate attack – underline and emphasize its horrors, and may, therefore the more clearly expose the sinfulness of war, but they do not modify or affect the fundamental theological argument. If war were to be civilized, restricted only to combatants, and waged under agreed conventions that would limit the grosser barbarities of nuclear warfare, it would still be wrong.

It is the duty, and the privilege, of the Christian not to be overcome of evil, but to overcome evil with good.

(ii) **Christian Non-Pacifism**
The Christian non-pacifist conviction is also rooted in a theology of the Cross. Abhorring war and the evils that stem from it, the non-pacifist rejects absolute pacifism because he believes that it obscures the Christian concept of love and tries to apply an individual ethic to a collective situation. Love, which manifests itself in self-sacrificial service, manifests itself also in a concern for social justice. In a sinful world, there are occasions when the claims of peace and justice conflict and a choice

must be made. Both the struggle for justice and the struggle for peace present a moral imperative, but justice has the prior claim, for there can be no lasting peace without it. The non-pacifist hesitates to arrogate to himself as a follower of Christ all the attributes of his Lord. The Cross and the Resurrection were the divinely ordained means of our salvation, but a means which derived their saving power from the fact that it was Christ who died and rose again. The problem with which the Christian non-pacifist wrestles is that of the victims of aggression. His motive is not self-preservation. He would be prepared to offer himself if that would ensure their salvation. It will not. If he, by his conscience, is prohibited form defending them, are they to be left defenceless?

The Christian non-pacifist does not justify every war. He is, indeed, a reluctant upholder of defensive warfare within very narrowly defined limits. But believing that God wills both justice and peace, he is not prepared to agree that invariably and inevitably pacifism is the will of God.

Deep Divergence, but Wide Agreement
It should be emphasized that the divergence between the convinced believers in these opposing judgements is far from one of total estrangement. They are united in their agreement that peace is to be earnestly desired and strenuously sought. Because the difference is between Christians, aware of each other's sincerity, we cannot rest merely with an agreement to differ. We must continue to debate and to pray together, in love and charity. Nevertheless, though the variance is not as wide as is commonly supposed, at the crucial point the divergence is deep. When the question is posed, 'In the event of wanton and unprovoked aggression, what is the duty of a Christian man?', the divergence remains.

International Police Action
The probable development of international police action under the authority of the United Nations introduces a new complication into the already complex situation. Many Christians would be prepared to accept, and support, an 'international police force' designed to prevent the spread of war by employing no more than a minimum of police action to separate combatants and to restore peace. A situation may, however, arise in which a United Nations police army would be instructed to use military force to impose peace. The pacifist would regard this as still contrary to his Christian obedience, but the non-pacifist would welcome it as a step toward a more just and impartial obstacle to extended warfare.

Liberty of Conscience
Should war come we realize that a grave decision will be demanded of the Christian. There will be those, sincere lovers of their country, whose inward conviction and loyalty to Christ compel them to oppose war in all circumstances. With equal sincerity and with a like inward constraint, others will feel the necessity of giving effect to obligations, commitments and loyalties of a national or international character which they deem binding on the body politic, and on themselves within it. The Methodist Church recognizes that, in present

circumstances, both decisions may express true loyalty to personal spiritual conviction, and an earnest endeavour to do the will of God and serve the highest interests of mankind. In view of this recognition, the Methodist Church will uphold liberty of conscience and offer unceasing ministries to all her sons and daughters, in whichever direction loyalty to inward convictions may carry them.

The Doctrine of the 'Just War'
Because pacifists are in a minority, the Christian pacifist has been compelled to understand and to state his position much more clearly and precisely than has the non-pacifist. Majority opinions are usually taken for granted. Those who share the general non-pacifist attitude to the responsibility of the Christian in time of war do not always realise that underlying it is a definite theological doctrine, the doctrine of the 'just war'. This is the carefully reasoned doctrine that a Christian may take part in war only when just means are used to defend a just cause. The important conditional clauses make it, therefore, essential that particular examination should now be given to the ways (if any) in which the use of nuclear weapons for mass destruction modifies the traditional theological concept.

The doctrine declares that for a war to be a 'just war' in the Christian sense it must:
(1) have been undertaken by a lawful authority;
(2) have been undertaken for the vindication of an undoubted right that had been certainly infringed;
(3) be a last resort, all peaceful means of settlement having failed;
(4) offer the possibility of good to be achieved outweighing the evils that war would involve;
(5) be waged with a reasonable hope of victory for justice;
(6) be waged with a right intention;
(7) use methods that are legitimate, i.e. in accordance with man's nature as a rational being, with Christian moral principles and internal agreements.

The use of nuclear weapons has, undoubtedly, brought a new dimension of terror to war. Bombs are now available which release 3,000 times the destructive power of the atomic bomb dropped on Hiroshima. Vast areas could be destroyed by a single blow. The destructive effects of these monstrous weapons are not confined to the immediate havoc of the explosions, but persist in the long-term contamination of the world by dangerous radio-active by-products.

It is immediately obvious that the use in war of nuclear weapons in the megaton range directly affects conditions (4), (5) and (7). The dreadful devastation caused by such weapons and the possibly more dreadful consequent and persistent effects of radio-active contamination, make it extremely doubtful if a war so waged could achieve a good outweighing the evil it would involve. If the result of such war is to make the world a desert and call it peace, it can no longer be presumed that there is a reasonable hope of victory for justice. Nor can it be argued that the extinction of a nation or a continent is in accordance with man's nature as a rational being or with Christian moral principles. In these circumstances, i.e., in war waged with such weapons, the 'just war' is impossible.

It must be noted that it does not therefore follow of necessity that the doctrine of the 'just war' as traditionally defined must be abandoned by the Christian non-pacifist. (The Christian pacifist contends that there cannot be a 'just war' in any circumstances, whatever the nature of the weapons used.) For the non-pacifist who believes that nuclear weapons of mass destruction will inevitably be used in the event of war the doctrine is no longer valid. But if, recognizing that there can be no victors in total nuclear war, potential combatant nations should agree to ban such weapons or to wage war with a limited range of graduated and controllable nuclear weapons, then the conditions of 'just warfare' could be observed ...

Document VI.15

Methodist Support for Freedom Fighting

Colin Morris, *Unyoung, Uncoloured, Unpoor* (London: Epworth Press, 1969), p. 19.

Post-colonial situations posed new questions for the churches over whether to support those who fought for freedom from oppressive governments. In Britain this was sharply raised by the unilateral declaration of independence by the white government in Southern Rhodesia in 1965. Later it was raised more generally by the World Council of Churches with their Programme to Combat Racism. Colin Morris was a Methodist missionary in Zambia, and wrote this in response to a young African in Zambia who asked whether it was right to become a freedom fighter in Rhodesia.

In true theologian's style, I'll give you a one-word answer to your question and then qualify it for a hundred and fifty pages, but at least I'll give you an answer first. Yes, I believe a Christian is justified in using violence to win freedom in Rhodesia; I know no other way he can get it. I fear innocent women and children will suffer, and I badly want to add 'which, God forbid', but that is a pious subterfuge, inviting the Almighty to stave off the worst consequences of a responsibly-made decision.

My life is not at risk, nor are any of the innocents who may get hurt my kinsfolk so it is an insufferable impertinence for me to give you any advice. My feeble excuse is that advice was asked for and not offered. I believe freedom fighters are justified in using any methods short of sadistic cruelty for its own sake to overthrow the Salisbury regime. I also believe your task is a near-hopeless one. But then, what else can you do? Go back to Rhodesia and they'll gaol you for life; stay in exile and you'll drag around, a half-man; fight them and you are almost sure to die.

Document VI.16

The Gulf War, 1991

URC, *Reports to Assembly*, 1991, pp. 164–5.

The invasion of Kuwait by Saddam Hussein of Iraq in 1990 prompted military intervention by the USA and the UK in support of Kuwait. Whilst this was generally supported by the churches, there was anxiety that the underlying issues were not being tackled, as this statement from the Church and Society Department of the United Reformed Church indicates.

3.3 On January 31, the Assembly Executive adopted a fuller statement prepared by the Department which was widely circulated; the following extracts contain the main emphases. As the battle ends, we pray for all, the powerful and the 'little people', who must play their part in building a just and lasting peace; the points of this earlier statement will still frame our continuing prayers and concern for the whole region.

'1. We share in the prayers for all engaged in, and those hurt by, the actual fighting, and for the leaders of all the nations.
2. We affirm our abhorrence of any suggestion that this conflict is between representatives of the religions of Islam, Christianity and Judaism. We call upon Christians in this country, through contact with congregations of other faiths, to resist any trend towards racial hatred or violence at this time.
3. We call on those who in time of peace prepared for war to plan even more determinedly for the peace which must follow this war.
We echo the calls now being made by church leaders and statesmen for a just peace which goes beyond a simple cease-fire.
There must be acknowledgement and genuine enhancement of the status of the United Nations, under whose indirect auspices the war is being fought, and without whose authorisation no future military action should ever be justified.
Any settlement should spare the common people of Iraq more humiliation and abuse – they have suffered enough.
The powerful nations, again within the UN forum, must commit themselves to address the several long-standing disputes in the Middle East, not just between Kuwait and Iraq, but in Lebanon, Cyprus and the 'occupied territories' disputed by Israel and the Palestinians.
A determined effort will be required by the international community to ensure redress for the increased economic hardships suffered by third world countries as a result of the conflict.
A similar effort will be required to care for and to restore the natural environment of the Gulf region.
The arms manufacturing and supply industries must be brought under some international monitoring and control.

4. In addition to our expectations of others, we commit ourselves also to the greater demands made at this time on Christians, lay and ordained, to care for the hurt and to work for true peace.

In these comments and commitments we would join with fellow-Christians of other traditions and in every land.

The just peace for which we all pray and strive has to be built out of the horror of this war, not without repentance and humility for actions in earlier times, but with that larger hope in the God and Father of our Lord Jesus Christ, the promised Prince of Peace.'

PART VII

SOCIAL ISSUES

Introduction

Probably the main social issue with which nonconformity was associated was temperance, usually equated with teetotalism. Historically the commitment was never complete, and whilst the Salvation Army could make teetotalism a condition of service for its officers the Baptist and Congregational Union Assemblies could only exhort. However, one strategem which was used by several nonconformist churches was to write a prohibition on the serving of alcoholic liquor into the trust deeds of chapels and halls. This was an internal measure; the main focus of attention fell on attempts to influence public policy. As the concern with poverty increased in the later nineteenth century, the conviction that reckless expenditure on alcoholic drink by the man in the household was a primary, preventable cause of poverty increased.

The Bible Christians' report in 1905 (**VII.1a**) was characteristically extreme in its language. Alongside the campaign to increase the number and size of Bands of Hope among the churches, it was concerned with Sunday closing of public houses as a legislative measure. It also illustrated the castigation of the Conservatives as a party of publicans – an allusion to the Licensing Act of 1904. One problem for the churches was the use of wine in Holy Communion, although the frequency of communion in most of the Free Churches was no greater than monthly, and sometimes quarterly. Enterprising manufacturers began to supply non-alcoholic communion wine (**VII.1b**), and this rapidly became the norm in the Free Churches.

In 1908, John Scott Lidgett caused controversy when, as President of the Wesleyan Conference, he sent a telegram to Lord Lansdowne, Leader of the Conservative Party in the House of Lords, saying that Wesleyan Methodism 'would not forgive or forget', if the Conservatives rejected the Liberal Government's Licensing Bill without proper discussion (**VII.2**). The Conference was already on record as being committed to the measure, and Scott Lidgett did not therefore regard this as interference in politics, which still concerned some Wesleyans. The Bill was nevertheless rejected, and Scott Lidgett described how this led Wesleyans to support the Parliament Act in a way which almost seemed to make temperance a more important issue for them than education (cf. **V.4**).

By contrast the Methodist Statement from 1951 (**VII.5**) was carefully worded to make it clear that abstention from alcoholic drinks was not a condition of membership in the Methodist Church; however, it was argued that it was a proper part of Christian discipleship, and scientific evidence about the effects of alcohol abuse was deployed in a way which was not done half a century earlier. The tone of the language was also very different from that in the Bible Christians' report. Nevertheless, in the later twentieth century total abstinence became less common as the consumption of wine increased among the middle classes, although it remained more common on official church occasions, even if the deeds of buildings did not prohibit the consumption of alcoholic drinks. Another driving force in the change was the sense that rigid avoidance of public houses intensified the class difference between church members and the working classes. The 1960 Licensing Act permitted Sunday opening of public houses, and began the reversal of the restrictive legislation earlier in the century.

The 1951 Declaration was the last of the total abstinence statements. In 1972 the Report on the Non-medical Use of Drugs saw alcoholism in the much wider setting of drug abuse. In 1975 it was admitted that many Methodists were not abstainers. Alcohol was still forbidden on Methodist premises and 'the juice of the grape' was to be used at Holy Communion. A later Report 'received' by Conference – *Through a Glass Darkly – Responsible Attitudes to Alcohol* (1987) – was much more moderate than the earlier hard-line approach. In 1999 the whole issue of total abstinence and the use of alcohol on Methodist premises was discussed at the Conference. The emphasis shifted from total abstinence to *responsible use*, but alcohol was still not permitted on Methodist premises.

The inter-war depression produced a new awareness of the significance of unemployment. The churches found different ways of helping the unemployed. In 1938 Dorothy Mellor gave a report on her work over more than ten years organising relief under the auspices of the Congregational Union (**VII.3**). There was still a lingering sense of the distinction between the deserving and the undeserving poor, and the focus was on helping church members rather than the unemployed generally. Nevertheless such action did mark more concerted efforts to remove poverty at home.

Another activity regarded as a cause of poverty was gambling. Nonconformists tended to be against betting on horses, and they were suspicious of football pools. From the Second World War there were increasing pressures to liberalise the gambling laws, notably by the legalisation of off-course betting on horses. In 1952 the Congregational Union Assembly approved a resolution against any moves to liberalise the law (**VII.6**), which emphasised both the destructive cost of gambling and the underlying moral issue of trying to get 'something for nothing'. The Methodist view at the end of the century was stated in 1995 (**VII.15**) following a report submitted in 1992. This tackled the distinction between private gambling and stock exchange activity and the privatisation of publicly owned enterprise in the light of the 1978 Royal Commission on Gambling and the gambling legislation which made their 1936 Report outmoded. Minor gambling and raffles were now allowed on Methodist premises. The National Lottery was condemned as a 'tax on the poor'.[1] A pamphlet, *The Winners' Shout, the Losers' Curse* (1997), was a statement of the Conference, 'accepted' but not 'adopted'. The work of Gordon Moody (1912–94) in pioneering group therapy and counselling typified by Gamblers Anonymous was a positive Methodist contribution to the problem.

The issue of divorce and remarriage concerned the churches from just after the First World War, when the possibility of making it easier to secure divorce was first canvassed. Sir Alan Herbert's Private Member's Bill of 1937 amplified the grounds for divorce and Legal Aid from 1950 made it available to more people. Further legislative changes in 1969 and 1973 removed the concept of a 'matrimonial offence', and made 'irretrievable breakdown' the primary ground for divorce. It was probably not surprising that the rate of divorce rose in the second half of the century, but few anticipated how dramatic that rise would be. The resolutions of the Methodist Conference in 1945 and 1948 (**VII.4**) reflected the affirmation of a traditional view of marriage but also awareness of the consequent issues: could Methodists who had been divorced remain in membership? and could they be remarried? No definitive position was taken, and the instruction was that such matters should be considered on a case-by-case basis. Although the Free Church position was perceived to be less dogmatic than that of the Church of England, the situation was not straightforward, and there was no guarantee that divorced persons could be remarried in church. The Presbyterian Church of England, which had affirmed the traditional view in 1946, revised its regulations in 1967 (**VII.10**), and it is interesting that the focus was the problem for ministers and the issue of ministerial conscience: the pastoral care of the divorcee seemed to come a rather distant second in consideration. (Perhaps surprisingly there was also less emphasis than in the Methodist provisions on a conciliar decision.) The Methodist regulations of 1998 (**VII.18**) reflected a situation in which divorce as such had to all intents and purposes ceased to be an issue.

Hard on the heels of divorce came the issue of homosexuality. The Wolfenden Committee recommended in 1957 that homosexual acts between consenting adults in private should cease to be a criminal offence, but legislation to this effect (with qualifications) was not approved until 1967. *Towards a Quaker View of Sex* was another of the publications of 1963 which set the religious world buzzing (**VII.7**). It was not concerned exclusively with homosexuality, although that had triggered the initial concern; it set out to consider the whole question of sexual morality and the group from the Society of Friends which produced the report suggested three principles on which that should be based, including the preservation of family life and the avoidance of exploitation of any person. The refusal to condemn homosexuality as sinful in itself was a landmark in thinking about the subject, even though this remained a minority view at the time. By the end of the century all the churches were having to face the issue, partly because of the question of whether ministers could engage in homosexual relationships, and partly because of the wider question of whether homosexual partnerships could be recognised by the Church. The resolutions adopted by the Methodist Conference on Human Sexuality in 1993 (**VII.16**) reflected a compromise on the issue; and the United Reformed Church was engaged in keen discussions on the same subject two or three years later.

The development of the female contraceptive pill made the use of contraceptives a public issue. Initially discussion of contraception was almost a proxy for a discussion of premarital sexual intercourse, since fear of pregnancy had always been regarded as the 'rational' or expedient reason for refraining from it, even if the moral argument was regarded as unconvincing. The Free Churches, in so far as they commented on the matter officially, generally followed the line reflected by the Presbyterian Church of England in 1965 (**VII.8**). The issue of the threat to life which so concerned Roman Catholic moral theologians did not figure largely in this discussion. Similarly, the issue of abortion, following the legalisation of abortion in certain circumstances by the Abortion Act of 1967 (a Private Member's Bill sponsored by David Steel), did not prompt the unequivocal condemnation among the Free Churches which it continued to receive from the Roman Catholic Church. The Methodist Statement of 1976 (**VII.11**) was one of the best summaries of thinking on this matter. Ironically, medical advances since 1967, in reducing the viable age for premature babies have helped to make a case for an amendment of the 1967 Act, at a time when politically and ecclesiastically the possibility of finding a consensus about change has diminished.

The Baptist report, *Living in a Secular Age* (**VII.9**), even though it was written as long ago as 1964, was a valuable contextualisation of the various issues already mentioned, indicating the way in which they are all related to the living of the Christian life. New issues were also arising as a result of medical advances. From the 1950s it became possible for people with various kinds of physical handicap to take a much more active part in life and to live longer, and this resulted in the need to make provision for them in the churches. Medical advances also sharpened the question of whether a Christian healing ministry is possible. An extract from a much longer Baptist report (**VII.17**) discussed these particular issues.

Finally, a series of issues which initially arose on the world scene had domestic consequences. Racism was originally perceived as an American problem, and the work of Martin Luther King Jr in the 1960s was widely admired. Only more slowly was it recognised that there was a British dimension. The reluctance of British churches to welcome West Indian immigrants has already been mentioned (**I.17**), but the more general fact of racism in British society came into prominence in the 1980s. The United Reformed Church's Declaration on Racism of 1987 (**VII.13**) reflected this concern. The economic problems of Britain in the 1970s as traditional industries went into decline and unemployment rose were seen to affect immigrant and other marginalised groups disproportionately. The civil disturbances which resulted in some places caused the Church and Society Department of the United Reformed Church to offer a reflection on issues of social justice in the same way in which the issue was analysed for Latin America or Africa (**VII.12**). These issues provided a new context for something which had concerned the churches for much longer – world poverty. The work of Christian Aid, originally one of the divisions of the British Council of Churches, increasingly focused on development work in countries of the 'Third World', as well as emergency aid in the case of famine, flood or war. The Presbyterian Church of England was one of the first Churches to respond to the suggestion that members should contribute 1 per cent of their income to this cause, and this was continued by the United Reformed Church after 1972. In 1992 this programme was relaunched under the title 'Commitment for Life' (**VII.14**). These areas were those in the whole range of social issues where actions speak louder than words.

Note

1   *Minutes of Methodist Conference*, 1996, p. 3.

Social Issues

Document VII.1

Early Twentieth-Century Teetotalism

(a) *The Minutes of the Bible Christian Conference*, 1905; (b) *Methodist New Connexion Magazine*, March 1906, quoted in K. Young, *Chapel* (London: Eyre Methuen, 1972), p. 163.

The first statement from the Bible Christian Conference is significant not only for the information it contains about the priority given to total abstinence, but also for its tone. This was a particular reaction to the Conservative government's Licensing Act of 1904. The second extract is a reminder of the way in which teetotalism created a market for non-alcoholic communion wine among nonconformists.

(a)
The annual returns indicate continued interest and activity in Temperance work. We are thankful to record an increase of 7 Bands of Hope, the total number now being 324. We have been urging for years past that every Sunday School should recognize the Band of Hope as an integral part of its work, and this recognition is being given in increasing measure, though the increase is not as rapid as we could wish to see it.

Will Elders' Meetings and Sunday School Teachers' meetings please note, as a great present day necessity, that there must be
A BAND OF HOPE IN EVERY CHURCH

Its purpose is to safeguard the children from the perils of the drink habit and the drink traffic. Who does not realize the necessity of this? Strong drink is England's curse and shame. For its sake the dearest ties are every day severed, the costliest sacrifices every day made; and the greatest sacrifice placed on the blood-stained altar of Bacchus is the life of England's children.

If the nation has not the moral sense to see the evil, to take measures for its removal, then the duty is laid all the more clearly and urgently on the Church of Christ to raise her voice in indignant protest, and to use every means in her power for the protection of its child-life, which is a nation's most precious possession.

Save the children!! That is the Church's watchword for the twentieth century. Our Bible Christian Church has an honourable record. Our fathers were among the first and foremost of Temperance Reformers. Our Chapels were open for the advocacy of teetotal principles when other places of worship were closed against them.

We are bound by the traditions of the past. As well as by the imperative needs of the present, to the principle and the practice of total abstinence.

The number of members in the Bands of Hope is 26,530. This is a decrease of 250, but the decrease is more than counter-balanced by the return of Sunday School scholars who are teetotalers. These number 34,953, or an increase of 2,403 on last year, while for the previous year the increase was 6,910.

It is a fact over which we greatly rejoice that the vast majority of children in our schools are teetotalers. If we can send them out into the battle of life as decided followers of Christ and pledged abstainers, we have done the greatest work possible for our day and generation.

The number of Temperance Societies is the same as last year, viz., 78. The membership is 5,508, an increase of 773. A large number of our churches have no separate temperance society for the reason that the church is a temperance society in itself, and also because many of our people are identified with one or other of the great temperance organizations of the country.

We have striven to obtain an approximate number of the members of churches who are total abstainers, but without success. The column for such a return is absolutely disregarded by some districts, in others only partially filled, so that no accurate statement can be made.

On the general and public aspects of the question every legitimate weapon has been used to fight the drink foe. The present Government, in alliance with the liquor traffic, has placed a new Licensing Act upon the Statute Book, which makes our work as Temperance Reformers more difficult than ever. It has lessened the power of magistrates in local areas in the control of licences, and has recognized the vicious principle of compensation as part of the law of the land. It is deeply felt by all the Free Churches, and by all who have the cause of temperance reformation at heart, that this Act must be vitally amended. Such legislation is worse than barren. It is pernicious and corrupting.

We eagerly long for the day when the nation shall have the opportunity to shake itself free from the incubus of a Government dominated by the priest and publican. In that day let every man amongst us exercise his franchise as in the sight of God and the Throne of Judgement. Justice! Freedom! Equality! Righteousness! These are lost ideals that wait for a time of restoration.

The Central Sunday Closing Association is taking steps to unite all the Temperance forces in the country to secure an English Sunday Closing Act during the next Parliament.

Most heartily do we support the proposal. In itself it is of the first necessity, and it would help, rather than hinder, other temperance reforms.

Sunday Closing would be an instalment of the legislation sought by all the temperance organizations. It is one of the few temperance reforms of which the people of Great Britain and Ireland have had actual experience; its undoubted success in promoting sobriety and good order in Scotland, Ireland and Wales gives the claim for its extension to England a pre-eminence over every other.

It is re-assuring in all our work and warfare to remember that 'the battle is the Lord's. The Lord of Hosts is with us, the God of Jacob is our refuge.' 'They that be with us are more than they that be with them.'

If defeat awaited us our duty would be the same; but we may hearten ourselves for the conflict by the confidence that victory is sure.

(b)
>
> PURE COMMUNION WINES
> their purity and freedom
> from Alcohol make them

the ideal Wines for use
in our Church Services.

*OVER 5,000 CHURCHES HAVE
ENDORSED BY REGULAR USE
THEIR EXCELLENCE & MERIT.*
Made entirely of sound Grape
Juice and absolutely undiluted.
Send 2/6 for four samples of
various kinds to F. Wright,
Mundy & Co, Kensington, London, W.

Document VII.2

The Licensing Bill of 1908

J. Scott Lidgett, *Reminiscences* (London: Epworth Press, 1928), pp. 66–8.

Nonconformist influence had persuaded the Liberal government to introduce a more restrictive Licensing Bill in 1908, which was defeated in the House of Lords. This account by Scott Lidgett of the Wesleyan reaction to this saga is interesting because of the traditional 'no politics' rule in Methodism.

Fighting for the Licensing Bill

The most dramatic event of the year had to do with the rejection of the Licensing Bill by the House of Lords at the mandate of a caucus of Peers that was held at Lansdowne House. The Government of the day had introduced the Bill in response to powerful pressure, especially of the Christian, and particularly of the Nonconformist, Churches. At the beginning of that year I had myself acted as spokesman of the National Council of Evangelical Free Churches on a deputation to the then Chancellor of the Exchequer, Mr Asquith, shortly afterwards to become Prime Minister. The main principles of the measure were laid before the Government and formed the bases of their Bill. The Wesleyan Methodist Temperance Committee alone secured more than a million signatures in support of it. The Conference at York, over which I presided, had passed a strong resolution in favour of the Bill, with only a handful of dissentients. So it was the Churches, with the Temperance Societies, that had put this controversial measure upon the Government, had organized support of it throughout the country, and, in particular, the Wesleyan Methodist Church stood officially committed to it through the overwhelming majority of the Conference. So official and overwhelming was this support that as President I arranged and presided over a crowded meeting held in Wesley's Chapel on behalf of the Bill. As the crisis approached, let it be remembered, the claim made was that the Bill should be fairly considered and fully discussed by the House of Lords. Instead of this a party meeting outside the House determined, at the instance of powerful vested interests, to slay the Bill outright and off-hand, without seeking to amend it.

Methodism Will Never Forget or Forgive
The news of this party political decision, which betrayed moral interests and flaunted the Churches, reached me at the Free Trade Hall just before speaking at the Anniversary of the Manchester Mission. I at once wrote a telegram to the Marquess of Lansdowne, the Conservative Leader in the Lords, to the effect that should the House of Lords reject the Bill on the Second Reading that act 'would never be forgotten or forgiven by the Wesleyan Methodist Church.' I showed the telegram to the Secretary of the Conference, the Rev. John Hornabrook, and, as he confirmed my judgement, I at once dispatched it. Subsequently I read it to the meeting in the Free Trade Hall, and immediately a burst of prolonged applause broke out, the whole audience standing, such as I have never witnessed at any meeting before or since. It will be seen that the demand was not made that the Bill should be passed as it stood, but only that it should be carefully considered, and that the Wesleyan Conference stood so committed to this support that I simply gave expression to its intense conviction on the matter. Yet the small minority of dissentients began to flood *The Methodist Recorder* with protests against the President of the Conference taking part in protests in politics! This campaign was fostered, for a time, behind the scenes, until, as he himself told me, Dr Henry J. Pope remonstrated against it, and pointed out its folly by suggesting, 'Don't you see that by doing this you are making him irresistible!' The warning took effect, and on the following Thursday, *The Methodist Recorder* announced that 'This correspondence is now closed.' For some months I was constrained in my platform addresses to expound and enforce the grave responsibility of the Christian Church when supreme moral interests are at issue in the public and political affairs of the nation.

Since considerations of moral judgement and not merely of political expediency are involved, I feel constrained to say that the action of the House of Lords brought nemesis in its track. Flushed by its success in securing the withdrawal of the Education Bill and defeating the Licensing Bill, the House of Lords went on to throw out the Budget. The result was the Parliament Act, and that result was in considerable measure brought about, not for constitutional or political reasons, but because of the indignation of multitudes who would not 'forget or forgive' the contemptuous rejection of a measure that was held by them to be vital to the moral progress of the Nation.

Document VII.3

Congregational Union Distress Fund

Congregational Year Book, 1938, pp. 209, 212–13.

The establishment of the Congregational Union Distress Fund in 1928 was very much the initiative of Dorothy Mellor, though it expanded subsequently from its Welsh origins. This was a report after ten years, illustrating the role of the churches in meeting the eonomic problems of the inter-war years.

It is, I understand, a privilege of advancing years to be allowed to reminisce, of which I am now taking advantage; for I have been turning up my original Distress Fund Accounts. They bring to mind most vividly, as only yesterday, the happenings of November, 1928. The look of surprise on Dr Berry's face when, after an evening spent with my husband and myself, I told him I was convinced that there was work for me in Wales, and he, knowing the need only then beginning, immediately put me into touch with four Welsh manses; the pathos and joy of that correspondence following; the preliminary appeal for money and clothes, circulated at first amongst Hertfordshire friends only; the amazing response; the delight of raising and distributing these gifts, aided that first week by Mrs Cartwright, now the very capable Secretary to the Unemployment Committee of the Christian Social Council; our house filled to overflowing; Christmas Eve 1928, the letter from Mr Johnes, begging me to remove the many bundles of clothes from his office in order that he might return there after the Christmas recess. I remember the Memorial Hall; my hunted existence until established in a vacated cloak-room, with the dungeon store underneath. The official establishment and then enlargement of Dr. Berry's Fund by the inclusion of a large number of churches in Monmouthshire and East Glamorganshire; the first development of the Fund to cover distressed areas in England; later on – London; in every case, smaller and less-known churches and areas were likely to be entirely omitted from the benefits of the various Public Funds; churches, too, which could not afford to help from their own Communion Moneys; manses with reduced stipends and widows with tiny incomes. Many folk were even beginning to bless the helping hand of the Congregational Union. I remember, too, the heroism unconsciously but invariably shown; the tragedies hidden often behind bare walls ...

And then I see Christmas Eve, 1936. Distress still abounding, unemployment with privation still rife, and yet a spirit of hope and cheerfulness in so many districts. I visualise 300 manses where a cheque from Headquarters has brought untold joy; some thousands of homes where a gift of a parcel of groceries through the church has brought a feeling of sureness that Christmas really has come; of thousands of children's voices made happy by a load of toys. I see, too, the quiet content in the heart of a lonely widow, who realizes with thankfulness that an account long unpaid can now be met; the gratitude of a life-server in the ministry, who, though old and finished, has not been forgotten. And all this made possible by the loving gifts both small and large of friends in and around our churches; those who, through the inspiration received, realize anew that Congregationalism implies serving others. I see, too, children parting with a precious toy that a comrade may have it and enjoy it; I see bands of young people carolling on a stormy winter night that money may be sent to us to distribute; I see parties of women armed with needles and thread spending hours in the making of garments for those who have known what it is to wear of the best; and I see whole churches reaching out and making new personal contacts in order to have real knowledge of those whose lot is made so hard. I visualize, too, a stream of boys and girls coming to London as to a strange city, feeling lonely and friendless, and immediately finding themslves members of a large fellowship, with an ever-open door of welcome.

And so the administration and boundaries of Dr. Berry's Distress Fund, centred eight years ago round four Welsh manses, have reached a further stage of development through the Additional Help Fund, the Adoption and the Transferee Schemes. May I just emphasize and slightly enlarge on what our Secretary has so concisely and clearly defined? Re the Additional Help: we are definitely aiming solely for those churches which provide, not only an excellent centre, but also the very necessary and requisite leadership. In no case (and this must again be emphasized) can this money, or indeed the Distress Fund generally, be utilized for the extinguishng of church debts.

For the 'adoption' scheme, we encourage it only if you are prepared to take over definitely. If you cannot provide toys at Christmas, nor a further supply of clothing according to the season, I must be notified. Spread your money throughout the year for your adopted area; do not disburse your entire collection at Christmas-time; keep some in hand; a large sum is entirely out of proportion to the gifts sent normally; £5 will provide 50 persons with groceries. Do strike personal contact with the adopted church at once. Don't send gifts first. If your church would prefer to join with other denominations in a big local effort, be sure the receivers at the other end include Congregationalists. You would be surprised at the number of Congregational churches who collect quantities of gifts from their own members to swell a town's efforts, and have no idea if our own folk are receiving even the tiniest percentage. If this *must* be done, notify me or else our minister at the other end, who will then be on the spot when allocation taks place. And remember, too, that one of the many advantages of Headquarters distribution lies in its privacy. Numbers of folk, both ministerial and lay, object to public help, and rightly so, but will accept it thankfully if sent by us.

Re the Transferees: I would like to thank our London ministers for their willing co-operation. I know it is more than worth while, for, apart from the actual loneliness often experienced, we have been able to trace girls who have determined to be on their own. We are also definitely able to visit them in their places of work, which keeps the treatment of them on a high level; the fact that a denomination takes the trouble to keep in touch with its young people is undoubtedly impressing a large section of the community. The church is playing her part both in the material and spiritual sides of this economic question. She is also, too, through the Christian Social Council, tackling the whole principle of showing the world the facts as they are can no longer be tolerated, but must be approached from the Christian standpoint.

And above all else, in my reminiscences, I see the guiding hand of a loving Father Who, through this period of sorrow and great tribulation, not yet over, and by the needs arising, has taught His children that all are members of one Brotherhood, sharing life's troubles and easing the burdens of all.

Social Issues

Document VII.4

Methodist Regulations Concerning Marriage and Divorce, 1948

Regulations of the Methodist Church regarding the Membership and Re-Marriage of Divorced Persons (Revised by Conference, 1948), in E. Rogers (ed.), *Declarations of Conference on Social Questions* (London: Epworth Press, 1959), pp. 124–6.

The Methodist Regulations regarding the membership and re-marriage of divorced persons, which were revised by Conference in 1948, illustrate the complexity of the issues which arose once divorce had become easier for ordinary people.

(i) The Christian Ideal of Marriage – The Conference proclaims and commends to the Methodist people the Christian ideal of marriage set out in its Declaration on the Christian View of Marriage and the Family and upheld in the statement on Divorce. It particularly emphasizes the binding and lifelong character of the marriage vows set forth in the Marriage Service, and enjoins that should one partner unhappily fail to keep these vows it is a Christian obligation on the other to do all that is possible for reconciliation.
(Minutes of Conference, 1945).

(ii) Regulation Regarding Continuance in and Membership of Persons who have been Divorced – If any member of the Methodist Church has been a party to divorce proceedings ending in the legal dissolution of marriage, whether Petitioner, Respondent, or Co-respondent, the question of continuance in membership shall thereupon be considered by the Leaders' Meeting of the Church with which the said member is connected. The Leaders' Meeting shall then refer the case and its recommendations to the District Discipline Committee for consideration of all the available evidence and for judgement. This judgement shall then be communicated to the Leaders' Meeting for action in accordance therewith. If the Leaders' Meeting is unable to accept the judgement of the District Discipline Committee, the case shall be referred to Conference. It shall be the responsibility of the Superintendent Minister to report any such case to the District Discipline Committee.
(Minutes of Conference, 1945).

(iii) Regulation Regarding Reinstatement in, or Admission to, membership of Persons who have been Divorced – The Methodist Church, mindful of the purpose for which it was raised up, and believing in the possibility of repentance and forgiveness, declares that any person so removed from membership under Regulation 2 may at any time be admitted again after application by such person to the same Leaders' Meeting, and the reference of such application to the District Discipline Committee for its consideration and judgement. Reinstatement shall only take place if the District Discipline Committee, in the light of all the relevant evidence, is satisfied that the person concerned is sincerely penitent and has made, or is prepared to make, such reparation as may be possible. The judgement of the District Discipline Committee shall duly be reported to the Leaders' Meeting for action in accordance therewith, and if the Leaders' Meeting is unable to accept the judgement of the District Discipline Committee, the case shall be referred to Conference. There shall be a right of appeal in all cases to the Methodist Conference.

Similar steps shall be taken in the case of divorced persons who have not previously been members of the Methodist Church but who desire to become members.

(Minutes of Conference, 1945).

(iv) Regulation Regarding Re-marriage of Divorced Persons – If a request is made by any person whose previous marriage has been dissolved, whether such a person is a member of the Methodist Church or not, to be married in a Methodist Church or by a Methodist minister elsewhere, or should a civil marriage already have been contracted by any such person, and a request made that a religious service in a Methodist Church may follow such a marriage, the request shall be considered by the minister concerned after he has interviewed both parties. Every endeavour must be made to uphold the principles and ideals embodied in the Conference Statement on divorce and the Conference Declaration on the Christian view of marriage and the family. Should the minister be in any doubt as to the proper course to take, he shall refer the matter to the ministers of the Circuit, who in their turn may refer any case about which there is doubt to a special Committee called together at the discretion of the Chairman of the District. Those other than ministers in Full Connexion with the Conference who may be requested to officiate at such marriages shall act under the direction of the Superintendent of the Circuit. In all cases the minister shall consult the Chairman of the District before the ceremony takes place. Under no circumstances does the Conference require a minister to officiate at the marriage of a divorced person should it be contrary to the dictates of his conscience so to do.

(Minutes of Conference, 1948).

Document VII.5

Methodism and Temperance in Mid-Century

The Declaration of the Methodist Church on Total Abstinence and Temperance Reform, (Adopted by Conference 1951) in E. Rogers (ed.), *Declarations of Conference on Social Questions 1932–1959* (London: Epworth Press, 1959), pp. 59–62.

The revised form of the Declaration adopted by Conference in 1951 was carefully worded to make it clear that abstention from alcoholic drinks is not a condition of membership in the Methodist Church; nevertheless it was argued that it is a proper part of Christian discipleship. The Declaration was also concerned with alcoholic abuse on a world scale. This was the last of the total abstinence statements.

The Conference has consistently appealed to the Methodist people to abstain from the use of intoxicating liquors as beverages, and in 1950 confirmed this appeal by approving the phrase 'For Total Abstinence and Temperance Reform' as part of the sub-title setting forth in summary form the work of the Department of Christian Citizenship. A commission so definite makes it imperative that the implications of the appeal should be fully understood by the Methodist people.

The Conference has not at any time imposed total abstinence from the use of intoxicating liquors as beverages as a 'condition of membership' of the Methodist Church. Nor does the reiterated appeal for total abstinence imply the imposition of such a condition. 'All persons are welcomed into membership of the Methodist Church who sincerely desire to be saved from their sins through faith in the Lord Jesus Christ and evidence the same in life and conduct and who seek to have fellowship with Christ Himself and His people by taking up the duties and privileges of the Methodist Church.' (*The Deed of Union*, Section 33 (a)).

The entry into the Church is a beginning, a first step in the Way which, by God's grace and the guidance of His Holy Spirit, leads the believing soul to fullness of life in Christ. Our appeal for total abstinence is addressed, in the first instance, to those who are members of the Methodist Church and have begun to walk in that way of life. The code of obligation to our neighbour, which demands that no hindrance should be put in the way of another's welfare, and the call to personal dedication, which means that body and mind should be kept perfectly fit for the Lord's service, are rules of life and conduct for the Christian which clearly follow from the teaching of Our Lord. They fully justify the refusal to compromise with the habit of drinking intoxicating beverages.

The generally accepted condemnation of drunkenness and immoderate indulgence in alcoholic beverages, which the Conference fully endorses, is not a sufficient answer to the many serious personal and social problems raised by this habit. The fact must be recognized that moderate use of alcoholic beverages may lead, and often has led, to excessive use, and certainly exposes the user to avoidable temptation. Moreover, for those who have accepted the yoke of Christ there is a three-fold obligation of commitment to God, love for one's neighbour, and discipline of self. Considered individually, alcoholic indulgence assails the highest centres of personality. It impairs conscience, judgement, and the sense of responsibility. Considered socially, alcoholic indulgence inflicts heavy loss and damage on the community in deterioration of character, diminution of health and efficiency, discord in domestic life, neglect and suffering of children, public disorder, the creation and intensification of poverty and economic waste, and in the undue influence of the liquor trade on public affairs. Considered both individually and socially, it thus adds one more avoidable hindrance to our fellowship with God.

The Methodist Church earnestly appeals to all within its pastoral oversight to practise total abstinence from alcoholic beverages, not as a burdensome duty, but as a privilege of Christian service. The Conference therefore reaffirms as follows its previous declarations of 1933 and 1948:–

(i) 'The Requirement of Christian Discipleship.'
In view of the Church's responsibility for the upbringing of a Christian order of life throughout the world, the Conference appeals to Methodists at home and abroad to abstain habitually from the use of intoxicating liquors as beverages. Example is service; and for this reason the Conference urges all our people to refrain, for Christ's sake, and for the common good, from the use of strong drink. The use of intoxicants on any occasion on Methodist Church premises is not permitted.

Christian discipleship is also concerned with the commerce in drink. The Conference urges the Methodist people to keep themselves free from complicity with a traffic the results of which are so injurious to the interests of religion, morality and social life. This recommendation should be borne in mind in the administration of our Circuits, and especially in the appointment of office-bearers.

(ii) 'Temperance Teaching and Total Abstinence Enrolment.'
Scientific and social research in recent years has abundantly confirmed the ancient judgement that indulgence in strong drink causes men to 'err in vision' and 'stumble in judgement.' The Conference directs that efficient Temperance teaching, based on the findings of science and their moral implications, shall be given in all Youth organizations associated with the Methodist Church; and that a systematic enrolment of total abstainers shall be undertaken from year to year in all our Sunday Schools and congregations.

The Conference accepts the judgement of the Royal Commission on licensing that 'every child ought to receive specific and systematic instruction as to the properties of alcohol, as in all other matters which may affect future health, so that the child may at least be in possession of sound material on which to form a personal judgement when years of discretion are reached'; and urges the Ministry of Education to continue to press upon all Local Education Authorities the importance of adequate Temperance instruction in the State schools, on the basis of the revised manual of instruction issued by the Board of Education. The Conference requests the governing bodies of all Methodist schools to make provision for adequate instruction on this subject ...

(iv) 'The Responsibilities of Christian Citizenship.'
The several objects of legislative reform approved by the Methodist Conferences in former years have been included, with few exceptions, in the programme of the Temperance Council of the Christian Churches of England and Wales. As it is essential that Temperance Reform should be pressed forward by the united action of the Churches, the Conference rejoices in this manifestation of unity and, recalling with thankfulness the part which Methodism has taken in the formation and work of the Council, commends its aims and labours to the whole-hearted support of our people.

Believing that the Church of Christ cannot condone the continuance of any wrong in the life of the State, the Conference resolves to support legislative change to the point necessary to secure, as far as legislative action can assure it, the complete and permanent eradication of the drink evil from the life of our nation and race.

Document VII.6

Congregationalists and Gambling, 1952

Congregational Year Book, 1953, pp. 100–101.

In May 1952 the Congregational Union Assembly received the following statement on Gambling, presented by the Life and Work Department, which was prompted by the Report of the recent Royal Commission. It largely reflected traditional attitudes to the subject.

The Life and Work Department desires to convey to the Assembly and to the Churches its judgment on the Report of the Royal Commission on Betting, Lotteries and Gambling.

1 It recognizes that the Report has made a serious attempt to grapple with an evil which is escaping adequate control by the Law.
2 It regrets that the Commission felt itself precluded from declaring its own ethical attitude to Gambling, and declares it does not share the ethical judgment on Gambling which seems implicit in the Report.
3 It regrets that the Commission confined itself almost exclusively to a consideration of the economic and financial effects of Gambling on both the gambler and society, and declares that the effects of gambling on both the individual and on society are more destructive than the Report suggests. In particular the Department regrets that the Report does not recognize that gambling involves attitudes of mind and practices and an absence of a sense of responsibility which are antagonistic to the ideal of mutual service which is the foundation of true democracy.
4 It regrets that the Report has isolated the act of gambling, and has nowhere considered the long-term influence thereof on sport and on children.
5 It regrets that by rejecting the figures concerning the total expenditure on Gambling supplied by the Central Churches Committee on Gambling, the Commission has only been able to indicate the number of people who do gamble and the amounts staked by them, but has precluded itself from recognizing the *strength* of the gambling propensity and the magnitude of the vested interests on gambling e.g. the provision of literature, etc.
6 It affirms therefore that owing to the omission of these factors from the Commission's Report, the Report itself cannot be regarded as an adequate treatment of the whole problem of Gambling or be accepted as a sound basis for

legislation. The Department further records its judgment that, by presenting gambling as a relatively harmless recreation, the Report will tend to encourage the practice.

7 The Department therefore reminds the Assembly and the Churches that, since the publication of the Report is likely to lead to an increase in Gambling, the work of the Churches in combating the evil will prove increasingly difficult, and that therefore an unambiguous witness is called for both on the part of the Churches and Church-members.

8 The Department therefore sees no reason to recommend the Assembly to depart from the resolution passed by last year's Assembly on the subject of Gambling.

Document VII.7

Towards a Quaker View of Sex, 1963

Alastair Heron (ed.), *Towards a Quaker View of Sex* (London: Friends Home Service Committee, 1963), pp. 40–42.

This report by a group of Friends was prompted by pastoral questions about homosexuality following the Wolfenden Report of 1957, but ranged much more widely over the issues of sexuality than any comparable document before. These are the main conclusions.

Those who have read so far will recognise how difficult it has been for us to come to definite conclusions as to what people ought or ought not to do. But although we cannot produce a ready-made external morality to replace the conventional code, there are some things about which we can be definite. *The first is that there must be a morality of some sort to govern sexual relationships.* An experience so profound in its effect upon people and upon the community cannot be left wholly to private judgment. It will never be right for two people to say to each other 'We'll do what we want, and what happens between us is nobody else's business.' However private an act, it is never without its impact on society, and we must never behave as though society – which includes our other friends – did not exist. Secondly, the need to preserve marriage and family life has been in the forefront of our minds throughout our work. It is in marriage that sexual impulses have their greatest opportunity for joyful and creative expression, and where two people can enter into each other's lives and hearts most intimately. Here the greatest freedom can be experienced – the freedom conferred by an unreserved commitment to each other, by loving and fearless friendship, and by openness to the world. In marriage, two people thus committed can bring children into the world, provide them with the security of love and home and in this way fulfil their sexual nature. Finally, we accept the definition of sin given by an Anglican broadcaster, as covering those actions that involve exploitation of the other person. This is a concept of wrong-doing that applies both to homosexual and heterosexual actions and to actions within marriage as well as outside it. It condemns as fundamentally immoral every sexual action that is not, as far as is humanly ascertainable, the result of a mutual decision. It condemns seduction and even persuasion, and every instance of coitus which, by reason of age or intelligence or emotional condition, cannot be a matter of mutual responsibility.

It is clear that we need a much deeper morality, one that will enable people to find a constructive way through even the most difficult and unpredictable situations – a way that is not simply one of withdrawal and abnegation. There are many who say that when people find themselves in a situation where it is difficult to be consistently moral, they must practise self-denial and 'bear their cross'. This is often the right way: but it is a serious misconception of the Cross to suggest that it is related only to self-denial.

Morality should be creative. God is primarily Creator, not rule-maker. Quakerism from the beginning rejected the idea of particular observances, rituals or sacrament, and instead regarded the whole of life's activities as potentially sacramental. It put aside dogmatic teaching and credal statements and emphasised instead the need for a search. It saw the possibility of discovering truth in the direct encounter of man with God in the silence of a Meeting for Worship where the religious community is gathered in a common discipline.

Every true Christian, of whatever branch of the Church, accepts that the whole of his life must be brought before God. The Society of Friends, originating as it did in an effort to restore wholeness and sincerity to Christianity at a time when the national Church had become largely formal, time-serving and corrupt, places particular emphasis on our individual and personal responsibility. We cannot accept as true a statement that is given us merely because it is given with the authority of tradition or of a Church. We have to make that truth our own – if it is a truth – through diligent search and a rigorous discipline of thought and feeling. Man is intended to be a moral being. That is not to say that he should accept a formal morality, an observance of *mores*, but that his actions should come under searching scrutiny in the light that comes from the Gospels and the working of God within us.

There have been periods in Quaker history when this effort to achieve consistency and integrity toppled over into a humourless scrupulosity, leading to a restricted life in which a pattern of conduct was secured at the expense of warmth and joy and creativeness. Friends, if they keep in mind the need to avoid this error, could help to discover that kind of conduct and inner discipline through which the sexual energy of men and women can bring health of mind and spirit to a world where man's energy always threatens to become destructive. We need a release of love, warmth and generosity into the world in the everyday contacts of life, a positive force that will weaken our fear of one another and our tendencies towards aggression and power-seeking.

This search is a move forward into the unknown; it implies a high standard of responsibility, thinking and awareness – something much harder than simple obedience to a moral code. Further, the responsibility that it implies cannot be accepted alone; it must be responsibility within a group whose members are equally committed to the search for God's will.

Perhaps our last words should be to those, equally aware of the tragedy, who may be distressed and put off by our rejection of a morality that has seemed to them a product of Christianity. We do know, from the intimate experience of several of us, that is is possible to give substance to the traditional code, to live within its requirements, enriched by an experience of love at its most generous and tender, and conscious of our debt to Christ in showing us what love implies. We would ask those who cannot easily follow our thoughts to recognise what has driven us – Christians and Friends, trying to live up to the high standard of integrity that our religious society asks of us – to our insistent questioning. It is the awareness that the traditional code, in itself, does not come from the heart; for the great majority of men and women it has no roots in feeling or true conviction. We have been seeking a morality that will indeed have its roots in the depths of our being and in our awareness of the true needs of our fellows.

We believe that there is indeed a place for discipline, but that it can only be fully healthy as well as fully Christian when it is found in application to the *whole* of life. The challenge to each of us is clear: accustom yourself to seeking God's will and to the experience of his love and power, become used in your daily life to the simple but tremendous spiritual fact that what God asks he enables, provided only and always that we will to do his will.

The men and women thus accustomed will not be less exposed to sexual difficulties – heterosexual or homosexual – than others whose lives are not 'under discipline' in this way. As we see it, the difference lies in their response to the claims of sexual urges. Whereas the emotional or 'moral' response focusses attention on the control of the sexual urge in isolation, the way of life we have described makes it likely that the particular sexual problem will be seen in the full context of ordinary daily living, and thus be kept in perspective as something for which God has not only a solution but a positive purpose.

Such positive purpose may – and often does – involve the acceptance of suffering by the person concerned. The Christian cannot escape the implications of the Cross. We have no unity with those who regard all tension and all frustration as being by definition bad or unhealthy: such a view is utterly without psychological foundation. The mental and spiritual well-being of a person depends rather on his or her developed capacity to deal with tensions and frustrations as and when they arise. In the power of the Holy Spirit, there are no dangers from which strength cannot be gained, no apparent disaster which cannot be transformed into spiritual opportunities.

Document VII.8

The Presbyterian View of Contraceptives, 1965

PCE, *Reports to Assembly*, 1965, p. 58.

The development of the contraceptive pill and its increasingly wide availability raised new questions. The Church and Community Committee of the Presbyterian Church of England reported in 1965, and the Assembly approved a resolution in substantially the same terms.

The Committee believes that the responsible use of contraceptives is in keeping with Christian conduct, and welcomes the wider publicity given to the problems of over population and to the value of family planning. At the same time, the Committee affirms its belief that:

(a) although the self discipline involved in abstinence from intercourse before marriage can be very costly and the pressures arising from arguments for experiment can be very difficult to resist, there is value in such abstinence;

(b) the use of contraceptives for intercourse before marriage is no true preparation for the married experience. Also it prejudices the possibility of that fidelity and trust, in later marriage, which are the privilege of husband and wife.

While the Committee recognises that contraceptives are rightly offered for sale in shops and through advertisements, it opposes, as potentially corrupting, the sale of appliances through slot machines in public places or in educational institutions.

Document VII.9

Living in a Secular Age, 1964

John Hough, *The Christian in a Secular Age* (London: Baptist Union, 1964), pp. 3–7.

John Hough was in charge of the Baptist Union Citizenship Department in the early 1960s and wrote this guide to contemporary Christian living, very much in the light of the early 1960s emphasis on secularity and religionless Christianity, as epitomised by John Robinson's *Honest to God*.

... Our problems about living as Christians are not just about the outcome of the high standards of conduct we profess as Christ's men and women. They are common to all who seek to find their way through the complex claims life makes upon them as members of family, community and nation. Political and economic unrest and perplexity beset those who are now striving in many parts of the world for new nationhood. Community responsibility is bedevilled as importunate admen compete against one another to guard and increase. The bonds of family life are strained by the fact that our homes tend to become no more than places where we can go to roost with the television next door to the garage. We have to learn afresh that charity like chastity begins at home. When men and women 'come of age' they do not attain responsibility overnight. They tend to exult in their new status and freedom – and they sometimes may have to pay a heavy price in debased ideals and character ... Christian thinking, whilst continuing profoundly to influence life in the community, cannot shake entirely free from pagan ideals. And on the other hand, when Christians think they see the way forward they find their ideas crushed by apathy or open hostility.

We know full well that Christian responsibility today demands a fresh search for a sense of personal holiness in every sphere of life in which Christians may honourably share. This renewal is demanded on two levels: our resolve wears thin, our enthusiasm flags, our visions fade; worn out machinery must be replaced. But, in addition, new moral situations demand new insights. 'New occasions teach new duties.' Every generation is called to different deeds of mercy...

As some problems and evils are lessened or abolished, others are created or aggravated. Consider for example how psychological studies are influencing the treatment of delinquency. Ideas of retribution have given way to methods of rehabilitation and restoration. The Church has as much need to study her attitude to crime and punishment as has the State in recent days. Modern treatment and legislation concerning mental and physical illness and handicap demands from the community new compassion insight and resourcefulness. What new decisions must be made in the face of drugs which may prolong or shorten life, or influence thought and temperament? Again, we find we are not only able to plan our environment, and the number of the world's inhabitants, but also the kind of people the world shall have. How, for example, are we to meet the possibility of choosing the sex of our children? How legitimate is it to apply to human reproduction, techniques long accepted in animal husbandry? There are other equally disturbing temptations to master our destiny. It is ten years since it was said that it was possible to manufacture a bomb 2,500 times as powerful as the one which devastated Hiroshima ten years before that. Now we have to reckon with thermonuclear weapons having an explosive power one million times more powerful than bombs used in the Second World War. A 10 megaton bomb, we are told, apart from fallout and genetic effects which may well prove incalculable, contains the equivalent of a train of railway wagons filled with high explosives stretching from London to New York. How we begin to confront this ultimate challenge to man's search for a nobler valuation of human life, conscious that the decision to use or withold this power may be vested in one small group, goes far beyond party political sentiment and allegiance.

Without glossing over the complexity of the issues, we have neither to glamorise good nor sensationalise evil in matters of family and community life. For example, the statistics relating to divorce, shocking as they may seem at a glance, do not necessarily suggest that there are fewer stable, successful marriage partnerships today than there were, say, half a century ago. Again, in some ways the attitude of many young people to sex and marriage is more wholesome now than it used to be, and the churches have become the largest and most influential voluntary bodies in the youth service. Or again, the fact that convictions for drunkenness among young people under 21 have trebled in the last ten years, must be weighed against increases in population and personal incomes, the influence of new forms of advertising which may not last, and the not inconsiderable proportion of people who are not habitual drinkers. A report published in April 1964 noted a decrease in drunkenness among people aged 18–21 on Merseyside and in the Birmingham and London areas.

It is true the present moral situation breeds new disagreement and confusion among Christians as they seek to be honest to God by being honest to man. But meantime the exciting feature is that the situation is driving many responsible Christians, provided that they have sufficient courage and trust, to a more searching examination of their traditional attitudes and values, that truth may be broken and refashioned. And Christians are seeing how much they *must* do together, and when they try to do so they discover new levels of fellowship and obedience to the Gospel.

We should not need to be reminded, as Professor Moule has said, that some moral decisions must be made corporately rather than individually: 'the normal organ of perception through which the Holy Spirit may be expected to speak with distinctively moral guidance is the Christian worshipping community listening critically.'

Our so called social service state obviously owes much to the inspiration of Christian outlook and action. Christians now must recognise how it is leading them on to fuller participation and responsibility for the statutory community services. There is of course the legal framework of social insurance, pensions, compensation and allowances ... Now responsibility is spilling over into another dimension. Real individual men, women and children make up the community. National Assistance is no longer to be grudgingly accepted as charity, but as a means of meeting exceptional needs outside the minimal framework of insurance. Wherever possible deprived children must be given the warm stimulus and comfort of home and family life. The traditional family doctor has been joined by a host of other professional social practitioners, skilled in the arts of human relationships ...

Our society needs Christians who will work out their search for a personal faith and for avenues of their new life in Christ by training as professional social workers, just as desperately as it needs recruits for the ministry, or R.I. specialists in day schools. Trained and gifted men and women who will undertake spare-time social work in voluntary and statutory bodies are as vital as those who will accept nomination for diaconates. The whole work has its monotony, and is rarely romantic: but it has it rewards. But there are two words of caution: voluntary social workers must have the humility and understanding to recognise problems they are unable to handle, lest they bungle by uninformed goodwill situations which may thereby become lastingly impaired; and secondly, service given must be skilled through proper training. Our faith has more to fear from those who shrink into the shell of organised religious life and thereby contract out of the wider social responsibilities than from those who try, however, falteringly, to discover Christ's will and presence in community need. We have to recognise the New Jerusalem even when there is no temple.

But Christians need to think out where their authority for their distinctive contribution lies. 'The sanctions of Sinai have lost their terrors,' we are told, 'and people no longer accept the authority of Jesus even as a great moral teacher.' (J. A. T. Robinson). The demands made upon Christians are always related to their rediscovery of the person and work of Jesus Christ. Christ enjoins the disciple to 'love as I have loved you,' not counting the cost. A Christian martyr of our own day has claimed 'when Christ calls a man, he bids him to come and die' (Bonhoeffer); it *is* so because God so loved the unlovely 'News of the World' world, that he gave.

There were times when Jesus resisted the cry for an absolute code of detailed responsibility, though such absolutes there surely are. In his last hours upon earth He urged upon his followers the fulfilment of the law in a new commandment of love. It is a daring ideal, demanding 'the courage to be new' (Robert Frost).

Document VII.10

Divorce and Remarriage, 1967

PCE, *Record of Assembly*, 1967, pp. 509–10.

The Presbyterian Church of England revised its regulations on divorce and remarriage in May 1967, although not without disagreement, as the *Record* illustrates.

The Assembly called for the Report of the Committee on the Church and the Community, which was submitted by the Revd. J. L. Cottle, *Convener*. On his motion, seconded by the Revd. J. Johansen-Berg, the Report was received.

The Convener then moved the following resolution:

The Assembly (a) accepts the 1967 regulations for Remarriage in Church, set out in the report; (b) instructs the appropriate Committee to advise and act upon point 6 regarding Congregational records; (c) repeals the regulations of 1946.

The Revd. F. D. McConnell, seconded by the Revd. G. Holland Williams, moved as an amendment:

1 The Assembly resolves as follows concerning the remarriage of divorced persons:
   (a) The Assembly authorises ministers, after serious consideration of the issues involved and when confident that it is right so to do, to solemnise the remarriage of a divorced person;
   (b) The Assembly instructs ministers, when preparing such a person for remarriage, to discharge their pastoral responsibility in such a way as to help that person and future partner to build up a truly Christian marriage within the life of the Church;
   (c) The Assembly requests ministers, in cases of exceptional difficulty in deciding upon an application for remarriage, to consult privately either another minister or one or two members of Session;
   (d) The Assembly declares that no minister shall be required to solemnise a remarriage against his conscience;
   (e) The Assembly repeals the regulations of 1946.

On being put to the vote this was agreed and became the substantive motion.

The Revd B. M. Pratt, seconded by the Revd. R. G. Walker, moved as an amendment:

Social Issues

The Assembly refers back to the Committee the matter of remarriage in Church to be considered in the light of the amendment, and asks for a further report to next Assembly.

On being put to the vote the amendment was defeated, and the substantive motion was adopted.

Document VII.11

Abortion, 1976

A Methodist Statement on Abortion adopted by the Methodist Conference of 1976, in D. Deeks (ed.), *Methodist Church Statements on Social Responsibility 1946–1999* (London: Methodist Church Division of Social Responsibility, 1992), pp. 1–4.

The Abortion Act of 1967 raised another set of issues. This Statement of 1976, found helpful by many doctors, is one of the most thorough discussions, which does not simply take an antagonistic stance.

Introduction
1. The question of abortion continues to exercise the thought, conscience and compassion of men and women. The area of the debate at this stage is limited to the period between conception and birth.
2. Abortion has at once moral, medical, legal, sociological, philosophical, demographic and psychological aspects. In addition, the Christian will seek to bring to the discussion insights and emphases which derive from his faith.

Theological Aspects
3. The Christian believes that man is a creature of God, made in the divine image, and that human life, though marred, has eternal as well as physical and material dimensions. All human life should therefore be reverenced. The fetus is undoubtedly part of the continuum of human existence, but the Christian will wish to study further the extent to which a fetus is a person. Man is made for relationships, being called to respond to God and to enter into a living relationship with Him. Commanded to love their neighbours, Christians must reflect in human relationships their response to God's love. Although the fetus possesses a degree of individual identity, it lacks independence and the ability to respond to relationships. All *persons* are always our 'neighbours'; other beings may call forth our loving care. In considering the matter of abortion, therefore, the Christian asks what persons, or beings who are properly to be treated wholly or in part as persons, are involved and how they will be affected by a decision to permit or forbid abortion.
4. It is of the essence of the Christian Gospel to stand by and care for those who are facing crises and to help them to make responsible decisions of doctors and nurses who find themselves unable to take decisions about their situation. It also respects the conscientious part in carrying out abortions.

5. In considering the question of abortion, Christians must never overlook the reality of human sin. This impairs judgement with the result that the abortion decision may be made in a context of selfishness, carelessness or exploitation. Human sin is also seen in attitudes and institutions which foster any debasing of human sexuality or are complacent to social injustice and deprivation. In facing these dimensions of failure and sin, Christians will work for an experience of spiritual renewal and a deeper understanding of the nature of human responsibility in the response made to the abortion.

The Issues Involved

6. On one side of the abortion debate is the view which seeks to uphold the value and importance of all forms of human life by asserting that the fetus has an inviolable right to life and that there must be no external interference with the process which will lead to the birth of a living human being. The other side of the debate emphasises the interests of the mother. The fetus is totally dependent on her for at least the first twenty weeks of the pregnancy and, it is therefore argued, she has a total right to decide whether or not to continue the pregnancy. It is further argued that a child has the right to be born healthy and wanted.

7. Both views make points of real value. On the one hand, the significance of human life must not be diminished; on the other hand, abortion is unique because of the total physical dependence of the fetus on the mother, to whose life, capacities or existing responsibilities the fetus may pose a threat of which she is acutely aware. It is necessary both to face this stark conflict of interests and to acknowledge that others are also involved – the father, the existing children of the family, the extended family, and society generally.

8. From the time of fertilisation, the fetus is a separate organism, biologically identifiable as belonging to the human race and containing all the genetic information. It will naturally develop into a new living human individual. A few days after fertilisation, implantation (or nidation) has taken place; it is significant that in the period before nidation a very large number of fertilised ova perish. At some time after the third month, the 'quickening' occurs – an event which is of significant, perhaps crucial, moment for the mother. Not earlier than the 20th week, the fetus becomes viable, *i.e.* able to survive outside the womb if brought to birth.

9. There is never any moment from conception onwards when the fetus totally lacks human significance – a fact which may be overlooked in the pressure for abortion on demand. However the degree of this significance manifestly increases. At the very least this suggests that no pregnancy should be terminated after the point when the aborted fetus would be viable. This stage has been reached by the 28th week and possibly by the 24th or even earlier. It would, in fact, be best to restrict all abortions to the first twenty weeks of pregnancy except where there is a direct physical threat to the life of the mother or when new information about serious abnormality in the fetus becomes available after the twentieth week. There is indeed also a strong

argument on physical, psychological and practical grounds to carry out abortions in the first three months wherever possible.

10. Because every fetus has significance, the abortion decision must neither be taken lightly nor made under duress. It is for this reason, as well as in her own long-term interests, that the mother should receive adequate counselling. This should enable her to understand what is involved in abortion, what are the alternatives to it and what are the considerations she should weigh before asking for a termination. The skills of social workers and the particular technique of counselling, as well as the responsible medical judgement of doctor and consultant, must therefore be engaged. The provision of this service should be a duty laid by administrative regulations on those approving abortions whether in the NHS or the private abortion clinics. This is another reason why abortion on demand is to be rejected.

The Abortion Act 1967

11. It is again to preserve the awareness of the significance of the fetus that the present form of the Abortion Act 1967 is of value. It retained the basic statement that abortion is unlawful, but indicated criteria which sufficiently altered the situation as to make abortion permissible. The intention behind the Act is therefore to be welcomed as it reflects a sensitivity to the value of human life and also enables serious personal and social factors to be considered.

12. These factors include, for example, the occasion when a pregnancy may pose a direct threat to the life or health of the mother. The probability of the birth of a severely abnormal child (where this may be predicted or diagnosed with an appreciable degree of accuracy) also provides a situation in which parents should be allowed to seek an abortion. It is right to consider the whole environment within which the mother is living or is likely to live. This will include the children for whom she is already responsible and there will be occasions when she is unable to add to heavy responsibilities she is already carrying. Again, there are social conditions in our country which are offensive to the Christian conscience, particularly those connected with bad housing and family poverty. These conditions must be improved; meanwhile it is clear that abortion is often sought as a response to the prospect of bearing a child in these and similarly intolerable situations. In the particular circumstances indicated in this paragraph, abortion is often morally justifiable.

13. The Abortion Act is nevertheless imperfect and requires clarification and amendment either by legislation or administrative regulations. Abortions should be limited to the first twenty weeks of pregnancy save in the exceptional cases to which reference has been made. Counselling must be offered in all cases. The profit motive must be reduced. There must be further consideration of the clause which allows abortion when the risks of continuing the pregnancy are greater than the risks in terminating it. This clause can be interpreted to justify abortion on demand. Unless the medical profession or suitable administrative regulations can ensure that this clause is

not used alone to authorise abortion on demand, the difficult task of amending the Act at this point must be attempted. There is little doubt that the responsible interpretation of the Act and the proper provision of abortion is more likely to be secured if a high proportion of terminations are carried out in NHS hospitals and not in private abortion clinics. The Methodist Church urged this in 1966. It again emphasises its concern.

14. Abortion must not be regarded as an alternative to contraception nor is it to be justified merely as a method of birth control. The termination of any form of human life can never be regarded superficially and abortion should not be available on demand, but should remain subject to a legal framework, to responsible counselling and to medical judgement. The Church, with others, must help to provide more adequate counselling opportunities. Society must also be sensitive to the burden it places on medical personnel, and not least upon nurses, by permitting abortion very freely. It must fully respect the conscience of those in the medical profession who feel unable to carry out terminations; though, on their part, they have a responsibility to put women who approach them in touch with alternative sources of advice.

15. The problems raised by abortion can be finally resolved only by a new and sustained effort to understand the nature of human sexuality and to encourage expressions of sexual relationships which are joyous, sensitive and responsible, and which do not tend to exploit others. Christians believe that in conception and birth, parents are pro-creators with God of new human life. They also affirm in the whole of their sexual relationships that identity-in-mutuality which is inherent in marriage and which argues so strongly for the permanence of the marriage commitment. In an imperfect world, where both individual and society will often fail, abortion may be seen as a necessary way of mitigating the results of these failures. It does not remove the urgent need to seek remedies for the causes of these failures.

Document VII.12

Social Justice, 1982

URC, *Reports to Assembly*, 1982, pp. 19–20.

From the 1970s the social consequences of Britain's industrial decline increased in importance in the churches' social agenda, accentuated by the feeling that the policies of Mrs Thatcher's Conservative government were making things worse rather than better. The United Reformed Church's Church and Society Department included this statement in its 1982 report.

3. **Social Justice** Following the debate on public expenditure at the 1981 Assembly, initiated by the Mersey Province, the July Executive Committee urged Synods, District Councils and local churches to find out about the impact

of current social and economic policies on community life in their areas and to urge Members of Parliament to defend the weakest members of the community.

4. Within a few hours of that meeting Toxteth was the scene of street riots caused by years of inner city neglect and decay. Other areas of the country were similarly affected by violent demonstrations, with considerable personal injury and destruction of property. The General Secretary wrote to the Prime Minister and leaders of the other political parties informing them of the Executive Committee debate.

5. Since then a few churches have written about the personal hardship and community despair in their areas as government policies and economic decline erode the social, educational and health services, and unemployment increases. The need to maintain law and order and the increasing frustration in the worst-hit communities create problems in policing and focus on the role of the police. Clearly in some areas there has been a break down of trust and many are worried that the police are not fully answerable to elected bodies. Certainly the troubles in Brixton and Toxteth involved serious mistrust of the police. Lord Scarman, in his report on the Brixton disorders in April 1981 spoke of 'the need for a concerted, better co-ordinated attack on the problems of the inner city', and observed 'the need to involve not just black people, but all the community, both nationally and locally, in a better directed response to these problems'.

6. While the Department has only received a few letters in response to the Executive Committee debate, as many were received protesting against the grant to the Liverpool 8 Defence Committee in Toxteth. The Liverpool 8 Defence Committee was formed by local people to 'defend' the community there against what they regarded as threats to their freedom and security. In the aftermath of the riots it arranged legal aid and proper representation for those who were arrested and charged. It gave assistance to those making claims for compensation for riot damage, it was involved in providing social activities particularly for young people, and it arranged transport for families and friends wishing to visit the remand centres and hospitals where many from Toxteth were taken during and after the disturbances. In offering a grant of £500 the BCC's Community and Race Relations Unit was making a positive gesture of support for those who have for years suffered from the effects of inner city neglect. In making the grant there was no implication of support for the violence which had erupted on the streets but rather a recognition that our whole society is implicated in neglecting some of its most disadvantaged citizens.

7. The events of 1981, with street disturbances in several inner city areas, challenge the churches in Britain to reassess their deployment policies and their use of resources. The Department welcomes the current discussion in the URC on new initiatives in mission and believes that high priority should be given to the urban poor.

8   It is now over a decade since the Government identified the 'indices of deprivation'. Among these were: multi-occupation of homes; large families; low income; poor health; unemployment; ethnic mixture. Communities having

these features were considered to need extra resources, through positive discrimination in their favour, if deprivation were to be overcome. Conflict and frustration in local communities has made the nation aware, almost too late, of the extent to which personal hardship, and the daily experience of disadvantage, can lead to alienation, especially where chronic unemployment affects localities that already suffer from poor housing and inadequate amenities. At national and local level there is a need for imaginative reshaping of policies to end disadvantage through redistributive approaches to taxation and welfare.

Document VII.13

Racism, 1987

URC, *Reports to Assembly*, 1987, pp. 22–3.

The WCC Programme to Combat Racism prompted greater awareness of continuing racism in Western societies. The United Reformed Church's Church and Society Department offered the following declaration on racism in 1987, which was adopted by the Assembly.

Declaration on Racism The Department believes that the Church should reaffirm its commitment to ridding church and society of racism. It therefore offers the following declaration and commends it for study at all levels of church life in the hope that it will encourage initiatives, policies, and programmes against racism:

The United Reformed Church believes that all people are created in God's image, free and equal in his sight.
Racism results where prejudiced attitudes of superiority over others are combined with the power to shape society.
Western civilisation is, and has long been, seriously flawed by racism.
British society nurtures racism through assumptions, stereotypes and organisational barriers, which deny black people a just share of power and decision making.
The Church displays racism by failing to adapt so that black people can share fully in its life, its outreach and its decision-making.
There is cause for celebration in church and society when black and white people learn to cooperate, share power and make decisions together and where new forms of community life are thus discovered.
The United Reformed Church commits itself to challenge and equip all its people to resist racism within themselves, within the church and within society as a whole and to train people and devote resources to this task.
The United Reformed Church pledges itself, as it shares in action against racism, to monitor and review at regular intervals what progress is being made in church and society.

Social Issues

Document VII.14

Commitment for Life, 1992

URC, *Reports to Assembly*, 1992, pp. 201–2.

Before the United Reformed Church came into being in 1972 its constituent churches had launched appeals to their members to raise money for world development. The target was fixed at 1 per cent of personal disposable income in the 1970s. In 1992 the programme was relaunched under a new title, 'Commitment for Life'.

COMMITMENT FOR LIFE
incorporating the world development (1%) appeal

1.1 *Commitment for Life* continues the emphasis placed on world development over the years by the United Reformed Church and its predecessor denominations. 25 years ago it might have been hoped that such an emphasis and this fresh presentation of an appeal in 1992 would not be needed.
But the United Nations paints a grim picture of our world:
one billion of our fellow human beings destitute;
3 billion without sanitation;
2 billion without safe water;
1.5 billion without any basic health care;
100m children of primary school age not attending school;
900m illiterate adults;
… and that income per head in sub-Saharan Africa and in Latin America **declined** during the 1980s which were relatively prosperous for us. According to UNICEF the deaths of 500,000 children are directly attributable to the crippling burden of Third World debt repayments.

1.2 Such is the global context. We have to consider also the eternal context, the clear commands of God to work for justice as the basis of peace, and to turn away from selfishness whether individual or corporate. 'When I was hungry …' remains the ultimate test for rich Christians in an age of hunger. Sin is not an abstract concept; it is a term descriptive of much of our life including 'the good we have left undone'. To live as forgiven sinners is our privilege; in Christ we are overwhelmed neither by the scale of human suffering nor by our own inadequacy. Rather, complacency is our danger, the subtle self-righteousness which overtakes forgiven sinners in every age and which our relative affluence does nothing to dispel. Let us then do good, and go on urgently doing good, feeling grateful not guilty.

1.3 This review seeks to reawaken the vision that has inspired the URC world development appeal throughout the years. With these fresh proposals we seek to tackle some of the misunderstandings that have arisen in the present appeal and to broaden its scope and reach. **We are calling *Commitment for Life* a programme rather than an appeal to counter one misconception, that it is only about money.**

2 THREE PRINCIPLES

2.1 **More than relief** First, insofar as we can distinguish between relief and development, the point is to attempt both, for the sake of the wretched of the earth.

From time to time disaster strikes, maybe a flood or earthquake or drought, and immense human suffering follows; though much of the suffering is preventable, nevertheless it is described as a 'natural disaster' and we all respond with compassion and collections. This relief is in line with the teaching of most religions and is certainly commended in the Bible.

Our responsibility for the weakest goes further, however. This is why development programmes are important, tackling the deeper effects of poverty by improving agriculture, schooling, clinics, economic opportunities, etc. This is why considerable effort goes into trying to persuade governments to increase the quantity and the quality of official aid and in the longer term to reorganise the economic order to deal with poverty itself. Just as in Britain we have moved beyond Poor Law relief and now expect certain basic needs for food, education, health care, security to be met and basic opportunities to be universally available, so we recognise that relief offers only temporary help to the poor across the world.

The URC world development appeal has supported longer-term development over the years, while at the same time members have also contributed generously to relief programmes directly. *Commitment for Life* will continue to concentrate on development.

2.2 **We benefit too** Individuals and churches who do participate fully in the appeal actually gain from it! At the heart of our discipleship is the principle that giving enriches the giver, that loving others brings us closer to God in peace and joy. Active involvement should produce an environment of worship (personal and corporate), a heightened awareness of the world and of God's purposes, and even a healthier lifestyle if we ask the right questions about our patterns of consumption.

The 1% element of personal giving is important – and this target is retained in the new programme. It is meant to be a symbol of a more open and satisfying life in which our response to poverty is not clouded by the guilt and frustration which can easily build up if we are constantly told that we are 'not doing enough'; rather it is part of our response to God as we share with others who can never repay us.

2.3 **Power to End Poverty** The third principle underpinning such an appeal is that it brings the church's fine words down to earth. It is relatively easy to talk about justice and peace, about love and hope. Any revised programme and appeal must help the church to interpret what these ideals actually mean in the world of hard decisions, of economics and international affairs, a world full of corruption and unworthy compromise, of vested interests and double-dealing. There is a connection between the upper room and boardroom, between the Servant-King and the President of the United States. Power must be used to

Social Issues

end poverty; the poor need an alternative PEP, initials familiar to people planning their own personal security. *Commitment to Life* can provide a framework in which the links can be explored.

2.4 **The world development appeal has been a response of faith; in this respect it remains the same – otherwise it does not deserve to take up so much time and energy and money. As a response of faith following the example and command of Christ himself, then we need to press ahead with the new programme.**

Document VII.15

Methodism and Gambling, 1992

A Methodist Statement on Gambling (Adopted by the Methodist conference of 1992), in D. G. Deeks (ed.) *Methodist Statements on Social Responsibility, 1946–1992* (London: Methodist Church Division of Social Responsibility, 1992), pp. 54–5, 59–62.

In 1992 a new report on Gambling summarised the changes since the 1936 Declaration, and drew a clear distinction between serious gambling and the use of what was technically gambling for fund-raising purposes. Interestingly one of the reasons for accepting this change was the development of ecumenical partnerships.

Recreational Gambling

19   At the time of the 1936 Declaration, recreational gambling was largely illegal and therefore unregulated ...

21   The legislation of the 1960s did not therefore simply legalise gambling – it decriminalised a vast, existing working-class practice. Formerly, betting was the recreation chiefly of men with little surplus income, for whom a short run of bad luck could be an irreversible disaster, both for them and their families. This activity was brought within the law at a time when relative prosperity and secure income minimised the harm that previously attached to low-income bettting.

22   Now many forms of recreational gambling have been legalised, and almost all are highly regulated. The principles of regulation were first laid down by the 1951 Royal Commission, with further elaboration by the 1978 Commission. and may be summarised as follows:

   a) To interfere with the individual as little as possible, while recommending measures to discourage socially damaging excesses and the incursion of crime.

   b) Facilities offered should respond to unstimulated demand, ie there should be little or no advertising.

   c) Gamblers should be made aware of what they may lose.

23   These principles have been embodied in legislation over thirty years, and they have totally reshaped the industry. The detailed examination of the industry

presented in *The Winner's Shout, the Loser's Curse* indicates that gambling is a limited, heavily regulated leisure pursuit. A majority of the population engage in some gambling activity, but this is largely trivial; serious gambling is pursued by rather small minorities. The activity is, overall, in a state of decline, and has been so almost since liberalisation in the sixties. Its share of the leisure market and its proportion of employees is decreasing. The number of casino and lottery players is shrinking, the number of football pool users is static, and only newspaper bingo is recruiting more players. There is much evidence that any attempt to expand the gambling market, as in the proposals for a National Lottery, will merely eat into existing gambling practice ...

Weighing the arguments

49 At first sight, the rigorist case seems overstated – understandably, given the social setting of its formation. It is clear that the distinctive Methodist view on gambling grew out of an active pastoral concern for the poorest in society. An ethical response was formed as that work grew. As suggested above, gambling can be a serious evil when an unregulated system battens upon financial insecurity. That concern has, it might be said, been permitted to inflate into a great doctrinal issue, which condemns the purchase of a raffle ticket as a denial of the Fatherhood of God, human solidarity and Christian fellowship. Similarly, the stark contrast between the self-indulgent gambler and the sacrificial life to which Christ calls us, implies a level of Christian ascetic practice which few, inside or outside the Church, would recognise as widespread.

50 It may also be countered that 'the winner's shout, the loser's curse' hardly describes most gambling outcomes. Stakes are modest; the pleasure and pain resulting are minor; losses are less cursed than regarded as a reasonable charge for this kind of entertainment. The rigorist argument is further weakened by the fact that it has not been defended or extended during the quarter-century over which gambling has become a legitimate leisure activity.

51 It can be claimed that [Ronald] Preston's liberal view pays inadequate attention to the seedier realities of the gambling world. In total, gambling is a minor part of the high degree of regulation which the traditional Methodist witness has helped to secure. It is also true that specific areas of gambling will continue to threaten serious harm; among those today are illegal betting and the inducement to the abuse of AWP machine play by young people. It is necessary to be continually alert to the industry's development.

52 It is necessary also to take both rigorist and liberal arguments seriously. On the one hand, the acquisitive nature of gambling – to enjoy a gain, through chance, at another's expense – can be destructive and demeaning to human relationships. On the other hand, it is clear that this consuming desire for gain at the expense of others is not the main motivation behind gambling, especially when it occurs in a fairly carefully regulated context. This is especially true in the case of the minor forms of fundraising which are often the cause of contention within the Methodist Church. This is certainly gambling, but the element of desire to gain is virtually absent.

53 It seems appropriate, therefore, to heed the experience of our tradition in our concern for the serious evils of gambling; but also to avoid the heavy-footed pursuit of the trivial.

Church Practice

54 From the above, it is clear that the Church will continue to regard gambling with concern. But changed circumstances since 1936, and especially since 1961, may encourage us in a cautious relaxation of our current rigour. Legislation has imposed a system of careful regulation on the gambling industry. Mild entertainment is the main outcome of most gambling activity, rather than greed, envy and financial ruin.

55 Opinion is naturally divided as to what the Methodist response should be to the significantly altered social context of gambling. Some will feel that a total ban on gambling should be sustained. Others suggest that the relaxation of the traditional Methodist stance is desirable on four grounds.

   a) **The Law**. The law now provides a reasonably clear guide as to what is of serious concern within gambling activity. A clear distinction is made between gambling which requires careful regulation, and relatively trivial activity in which gain at the expense of others is not a serious consideration – the whole area of minor fundraising, as described in paragraphs 28–31 above [not reprinted].

   b) **The practice of other churches**. Methodists are aware that other churches, notably the Anglicans and the Catholics, do things differently. This is particularly true where Methodists are involved in Local Ecumenical Projects, and other instances in which they share buildings and a Christian life together. Some Methodists are embarrassed at what they themselves feel to be an eccentric view of the practice of other churches. There is a concern that Methodism should no longer be sharply distinctive in this way.

   c) **Other people's practice**. The Church is increasingly involved with a wide range of social groups who use our premises. Again, many Methodists are concerned to find themselves associated with a moralising view towards minor forms of gambling that they do not themselves share.

   d) **Methodist Practice**. It is clear that many Methodists see no harm in the kind of minor forms of gambling that are not required to be licensed, like the purchase of raffle tickets at private functions. A survey carried out in one circuit found that a third of Methodist members gambled, and that they distinguished very clearly between this as a harmless social activity, and gambling with a desire to gain at the expense of others. It is also felt that our failure to distinguish between the serious and the trivial weakens our case against, for instance, the lack of regulation of gaming machines, and proposals for a national lottery.

56 It is therefore proposed that the Methodist Church should adopt a largely common-sense distinction between what constitutes serious gambling, and what is merely a trivial activity which aims at minor fund raising, and in which

the desire to win at the expense of others is generally absent. This is broadly the view that informs the law on gambling, with the serious anomaly of the law on Amusements with Prizes Machines. To distinguish thus between serious and trivial forms of gambling practice is to reinforce and renew the Methodist witness on this question rather than to weaken it.

57 It is therefore suggested that those minor gambling activities which are permitted at exempt and non-commercial entertainments, as described at paragraphs 28–31 above, should be allowed on Methodist premises, with the following prohibitions: that Amusement with Prizes machines are not permitted on Methodist premises; and that prizes awarded in the context of Amusements with Prizes shall not be cash prizes.

58 It is important at this point to distinguish between our view of minor gambling on the one hand, and our view of stewardship on the other. **The aim of this proposed relaxation is to remove the heavy hand of censure from trivial sorts of gambling; it is emphatically not to legitimise a whole new range of fund-raising activities.** The Methodist Church depends on the serious commitment of its people to the stewardship of their resources. To gamble without thought of the small gain on offer may be no great matter; to give little, by whatever means, is a serious failure of Christian commitment.

59 It seems unlikely that any further degree of regulation would reduce the number of people who suffer serious harm from gambling except in the area of AWP Machine abuse; it is much more likely that closer regulation would increase illegal gambling, with a consequent expansion of harm. It must be expected that the number of those harmed will not abate. The Methodist people must therefore continue, with others, in its pastoral vocation to heavy and compulsive gamblers.

Conclusion

60 It is important to recognise that what is at issue both in recreational gambling and in the stock market is not merely the activity itself, but the motives and intentions of the participants. Most recreational gamblers want fun, and if possible, a win. This is even more the case when stakes are low, a good cause is helped, and the question of gain does not seriously arise. Most participants in the stock market look for the best possible return on their resources. Each area is subject to extensive abuse, and each needs to be closely regulated, but this scrutiny will probably be more effective if the different areas, their vices and regulatory systems are seen as largely separate fields of concern.

Document VII.16

Methodism and Human Sexuality, 1993

Resolutions on the Human Sexuality Report adopted in 1993, in *Minutes of the Methodist Conference*, 1993, pp. 1–2.

Social Issues

By the 1990s the churches were being pressed to say where they stood on questions of homosexuality as the number of people who 'came out' and declared that they were gay or lesbian increased. This Statement clearly holds in tension two views of sexuality. It can be compared with the Statement of the Bishops of the Church of England and the Statement of the Lambeth Conference of 1998, and also reports to the United Reformed Church General Assembly in the mid-1990s.

1 The Conference adopted the following resolutions on the Human Sexuality Report.
   (1) The Conference affirming the joy of human sexuality as God's gift and the place of every human being within the grace of God, recognizes the responsibility that flows from this for us all. It therefore welcomes the serious, prayerful and sometimes costly consideration given to this issue by the Methodist Church.
   (2) All practices of sexuality which are promiscuous, exploitative or demeaning in any way are unacceptable forms of behaviour and contradict God's purposes for us all.
   (3) A person shall not be debarred from the church on the ground of sexual orientation in itself.
   (4) The Conference reaffirms the traditional teaching of the Church on human sexuality; namely chastity for all outside marriage and fidelity within it. The Conference directs that this affirmation is made clear to all candidates for ministry, office and membership, and having established this affirms that the existing procedures of our church are adequate to deal with all such cases.
   (5) The Conference resolves that its decisions in this debate shall not be used to form the basis of a disciplinary charge against any person in relation to conduct alleged to have taken place before such decisions were made.
   (6) The Conference recognizes, affirms and celebrates the participation and ministry of lesbians and gay men in the church. Conference calls on the Methodist people to begin a pilgrimage of faith to combat repression and discrimination, to work for justice and human rights and to give dignity and worth to people whatever their sexuality.

Document VII.17

Baptists and Disability

Complete In Christ (Didcot: Baptist Union, n.d.), pp. 52–64.

Medical advances in the second half of the century meant that disabled people were no longer housebound. Again a new range of issues were raised for the churches, as this Baptist publication indicates; and by the end of the century legislation was requiring churches to be adapted for those with disabilities.

BEING NEUTRAPENIC

Sometimes the side effects of treatment create their own disabilities (and vocabulary!): the suppression of normal immune reactions by chemotherapy brings its own problems, some relevant in the church context.

> During the most vulnerable periods we used to get to church during the first hymn and slip out again while the final hymn was being sung. Once I even sat upstairs ... on my own to avoid contact with potential coughs and colds. I found this rather depressing, as though my worship was only half completed. It made me realize that for me 'going to church' consists of two equally significant components, the social contact with my fellow members being just as important as being present at the service. This was much improved when friends realized that a simple cold would be likely to develop into something rather serious if I caught it. I began to sit in my usual place again and at the end of the service people used to gather around me ... They used to make a wide circle and we would shout conversation across to each other and laugh at the situation together.
>
> One thing which did worry me was 'Had the communion cups been thoroughly washed up?' 'Who last used this cup?' This slight anxiety somewhat spoilt the joy of being able to participate in communion ... heightened even more when we were worshipping at Anglican churches with a common cup. Instead of concentrating on the service I found myself praying, 'Please, God, don't let me catch any bugs'. I know that it made my husband feel anxious too.
>
> [When able to return to the church hall]
> Having to be seated was very hard. Not being on a level with everyone else made it so difficult to join in conversations and as people rushed around one could easily feel overlooked. Not being able to move from place to place was an awful disadvantage too. I never experienced this sort of frustration when out in the wheelchair in the secular world. There I never met with anything other than smiles, helpfulness and a sense of inclusion. It was easier when I had remained in the church and people had formed the circle around me. I am sure that it is all a question of body space and neck angles!

PART OF THE CHURCH'S LIFE

It is easy to feel left out and overlooked on the fringe of church life, but people with severe disabilities can be well integrated and a creative force in the church, drawing out other's gifts, as well as contributing their own.

Baptism by immersion may present problems, though the Baptist Times occasionally shows how churches and candidates surmount them. If people fuss too much about 'how?', candidates may find it easier to decide against immersion – and bear the pain of being 'different'.

For people with disabilities, who often need to receive help, it is especially precious to be able to serve. After many years in ministry, Howard Williams once remarked to me that he was 'constantly amazed by the contribution to the church of people who could easily be excused any extras'. I remember Annie, a street-wise old saint with weak heart and little sight, who still did the washing up at church every Sunday and loved to run the tuck shop for a tough inner-city Boys' Club midweek.

Another active church member has a weak right side and speech defect resulting from whooping cough in babyhood. Baptized at fourteen, she has served as Sunday School teacher, Girls' Brigade officer, and on the Pastoral Care Team. She enjoys helping with her present church's annual 'Holiday at Home' for those who cannot go away, including disabled people. She writes: 'If there is a message I can give ... perhaps it is this: Do give people with disabilities a chance to lead a normal life. Give help when it is needed, but please remember that these people want to be one of you, not set apart'.

In another church a young woman finds the limitations of a spinal injury hard: 'I used to enjoy going on the weekend retreats ... but I find this difficult now ...' People know she has a serious problem, and she values the support and encouragement they give her, but that does not stop her minding that she cannot 'pull her weight':

> I also enjoyed helping with Sunday lunches at church but when my back problem flared up again I had to let them down, which caused me much distress as I felt a failure, although everyone was very kind and understanding. When I do help with lunches I try and do most that's asked of me, but I do have problems lifting ... [and] I'm embarrassed to say I can't do it.

There is a delicate balance in this. As another says:

> The disabled person has to beware of disabling their self-esteem by believing certain tasks are beyond them when with some application the over-facing problem can be tackled successfully. Other people have to have the sensitivity on the one hand to be aware of and anticipate the disabled person's limitation, and on the other to know when and how to encourage them to achieve a task ... The key consideration for the church is to exercise a vigorous policy of inclusiveness in its attitude toward the disabled, rather than the exclusiveness which has prevailed in the past. An illustration of this is that a member with cerebral palsy has recently produced our church Christmas card. His disability means he has no use of his arms and hands; his ability meant that he produced the cover design, lay-out and inside text by computer – all done with two toes on his left foot!

Sport is another important communal activity; what is possible will vary. Sports which rely on precision and skill rather than strength can boost confidence. Bowls, ten-pin bowling, snooker, billiards, and table-tennis may be good; and outdoor sports like sailing, riding, karting, and even motor sports are within the ability of many. People unable to run may win races in the swimming pool.

HEALING – THE VEXED ISSUE

Many contributors have mentioned problems over the way healing ministry is often understood. One minister, physically disabled from birth, writes:

> A problem that often arises in the church is that people who are very committed to the healing ministry see the disabled as ripe for it. They can often cause spiritual depression by their insistence on laying on of hands when it is the disabled person who has taken his condition to the Lord, asking for the ability to cope with and triumph over his limitations, and learned to live with them. That is the realistic experience of healing.

Another minister had no crisis of faith as a result of prolonged suffering, but felt vulnerable in relation to healing ministry: 'Handled with an inadequate theology of suffering, it can seem like a lottery'.

A third minister writes:

> While the Lord has not healed me, despite prayers of many people at different times, I have found peace in the acceptance and reality of the Lord's reply to Paul, 'My grace is sufficient'. Many years ago my chest consultant commented that I should not humanly be able to do the things I did or take on the work load I was able to. And I worked for many years more after that. Healing may often be more in the mind and soul than in the body.

There can also be a cruel sense of failing your family, friends and church, when they are praying for your healing and you fail to recover. Some people when close to death experience great distress from this sense of letting the side down. They may even come to dread visits from those friends from whom support might have been expected.

Of course we should pray for our friends, but physical healing does not always follow as the answer to fervent prayer. It is very hard to be told, as was a friend of mine recently, that you have not 'been healed' because your family and friends have not been praying in the 'right' way. Those who lead in healing ministry may be careful about their understanding and expectations, but simplistic interpretations are still around. So many contributors have raised the pain they have experienced in this respect that it has to be mentioned here.

Document VII.18

Marriage and Divorce, 1998

Standing Order 011A 'Marriage', in *The Constitutional Practice and Discipline of the Methodist Church, vol.* ii, 1998, p. 279.

This Standing Order was adopted by the Conference of 1998, replacing the previously numbered SO 830. It reflects a shift in the focus of concern by comparison with fifty years before. Book VI, Part 9, of *The Constitutional Practice and Discipline* also includes advice about marriage preparation and appropriate consultation including inter-faith marriages, and marriages where the parties request two ceremonies in churches of different denominations which must take place on the same day.

(1) The Methodist Church believes that marriage is a gift of God and that it is God's intentions that a marriage should be a life-long union in body, mind and spirit of one man and one woman. The Methodist Church welcomes everyone, whether or not a member, who enquires about an intended marriage in any of its places of worship.

(2) Divorce does not itself prevent a person being married in any Methodist place of worship.

(3) Under no circumstances does the Conference require any person authorised to conduct marriages who is subject to the discipline of the Church as a minister, deacon, probationer or member to officiate at the marriage of a particular couple should it be contrary to the dictates of his or her conscience to do so.

(4) A minister, deacon, probationer or member who is authorised to conduct marriages but who for reasons of conscience will never officiate at the marriages of couples in particular circumstances shall refer such couples to an authorised colleagues who is not so prevented.

(5) The Methodist Church opposes discrimination on the basis of gender or race. Accordingly, if a couple is seeking to be married in a Methodist place of worship no objection to the performance by a particular minister, deacon, probationer or member of any duty in respect of their proposed marriage shall be entertained on such a ground. No minister, deacon, probationer or member shall perform the relevant duty or duties in place of the other person concerned or otherwise assist the couple to make the objection effective.

PART VIII

CHURCH UNITY

Introduction

The significance of church unity in twentieth-century nonconformist history is one of the most striking differences from previous centuries. It is difficult to imagine the topic justifying a separate chapter in any earlier volume in this series. There had been moves for closer co-operation between the Baptist and Congregational Unions at the end of the nineteenth century, and some union churches were formed. The beginnings of a coming together of the separated branches of Presbyterianism and Methodism also date back to the last part of the nineteenth century. But the twentieth century saw the decisive moves, even though less was achieved in the end than many had hoped.

The coming together in 1900 of the Free Church of Scotland and the United Presbyterian Church was anticipated south of the border, when the United Presbyterian congregations in England joined with the Presbyterian Church in England (which after the Disruption of the Church of Scotland in 1843 maintained closer links with the Free Church than the established Church) to form the Presbyterian Church of England in 1876. The congregations of the Church of Scotland in England remained a separate presbytery all through the twentieth century.

Nonconformists started to meet together in the 1890s through the annual Free Church Congresses (imitated from the Anglican Church Congress) and in 1896 the National Council of Evangelical Free Churches was formed. This drew together the local Free Church Councils in many parts of the country, but it did not provide a meeting place for the national leaderships of the churches. J. H. Shakespeare, General Secretary of the Baptist Union, called for the establishment of a Federal Council, which could provide such a meeting place, when he was Chairman of the National Council in 1916. This led to the formation of the Federal Council of Evangelical Free Churches in 1917. In his book, *The Churches at the Cross-Roads* (1918), Shakespeare described his thinking and hopes (**VIII.1**), arguing that federation was a viable alternative to organic union as a way forward. In a later chapter he described his assumption that the acceptance of episcopacy was essential if any kind of union with the Church of England was to be achieved. Shakespeare was more far-sighted and more prepared to be realistic than many other nonconformists of his own day and since; but his words, written, it should be noted, before the Lambeth Appeal of 1920, found no echoes at the time. and provoked hostility among his Baptist colleagues; and he retired due to ill health in 1924.

One of the early actions of the new Council was to invite the member churches to co-operate to avoid overlapping in church extension (**VIII.2**). The Congregational Union Assembly accepted this policy, which was similar to the policy they had sought to adopt with the Baptist Union before the First World War.

The Lambeth Conference of 1920 issued 'An Appeal to all Christian People', which led to a series of conversations with representatives of the Federal Council.[1]

These conversations were very positive, but progress came to a halt over the status of the Free Churches' ministry. Although A. C. Headlam, later Bishop of Gloucester, felt that it might have been possible to suggest that recognition of the Free Church ministry did not depend on actual or conditional episcopal ordination, Archbishop Lang believed that this would have gone beyond what the Lambeth Conference of 1920 had agreed. Not surprisingly the Free Churches unanimously rejected any proposal which cast doubt on the validity of their existing ministry, and the conversations concluded in 1925. The Response of the Federal Council itself (**VIII.4**) is carefully measured, acknowledging the positive achievements of the conversations as well as the outstanding problems. The same problems explain the General Synod's failure to secure the necessary majority for the Covenant Proposals in 1981; the history of the reformed Church of England of the sixteenth to the eighteenth centuries had been forgotten.

The different Methodist churches began to come together in the Empire before anything happened in Great Britain. Then, in 1907, the Methodist New Connexion, Bible Christians, and United Methodist Free Churches united to form the United Methodist Church. A wider union was mooted by some Wesleyans in 1913, and serious negotiations between the Wesleyan Methodist, Primitive Methodist and United Methodist Churches began in 1918.[2] Constitutional issues such as the ratio of ministers and lay people in the Conference, the relation between the two sessions of Conference, with the Wesleyan demand for a continuing ministerial or 'pastoral' session, the cessation of the 'Legal Hundred' of ministers to endorse legally Conference decisions, the annual Presidency by a minister with a lay Vice President, and even lay presidency at Holy Communion in certain circumstances were solved reasonably quickly. The doctrinal arguments were over the role of scripture and Wesley's sermons and *Notes on the New Testament*. The Primitive Methodist biblical scholar, A. S. Peake, held the *Notes* to be outmoded. The 1924 wording acknowledging the 'Divine revelation recorded in the Holy Scriptures' as the 'supreme rule of faith and practice' is typical of Peake – he did not believe that the Bible was the revelation itself. Peake's view was largely shared by Wesleyans such as Sir Robert Perks, and by many United Methodists.

The first report was presented to the various Conferences in 1919, and the first version of the Scheme was published in 1920. Three revisions followed in 1922, 1924 and 1926. The statements of 1926, which became the basis of the doctrinal clauses of the Deed of Union, were clearly influenced by Lidgett, Peake and Maldwyn Hughes. It was stated that the Wesley material was not intended to impose a system of formal or speculative theology on Methodist preachers but to set up standards of preaching and belief. The Deed of Union enabled liberals and conservatives in theology to remain in one church but it was also typical of an age of theological imprecision. Only on 27 July 1928 did the ministerial (Pastoral) Session of the Wesleyan Conference obtain – just – the required 75 per cent majority. The Primitive Methodists had larger majorities in favour, although they had minorities who feared Wesleyan dominance and too high a status accorded to ordained ministers.

An Act of Parliament was secured in 1929 and the Deed of Union was approved by the three Methodist Churches so that the united Church could be inaugurated in 1932. Each Church held its final Conference in the summer of 1932 and the united Conference assembled on 20 September 1932 at the Albert Hall when the Deed of Union was signed in the presence of the Duke and Duchess of York.

Peake was a key figure in the theological basis of the union (**VIII.5**). His one-volume *Commentary on the Bible*, published in 1920, did much to popularise critical views of scripture. Leading Wesleyans testified to his influence. Other Wesleyans, led by J. E. Rattenbury, initially opposed union (**VIII.3**), and picked out Peake as their target. The main reason for their opposition, however, was that they preferred reunion with the Church of England, and so long as this option appeared to remain open, as a result of the Lambeth Conversations, they were hesitant to complicate matters by moving in the direction of other Methodists who lacked the same reverence for John and Charles Wesley. Thus Rattenbury suggested that the problem was a difference of *viewpoint*, rather than a difference of doctrine. However, they were eventually won over and unlike Presbyterian reunion in Scotland there were no continuing splinter groups. The essential provisions of the Deed of Union in relation to doctrine and membership (**VIII.6**) were stated to be unalterable, which was one reason for the Methodist Church Act of 1976 (**V.20**) but also reflected the problems of securing agreement. A striking testimony to Methodist Union came from a former Primitive Methodist, Edward Rogers, shortly before he died in 1997 (**VIII.7**).

In 1934 there was a depressing report to the Baptist and Congregational Unions about how union churches had been faring (**VIII.8**). The observed tendency of such churches to identify with one or other of the two partners, seen particularly in their baptismal practice and the tendency to call ministers from one tradition rather than the other, is an interesting reflection on the church life of the time. The same tendency was not so pronounced in relation to Local Ecumenical Partnerships from the 1960s, which probably indicates that ecumenism was both more novel and less of a priority before 1945. Although both sides wished to continue the experiment, there were no great hopes of its extension. It was, in fact, in the 1930s that the Congregational Union engaged in its first set of union conversations with the Presbyterian Church of England, but without success. Ecumenical attention among Congregationalists and Methodists in the 1930s was fixed upon South India and the negotiations for union there with the Church of England, which included the acceptance of episcopacy. At home, in January 1935 a 'Sketch of the Constitution of a Reunited Church' was published, which was discussed in the Convocations of Canterbury and York, and by the Federal Council. An amplified Scheme was published in 1938, but discussion of it was lost in the outbreak of the Second World War.

The National Council and the Federal Council of the Free Churches were successfully merged in the Free Church Federal Council in 1940. The doctrinal basis of the former Federal Council was taken as the basis for the new body (**VIII.9**). In retrospect it is striking that this should have been felt necessary, particularly in such detail. The major British churches joined the World Council of Churches in Process of Formation from 1938, though its inauguration had to wait until after the war, in 1948, at Amsterdam. The British Council of Churches was formed in 1942, thereby bringing the Church of England and the Free Churches together into a common forum, with the Church of Scotland, the other Scottish churches, and churches in Wales and Ireland. The Roman Catholic Church was not, of course, a member at this stage, although Cardinal Hinsley was probably the most ecumenically minded Archbishop of Westminster for half a century. The experience of war, especially the consequences of bombing, brought many local churches together in quite new ways, through sharing buildings.

After the war there was a further round of conversations between the Congregational Union and the Presbyterian Church of England. Although the time was not felt to be ripe for union, a Covenant was agreed between the two Churches in 1951 (**VIII.10**), to encourage closer relationships wherever possible, the sharing of ministers and new joint congregations.

The primary initiative in this period, however, came in Archbishop Fisher's University Sermon at Cambridge in November 1946, when he suggested that the Free Churches might be prepared 'to take episcopacy into their system' as a means towards intercommunion. Fisher had been put off by the trouble which the formation of the Church of South India had caused in the Anglican Communion. The four Anglican dioceses which joined were, in effect, excluded from the Anglican Communion until all the ministers in the new Church of South India were episcopally ordained. This was because, although the new Church was episcopal from the outset, the existing Methodist and Congregational ministers were recognised without any re-ordination taking place. Anglo-Catholics petitioned the Archbishop of Canterbury until the last moment to stop the process going ahead – though it is not clear that he could have done – but he refused. Fisher concluded that intercommunion would be a safer goal, and he offered this prospect to the Free Churches. A Joint Committee was set up, which produced the report *Church Relations in England* in 1950.

It is not surprising that Baptists, Congregationalists and Presbyterians, who might possibly have been prepared to adopt episcopacy in a united Church, could see no point in making their existing churches episcopal without further steps towards union. Methodists, however, agreed to discuss matters further, and this led to the Anglican-Methodist conversations. A preliminary report was published in 1958, which suggested a two-stage scheme: first, the mutual recognition of ministries, with full union later. A Report of 1963 proposed a Service of Reconciliation (**VIII.12**). The central feature of this was a deliberately ambiguous act by which the ministers of the two Churches were mutually welcomed. Bishops were to lay hands on Methodist ministers, but not with words of ordination. This attracted the hostility both of those who felt that it implied ordination and of those who felt that it was not sufficiently clear that it was. Four of the Methodist members recorded their dissent (**VIII.13**), including Kingsley Barrett who was probably the leading Methodist biblical scholar of his day. In the years following various attempts were made to clarify and refine the proposals, and a formal Scheme was produced in 1967. Some more radical Methodists thought that the issues were irrelevant, either in the wider world scene or in the problem areas of urban Britain

(**VIII.14**). Archbishop Fisher, after his retirement, attacked the final version of the Scheme because the goal had changed to organic union, which was precisely what his November 1946 sermon sought to avoid. The Proposals failed to secure the necessary majority from Anglicans in the Church Assembly in 1969. A slightly revised version was submitted to the new General Synod, but in 1972 the Scheme again failed to secure the necessary majority, some twenty-five years after Fisher's first proposal. Although it was not the only thing happening ecumenically, twenty years – say, half the ministry of an average minister – had been taken up with the discussion of proposals which eventually failed.

The Church of England's unwillingness to compromise on anything for the sake of union may be contrasted with the kinds of change which were being contemplated in the Free Churches. An example was the address given to the 1962 Annual Conference of Churches of Christ in Nottingham by their representative at the World Council of Churches Assembly at New Delhi in 1961, James Gray (**VIII.11**). Only in 1956 had the Churches of Christ Annual Conference recommended its churches to consider inviting to Holy Communion (which Churches of Christ celebrated weekly) those who had not been baptised as believers. Gray concluded that the discussions at New Delhi did not suggest that the major churches of the world were likely to abandon infant baptism. It may seem surprising that he ever thought they would; but the discussion after the Second World War, and particularly Karl Barth's support for believers' baptism, had led some to suppose that a shift in thinking might be likely. Gray's key point was that churches planted in new estates would increasingly be the only Free Church in the area, and therefore would need to cater for all; hence he proposed that in such situations people might be admitted to membership without being baptized as believers. This was no new thing for 'open membership' Baptist churches, but it was for the sacramentally more conservative Churches of Christ. The address was significant because it demonstrated anxiety about changes which the next generation would see as essential, and also because it showed that greater importance was attached to the unity of the Church than to the preservation of particular denominational traditions.

The British Faith and Order Conference held at Nottingham in 1964 captured the new mood of optimism about the ecumenical outlook. The resolution, approved by a large majority, in favour of covenanting for union, if possible by Easter Day 1980 (**VIII.15**), expressed the enthusiasm of a Conference which included a broad spread of representation from the member churches of the British Council of Churches. The second half, concerning areas of ecumenical experiment, ecumenical group ministries and similar matters where some kind of immediate progress could be made, attracted less opposition and in the long run was to be the more important. It led to the Sharing of Church Buildings Act of 1969, which was a major step forward in ecumenical co-operation; areas of ecumenical experiment were renamed Local Ecumenical Projects and later Local Ecumenical Partnerships, and were particularly significant in new towns such as Swindon or Milton Keynes.

In 1963 Congregational–Presbyterian conversations began again, resulting in a joint Statement of Church Principles. As a result of the impetus of the Nottingham

Conference, Churches of Christ were invited to send observers to the conversations in 1966, and the Basis of Union of what became the United Reformed Church was drafted in such a way that it would not be necessary to delete, but only to add, material if Churches of Christ were to join. The United Reformed Church Act of 1972 (**VIII.16**) was carefully drafted to deal with property matters only, it being acknowledged that it was for the Church to decide on matters of doctrine. The united Church came into being in October 1972. More then two-thirds of the churches of the Congregational Union voted to join, as the Scheme of Union required. Two groups of churches were formed from the minority – the Congregational Federation and the Evangelical Fellowship of Congregational Churches; and some churches stayed outside all the groups. The Uniting Assembly resolved to open negotiations for union with Churches of Christ, and proposals were produced in 1976. The Churches of Christ just failed to secure the required majority, and so the Association of Churches of Christ was dissolved to allow the congregations to move in the direction they wished. Hence in 1981 the Re-formed Association of Churches of Christ, which were the majority, joined with the United Reformed Church; and most of the other congregations formed the Fellowship of Churches of Christ. The Statement of the Nature, Faith and Order of the United Reformed Church as agreed in 1981 (**VIII.17**) contained the agreed understanding of the Church. Later, conversations were held with the Congregational Union of Scotland and although the proposals failed to gain a sufficient majority in Scotland in 1988, the majority of congregations did join the United Reformed Church in 2000, with a slightly revised Basis of Union (**VIII.18**).

In the summer of 1972 after the second failure of the Anglican–Methodist Scheme and before the inauguration of the United Reformed Church, a Church Leaders' Conference was held in Birmingham. Archbishop Michael Ramsey looked for future leadership in the ecumenical movement from the United Reformed Church. It was agreed to pursue the goal of a Covenant in England, which had been suggested at the Nottingham conference eight years before. A Churches' Unity Commission was set up which, for the first time, included the Roman Catholic Church. Dr John Huxtable, joint General Secretary of the United Reformed Church, was appointed as Secretary. In 1976 the Commission published Ten Propositions on Visible Unity (**VIII.19**), and invited responses from the Churches. Five of the churches agreed to go forward: the Church of England, the Methodist Church, the United Reformed Church, the Moravian Church and Churches of Christ. The thoughtful response from the Baptist Union explaining why they felt unable to go further (**VIII.21**) aptly summarised the position of those who on ecclesiological grounds did not feel able to commit themselves to the quest for organic union. It also reflected the shift which was taking place among Baptists, with evangelical (and sometimes charismatic) voices gaining ground at the expense of ecumenical voices. What would J. H. Shakespeare have made of it?

Separate discussions had been taking place in Scotland and Wales over a possible covenant. (One important intervention at the Nottingham Conference had been an amendment, moved by Professor J. K. S. Reid from Aberdeen, to the original proposal for a covenant, which inserted the words 'in appropriate groupings such as nations'.) The Scottish discussions produced a lengthy theological document over some fifteen years, which was eventually rejected by the Church of Scotland. In Wales, events moved more quickly and a Covenant was agreed and accepted in 1975 (**VIII.20**). The pattern of the document, which coupled a series of recognitions with a series of commitments to go further, was significant. While the agreements reached were significant, it could be argued that the important matters were all contained in the 'intention' clauses.

The proposed English Covenant, which was published in 1980, reflected a rather different approach. The Introduction to the Proposals (**VIII.22**) was signed by all but three Anglican members. The centre-piece was a three-part Order of Service for the Inauguration of the Covenant, which it was envisaged would actually initiate the required mutual recognition of ministries – the elusive goal since the Lambeth conversations of the 1920s. Hence the inaugural service included the ordination of new bishops and ministers at the same time as recognition was extended to those exercising a quasi-episcopal role in the Methodist and United Reformed Churches – District Chairmen and Provincial Moderators. Some in the United Reformed Church opposed the proposed episcopal structure for the future, though the requisite majority in favour was achieved in the General Assembly. Similarly in the Church of England there was opposition to the recognition of those exercising a quasi-episcopal role without their actually becoming bishops; but more significant was the opposition to the recognition of women ministers which the covenant would involve. The General Synod in 1982 failed to secure a two-thirds majority in favour in the House of Clergy, despite succeeding in the Houses of Bishops and Laity, and so the Covenant proposals fell. This was one occasion when episcopal leadership was not followed!

The same year saw the publication of the report, *Baptism, Eucharist and Ministry*, by the Faith and Order Commission of the World Council of Churches, often referred to as the Lima Report because it was agreed at a Commission meeting at Lima in Peru. This registered a higher degree of consensus on these disputed matters than before, and gained added significance from the fact that the Roman Catholic Church was a full member of the Faith and Order Commission, although not of the World Council of Churches. Responses to the report were invited from the member churches of the Council and others, and most of the British Churches responded. The response of the Society of Friends (**VIII.23**) probably summarised Quaker thinking towards the end of the twentieth century on these matters more completely than any other document. There was nothing new in the Response, and in some respects it demonstrated the same determined refusal to move from past positions as some Anglican responses in ecumenical affairs.

Towards the end of the 1980s a process, entitled 'Not Strangers but Pilgrims', was initiated to review the British Council of Churches so as to make it possible for the Roman Catholic Church to become a full member. This resulted in a smaller institution, Churches Together in Britain and Ireland, with separate bodies for each of the four nations, the English one being entitled Churches Together in England. Responsibility for local ecumenism, which with the collapse of national initiatives had become the main area of development in the last quarter of the century, moved to Churches Together in England. This particularly applied to Local Ecumenical Projects or Partnerships (LEPs), the number of which continued to increase steadily in England (**VIII.25**). The Baptist Union and the Methodist Church reached an agreement on baptismal policy in LEPs where both of them were partners (**VIII.24**). The Basis of Union of the United Reformed Church, which included those who believe only in believers' baptism *and* those who believe also in infant baptism, did not permit the baptism as a believer of someone already baptised in infancy; whereas clause 4 of the Baptist–Methodist agreement did permit it if the person concerned transferred to the Baptist roll. The significance of LEPs for the United Reformed Church, which had a higher proportion of its congregations involved in them than any other church, was carefully assessed in 1996 (**VIII.26**). Churches Together in England initiated a process entitled 'Called to be One' in the later 1990s, inviting responses from the churches. The United Reformed Church identified some of the key issues (**VIII.27**); but nothing resulted from the process.

At the very end of the century, after initial informal discussions between the Methodists and the Church of England, formal talks took place which led to proposals for a Covenant between the two Churches, which was inaugurated in 2002. What made this possible was the Methodist Conference's adoption of the report on Episcopacy (**II.19**). There were also informal discussions between the Church of England and the United Reformed Church, and between both Churches and the Methodist Church, but these have not yet led to any more formal conversations between the Church of England and the United Reformed Church. Part of the impetus for this was the series of agreements which the Church of England or the Anglican Churches in Britain and Ireland had made with protestant churches in Germany, Scandinavia and France. These created relationships between those churches and the Church of England which are the same as those between the continental churches and the United Reformed Church, principally through the Leuenberg Agreement between Lutheran and Reformed Churches in Europe of 1973. The Anglican–Methodist Covenant brought this mixture of relationships into the heart of English nonconformity.

Notes

1 The documents produced by these Conversations and the Churches' responses to them are reproduced in Bell (1924 and 1930).
2 The negotiations are outlined in: Davies (1983), pp. 333–40; Kent (1966), pp. 1–43; Currie (1968), pp. 248–89; Turner (1985), pp. 194–214.

Document VIII.1

Shakespeare's Vision of Free Church Unity, 1918

J. H. Shakespeare, *The Churches at the Cross-Roads* (London: Williams & Norgate, 1918), pp. 117–26, 166–84.

J. H. Shakespeare was General Secretary of the Baptist Union and his initiative as Chairman of the National Free Church Council led to the formation of the Federal Council of Free Churches in 1917. Here he sets out his broader vision for unity, including the question of episcopacy.

I have already said that the churches cannot face the new time upon which they are entering, with its new problems and moral demands, in any spirit of hopefulness unless they close their ranks. They must not attempt to carry with them the lumber of the past. The temper and attitude of the modern mind towards Church divisions is such that unrelieved denominationalism will involve inevitable and increasing loss. The churches must seek unity and establish closer relations that religion itself may be saved ...

In the year 1916, from the Chair of the National Free Church Council I made definite proposals for closer relations between the Free Churches. The question was brought before the Annual Assembly or Conference of each, and representatives were duly appointed to consider the possibilities and implications of Free Church union, and to prepare a scheme. Eighty-one delegates were appointed, and there was not a single absentee from the Conference which was held at Mansfield College, Oxford, in September of the same year. We who met together discovered one thing at the outset, if we did not know it already, that the desires of no one representative group could be exactly or entirely satisfied. Granted that there must be no sacrifice of principle, yet there must be give and take ...

Two distinct methods were considered, that of corporate union and the way of federation. Some who were present advocated the former, and clearly, if it were possible, it had great advantages ... It was known that the Presbyterians, Methodists and Congregationalists of Canada were preparing plans for a corporate union under the name of the United Church of Canada. Nor could there be any doubt that such a method would strike a more ringing note of unity than the tentative and moderate proposal of federation. It would have been hailed by many with more enthusiasm, and would have been a more effective remedy for sectarian evils of waste and competition than anything else. Its appeal to the outsider would have been overwhelming, and it would have simplified the religious position in the country beyond all reckoning. Imagine what it would have meant in the history of our time if the chapter of separation could have been closed, and the principles and resources of the Free Churches could have been represented by one Church, its mighty spirit taking a new form, no longer obscured by divisions or a false emphasis, but fitted to enter in with a single eye and purpose at the open door of the vast opportunity of the new time. Such a vision hung for a brief moment over the Conference and then vanished. The moment was not ripe for corporate union.

The way of federation remained, and it is now before the Free Churches ...

Federation is a silken thread and not an iron chain. The fundamental idea is that the autonomy of each constituent part shall be respected, and that whatever is of permanent value in its distinctive witness, order and institutions, shall be preserved. It ought not to pass the wit of man to find a way in which the gains and fruits of history should be secured, and the best elements of all the Churches contributed to the common stock. Federation stands 'for the fuller, richer and more various life' of the Churches which compose it. It aims at the practical reconciliation of autonomy with co-operation, liberty with order and unity with diversity ...

I do not maintain that federation is a final goal, or that it is an ideal solution. There are ideals that we must be content to leave with God, believing that He will bring them to pass ... The value of federation will depend in the long run upon whether the interpretation we give to it is large and generous. We may play with it and make of it only a 'flickering expedient' or we may regard it as an intermediate step, not as a stopping-place, leaving it to another generation to walk in the light God shall give, while we walk in ours ...

I pass now from the proposals for federation to discuss the question of the reunion of the Evangelical Free Churches with the Church of England ...

A different spirit is abroad. There is a longing for unity. The power of prayer and Christian love is inexhaustible. It is illustrated on every hand. A bishop of the Church of England has preached from a Baptist pulpit. On the Sunday appointed for intercession, in many places a Free Church minister preached in a Parish Church. In one cathedral, at least, clergymen and ministers alternately conducted a service for half-an-hour each through the larger part of the day. It is a time of national burden and sadness. In every home there is sorrow and mourning, and in many there is death. In the storm which is sweeping the world nations, classes and individuals are coming closer together ...

Each has a contribution of incalculable value to make to the other. The Church of England lays the chief emphasis upon the Church, and on the other hand there can be no doubt that in the Free Churches the Church tends to become a shadowy idea. It degenerates into a congregation assembled to listen to one man. If the preacher has no message, no gift in prayer, the Free Churchman in the pew is inclined to think that he has received nothing ...

The tradition of the Church of England is one of reverence and beauty and order; of worship carried on generation after generation in words that have become sacred. Every priest of the Church of England is under the spell of this tradition ... The tradition of the Free Churches is of freedom, of personal responsibility, and of the free access of the soul into the presence of Christ, and every member of every little village chapel is strengthened and uplifted by it ... But is there not a larger tradition – a common tradition? Can we not enter into a wider heritage in which reverence and freedom, order and beauty, the Church and the individual, have their rightful place? Freedom and authority – but order is the union of both ...

And now I come to the crux of the whole problem of reunion, the question of episcopacy. It is no use concealing my conviction that reunion will never come to pass except upon the basis of episcopacy. I did not think so once, but that was simply because I did not understand it.

The Churches fall into two main groups, and these groups are based the one on an evangelical and the other on an institutional conception of the Church. The first, or evangelical, hold that the Church of Christ is constituted by the Gospel and that its continuity is in evanglical experience. That is to say, the Church is the extension of the Incarnation, preserves the Faith, is endued through the gift of the Holy Spirit with supernatural power, and repeats in all its members, age after age, the miracle of regeneration. The second, or institutional, hold that the Church of Christ is constituted by episcopacy, not on a secular principle of expediency or through the mechanical transmission of grace, but by the institution of Christ Himself. 'The Episcopate,' says Dr. Gore, in *The Church and the Christian Ministry*, 'with its claim of an apostolic succession, is ... an essential and inviolable element of Christianity'...

If reunion can only be effected by an admission on the part of the Free Churches that the very existence of the Church depends upon a particular form of government, episcopal or any other, then the way to unity is finally and for ever barred. The Free Churches may admit that episcopacy is of the *bene esse*, but never that it is of the *esse*, of the Church ... The records of the New Testament and of the Primitive Church reveal traces of three forms of government – episcopal, presbyteral and congregational. Probably the infant Church, immature and beset by foes, was feeling its way under the guidance of the Spirit to a unity of administration with which it could confront imminent perils ... To a Free Churchman it is inconceivable that our Lord should have made any form of government essential to the Church, and yet have left its necessity so obscure that Christian scholars of the rank of Hort and Plummer and Gwatkin cannot find it, and, indeed, find the opposite...

From the other side, it is an idle dream that unity can be secured between the Church of England and the Evangelical Free Churches except upon the basis of episcopacy. I agree with Dr Armitage Robinson that 'it is, humanly speaking, inconceivable that unity can be re-established on any other basis.' Of course, I do not mean episcopacy as we see it in history, monarchical, prelatical and unconstitutional. We may toy with the question, and find countless points of agreement, but when we get to close quarters, we learn that to seek any other basis than episcopacy is a pure waste of time. Free Chuchmen may regret that it is so. They may, and do, wish that the attitude of the episcopal to the non-episcopal Churches was, in respect to all questions of ministry and sacraments, like that of non-episcopal to one another. But the fact remains that any widespread attempt to surrender episcopacy would inevitably break up the Church of England; and its evangelical members, no less than its Anglo-Catholic, value episcopacy far too much to let it go; and that no responsible Anglican leader has any intention of forfeiting the mediating position which the English Church holds as between East and West ...

But do we not feel that we must face the greatest question of all? Is there any reality in the doctrine of the Holy Ghost as the guide and teacher of truth, and if so, can we believe that a form which goes back to the beginning of Christian history, and has taken its place 'in the greater part of Christendom as the recognized organ of the unity and continuity of the Church,' arose without the guidance of the Spirit? or, on the other hand, can we believe that the guidance of the Spirit has been so completely withheld from the non-episcopal Churches that they have gone quite astray? The true dimensions of the Church will appear only as we bring together the historic past and the Divine working in the present age. Unity will be reached 'not by the method of human compromise, not by grudging concession, but by a willing acceptance for the common enrichment of the united Church of the wealth distinctive of each.'...

Document VIII.2

Overlapping of New Churches

Congregational Year Book, 1923, p. 14.

One of the perennial problems for the Free Churches had been competition in church extension. This proposal to avoid it was adopted by the Congregational Union Assembly in 1922.

2. – OVERLAPPING

(i) 'That the Federal Council consider it desirable that steps should be taken to avoid overlapping or competition in regard to Church Extension in new districts.

(ii) 'That the policy of the Federal Council is not the setting up of inter-denominational or undenominational churches in new districts, but rather of churches connected with a particular denomination.

(iii) 'That it be remitted to the Continuation Committee to take, with as little delay as possible, such steps as it seems desirable to secure co-operation between the Denominations with regard to Church planting in new and growing districts, including perhaps consultation with the Church Extension authorities of the federating Denominations.

(iv) 'That the Continuation Committee be asked to submit this policy to the Denominations with a view to adoption by them, and also to invite the Denominations to commit to the Federal Council the carrying out of the policy.'

Document VIII.3

Opposition to Methodist Union in Wesleyanism

J. E. Rattenbury, *Methodist Recorder*, 8 June 1922, reprinted in R. E. Davies, A. R. George and E. G. Rupp (eds), *A History of the Methodist Church in Great Britain*, vol. iv (London: Epworth Press, 1988), pp. 634–41.

Negotiations for Methodist union began soon after the end of the war. Dr J. E. Rattenbury was, for a time, one of the leading opponents of the union scheme in Wesleyanism, and here states the case for the 'other side' against Dr A. S. Peake's criticisms.

... Dr Peake takes objection to one sentence of the Manifesto because he says it doesn't state facts. I do not think Dr Peake has read this sentence fairly. But I have to admit that some of our own ministers have refused to sign the Manifesto because they hold Dr Peake's views as to its meaning. This apparently ambiguous sentence has lost us many signatures, so Dr Peake should be pleased! ...

Here are the words he criticises so severely:– 'We hold that the view-point of Wesleyan Methodism is essentially different from that of the other Methodist Churches in regard to doctrinal standards, the Sacraments, forms of worship, the ministry, party politics, and other matters of the first importance.'

The vital word in this sentence is the word 'view-point'. Our statement is not that there is an essential difference in doctrine, but in view-point. 'View-point' obviously means the point from which things are viewed. This view-point is different by reason of our history, and separate corporate experience, and, we think, so distinctive that Union will be impossible until there is a much better understanding. Therefore we think the time is not ripe for union, and that attempts to press it now are unduly precipitant...

Take Politics. Each Church contains people of different political parties, although the variations have been more marked in the Wesleyan than the other Churches. But can there be any question that Wesleyans and Primitives have regarded, and do regard, politics from a different corporate point-of-view? The Wesleyan Conference has always been reluctant to speak as a Conference on political questions, because it corporately supported no party. It has indicated strongly that its Chapels should not be used for political meetings, and has even disapproved the use of Public Halls like the Central and Kingsway Halls for such purposes. Nothing has characterized Wesleyan Methodism more than its determination not to support, as a Church, a particular party, or commit itself to a political policy, even where the majority of Wesleyans have approved of it, if such a committal lays it open to a charge of supporting a party. Can this really be claimed of Primitive Methodism? I hardly think Dr Peake would make the claim. I am arguing neither for the Wesleyan nor against the Primitive position in respect to the duty of the Church in the political sphere. But I shall need very forceful evidence to convince me that there is no difference in point-of-view.

Take Forms of Worship. Of course, it is true that the normal Nonconformist type of worship is commonest in Wesleyan Chapels, and it is practically universal in Primitive Methodist Chapels. But we have used the Anglican Liturgy in many of our Chapels from the beginning on Sunday mornings. And we use Liturgical forms in the Sacraments. Our only authorized form of service for Holy Communion in England is a very slightly altered version of the Anglican rite. In these matters thousands of Wesleyans would greatly resent any change – particularly in Holy Communion. How can a Church like Primitive Methodism view these things from our standpoint? Of course, there are Wesleyans who would prefer the Primitive Methodist methods, and what we fear is, not that Liturgies would be immediately abolished, but that the left-wing Methodists would be so enormously re-inforced, that the old-fashioned Wesleyan would lose the distinctive Wesleyan history he prizes...

Take Doctrine. This, I am informed, is the point on which Dr Peake is most chagrined by the Manifesto. To my mind it is the point in which our attitude is most defensible. When I saw the first draft of the Manifesto, I admit I questioned the meaning of the phrase. The reply which convinced me of its fairness, and still convinces me, was, 'The United Methodist Church has taken power to change its doctrine once every ten years.' This, to my mind, expresses a view-point which is not ours.

A study of the amendments in the 1921 Synods of the United Methodist Church particularly, but also of some Primitive Methodist Synods, will illustrate a point-of-view on this matter very different from that of the Wesleyan Synods.

I venture to assert that the view-point of Dr Peake himself is not that of Wesleyan Methodists on this subject. He has always insisted in Committee on the Representative Session of the Conference – and so far he has got his way – being the final authority in doctrine, because doctrine is a matter for the whole Church. I say emphatically that, right or wrong, this has never been the view-point of Wesleyan Methodism! Wesleyan Methodism has never considered the people as judges on doctrine, not because it despised the people, but because it never has imposed doctrinal tests upon them, always safeguarding religion from intellectual assents, and insisting that constitutional Christianity only implied doing all the good you can, abstaining from all harm, and attending the means of grace.

Document VIII.4

Federal Council Response to Lambeth, 1925

Resolutions adopted by the Annual Assembly of the Federal Council of the Evangelical Free Churches of England, 21–23 September 1925, in G. K. A. Bell, *Documents on Christian Unity, Second Series*, Oxford, 1930, pp. 98–102.

The conversations between representatives of the Federal Council of Free Churches and the Church of England followed the Lambeth Conference's 'Appeal to all Christian People' in 1920. They came to grief over the Church of England's insistence that Free Church ministers should be reordained by bishops as a condition of recognition. This reply in 1925 marked the end of the conversations.

I   The Council receives the Report, without thereby being committed, any more than in previous years, to all the statements and opinions contained therein. In so doing, it thanks the Anglican representatives on the Joint Committee for the care, conciliation, and candour with which they have considered and replied to the questions submitted on behalf of the Free Churches.

II   The Council concurs in the opinion given in the Report, and approved by the Anglican representatives and its own, that it is desirable to bring to a pause the conferences which have been taking place, in order that the various documents issued by the Joint Committee and the positions agreed on or proposed may be more deliberately considered by the Churches concerned and by the Christian mind of the country. In concurring in this, the Council expresses its deep thankfulness for the spirit of unbroken friendliness which has prevailed thoughout the whole proceedings of the Joint Comnmittee for four years; and it desires to make clear that such suspension of formal meetings at Lambeth is not to be taken to mean any rupture in this friendly relationship, or any closing of the door against the resumption of conference when God's Spirit may seem to invite to this step.

III   In view of the termination of the present series of conferences the Council discharges the Committee. It resolves to appoint a Committee of Reference on the Lambeth Appeal (to be nominated by the Standing Committee) to elucidate any points of inquiry which may arise, and generally to watch over the situation, but without power to resume formal conference till so authorized by the Council.

IV   In view, further, of the termination of these conferences, the Council, for the information of the Churches which it represents, may fitly at this stage recall and briefly comment on the main positions regarding faith and order which have been explored by the Joint Committee. It will suffice to mention, at present, four topics:

(i) The large measure of agreement between the Churches concerned on vital and fundamental matters of *faith* is to be recognized, valued, and emphasized. On the strength of this alone, the Free Churches declare their readiness to join with their Anglican brethren not only in moral and social, but also in religious and evangelical work wherever possible.

(ii) On the issue of *polity*, the Joint Committee was agreed that an episcopacy, not of its present character, but of a 'constitutional' character, should be an essential element in the order of the United Church, place being 'similarly' given to elements of presbyteral and congregational order as equally essential elements; and this proposal is to be taken not in one part of it only, but in its entirety. Suggestions as to how a 'constitutional episcopate' can be reconciled with the presbyteral and congregational elements are made in memoranda accompanying this

Report, but it is important to notice that neither the Joint Committee nor the Council is committed to these details.

(iii) On the matter of *recognition*, regarding which the Free Church representatives have from the first meeting at Lambeth desired some declaration of the Anglican view, special note should be taken of the following statement made by the Anglican representatives in their first memorandum on the 'Status of the Free Church Ministry':

'It seems to us to be in accord with the Lambeth Appeal to say, as we are prepared to say, that the ministries which we have in view in this memorandum, ministries which imply a sincere intention to preach Christ's Word and administer the Sacraments as Christ has ordained, and to which authority so to do has been solemnly given by the Churches concerned, are real ministries of Christ's Word and Sacraments in the Universal Church.'

This explicit and considered recognition of these non-episcopally ordained ministries as *(a)* evangelical, *(b)* sacramental, and *(c)* not schismatic but within the Church – whatever further questions as to the extent of their 'authorization' may be subsequently raised – is to be welcomed; and, if its significance is fully recognized, and if practical effect is given to its terms, it should mark a stage in the whole discussion between the Anglican and the Free Churches, and will prove a valuable basis for further progress if and when conferences are resumed.

(iv) It must, however, be observed that, on this subsequent question of *authorization* the Anglican representatives seem still inclined, despite the declaration above quoted, to insist that Free Church ministers accept ordination – at least in the form known as *sub conditione* – at episcopal hands. The Free Church representatives on the Joint Committee intimated that there is, in their view, little or no prospect of this being accepted by any non-episcopal Church. With this view the Council agrees; and it takes leave to say that it would deeply regret if the fortunes of the Lambeth Appeal, so far as non-episcopal Christendom is concerned, were finally bound up with a proposal so unconvincing and so unpromising as that of requiring the ordination to the ministry of Christ's Word and Sacraments in the Church of men explicitly acknowledged to be in that very ministry. The question of authorization must be answered by some other means than ordination. It is, therefore, to be noted with satisfaction that the Anglican memorandum does not exclude the alternative method of a 'commission' which shall be *(a)* mutual and *(b)* unambiguously not an ordination. This is the line which is being followed wherever today union between Churches is being achieved. It should, however, be recognized that on this question the Anglican Church has peculiar difficulties to consider; and the issue is one which, therefore, is not to be pressed to an immediate decision. (There are other matters of high importance in the report and its accompanying memoranda, but these, having been less fully dealt with, need not be referred to here.)

V   In conclusion, the Council, reviewing the whole of the conversations which have taken place – which have been carried on for a much longer period and in a far more conciliatory spirit than in any previous meetings between Conformity and Nonconformity in England – records its assurance that these conferences have done much to bring representative members of the Churches concerned into closer fellowship and to a better understanding of each other's position; and, further, that they have prepared the way to further progress towards unity in the future, To avoid misunderstanding, it may be well to state that the discussions have been in no sense negotiations for reunion, but have been intended simply to elucidate the meaning of the Lambeth Appeal and to indicate on what lines reunion, if desired, might possibly be effected. Believing that the Spirit of God is, in these days, manifestly drawing more closely together all who name the Name of Christ as Lord and Saviour, and impressed with the urgent call to unity in face of the moral and religious problems of the world, the Council anew commends the whole matter to the mind and heart and conscience of Christian people, particularly the people of the Churches which it represents. And it prays that grace and mercy and peace from our Lord Jesus Christ may be with the brethren with whom it has been in conference, with the great Church which they represent, and with the whole Church of God.

Document VIII.5

Peake on Methodist Union

Leslie S. Peake, *Arthur Samuel Peake* (London: Hodder & Stoughton, 1930), pp. 162–6.

The Primitive Methodist layman, A. S. Peake, was one of the keenest advocates of Methodist union and played a decisive role in the formation of the various plans, though his death in 1929 meant that he did not live to see his dream accomplished.

During the early part of the campaign Peake's chief task consisted in expounding his six reasons why Methodist Union should become part of the recognised policy of the Methodist Churches.

1   He was convinced from his study of the New Testament that Union was the will of Christ. Separation might sometimes be a positive duty, as in the case of the Reformation, but grave was the responsibility and heavy the guilt of those who made it inevitable. It was Christ's ideal for His Church that it should be one both in spirit and in organisation...
2   Peake could see no legitimate reason why Churches that were so similar in doctrine and in organisation should remain apart at a time when every effort

was needed to stem the tide created by the triple alliance of materialism, indifference, and positive evil ... It was always fatal for a Church to coddle its denominationalisms.

3 Peake felt very keenly the taunts made by the outsider that the Church had lost its power for good because it was an organisation divided against itself. His seat on the Commission conducted by the Army and Religion Enquiry had been an eye-opener in this respect ... 'The men who faced the grim realities of life and death on the battlefield are in no mood to be patient with our sectarian spirit and they bid us set our own house in order before we preach a League of Nations'...

4 Peake was certain that the evangelisation of England would receive a new impetus if the Methodist Churches could lead a united attack against the forces of evil. He believed that the ignorance in which the masses dwelt was in no small degree due to the fact that the Christian religion had so many sects to expound it. He believed, too, that the real weakness of the Church, especially as it affected its young people, was being masked by the policy of division. Each Church had its own constituency; it took it for granted that other Churches had theirs; it had no means accordingly of knowing how vast was the number of those who were outside the Churches altogether...

5 Peake realised that there was a big movement in the direction of Union in many departments of life. In view of this centripetal tendency, it was necessary that the three Methodist Churches should, if possible, combine their forces. The striking success of Methodist Union in the Colonies had won the applause of its stoutest opponents ...

6 He was confident that Methodist union was the first move towards the Reunion of Christendom.

Document VIII.6

The Methodist Deed of Union, 1932

The Minutes of the Uniting Conference, 1932, pp. 286–306.

The Deed of Union as adopted by the Uniting Conference has been amended on several occasions by Conference, apart from clause 30 about Doctrine and clause 36 about Membership.

30. Doctrine – The doctrinal standards of The Methodist Church are as follows:

The Methodist Church claims and cherishes its place in the Holy Catholic Church, which is the Body of Christ. It rejoices in the inheritance of the Apostolic Faith and loyally accepts the fundamental principles of the historic creeds and of the Protestant Reformation. It ever remembers that in the Providence of God Methodism was raised up to spread Scriptural Holiness through the land by the proclamation of the Evangelical Faith and declares its unfaltering resolve to be true to its Divinely appointed mission.

The Doctrines of the Evangelical Faith, which Methodism has held from the beginning and still holds are based upon the Divine revelation recorded in the Holy Scriptures. The Methodist Church acknowledges this revelation as the supreme rule of faith and practice. These Evangelical Doctrines to which the Preachers of The Methodist Church both Ministers and Laymen are pledged are contained in Wesley's Notes on the New Testament and the first four volumes of his sermons.

The Notes on the New Testament and the 44 Sermons are not intended to impose a system of formal or speculative theology on Methodist Preachers, but to set up standards of preaching and belief which should secure loyalty to the fundamental truths of the Gospel of Redemption and ensure the continued witness of the Church to the realities of the Christian experience of salvation.

Christ's Ministers in the Church are Stewards in the household of God and Shepherds of His flock. Some are called and ordained to this sole occupation and have a principal and directing part in these great duties but they hold no priesthood differing in kind from that which is common to all the Lord's people and they have no exclusive title to the preaching of the gospel or the care of souls. These ministries are shared with them by others to whom also the Spirit divides His gifts severally as He wills.

It is the universal conviction of the Methodist people that the office of the Christian Ministry depends upon the call of God who bestows the gifts of the Spirit the grace and the fruit which indicate those whom He has chosen.

Those whom The Methodist Church recognizes, as called of God and therefore receives into its Ministry shall be ordained by the imposition of hands as expressive of the Church's recognition of the Minister's personal call.

The Methodist Church holds the doctrine of the priesthood of all believers and consequently believes that no priesthood exists which belongs exclusively to a particular order or class of men but in the exercise of its corporate life and worship special qualifications for the discharge of special duties are required and thus the principle of representative selection is recognized.

The Preachers itinerant and lay are examined tested and approved before they are authorized to minister in holy things. For the sake of Church order and not because of any priestly virtue inherent in the office the Ministers of The Methodist Church are set apart by ordination to the Ministry of the Word and Sacraments.

The Methodist Church recognizes two sacraments namely Baptism and the Lord's Supper as of Divine Appointment and of perpetual obligation of which it is the privilege and duty of Members of The Methodist Church to avail themselves.

31. Doctrinal Standards Unalterable – (a) The Conference shall not have any power to alter or vary in any manner whatsoever the clauses contained in this Deed which define the doctrinal standards of The Methodist Church.
(b) The Conference shall be the final authority within The Methodist Church with regard to all questions concerning the interpretation of its doctrines ...

33. Basis of Membership (Formerly Clause 36) – (a) All persons are welcomed into membership of The Methodist Church who sincerely desire to be saved from their

sins through faith in the Lord Jesus Christ and evidence the same in life and conduct and who seek to have fellowship with Christ Himself and His people by taking up the duties and privileges of The Methodist Church.

(b) It is the privilege and duty of Members of The Methodist Church to avail themselves of the two sacraments namely Baptism and the Lord's Supper. As membership of The Methodist Church also involves fellowship it is the duty of all Members of The Methodist Church to seek to cultivate this in every possible way. The Weekly Class Meeting has from the beginning proved to be the most effective means of maintaining among Methodists true fellowship in Christian experience. All Members of The Methodist Church shall have their names entered on a Class Book shall be placed under the pastoral care of a Class Leader and shall receive a quarterly ticket of membership.

(c) According to Methodist usage the Sacrament of Baptism is administered to infants and regular oversight should be given by the local Church and its Minister to all who have been dedicated to God by this sign. If any have not received Christian Baptism that Sacrament should be administered either before or in connection with the Recognition Service.

(d) After a probation of not less than three months those approved shall be admitted to full membership by the Leaders' Meeting and be publicly recognized at a service conducted by the Minister in the presence of the Church at the earliest opportunity which shall be followed by the administration of the Lord's Supper.

(e) Any Member of The Methodist Church, who without sufficient reason persistently absents himself from the Lord's Supper and from the meetings for Christian Fellowship shall be visited by both his Leader and his Minister. The name of any such person who by such prolonged absence severs himself from Christian Fellowship shall be removed by the Leaders' Meeting from the Class Book and he shall thereupon cease to be a Member of The Methodist Church.

(f) In connection with the Societies of The Methodist Church classes shall be generally established which shall directly provide for the religious instruction of young people. The object of these classes shall be to secure the decision of children for Christ their instruction and training in Christian Doctrine and ethics and the development in Christian experience and character. The Holy Scripture shall be the basis of instruction and these classes shall be met wherever possible weekly.

Document VIII.7

A Primitive Methodist in the Methodist Church, 1997

Edward Rogers, 'Memoirs of Primitive Methodism', *The Methodist Recorder*, 18 September 1997.

The Revd Edward Rogers (1909–97) was General Secretary of the Christian Citizenship Department, later Division of Social Responsibility, and President of the Conference in 1960. This describes the movement from one world into another.

Church Unity

At the age of five or thereabouts I joined the primary department of the Fleetwood Mount Road Primitive Methodist (PM) Church's Sunday School. In my early teens I joined the weekly meeting of the Christian Endeavour (CE) Society.

CE headquarter prepared a list of topics to be discussed during the year. We had to be active participants. According to rota, one would lead the worship. Similarly, each would speak about the topic set for his or her week, there was no choice. You might strike lucky with an easy theme – or you might not. Easy or tough, you had to have a go at it. CE was an excellent preparatory school for local preachers.

Accepted as a candidate for the Primitive Methodist ministry, I went to Hartley College for training. I left college, a year after Methodist Union, as a Methodist without prefix. It did not make much immediate difference. I spent the whole of my probation in charge of churches in Poplar and the Isle of Dogs, in the East London Mission circuit, composed exclusively of ex-PM mission churches.

I went on to a rather curious appointment as superintendent of the Bakewell circuit, under the benevolent and unobtrusive oversight of Benson Perkins, then Chairman of the Sheffield District. I had the pastoral care of nine small churches. They were all ex-PM. I had been in the Methodist ministry for seven years until, stationed in the Sutton Park circuit, I served in a predominantly ex-Wesleyan circuit – and even then my main church, Erdington High Street, was ex-PM.

But I had also two smaller ex-Wesleyan churches under my care; in Kingsbury and Bodymoor Heath for the first time I presided at the Lord's Supper following a set, printed order of service.

In my home church in the days of my youth the supper was a sort of appendix, tacked on infrequently after a Sunday morning service had concluded. The presiding minister, though always quoting the Gospel record of the Passover meal of Jesus and the disciples, devised his own order of service. Seventy years ago, as older readers will recall, the Sunday evening service was by far the better attended. Morning congregations were usually thin, but even so most of those present departed without participating in the supper. It was tacitly assumed that it was an observance for the particularly devout only.

The Christian festivals were observed, but without special emphasis. More was made of Christmas as the years passed. Churches in the Manchester area arranged Whitsun walks on the Monday – Sunday School children in procession through town or city centres – but, generally speaking, the festivals were not the high points of the year. The great days were the Sunday School anniversary and the harvest thanksgiving. A door would be opened at the rear of the already commodious gallery to reveal a large room into which the overflow of the congregation would be crammed.

For the anniversary the children were seated in benches in tiers at the front of the church. Braver souls sang solos or delivered edifying poems. Many of the children took up the offertory each first putting a shilling into his or her collection bag. It was, at that time, no small sum. Nobody mentioned it, but everybody knew the score: 'No shilling, no collection bag.'

For harvest there was the usual vast array of fruit and vegetables; but it was the result of Monday's sale of the produce for church funds that really mattered. We knew that we could pull in more than the Wesleyans or the Congregationalists. We always did. But would we be up or down on our result of the previous year? I still remember the occasion when a determined steward paid £5 for one apple just to make sure we were up.

For those of us in the pews the main impact of the wider Church came from the District Synod. Somewhere in the distance there was a Conference. The President toured the Connexion, leading rallies and preaching sermons. Conference issued statements on social and ecclesiastical issues; most of them, as we would expect from PM sources such as on stationing and discipline, that the synods had not resolved.

Stationing? Yes. When a minister was appointed to his first circuit he almost invariably continued his ministry in the District of that circuit. So stationing was very largely and fairly easily arranged within and by the synod.

Synod then was not the present one-day mainly business meeting. It lasted over a weekend. It did essential business, though one hardly noticed it, for it was primarily a vehicle for evangelism. Two or three star speakers inspired an evening rally. Guest preachers took the Sunday services. Usually there was also some special extra. When synod came to Fleetwood we always invited Madame Katie Peters to sing to us. On the whole this sort of synod, not confined to delegates, was a pleasure.

Primitive Methodism was practising subsidiarity long before we heard the word. Each level – local church, circuit, synod, conference – made its contribution to the work and witness of the church. Doing our own thing in our own way, not overawed by rule and regulation, we prided ourselves at union that we would be offering freedom and flexibility to Methodism.

For example many Wesleyan circuits adhered to the tradition of a fixed three year period for ministerial appointments. The Prims did not. If circuit and minister were content, a minister could serve a circuit for as long as both desired. From the time I began to notice such things until and during my term in Hartley College, Mount Road had two ministers only; James Burton and James E. Philippson – a span of 20 years.

I have not delved into the details of pre-union negotiations. What emerged has all the marks of compromise: a slightly longer set period with allowance, very strictly controlled, for an also slightly longer extension.

Since then, step by step, and very short steps, there has been continuous relaxation. It is no longer exceptional for a minister to serve a circuit for seven years; but there is still no general satisfaction with the system. Noting the trend I begin to wonder if we shall eventually adopt the old PM practice.

In this admittedly personal survey I have written of the contribution made by Primitive Methodism to the United Church. It would be ungracious not to acknowledge that we have also received; notably in setting more frequently a well-ordered celebration of the Lord's Supper in the heart of our worship.

Document VIII.8

Congregational-Baptist Union Churches, 1933

Congregational Year Book, 1934, pp. 81–2.

Joint Congregational-Baptist churches had existed since the late nineteenth century. This report to the Congregational Union in 1933 suggested that there needed to be more active supervision if their genuinely united nature was to be preserved.

... *'Union' Churches*.
The Committee has also made inquiries of the County Secretaries of both denominations, and other persons, as to the spiritual effectiveness of Union Churches, and the nature and extent of their support of outside work, and especially of the work of the Baptist Missionary Society and the London Missionary Society.

We summarise a mass of correspondence in the following terms:–

We have received reports from more than twenty counties with reference to the experiences of Union Churches numbering about fifty.

To the question whether such Churches remain real Union Churches the majority answer 'No.' With the passing of time Churches tend to become definitely associated with one denomination only.

In about half of the so-called Union Churches provision is made for the rite of baptism as administered by both Churches, but one or other form of the rite tends to fall into desuetude. About one-quarter of these Churches, and these are the stronger numerically and financially, subscribe to the missionary and denominational funds of both Unions.

Unless there is some provision in the Trust Deed for the alternation of ministers of the two denominations, as Churches move into alignment with one or other denomination they tend to seek ministers from its accredited list only.

The bulk of the testimony received is against the advisability of the formation of Union Churches under existing conditions.

Bearing this testimony in mind, the Committee cannot take the responsibility of recommending the formation of Union Chuches, but it does believe that they are an important experiment which may under favourable conditions have even more important developments. Their position is at present rather uncertain. When such churches are formed the tendency is for them to be regarded as 'attached' rather loosely to both denominations without either denomination assuming any real responsibility for them.

The Committee therefore recommends that the two Unions should take a more active interest in them by appointing a Joint Committee which should consider their difficultes and seek to elucidate the lessons learned in their experience with a view to future policy.

The present cost of building new Churches and the undesirability of seeming rivalry in new districts appear to indicate a field for common action, with the full support of both denominations for local effort where Union Churches are already desired, and, it may be, for fostering such local effort and feeling.

Neither Union seems definitely to have made up its mind as to whether and under what conditions, Union Churches are desirable and should be encouraged. The demand in many quarters for a fuller realisation of our unity in Christ suggests that this problem should be squarely faced.

The Committee has considered what in its judgment would be the most helpful form of constitution for a Union Church under present conditions and recommends as follows:–

Where there is a local desire for a 'Union' Church of Baptists and Congregationalists, the Church should be based on the following or similar principles, and should then in case of need be eligible to receive financial aid from appropriate funds, both Baptist and Congregational.

Suggested Constitution of 'Union' Church.
1. The property to be held in trust by the Baptist and Congregational Unions jointly.
2. The minister to be chosen alternately from the accredited lists of the two Unions.
3. The rite of baptism should be administered in both modes recognised by the two denominations, the choice of the mode being left to the personal conviction of those desiring its administration for themselves or their children, and no distinction should obtain among Church members on the ground of a preference for either mode. There should be on occasion specific teaching on the importance of baptism and on the views of both denominations with regard to the rite.
4. Membership of the Church and admission to the Lord's Table should be open to all Christians.
5. The collections and contributions of the Church for missionary and denominational funds should be equally divided between the agencies of the two denominations, but any member of the Church should be able to 'earmark' his personal contribution to any particular agency.

    The Church should pay 50 per cent of the Union fees ordinarily payable to each denomination.
6. If an officially recognised Church of either denomination should come into existence within one mile of the existing Union Church, then the latter should be free, provided that three-fourths of its members so agree, to declare that henceforth it shall cease to be a Union Church and be affiliated to the other denomination only.

Document VIII.9

The Free Church Federal Council, 1940

Free Church Federal Council Constitution (London, 1940), pp. 1–4.

In 1940 the National and Federal Councils of Free Churches combined to form the Free Church Federal Council. The doctrinal statement of the Federal Council was preserved for the new body.

2 OBJECTS

(1) To express the essential unity in Christ of the Evangelical Free Churches of England and Wales.
(2) To secure their federation on the basis of their common Evangelical faith, each denomination retaining liberty to fulfil its own distinctive witness and mission.
(3) To foster their fellowship in worship and work, to co-ordinate their counsels, activities and resources for the evangelisation of the people and the extension of Christ's Kingdom in every sphere of life.
(4) To maintain the spiritual testimony of the Free Churches, to uphold full religious liberty and to take action when authorised to do so in matters affecting the responsibilities and rights of the federated Churches.
(5) To promote fellowship and united action where possible with other branches of the Church throughout the world.

3 DOCTRINAL STATEMENT

The Declaratory Statement of Common Faith and Practice adopted on March 26th, 1917, as a doctrinal basis of the former Federal Council of Evangelical Free Churches of England shall be the doctrinal basis of the Free Church Federal Council. The full statement is as follows:–

(1) The Evangelical Free Churches of England claim and cherish their place as inheritors, along with others, of the historic faith of Christendom, which found expression in the ecumenical creeds of the early and undivided Church; and this Declaratory Statement does not profess to be a comprehensive creed, but is a declaration of such truths as in the circumstances, it seems proper to rehearse and emphasise.
(2) It is an essential element in the proposals for federation that each of the federated Churches should preserve its own autonomy as regards faith and practice; this Statement, therefore, is not to be imposed as a disciplinary standard on any of these Churches, nor, on the other hand, does it supersede or in any way alter the place of whatever doctrinal standards any of these Churches may maintain in their constitution.

I

There is One Living and True God, Who is revealed to us as Father, Son and Holy Spirit; Him alone we worship and adore.

II

We believe that God so loved the world as to give His Son to be the Revealer of the Father and the Redeemer of mankind; that the Son of God, for us men and for our salvation, became man in Jesus Christ, Who, having lived on earth the perfect human life, died for our sins, rose again from the dead, and now is exalted Lord over all; and that the Holy Spirit, Who witnesses to us of Christ, makes the salvation which is in Him to be effective in our hearts and lives.

III

We acknowledge that all men are sinful and unable to deliver themselves from either the guilt or power of their sin; but we have received and rejoice in the Gospel of the grace of the Holy God, wherein all who truly turn from sin are freely forgiven through faith in our Lord Jesus Christ, and are called and enabled, through the Spirit dwelling and working within them to live in fellowship with God and for His service; and in this new life, which is to be nurtured by the right use of the means of grace, we are to grow, daily dying unto sin and living unto Him Who in His mercy has redeemed us.

IV

We believe that the Catholic or Universal Church is the whole company of the redeemed in heaven and on earth, and we recognise as belonging to this holy fellowship all who are united to God through faith in Christ.

The Church on earth – which is One through the Apostolic Gospel and through the living union of all its true members with its one Head, even Christ, and which is Holy through the indwelling Holy Spirit Who sanctifies the Body and its members – is ordained to be the visible Body of Christ, to worship God through Him, to promote the fellowship of His people, and the ends of His Kingdom, and to go into all the world and proclaim His Gospel for the salvation of men and the brotherhood of all mankind. Of this visible Church, and every branch thereof, the only Head is the Lord Jesus Christ; and in its faith, order, discipline and duty it must be free to obey Him alone as it interprets His holy will.

V

We receive, as given by the Lord to His Church on earth, the Holy Scriptures, the Sacraments of the Gospel, and the Christian Ministry.

The scriptures, delivered through men moved by the Holy Ghost, record and interpret the revelation of redemption, and contain the sure Word of God concerning our salvation and all things necessary thereto. Of this we are convinced by the witness of the Holy Spirit in the hearts of men to and with the Word; and this Spirit, thus speaking from the Scriptures to believers and to the Church, is the supreme Authority by which all opinions in religion are finally to be judged.

The Sacraments – Baptism and the Lord's Supper – are instituted by Christ, Who is Himself certainly and really present in His own ordinances (though not bodily in the elements thereof), and are signs and seals of His Gospel not to be separated therefrom. They confirm the promises and gifts of salvation and, when rightly used by believers with faith and prayer are, through the operation of the Holy Spirit, true means of grace.

The Ministry is an office within the Church – not a sacerdotal order – instituted for the preaching of the Word, the ministration of the Sacraments and the care of souls. It is a vocation from God, upon which therefore no one is qualified to enter save through the call of the Holy Spirit in the heart; and this inward call is to be authenticated by the call of the Church, which is followed by ordination to the work of the Ministry in the Church. While thus maintaining the Ministry as an office, we do not limit the ministers of the New Testament to those who are ordained, but affirm the priesthood of all believers and the obligation resting upon them to fulfil their vocation according to the gift bestowed upon them by the Holy Spirit.

VI

We affirm the sovereign authority of our Lord Jesus Christ over every department of human life, and we hold that individuals and peoples are responsible to Him in their several spheres and are bound to render Him obedience and seek always the furtherance of His Kingdom upon earth, not however, in any way constraining belief, imposing religious disabilities, or denying the rights of conscience.

VII

In the assurance given us in the Gospel, of the love of God our Father to each of us and to all men, and in the faith that Jesus Christ, Who died, overcame death and passed into the heavens, the first-fruits of them that slept, we are made confident of the hope of Immortality, and trust to God our souls and the souls of the departed. We believe that the whole world must stand before the final Judgment of the Lord Jesus Christ. And, with glad and solemn hearts, we look for the consummation and bliss of the life everlasting, wherein the people of God, freed for ever from sorrow and sin, shall serve Him and see His face in the perfected communion of all saints in the Church triumphant.

These things, as all else in our Christian faith, we hold in reverent submission to the guidance and teaching of the Holy Spirit Who is Truth, and we shall ever seek of Him enlightenment and grace both to unlearn our errors and also more fully to learn the mind and will of God, Whom to know is life eternal and to serve is perfect freedom.

And being thus called of God unto the presence of His redeeming love wherein He is delivering the world from sin and misery and is reconciling all things to Himself in Jesus Christ, and being animated with faith in the final triumph of our Lord, we set before us as our end and aim to carry the Gospel to every creature and to serve and stablish, in our land and throughout the earth, His reign of righteousness, joy and peace.

Grace be with all those who love our Lord Jesus Christ in sincerity. And to God be glory in the Church by Christ Jesus, throughout all ages, world without end. Amen.

Document VIII.10

The Congregational–Presbyterian Covenant, 1951

Congregational Year Book, 1952, pp. 98–9.

Following the failure of the second round of Congregational–Presbyterian talks after the war, the two churches decided to make a Covenant, which was accepted on 9 May 1951.

A joint session of the Assemblies of the Presbyterian Church of England and the Congregational Union of England and Wales was held at 10 a.m.

The following Declaration, which had been accepted by both Assemblies a year ago, was read by Dr. Whitehorn, M.B.E., and members of both Assemblies stood in sign of their acceptance of it:

WHEREAS

The Congregational Union of England and Wales and the Presbyterian Church of England in the year of our Lord 1945 did appoint representatives jointly to consider the possibility of a union of the two and, if possible to prepare a Scheme of Union, and these representatives have produced a report and prepared a scheme which have been considered by the two appointing bodies, and there is at this time no sufficient agreement to warrant the consummation of union upon the basis of the proposed scheme;

NEVERTHELESS

The two denominations are of one mind that they should enter into a closer relationship with one another and more effectively co-operate together;

NOW THEREFORE

The Congregational Union of England and Wales and the Presbyterian Church of England, acting as they believe under the guidance of the Holy Spirit, declare before God and the world that, sharing the Christian faith and inheriting the Reformed tradition, they do enter into a new and solemn relationship, covenanting with God and each other to take counsel with one another as the Spirit may direct, and to seek all opportunities from their mutual co-operation in the service of the Lord Jesus Christ Whom they acknowledge to be sole Head of the Church.

A sermon was preached by Dr Douglas Horton, M.A., Minister and Secretary of the Congregational Christian Churches of the United States of America. Prayer was offered by the Rev. S. Maurice Watts, B.D. Dr Bacon presided over a Communion Service, with which the session culminated, and at this service the Prayer of Thanksgiving was led by Dr Nathaniel Micklem, M.A. Dr John Short, M.A., Ph.D., and the Rev. Herbert Stephenson, M.A., presided over tables in the gallery.

Document VIII.11

Churches of Christ and Unity, 1962

J. Gray, *Implications of New Delhi for Churches of Christ* (Birmingham: Berean Press, 1962), pp. 17–26.

This address, given at the Annual Conference of Churches of Christ in 1962 by their representative at the New Delhi Assembly of the WCC in 1961, marked a turning point in their involvement in the ecumenical movement.

The most difficult and the most challenging consequences of our involvement in the Ecumenical Movement are in the field of relations between our Churches as an organized body and other denominations...

The Ecumenical Movement is only possible because there is underlying agreement on three principles:

(i) The true nature of the Church can be manifested only in unity. On this principle all thinking Churches of Christ members in every generation of our history would be at one. To have it so widely and openly recognized is a major advance in the cause of reunion.

(ii) Because there is division within the Body of Christ on earth it is impossible for separated communions or for any one of them to manifest the fulness of the life of the Body. This truth we have not always recognized: we have tended to think that *we* as a body of Churches could restore Apostolic Christianity within our own Churches whatever was happening to other Christian bodies; and this has often led to a sense of self-righteous superiority and to spiritual blindness – blindness to our own defects and to the supremely important fact that in the New Testament period, which we have taken as normative, all Christians and all Churches were manifestly one, all in communion with one another (in spite of tensions), and all acknowledging loyalty to the One Lord and His Apostles (in spite of the painful controversies of a period of rapid growth and formative thought and activity)...

(iii) Each of the Communions represented in the Ecumenical Movement embodies and mediates a measure of the truth and life of the Catholic Church of Christ, though all in varying ways and degrees fail to embody elements which belong to that truth and life...

In the light of this the problem of achieving Christian union is that of each Church recognizing the limitations of its own apprehension and embodiment of the fulness of Christian truth, bringing its clear insights and evident treasures to the common wealth of the whole Great Church, and gradually learning to enter into the treasures of other Churches ...

The Ecumenical Movement ... places the responsibility squarely on the shoulders of the separate Churches; and we cannot be content, any of us, to continue indefinitely sharing the Ecumenical fellowship while guarding jealously our status as a separate body ...

We must therefore pledge ourselves to a constant re-examination of our 'position and plea,' and of our relations with other Churches, lest we be found, despite our high-sounding protestations, to be hindering and not furthering that unity for which we pray ... To advance this process I make the following suggestions for your serious consideration:

(i) The time has surely come for all our Churches to give a higher priority to local ecumenical activities ...

There is ample scope and a good deal of established experience: inter-church groups for prayer and study; services during Holy Week and the Week of Prayer for Christian Unity, at Christmas and New Year; co-operation in Inter-Church Aid and Refugee work, in Evangelism and Visitation campaigns, Women's World Day of Prayer, the British and Foreign Bible Society, etc ...

(ii) The time has come when we need *to reconsider our ordering of worship in relation to the Ecumenical Movement.* We have in our traditional Communion Service a precious medium of worship. Derived as it is from the order preserved by Justin Martyr in the second century (for there is the most scanty material in the New Testament for anything like an order of service), and embodying all the elements of the truly catholic orders of the early centuries, it is capable of the most exalted use.

But in the ecumenical setting of today we should beware of limiting too rigidly the form of service and the kind of prayers we use, as if everything each local church does in its Communion Service were laid down by the Apostles and any divergence from it is apostasy. We are often in fact guilty of this: and it is the essence of a sectarianism from which we think ourselves emancipated. A generation ago few, if any, of our Churches used the Lord's Prayer corporately, and theological reasons were sometimes advanced to justify this neglect; but I suspect the operative reason was that other Churches used it and therefore we must not ...

(iii) A third implication is *in the delicate field of Intercommunion and the recognition of the Church-membership of other Christians.* The agonizing re-appraisal of our traditional Close Communion position which has gone on for a generation has resulted in the acceptance of the practice of Guest Communion ...

We are driven to consider also the further issue of the practical implications of our recognition of members of other Churches as Christians. So far as I know no Church of our Association has ever recognized anyone as a member who has not been baptized as a believer, openly confessing Christ as His Lord ... There is no possibility, as I see it, of our Churches moving from this position, for it is bound up with our most cherished convictions.

Nevertheless I suggest we are being driven to reconsider even this, so far as churches in new housing areas are concerned. Under present-day conditions of building in new towns or new estates, it is almost always necessary for sites for new churches to be allocated by a local authority; and the Roman Catholic Church, the Church of England, and the Free Churches are the three units usually considered for this purpose. This means that we face a new situation in relation to other Churches: if we are allocated a site it is very hard to contemplate planting on it a Church of Christ which will not admit to its membership other Free Church people who live in the area thus ignoring the new situation; and if this were the declared policy beforehand it is highly unlikely that a site would be offered to us.

... I believe that where an opportunity does arise for us to enter such an area we need to respond to the new ecumenical setting by a radically new attitude. A church in such an area exists to serve the community, and it is imperative to express there the felt unity of all Christian Churches by a welcoming attitude towards all Christian people ...

I suggest we should take a further step as an extension of the ecumenical attitude expressed in Guest Communion, namely that those baptized as infants and later confirmed or otherwise admitted into full membership of their own Church, should, if they desire to associate themselves with the new Church of Christ, be welcomed as *Guest Members*. The assumption might be that they are Methodists, Congregationalists, etc., in temporary fellowship with the Church of Christ, as they are living some distance away from a church of their own denomination. This concept of Guest Membership seems preferable to that of Associate Membership, which suggests paying a smaller subscription and not being quite a full member. Guest Members would have all the privileges of membership, except that all appointed as Deacons (men or women) or Elders should be baptized as believers.

It would be understood that the practice of Churches of Christ is Believers' Baptism, and that no other form of Baptism would be practised; and this would be witnessed to by the open baptistry in the church building.

It may be that such a policy would need periodic review, and the terminology is only tentatively suggested; it would certainly need careful and loving application, and wise leadership. But it would be a sincere attempt to maintain our traditional conviction and to respond to the Holy Spirit's leading in the growing together of all Christians in this generation. It would of course lead to a re-examination of our practice in long-established Churches; and this we must also face. But it seems to me there is a clear case in new areas for some such bold and Christian policy; and I make a plea that it should be prayerfully considered, and – I earnestly hope – without provoking charges of heresy.

Document VIII.12

Anglican–Methodist Proposals, 1963

Conversations between the Church of England and the Methodist Church: A Report (London: Church Information Office and Epworth Press, 1963), pp. 37, 38, 43, 47.

The Report of the Anglican–Methodist Conversations of 1963 elaborated the two-stage proposal first floated in 1958, whereby the ministries of the two churches would be reconciled first, and full corporate union would follow later. The proposed Service of Reconciliation therefore attracted most comment.

(i) The Service of Reconciliation.

(a) The service has been constructed on the principle that there should be a formal reception of the members and ministers of each Church by accredited representatives of the other, performed in such a way as will enable each member to communicate and each bishop, priest and minister to officiate in either church. No denial of any gift or grace already received is intended on either side, and for this reason an attempt has been made to avoid the use of any prayer or substantial part of a prayer which has already been said over those for whom it is now used.

(b) It is assumed that after this service has been held there will be full communion between the two Churches and as close an integration of their life and work as may be possible until the time when complete union can be brought about.

(c) The service will be followed as soon as possible by the consecration of certain Methodist ministers to the episcopate, and thereafter ordinations in the Methodist Church will be performed by bishops assisted by other ministers. It is desirable that before this happens the Church of England and the Methodist church should jointly revise their respective ordinals, so that by the use of a service of ordination which is common to both Churches unity may be furthered, and ground for suspicion and criticism removed. The Ordinal of the Church of South India offers an example of what might be done ...

Declaration of Intention

... In the union of ministries neither of us wishes to call in question the reality and spiritual effectiveness of the ministry of the other Church. We believe that both our ministries have, in response to prayer, been blessed and used by God. But we recognize that there has been disagreement between us over what has been God's will for his Church, we wish to share each in the spiritual heritage of the other, and we wish to assure to our united Churches a ministry fully accredited in the eyes of all their members and, so far as may be, of the Church throughout the world.

(ii) Rubrics and statement of reception of Methodist ministers by Anglicans and Anglican ministers by Methodists:

Then shall the Bishop lay his hands on the head of each of the Methodist ministers in silence. After he has laid hands upon all of them the Bishop shall say:

We receive you into the fellowship of the ministry in the Church of England. Take authority to exercise the office of priest, to preach the Word of God and to minister the holy Sacraments among us as need shall arise and you shall be licensed to do ...

... Then shall the Presiding Minister lay his hands upon the head of each bishop and priest in silence. After has laid hands upon all of them, the Presiding Minister shall say:

We receive you into the fellowship of the ministry in the Methodist Church. Take authority to exercise the office of a minister, to preach the Word of God and to minister the holy Sacraments among us as need shall arise and you shall be appointed to do.

Document VIII.13

Methodist Dissentients, 1963

Conversations between the Church of England and the Methodist Church: A Report (London: Church Information Office and Epworth Press, 1963), pp. 51ff.

Four of the Methodist members of the Anglican–Methodist conversations dissented from the Report: Professor Kingsley Barrett of Durham University; Dr Thomas E. Jessop, Emeritus Professor of Philosophy in the University of Hull (Vice President of Conference 1955); the Revd Dr Norman H. Snaith, formerly Principal of Wesley College Leeds, President of Conference 1958 and the Revd Thomas D. Meadley, Principal of Cliff College. This is the substance of their dissenting note.

The writing of this part of the report has not been undertaken lightly or captiously, but with a sense of deep regret and heavy responsibility. Those who are responsible for it desire to bear witness to the spirit of understanding and friendliness that has prevailed during the conversations; more, to a spirit of Christian fellowship which itself lends an air of unreality to the mechanical and legalistic devices proposed in order to obtain what already exists. They wish also to make clear beyond any possibility of misunderstanding or cavil their concern for the proper unity of the Church (which need mean neither uniformity nor unity of organisation). They seek such unity; only they do not believe that it is to be found in a scheme which, though well-intentioned, is in principle sectarian and exclusive, and would in practice lead to certain division in the Methodist Church, and could conceivably lead to division in the Church of England also ...

Scripture and Tradition

The discussion of this fundamentally important subject ... does not recognize adequately the pre-eminent and normative place of scripture, or set out satisfactorily its relation to tradition. All Churches have traditions, for no body of men can exist long without accumulating them, but they are of mixed value, containing both truth and falsehood, good and evil. They are thus not without use, but must continually be sifted and tested by scripture. It is true that scripture interprets (and not infrequently condemns) tradition rather than that tradition interprets scripture. In a word, tradition represents the worldliness of the Church, scripture points it to its supernatural origins and basis. All Christians have much to learn from the past, but it is their perpetual obligation to bring their inherited customs, institutions, and traditions to the bar of scripture, by which Christ rules in his Church ...

Episcopacy

... It is evident that the only kind of episcopacy that will qualify Methodism for communion with the Church of England is the so-called historic episcopacy. To discuss other kinds of episcopacy is therefore beside the point ...

Historic episcopacy is so essential to the proposals contained in this report that it is necessary, in all charity, to make a few comments on it:

(a) Historically it is incapable of proof – 'a fable which no man ever did or could prove' as John Wesley said of the apostolic succession.

(b) It has notoriously failed to act as the safeguard it is claimed to be. This is sufficiently illustrated by the history of the medieval and renaissance papacy.

(c) Methodists have consistently, and rightly, claimed that their Church is one with the Church of the apostles, saints, and martyrs, without the aid of any material succession. The Christian heritage is in faith and life, not in institutions.

(d) For what outward continuity may be worth, most Methodists would prefer to be visibly one with the Churches of the Reformation than with medieval and un-reformed Christendom.

(e) If the hope of further union, on the basis of the historic episcopate, is canvassed, it must be recalled that the largest Episcopal Church in the world believes that the Church of England does not have, and therefore cannot impart, the historic ministry.

(f) Far more important than any of these points is the fact that historic episcopacy is completely without support in the New Testament. This negative observation is itself sufficient to show that no ecclesiastical body has the right to demand participation in historic episcopacy, as a qualification for communion or union with itself. Further, we are bound to conclude that the belief that the full and true being of the Church is dependent upon its possession of historic episcopacy is inconsistent with the New Testament doctrine that the existence of the People of God depends wholly upon God's gracious election, grasped by faith only.

(g) There is little help in the (limited) 'liberty of interpretation' offered ... Actions speak louder than words, and an interpretation of episcopacy as (i) the historic episcopacy, and (ii) absolutely indispensable to the Church of the future, is presupposed by the proposals contained in the report.

Ordination
It is not the purpose of this paragraph to discuss the meaning of ordination, but to draw attention to the meaning, and crucial importance, of the Service of Reconciliation ... In its essential structure this Service consists of two reciprocal acts, by which Methodist ministers and people are received into the Church of England, and Anglican ministers and people are received into the Methodist Church.

In the former act prayer is offered that the ministers may be endued according to their need 'with grace for the office of priest in the Church of God'. Subsequently the bishop lays his hands on the head of each minister, and says, '... Take authority to exercise the office of priest ...'. There can be no doubt that this act is capable of being, and in some quarters certainly will be, interpreted as an act of ordination ...

... Methodists have no right to lay their hands on Anglicans, and most Methodists would not wish to do so; they can pray for them without the aid of this superfluous act. The only satisfactory solution would be for neither party to lay hands on the other; in this way it would become unambiguously clear that ordination was not in mind. This course has, however, been explicitly rejected. There must be episcopal laying on of hands. It is impossible to doubt that whatever else the rite implies it confers episcopal ordination; and this (a) means a mechanical and almost magical view of ordination, and (b) casts an intolerable (though certainly unintended) slur on Methodist ordinations and ministries in the past ...

Priesthood
... The word *priest* as a description of the minister is unfamiliar in Methodism. A mere difference in terminology would not necessarily be a stumbling-block; but in fact more is involved. Whatever the etymology of the English word *priest*, in this report it means more than *presbyter*. It is expressly connected with sacrificial views of the Eucharist, and with the power to pronounce absolution ... Priest must be understood as *hiereus*, a word the New Testament applied to Christ, but never to ministers ...

Sacraments
The normal officiant at the sacraments will be a minister, not because he is a special kind of priest but because the sacraments are bound up with preaching and pastoral work. It will, however, be clear that if the points made above are correct the Church of England is wrong in viewing lay celebration of the sacraments as 'a grave problem' ... To say this is not to seek frequently lay celebration of communion in practice, but to assert the belief that as a matter of principle the Methodist Church is right in allowing the possibility of it ...

... When Stage II is reached, Methodism will exist only as part of a new Church, and, since this new Church can come into being only on the basis of the 'strictest invariability' of episcopal ordination, it is very improbable that it will be in communion with non-episcopal Churches ... Methodists will then no longer be in full communion with their reformed and evangelical brethren in the other Free Churches.

Conclusion

... Some of the differences between catholic and protestant represent reconcilable differences of viewpoint; in others, one must be right and the other wrong. In these circumstances, to move from a Church committed to the evangelical faith into a heterogeneous body permitting, and even encouraging, unevangelical doctrines and practices, would be a step backward which not even the desirability of closer relations could justify ...

Document VIII.14

Methodist Radicals

(a) Colin Morris, *Include Me Out* (London: Epworth Press, 1968), pp. 7, 38; (b) John J. Vincent, *Here I Stand* (London: Epworth Press, 1967), p. 59.

While controversy raged over the Anglican–Methodist proposals after 1963, some Methodists thought there were other things which were more important. Colin Morris was first President of the United Church of Zambia and President of the Methodist Conference in 1976. His book was written over a weekend as a tract for the times. John Vincent was at this time (1967) Superintendent of the Rochdale Mission; he founded the Urban Theology Unit in 1970 and was President of the Methodist Conference in 1989.

(a)
The other day a Zambian dropped dead not a hundred yards from my front door. The pathologist said he'd died of hunger. In his shrunken stomach were a few leaves and what appeared to be a ball of grass. And nothing else.

That same day the arrival of my *Methodist Recorder*, an issue whose columns were electric with indignation, consternation, fever and fret at the postponement of the final Report of the Anglican-Methodist Unity Commission. Until that morning I had been enjoying the war that the issue had sparked off, and, indeed, had sent aloft the odd missile of my own.

It took an ugly little man with a shrunken belly, whose total possessions, according to the Police, were a pair of shorts, a ragged shirt and an empty Biro pen, to show me that this whole Union affair is the great Non-Event of recent British Church history ...

Let it be so much as whispered that Billy Graham is *en route* for Britain to conduct an evangelical campaign and some of the best brains in the Church mobilize themselves to do a demolition job on him before he even sets foot off the boat at Southampton. The air is thick with accusations and counter accusations and any apparent set-back in his fortunes is greeted with jubilation. Other sectors of the Church showed the same malicious and destructive spirit following the publication of *Honest to God*. A Church, which can afford to pour that much energy down the sewer has too much time on its hands. And in the polluted atmosphere of clever malice that hangs over the Church at such times, our claim to offer a Gospel of reconciliation rings as hollow as the sales-pitch of a bald-headed man selling hair restorer.

(b)
Is this moment not perhaps *a time of darkness for the Church*? Are there not periods of the absence of God, of blind atheism? And do not such periods sometimes herald 'a new form of Christ appearing in the world'? Those who have lived with the assumptions of the ecumenical movement all their lives must beware of the temptation to fulfil in their old age that which already belongs to yesterday. At all events, we must not conclude unions, patchings-up and rationalizings which belong to a period of confident denominationalism, but which are essentially irrelevant to the present world. They may well be also irrelevant when the light of God's new day breaks thorough. But that new day can only come on the other side of the darkness of crucifixion; and we cannot be crucified while we are still boasting about our 'gifts' and 'what God has done for us'. Perhaps we have to begin by saying, not that we are all so rich that we can treat each other, but rather that we have all *lost* the Lord. Out of weakness, exhaustion, frustration and self-sacrifice we shall find each other's hands and be crucified and perhaps rise again with another 'Body' altogether.

Document VIII.15

The Nottingham Faith and Order Conference, 1964

Unity Begins at Home (London: SCM Press, 1964), pp. 77–9.

The Faith and Order Conference held by the British Council of Churches at Nottingham in 1964 had five Sections. These are the resolutions from Section V, 'All in each place', which profoundly influenced the shape of British ecumenism for the next half-century. About 500 people attended the Conference, of whom 476 were delegates: only votes against and abstentions were counted.

A

1   United in our urgent desire for One Church Renewed for Mission, this Conference invites the member churches of the British Council of Churches, in appropriate groupings such as nations, to covenant together to work and pray for the inauguration of union by a date agreed amongst them

Conference: 5 against, 12 abstained.
Official delegates: 5 against, 8 abstained.

2   We dare to hope that this date should be not later than Easter Day, 1980. We believe that we should offer obedience to God in a commitment as decisive as this.
Conference: 53 against, 18 abstained.
Official delegates: 41 against, 14 abstained.

3   We urge that negotiations between particular churches already in hand be seen as steps towards this goal.
Conference: none against, 8 abstained.
Official delegates: none against, 7 abstained.

4   Should any Church find itself unable to enter into such a covenant we hope that it will state the conditions under which it might find it possible to do so.
Conference: none against, 6 abstained.
Official delegates: none against, 5 abstained.

5   Since unity, mission and renewal are inseparable we invite the member churches to plan jointly so that all in each place may act together forthwith in common mission and service to the world.
Conference: 2 against, 1 abstained.
Official delegates: 1 against, none abstained.

B

Recognizing that visible unity will only be realized as we learn to do things together both as individuals and as congregations, this Conference invites the member churches of the British Council of Churches to implement the Lund call to 'act together in all matters, except in those in which deep differences of conviction compel them to act separately'. In particular it requests them:

1   To make every effort to promote the common use of church buildings, and to set up whatever machinery is necessary to implement this;

2   To declare that the following activities should be carried out jointly, or (where this is not possible for deep reasons of conscience) co-ordinated, namely: 'learning together' (including local ecumenical study conferences and Faith and Order groups), lay training, youth work, children's work, men's and women's organizations, local church publications, Christian Aid, programmes of visiting, concern for and service to the whole life of the local and wider community;

3   To designate areas of ecumenical experiment, at the request of local

congregations, or in new towns and housing areas. In such areas there should be experiments in ecumenical group ministries, in the sharing of buildings and equipment, and in the development of mission.

Vote on B 1, 2, 3: unanimous.

Document VIII.16

United Reformed Church Act, 1972

Elizabeth II 1972, c. xviii.

The formation of the United Reformed Church in 1972 required an Act of Parliament, but its purposes were carefully limited to making provision for the transfer of property and trusts to the new Church, as the preamble to the Act indicates.

Whereas –

1   The Congregational Church in England and Wales (hereinafter called 'the Congregational Church') is a voluntary unincorporated association of autonomous groups of persons (known as 'churches') of the congregational denomination the affairs of which are regulated by a council and an assembly:
2   The Congregational Union of England and Wales (Incorporated) is a company limited by guarantee having for its main object the promotion of evangelical religion according to the principles and usages for the time being of the congregational denomination and having power to act as trustee of any property vested in the company:
3   The incorporated associations whose names are set out in Part I and the second column of Part II of the First Schedule to this Act and in paragraphs (d) to (g) inclusive of subsection (3) of Section 12 (Property held in trust for the congregational denomination) of this Act are companies limited by guarantee (or otherwise limited) having objects and powers similar to the objects and powers of the Congregational Union of England and Wales (Incorporated):
4   The associations whose names are set out in the first column Part II of the First Schedule of this Act are voluntary unincorporated associations of churches of the congregational denomination within particular counties or areas formed for the purpose of mutual guidance and assistance:
5   The church or denomination known as the Presbyterian Church of England (hereinafter called 'the Presbyterian Church', is a voluntary unincorporated association of persons organised for the purpose of Christian worship, instruction, fellowship and work into groups (known as 'congregations') having a form of church government administered through representative councils or courts known as Sessions, Presbyteries and the General Assembly of which the last mentioned is the supreme court whose decisions are final and binding upon the whole Presbyterian Church:

6   The Presbyterian Church of England Trust is a company limited by guarantee having for its main object the carrying on, promotion and furtherance of religious or other charitable work directed to the advancement and support of the Presbyterian Church and having power to act as trustee of any property vested in the company:

7   The Assembly of the Congregational Church and the General Assembly of the Presbyterian Church being convinced that the will of God is a union of their respective churches or denominations have for many years been engaged in discussions towards the achievement of that end:

8   The said discussions culminated in the preparation of a Scheme of Union (hereinafter called 'the Scheme') which was approved by the Assembly of the Congregational Church on the eleventh day of May One thousand nine hundred and seventy-one and by the General Assembly of the Presbyterian Church on the same day:

9   The Scheme provides for the formation of a united church or denomination under the name of the United Reformed Church (Congregational-Presbyterian) in England and Wales (hereinafter called 'The United Reformed Church') if the procedures and conditions defined and declared in the Scheme are satisfied:

10   The formation of the United Reformed Church must involve the variation of trusts of property held for or for the purposes (amongst other bodies) the Congregational Church, churches and associations of churches and of the Presbyterian Church and of the organisations and associations of that church or denomination:

11   It is expedient that the variations of trust for which provision is made in the Act should be made if the United Reformed Church is formed:

12   It is further expedient that the other provisions of this Act (being provisions incidental to or consequential upon the formation of the United Reformed Church) should be enacted:

13   And whereas the purpose of this Act cannot be effected without the authority of Parliament:

May it therefore please Your Majesty that it may be enacted, and be it enacted, by the Queen's most Excellent Majesty, by and with the advice and consent of the Lords Spiritual and Temporal, and Commons in this present Parliament assembled, and by the authority of the same, as follows:–

Document VIII.17

United Reformed Church Schedule D

The Manual, 2nd edn (London: United Reformed Church, 1984), pp. 10–11.

The statement concerning the nature, faith and order of the United Reformed Church is read aloud at ordination and induction services. This is the version approved in 1981 after the majority of Churches of Christ had joined the United Reformed Church.

Church Unity

1. The United Reformed Church confesses the faith of the Church catholic in one God, Father, Son and Holy Spirit.

2. The United Reformed Church acknowledges that the life of faith to which it is called is a gift of the Holy Spirit continually received in Word and Sacrament and in the common life of God's people.

3. The United Reformed Church acknowledges the Word of God in the Old and New Testaments, discerned under the guidance of the Holy Spirit, as the supreme authority for the faith and conduct of all God's people.

4. The United Reformed Church accepts with thanksgiving the witness borne to the catholic faith by the Apostles' and Nicene Creeds, and recognises as its own particular heritage the formulations and declarations of faith which have been valued by Congregationalists, Presbyterians and members of Churches of Christ as stating the Gospel and seeking to make its implications clear.

5. The United Reformed Church testifies to its faith, and orders its life, according to the Basis of Union, believing it to embody the essential notes of the Church catholic and reformed. The United Reformed Church nevertheless reserves its right and declares its readiness at any time to alter, add to, modify or supersede this Basis so that its life may accord more nearly with the mind of Christ.

6. The United Reformed Church, under the authority of Holy Scripture and in corporate responsibility to Jesus Christ its everliving head, acknowledges its duty to be open at all times to the leading of the Holy Spirit and therefore affirms its right to make such new declarations of its faith and for such purposes as may from time to time be required by obedience to the same Spirit.

7. The United Reformed Church, believing that it is through the freedom of the Spirit that Jesus Christ holds his people in the fellowship of the one Body, upholds the rights of personal conviction. It shall be for the church, in safeguarding the substance of the faith and maintaining the unity of the fellowship, to determine when these rights are asserted to the injury of its unity and peace.

8. The United Reformed Church declares that the Lord Jesus Christ, the only ruler and head of the Church, has therein appointed a government distinct from civil government and in things spiritual not subordinate thereto, and that civil authorities, being always subject to the rule of God, ought to respect the rights of conscience and of religious belief and to serve God's will of justice and peace for all humankind.

9. The United Reformed Church declares its intention, in fellowship with all the churches, to pray and work for such visible unity of the whole Church as Christ

wills and in the way he wills, in order that people and nations may be led more and more to glorify the Father in heaven.

Document VIII.18

Basis of Union of the United Reformed Church

The Manual, 6th edn (London: United Reformed Church, 2000), pp. A1–A9.

The Basis of Union is concerned with the Nature and Faith of the Church, and the Ministry and the Sacraments. The conciliar structure of the Church is a separate section. This version is that of 2000, after union with the Congregational Union of Scotland and the change into inclusive language.

The Church and The United Reformed Church

1   There is but one Church of the one God. He called Israel to be his people, and in fulfillment of the purpose then begun he called the Church into being through Jesus Christ, by the power of the Holy Spirit.
2   The one Church of the one God is holy, because he has redeemed and consecrated it through the death and resurrection of Jesus Christ and because there Christ dwells with his people.
3   The Church is catholic or universal because Christ calls into it all peoples and because it proclaims the fullness of Christ's Gospel to the whole world.
4   The Church is apostolic because Christ continues to entrust it with the Gospel and the commission first given to the apostles to proclaim that Gospel to all peoples.
5   The unity, holiness, catholicity and apostolicity of the Church have been obscured by the failure and weakness which mar the life of the Church.
6   Christ's mercy in continuing his call to the Church in all its failure and weakness has taught the Church that its life must ever be renewed and reformed according to the Scriptures, under the guidance of the Holy Spirit.
7   The United Reformed Church humbly recognises that the failure and weakness of the Church have in particular been manifested in division which has made it impossible for Christians fully to know, experience and communicate the life of the one, holy, catholic, apostolic Church.
8   The United Reformed Church has been formed in obedience to the call to repent of what has been amiss in the past and to be reconciled. It sees its formation and growth as a part of what God is doing to make his people one, and as a united church will take, wherever possible and with all speed, further steps towards the unity of all God's people.
9   The United Reformed Church testifies to its faith, and orders its life, according to this Basis of Union, believing it to embody the essential notes of the Church catholic and reformed. The United Reformed Church nevertheless reserves its right and declares its readiness at any time to alter, add to, modify

or supersede this Basis so that its life may accord more nearly with the mind of Christ.

10 The United Reformed Church, believing that it is through the freedom of the Spirit that Jesus Christ holds his people in the fellowship of the one Body, shall uphold the rights of personal conviction. It shall be for the church, in safeguarding the substance of the faith and maintaining the unity of the fellowship, to determine when these rights are asserted to the injury of its unity and peace.

The United Reformed Church and the Purpose of the Church

11 Within the one, holy, catholic, apostolic Church the United Reformed Church acknowledges its responsibility under God:
   - to make its life a continual offering of itself and the world to God in adoration and worship through Jesus Christ;
   - to receive and express the renewing life of the Holy Spirit in each place and in its total fellowship, and there to declare the reconciling and saving power of the life, death and resurrection of Jesus Christ;
   - to live out, in joyful and sacrificial service to all in their various physical and spiritual needs, that ministry of caring, forgiving and healing love which Jesus Christ brought to all whom he met;
   - and to bear witness to Christ's rule over the nations in all the variety of their organised life.

The Faith of the United Reformed Church

12 The United Reformed Church confesses the faith of the Church catholic in one God, Father, Son and Holy Spirit. It acknowledges that the life of faith to which it is called is a gift of the Holy Spirit continually received in Word and Sacrament and in the common life of God's people. It acknowledges the Word of God in the Old and New Testaments, discerned under the guidance of the Holy Spirit, as the supreme authority for the faith and conduct of all God's people.

13 The United Reformed Church believes that, in the ministry of the Word, through preaching and the study of the Scriptures, God makes known in each age his saving love, his will for his people and his purpose for the world.

14 The United Reformed Church observes the gospel sacrament of baptism into Christ as a gift of God to his Church, and as an appointed means of grace. Baptism is administered with water in the name of the Father and of the Son and of the Holy Spirit. It is the sacrament of entry into the Church and is therefore administered once only to any person.

When the Church observes this sacrament it makes explicit at a particular time and place and for a particular person what God has accomplished in Christ for the whole creation and for all humankind – the forgiveness of sins, the sanctifying power of the Holy Spirit and newness of life in the family of

God. In this sacrament the Church affirms its faith in the action of God in Jesus Christ; and takes corporate responsibility for those receiving baptism, promising to support and nourish them as it receives them into its fellowship. Baptism may be administered in infancy or at an age of responsibility. Both forms of baptism shall be made available in the life of every worshipping congregation. In either case the sacrament of baptism is a unique part of the total process of Christian initiation. When baptism is administered at an age of responsibility, upon profession of faith, those baptised enter at once upon the full privileges and responsibilities of membership. When baptism is administered to infants, upon profession of faith by their parent(s), they are placed under the nurture of the Church that they may be led by the Holy Spirit in due time to make their own profession of faith in Christ as their Saviour and Lord, and enter upon the full privileges and responsibilities of membership. These two patterns of Christian initiation are recognised by the United Reformed Church.

The profession of faith to be made prior to baptism by a believer or at an age of responsibility by one baptised in infancy is indicated in Schedule A.* This profession, and its acceptance by the church which shares in it, is a necessary part of the process of initiation and whenever possible it should be made at a celebration of the Lord's Supper.

The United Reformed Church includes within its membership both persons whose conviction it is that baptism can only be appropriately administered to a believer and those whose conviction it is that infant baptism also is in harmony with the mind of Christ. Both convictions are honoured by the church and both forms of baptism are understood to be used by God in the upbuilding of faith. Should these differences of conviction within the one church result in personal conflict of conscience it will require to be pastorally reconciled in mutual understanding and charity, and in accordance with the Basis of Union, in the first instance by the elders' meeting of the local congregation, and if necessary by the wider councils of the church. Whether the baptism is of an infant or a believer, whether it is by pouring or immersion, it shall not be such to which a conscientious objection is taken either by the person administering baptism, or by the person seeking it, or by the parent(s) requesting it for an infant.

[* Admission to the full privileges and responsibilities of membership of the Church shall be in accordance with paragraphs 2(1) and 2(2)(vi) of the structure and with Schedule A.]

15 The United Reformed Church celebrates the gospel sacrament of the Lord's Supper. When in obedience to the Lord's command his people show forth his sacrifice on the cross by the bread broken and the wine outpoured for them to eat and drink, he himself, risen and ascended, is present and gives himself to them for their spiritual nourishment and growth in grace. United with him and with the whole Church on earth and in heaven, his people gathered at his table present their sacrifice of thanksgiving and renew the offering of themselves, and rejoice in the promise of his coming in glory.

16 The United Reformed Church gives thanks for the common life of the Church, wherein the people of God, being made members one of another, are called to love and serve one another and all people everywhere and to grow together in grace and in the knowledge of the Lord Jesus Christ. Participating in the common life of the Church within the local church, they enter into the life of the Church throughout the world. With that whole Church they also share in the life of the Church in all ages and in the communion of saints have fellowship with the Church triumphant.

17 The United Reformed Church at the date of formation confesses its faith in the words of this statement:–

We believe in the one living and true God, creator, preserver and ruler of all things in heaven and earth, Father, Son and Holy Spirit. Him alone we worship, and in him we put our trust.

We believe that God, in his infinite love for men, gave his eternal Son, Jesus Christ our Lord, who became man, lived on earth in perfect love and obedience, died upon the cross for our sins, rose again from the dead and lives for evermore, saviour, judge and king.

We believe that, by the Holy Spirit, this glorious Gospel is made effective so that through faith we receive the forgiveness of sins, newness of life as children of God and strength in this present world to do his will.

We believe in the one, holy, catholic, apostolic Church, in heaven and on earth, wherein by the same Spirit, the whole company of believers is made one Body of Christ, to worship God and serve him and all men in his kingdom of righteousness and love.

We rejoice in the gift of eternal life, and believe that, in the fullness of time, God will renew and gather in one all things in Christ, to whom, with the Father and the Holy Spirit, be glory and majesty, dominion and power, both now and ever.

18 The United Reformed Church, under the authority of Holy Scripture and in corporate responsibility to Jesus Christ its everliving head, acknowledges its duty to be open at all times to the leading of the Holy Spirit and therefore affirms its right to make such new declarations of its faith and for such purposes as may from time to time be required by obedience to the same Spirit.

At the same time the United Reformed Church accepts with thanksgiving the witness borne to the catholic faith by the Apostles' and Nicene Creeds. It recognises as its own particular heritage the formulations and declarations of faith which have been valued by Congregationalists, Presbyterians and members of Churches of Christ as stating the Gospel and seeking to make its implications clear.*.

[*   e.g. Among Presbyterians: The Westminster Confession, 1647; A Statement of the Christian Faith, 1956.

Among Congregationalists:

in England and Wales: The Savoy Declaration, 1658; A Declaration of Faith, 1967.

in Scotland: A Statement of Faith, 1949.

Among Churches of Christ: Thomas Campbell's Declaration and Address, 1809.]

Ministry in the United Reformed Church

19 The Lord Jesus Christ continues his ministry in and through the Church, the whole people of God called and committed to his service and equipped by him for it. This service is given by worship, prayer, proclamation of the Gospel, and Christian witness; by mutual and outgoing care and responsibility; and by obedient discipleship in the whole of daily life, according to the gifts and opportunities given to each one. The preparation and strengthening of its members for such ministry and discipleship shall always be a major concern of the United Reformed Church.

20 For the equipment of his people for this total ministry the Lord Jesus Christ gives particular gifts for particular ministries and calls some of his servants to exercise them in offices duly recognised within his Church. The United Reformed Church recognises that Christ gives himself to his Church through Word and Sacrament and through the total caring oversight by which his people grow in faith and love, the exercise of which oversight is the special concern of elders and ministers. Those who enter on such ministries commit themselves to them for so long as God wills: the United Reformed Church having solemnly acknowledged their vocation and accepted their commitment shall appoint them to their particular ministry and give them authority to exercise it within the church, setting them apart with prayer that they shall be given all needful gifts and graces for its fulfilment, which solemn setting apart shall in the case of ministers and elders be termed ordination.

21 Some are called to the ministry of the Word and Sacraments. After approved preparation and training, they may be called to be ministers of local churches, or missionaries overseas, or to some special and approved ministry, and are then ordained and inducted to their office. They are commissioned to conduct public worship, to preach the Word and to administer the Sacraments, to exercise pastoral care and oversight, and to give leadership to the church in its mission to the world. Their service may be stipendiary or non-stipendiary, and in the latter case their service is given within the area of a District or area Council and in a context it has approved.*

[* Those persons who, at the time of unification serve as Registered Pastors and are so recognised by the Congregational Union of Scotland, may continue in that service under the same conditions. Such persons shall be authorised by an area council to preside at the sacraments and to serve as members of that area council. They may seek further training with a view to applying for recognition as ministers.]

22 Some are called to be elders. They share with ministers of the Word and Sacraments in the pastoral oversight and leadership of the local churches,

taking counsel together in the elders' meeting for the whole church and having severally groups of members particularly entrusted to their pastoral care. They shall be associated with ministers in all the councils of the church. Elders elected by the church meeting are ordained to their office and are inducted to serve for such limited period as the church which elects them shall determine. All elders are eligible for re-election, and those elected shall enter upon their office by induction. On moving to another local church an ordained elder is eligible for election by that church to the elders' meeting, and, if so elected, is inducted. The ordination and induction of elders shall be carried out in the course of public worship by a minister of the local church (or, during a pastoral vacancy, by the interim moderator) acting with the serving elders (see Schedule B).*

[*   Within the Synod of Scotland those office bearers who fulfil the functions of the United Reformed Church eldership will be called elders, or by local church meeting decision, may retain their existing titles. Such persons will be recognised as elders for all purposes by the wider councils of the Church.]

23 All other ministries recognised by the uniting churches at the date of unification (as defined by the United Reformed Church Act 1981) shall continue to be exercised in the United Reformed Church without further commissioning, subject always to the decisions of the General Assembly. The United Reformed Church shall determine from time to time what other ministries may be required and which of them should be recognised as ministries in the whole church. It shall decide how those who are to exercise them shall be set apart.

24 The worship of the local church is an expression of the worship of the whole people of God. In order that this may be clearly seen, the United Reformed Church shall (a) take steps to ensure that so far as possible ordained ministers of the Word and Sacraments are readily available to every local church; (b) provide for the training of suitable men and women, members of the United Reformed Church, to be accredited by district or area councils as lay preachers; (c) make provision through district councils, in full consultation with the local churches concerned, for the recognition of certain members of the United Reformed Church, normally deaconesses, elders or accredited lay preachers, who may be invited by local churches to preside at baptismal and communion services where pastoral necessity so requires. The pastoral needs of each situation shall be reviewed periodically by the district or area council in consultation with the local church. Apart from ordained ministers of the United Reformed Church and of other churches, only such recognised persons may be invited.

The provisions of paragraph 24 are intended to establish the principle that worship should be led by representative persons recognised by the wider church as well as by the local church. The provisions do not prevent the congregation assembled for baptismal or communion service from themselves appointing, as a church meeting, a suitable person to preside at the celebration of the sacrament in a case of emergency, for example if the expected president is taken ill or held up in travel. The provisions do not require such an action rather than a postponement of the baptismal or communion service if that seems preferable.

25 The ordination and induction of ministers shall be in accord with Schedules C and D. Appropriate affirmations of faith shall also be made by those entering upon other ministries within the life of the church. In the United Reformed Church all ministries shall be open to both men and women.

The totality of ministers who fall within any of the categories defined in Schedule E, Paragraph 1 and are in good standing may be referred to as the Roll of Ministers. Ministers shall conduct their ministry according to the criteria set out in Schedule E.

[Schedules A, B, C, and E are not reprinted.]

Document VIII.19

Ten Propositions, 1976

Visible Unity: Ten Propositions (London: Churches' Unity Commission, 1976), pp. 1–2.

The Churches' Unity Commission submitted Ten Propositions to the Churches for their comment and reactions in 1976.

1 We affirm our belief that the visible unity in life and mission of all Christ's people is the will of God.
2 We therefore declare our willingness to join in a covenant actively to seek that visible unity.
3 We believe that this search requires action both locally and nationally.
4 We agree to recognize, as from an accepted date, the communicant members in good standing of the other covenanting Churches as true members of the Body of Christ and welcome them to Holy Communion without condition.
5 We agree that, as from an accepted date, initiation in the covenanting Churches shall be by mutually acceptable rites.
6 We agree to recognise, as from an accepted date, the ordained ministries of the other covenanting Churches, as true ministries of word and sacraments in the Holy Catholic Church, and we agree that all subsequent ordinations to the ministries of the covenanting Churches shall be according to a Common Ordinal which will properly incorporate the episcopal, presbyteral and lay roles in ordination.
7 We agree within the fellowship of the covenanting Churches to respect the rights of conscience, and to continue to accord to all our members, such freedom of thought and action as is consistent with the visible unity of the Church.

8   We agree to continue to give every possible encouragement to local ecumenical projects and to develop methods of decision making in common.
9   We agree to explore such further steps as will be necessary to make more clearly visible unity of all Christ's people.
10   We agree to remain in close fellowship and consultation with all the Churches represented on the Churches' Unity Commission.

(NB 'an accepted date' refers to a time agreed by those who accept the Covenant, to implement consequent actions.)

Document VIII.20

The Welsh Covenant, 1975

Churches Together in Pilgrimage (London: British Council of Churches, 1989), p. 74.

The Nottingham Faith and Order Conference had encouraged the churches to covenant together 'in appropriate groupings such as nations'. The Covenant which the Church in Wales, the Presbyterian Church in Wales, the Methodist Church and the United Reformed Church, together with a number of Baptist Churches, entered in 1975 is given here.

Confessing our faith in Jesus Christ as Lord and Saviour, and renewing our will to serve his mission in the world, our several churches have been brought into a new relationship with one another. Together we give thanks for all we have in common. Together we repent the sin of perpetuating our division. Together we make known our understanding of the obedience to which we are called:

1 (a) We recognize in one another the same faith in the gospel of Jesus Christ found in Holy Scripture, which the creeds of the ancient Church and other historic confessions are intended to safeguard. We recognize in one another the same desire to hold this faith in its fullness.
   (b) We intend so to act, speak, and serve together in obedience to the gospel that we may learn more of its fullness and make it known to others in contemporary terms and by credible witness.
2 (a) We recognize in one another the same awareness of God's calling to serve his gracious purpose for all mankind, with particular responsibility for this land and people.
   (b) We intend to work together for justice and peace at home and abroad, and for the spiritual and material well-being and personal freedom of all people.
3 (a) We recognize one another as within the one Church of Jesus Christ, pledged to serve His Kingdom, and sharing in the unity of the Spirit.
   (b) We intend by the help of the same Spirit to overcome the divisions which impair our witness, impede God's mission, and obscure the gospel of

man's salvation, and to manifest that unity which is in accordance with Christ's will.

4 (a) We recognize the members of all our churches as members of Christ in virtue of their common baptism and common calling to participate in the ministry of the whole Church.

(b) We intend to seek that form of common life, which will enable each member to use the gifts bestowed upon him in the service of Christ's Kingdom.

5 (a) We recognize the ordained ministries of all our churches as true ministries of the word and sacraments, through which God's love is proclaimed, his grace mediated, and his Fatherly care exercised.

(b) We intend to seek an agreed pattern of ordained ministry which will serve the gospel in unity, manifest its continuity throughout the ages, and be accepted as far as may be by the Church throughout the world.

6 (a) We recognize in one another patterns of worship and sacramental life, marks of holiness and zeal, which are manifestly gifts of Christ.

(b) We intend to listen to one another and to study together the witness and practice of our various traditions, in order that the riches entrusted to us in separation may be preserved for the united Church which we seek.

7 (a) We recognize in one another the same concern for the good government of the Church for the fulfilment of its mission.

(b) We intend to seek a mode of Church government which will preserve the positive values for which each has stood, so that the common mind of the Church may be formed and carried into action through constitutional organs of corporate decision at every level of responsibility.

We do not yet know the form union will take. We approach our task with openness to the Spirit. We believe that God will guide his Church into ways of truth and peace, correcting, strengthening, and renewing it in accordance with the mind of Christ. We therefore urge all our members to accept one another in the Holy Spirit as Jesus Christ accepts us, and to avail themselves of every opportunity to grow together through common prayer and worship in mutual understanding and love so that every place they may be renewed together for mission.

Accordingly we enter now into this solemn Covenant before God and with one another, to work and pray in common obedience to our Lord Jesus Christ, in order that by the Holy Spirit we may be brought into one visible Church to serve together in mission to the glory of God the Father.

Document VIII.21

Baptists and the Ten Propositions, 1977

Visible Unity in Life and Mission in R. Hayden (ed.), *Baptist Union Documents, 1948–1977* (London: Baptist Historical Society, 1980), pp. 193–201.

> This response from the Baptist Union Council, based on responses from nearly 1,000 churches, declined to proceed to the further stage of covenanting. However, it is not hostile to the objective of visible unity and raises a series of significant questions.

The Churches' Unity Commission seeks from those Church bodies that created it definitive answers to the Ten Propositions tabled in 1976. The Baptist Union Council, as one such body, has had to consider what its response should be and – equally importantly – how that response should best be framed. At the outset, two controlling factors require emphasis.

In the first place, it must be recognised that the Council cannot of itself commit any church in membership with the Baptist Union to entry into the proposed Covenant. Local congregational decision is finally decisive. The responsibility of the Council is to recommend to the churches of the Union a response.

It is our clear judgement that at present no unqualified recommendation to accept the Ten Propositions can be made. We have formed this judgement in the light of provisional responses from our churches and of certain issues elaborated later in this document.

In the second place, it is arguable that any seriously qualified recommendation or response would not only be difficult to frame but also fail to serve the serious enterprise on which we are engaged. We recognise that the Propositions alone contain the questions to be addressed and that it is open to us to react negatively to some and affirmatively to others. Yet we cannot judge such a procedure to be finally helpful in charting possibilities for the future. We further recognise that the 'commentary' and other clarificatory material issued by the Commission do not strictly belong to the questions posed. Yet it would be unrealistic to return a response that failed to give very serious weight to all such background understanding.

It is our clear judgement however that, rather than attempting isolated reactions to each individual proposition seriatim, some constructive indication should be offered as to the understandings upon which we might in fact feel it possible to make positive recommendations for 'covenanting' to our churches.

A. UNITY

We gladly reaffirm our belief that the *visible unity in life and mission* of all Christ's people is the will of God (*Proposition 1*) and recognise that the search for such unity must involve action both locally and nationally (*Proposition 3*). We are aware that there are those who believe that to embark with seriousness on this road is properly and inevitably to plot a course for 'organic union'; and within the flexible framework of covenanted commitment there is clearly and rightly room for two or more denominations to negotiate a 'union' should they at any point judge this to be their Christian obedience. We are also aware that some suspicions of organic union may on the one hand merely reflect the mood of our time and may on the other hand be used to sanctify withdrawal from costly, meaningful and effective action. Yet we are alarmed by the apparently inexorable way in which (not only outside our own ranks) discussion and debate have failed to give controlling weight to the significant phrase 'in life and mission'. Therefore:

It is our conviction that as much hard thought needs to be given to the implications of defining the goal of visible unity in terms of the phrase 'in life and mission' as has been devoted over the decades to drafting schemes of organic union.

In this connection we would make our own the words of the C.U.C. commentary on Proposition 1:

> 'Structures must faithfully express such unity as already exists, foster and facilitate the fuller measure of unity we may come to recognise as ours, and set us free to undertake our common mission in and to the world.'

We believe that these perspectives must increasingly challenge us all and dictate the *shape* of any movement into visible unity. It is in terms of this understanding that we would interpret and assent to *Proposition* 9 which speaks of agreement 'to explore such further steps as will be necessary to make more clearly visible the unity of all Christ's people'.

B. MEMBERSHIP

1   Mutual recognition of communicant membership is fundamental to any movement into visible unity. The implementation of it (in terms of *Proposition 4*) in some of our churches, were they to desire it, would require legal changes to be made. In itself, however, this proposal would and should command widespread acceptance provided only that as much serious thought be given to the request that a member should be 'in good standing' as is clearly being given to the requirement of the practice in the future of the 'mutually acceptable rites' of initiation.

2   Such 'mutually acceptable rites' are set forward (*Proposition* 5) as necessary requirements of the post-covenant situation. The C.U.C. 'explanatory note' indicates the basic elements of the total initiatory process and the way in which any temporal division of that process should be structured. We are invited to recognise that no supplemental initiatory rite should be required of those seeking to move from one covenanted Church to another.

   We do not believe that such a requirement necessarily provides any finally insuperable barrier for Baptists. It must, however, be made clear on what grounds and within what context progress might at this point be made. Most Baptists would approach the issue of the recognition and reception of members of paedobaptist Churches by reference to whether or not a faith response to the Gospel of the grace of God in Christ had in fact been made. The 'mutually acceptable rites' as outlined by C.U.C. all make essential provision for such a response. That being so, reception and recognition might readily be envisaged. This is the positive side of the situation.

   Yet it would be dishonest to pass over the negative side, namely that no automatic recognition of infant baptism as true baptism is necessarily being given. We do not understand Proposition 5 as requiring such a recognition. We do however believe that it would be costly delusion to imagine that the creation of mutually acceptable rites of initiation indicates profound theological agreement on the baptismal issue. The Faith and Order Commission of the W.C.C. has recently come to recognise that the extent of emerging consensus here may have been overestimated.

We judge that acceptance of Proposition 5 will lack integrity unless all are clearly committed to a continued grappling with the real theological divergences that remain.

3 It is in this context that we take up the matter of 'rights of conscience' (*Proposition 7*). Questions relating to baptism point to but one of many areas in which difficulties may arise. Since, however, it is an area of special concern to Baptists it may usefully constitute a test case. We are assured in the Commission's extended comments on Proposition 7 that no diminution of existing individual freedom of thought and conscience is envisaged. We are also reminded that covenanting Churches are bound by the terms of the covenant entered. How might this apply on the baptismal front?

Within limits the answer seems clear and coherent. If the terms of the covenant include the practice of mutually acceptable initiatory rites, then covenanting Baptist churches must observe the unvarying practice of baptism. Such a requirement may expose existing tensions among Baptists, but it seems wholly reasonable to claim that a community must come to terms with its own 'corporate' conscience *prior* to covenanting. It may not as a community expect freedom to breach commitments freely accepted.

Where so-called 'rebaptism' is concerned, however, the answer is not obviously as clear-cut. We judge that, whilst any Baptist church which covenants would remain free to preach believers' baptism, a claim of freedom, on grounds of conscience, to urge believers' baptism on individual paedobaptists seeking transfer of membership would negate the covenant relationship itself (as in the case of other Churches wishing to present their customary rites) and that therefore such an issue of conscience must be faced and settled prior to entry into covenant. However, we could not commend to our churches any covenant which involved a bar to the administration of believers' baptism in the case of a paedobaptist whose conscience might lead him or her to the conclusion that fidelity to Scripture and the Gospel required such baptism.

We are clear that the exercise of responsible pastoral freedom must be preserved at this point and possibly others precisely because the covenant is not based on real theological agreement on the baptismal issue.

C. MINISTRY

1 Mutual recognition of membership finds its inevitable counterpart in mutual recognition of ministries. At this point mutual recognition of existing ministries is seen as indissolubly tied to a movement into the future involving for all

Churches in the post-covenant situation ordinations 'according to a Common Ordinal which will properly incorporate the episcopal, presbyteral and lay roles in ordination' (*Proposition 6*). As to the Common Ordinal, it is plain that what is envisaged is not a total uniformity of practice but rather an Ordination Service which, on the basic of agreement on its intention would contain reading and proclamation of the Word of God, a common Ordination Prayer, and a common form for the Presentation and Examination of candidates. Even this measure of verbal inflexibility would present problems to some Baptists and would need to be a matter of careful and open discussion. It is clear, however that the basic issue arises in connection with the requirement of proper provision for 'episcopal, presbyteral and lay roles' in ordination. The introduction of the word 'episcopal' poses the central problem. The Commission's document 'The Meaning and Implications of Proposition 6' makes clear that it is speaking of the 'historic episcopate' and, in this connection tables Method A and Method B as alternatives.

Method A involves for the Churches conventionally described as 'non-episcopal' the creation of an episcopal ministry distinguishable from the presbyteral ministry already possessed. The setting apart of such episcopal ministers (bishops) would begin within the Service of Worship which contained the act of covenanted commitment and would be an action in which representatives of 'episcopal' churches would share. In any subsequent ordination to the presbyteral ministry of word and sacraments, an episcopal minister of the denomination concerned would be centrally involved.

Method B involves the participation of a bishop from one of the convenanted 'episcopal' Churches in the ordination of presbyters within 'non-episcopal' Churches – with appropriate reciprocal participation in ordinations within 'episcopal' Churches.

History, tradition, and conviction combine to render such proposals extremely suspect in Baptist eyes. The inevitable introduction of the word 'bishop', laden as it is with the controversies of the centuries, prompts a negative reaction which must be imaginatively understood. More serious still is the felt lack of weighty and convincing argument for the attaching of such overriding importance to the existence or establishment of an episcopal order of ministry. In this matter, the New Testament scarcely speaks with a clear and decisive voice; the argument from antiquity is one that defenders of an episcopal order of ministry might be reluctant to apply on other issues; the claim of 'proven worth' depends upon a particular and contestable reading of history.

2   It would therefore be easy for us to return a simple negative to both the Commission's proposals. To do this, however, would neither assist the Commission nor do justice to some of our own deepest convictions There are affirmations we need to make. We are wholly mindful of the importance of an apostolic succession for the health of the Church of God. The unity of the Church is a unity in space and time as well as reaching beyond. Links with apostolic foundations must be plain and enduring. Yet exactly in this

connection Baptists will join with others in pointing to an apostolic succession in scriptural faith, proclamation, life and mission.

Equally we are mindful of the significance of the exercise of episcopal functions for the health of the Church of God. The truth of the Gospel must be safeguarded and maintained. Caring oversight of the People of God must find proper expression. A focus of continuity is important. Yet exactly at this point Baptists will see the realities of episcopacy manifested *in corporate fashion* in church meeting, associations and councils, and *focussed* for particular purposes in an honoured presbyteral ministry of word, sacraments and pastoral care. They will acknowledge that such understandings have sometimes been obscured. They will not conclude that the essence of episcopacy is lacking among them.

What then is lacking? Contemporary voices urge us to believe that it is the historic episcopate understood as 'the fulness of the sign of apostolic succession' (see W.C.C. Faith and Order Paper No, 73, *One Baptism, One Eucharist, and a Mutually Recognised Ministry*, p. 56 and *passim*). Whatever meaning is to be read into this somewhat ambiguous phrase, the question has to be asked as to whether the recovery of this 'sign' is an indispensable prerequisite not merely for organic union but for the mutual recognition on which we are in fact engaged. The Faith and Order Paper referred to above concludes:

> 'Churches (with episcopal succession) should also consider the desirability of recognizing some ordained ministries that exist apart from an episcopal succession but which embody a succession of ordained ministers who combine in their ministries the functions of both bishop and presbyter. It may also be possible to recognize some ministries that do not claim a formal episcopal or episcopal-presbyteral succession but that in fact exist with the express intention of maintaining a succession in the apostolic faith' (p. 56).

We desire to press this question upon the Commission and through it upon our episcopal brethren with a view to obtaining a considered and argued response.

3   It may of course be the case that in the last analysis we have to face a conviction that the essential role of a bishop, whatever else may be finally dispensable, is that of 'ordainer' and that, provided that this function is exercised, the minimal condition for 'recognition of ministries' has been fulfilled.

It is because Method B, whatever its expressed intention, lends itself so readily to this understanding and suggests too easily the severance of the episcopate from its whole churchly context and from the rich texture of meanings and relationships that alone give it life that we cannot recommend it.

As a temporary measure in limited local situations a case might be made for it. In the context of a national covenant we believe it does justice neither to 'episcopal' nor to 'non-episcopal' convictions.

4 We do however detect the Commission speaking with a more meaningful and persuasive voice. The significant elements of episcopacy already present in the life of 'non-episcopal' Churches are explicitly recognised. In Method A, the establishment of a distinct and distinguishable episcopal ministry is commended to 'non-episcopal' Churches on the ground that the health and life of the Church has been found to require, beyond corporate expressions of episcopacy, the setting apart of some to a unifying office of particularly wide and heavy responsibility calling for special gifts of mind and spirit. No dogmatic theory is argued. No fixed pattern is prescribed. To such an emphasis Baptists are not strangers. In recent decades they have found themselves recognising something of this need and setting aside men to meet it. In many fundamental respects, episcopacy in this personalised sense, far from being a foreign body, can lay claim to recognition as a prized and familiar feature of Baptist common life.

If these things are so it may fairly be asked why we are not able to recommend our churches to covenant on the basis of Method A. Three reasons at least must be noted:

In the first place, we have already indicated that we are not yet convinced that mutual recognition of ministries must or should depend upon the existence or creation of a distinct episcopal order, and therefore seek a considered response on this issue.

Secondly, we are acutely aware that there is here opened up a complex area of discussion which we and our churches have scarcely begun to consider in the more open terms in which the issues now confront us.

Thirdly, it is important to make clear in what context such consideration for us would be pursued. We are not convinced that we lack some unchanging feature of church order. Rather do we remember that the visible unity being sought is a 'visible unity in life and mission'. We have to ask ourselves what, in the purpose of God, will best serve 'life and mission' in the coming days. We have to discern whether or not we are being called to pioneer from and within our Association life a distinguishable form of episcopal ministry which the existing 'episcopal' Churches would be able to recognise as such yet which, at the same time, would both contribute to the health of Christ's People and serve their missionary calling.

It will be clear that there are too many uncertainties and matters needing further clarification to allow of an immediately positive recommendation.

D. COVENANTING

We are invited by the Commission to move towards visible unity in covenant relationship with others (*Proposition 2*). That might seem an unexceptionable step to take. Yet it would be agreed that it must lack meaning given the reservations on other points we have felt it necessary to table. It may, however, still be relevant and important to explore and expose certain realities implicit in such covenant commitment and to comment upon them. The nature and content of the Service of covenanting therefore demands attention.

Prior procedural, even legal, steps are implied. Yet the heart of the matter lies in a solemn act of covenanted commitment before God which, for the partners sharing in it, both involves a specific pledge to continue together in movement into that visible unity which Christ intends for his Church, and signalises, seals and expresses mutual recognition and acceptance of one another as true Churches and, in particular, mutual recognition of membership and ministry. Acceptance of one another as true Churches must in this context be expressive of a thankful recognition that, in sufficient measure, a common Faith is shared.

Given these things, we still judge it important that two further points be made. On the one hand, we see mutual recognition of membership and ministries as in the last resort contained within the mutual acceptance of one another as true Churches. 'Ministry' must not be sundered from 'membership' nor either from 'Church'. There are not three separate 'recognitions' based on three separable agreements and requiring three separable reconciling acts.

The act of covenanted commitment must itself portray and not obscure this wholeness and interpenetration.

On the other hand, we see a danger that covenanting may too easily be framed in terms that suggest it is essentially a matter of human decisions – though made in the presence of God. We therefore judge it important that the centrality of the action of God be stressed. Covenanted commitment is a decisive happening profoundly affecting the past, present and future of the partners involved. All recognise and are recognised. All receive and give. All are ushered into a future in which each is mandated to foster, continue and express a new measure of fullness and universality. Yet such high claims can surely have integrity and reality only if they are rooted in submission to the surprising grace of God. Our 'mutual recognition' is but the echo of His recognition of us all. Our 'giving and receiving', rightly understood, is *his* condescension to our *common* need. To take such a perspective seriously may be the surest way to discipline over-anxious concern to establish what one possesses and another lacks.

We conclude therefore that the act of covenanted commitment can only bear the weight attached to it if the primary emphasis falls upon what God has done and is doing to us all. Thus the act should in tone as well as context be doxological rather than declaratory.

E. THE LOCAL AND THE UNIVERSAL

What we are bold to believe God may do for us and with us is one thing. We have indicated our belief that it is this perspective that must explicitly control the framing of any act of covenanted commitment. It is another thing to make concrete and specific progress in unity within any situation of mutual commitment into which the Churches may move,

Here the Commission speaks in terms of encouragement of local ecumenical projects and development of methods of decision-making in common (*Proposition*

8). Local ecumenical projects may be seen as one expression of the search for visible unity in life and mission; and the test of any such project remains whether it has promise of serving this goal. Common decision-making similarly presents itself as a realistic indication of the genuineness and effectiveness of covenant commitment. At these points, however, more basic questions intrude. Methods of common decision-making are important. Yet for their development there is required some measure of common understanding with regard to decision-making itself.

Probably most Christians would be in broad agreement that the Church is to be understood theologically as both universal and local, that the Church universal is not an aggregate of local churches, that there is the one universal Church which 'in locality' finds visible concretion. Certainly there will be variations of understanding and practice in the definition and expression of the term 'local'. For some it will suggest the word 'diocese', for others the word 'congregation'. Already potential divergences as to the essential place of decision-making begin to appear.

The much more serious problems, however, emerge as the movement away from the 'local' takes place. Some may be found speaking of 'higher courts' of the Church as centres of authority to which decisions may or must be referred. In so far as legal sanctions are characteristically attached to national bodies it might seem that the 'Church national' is being accorded a theological significance equal to or greater than the 'Church local' or the 'Church universal', Because we sense that in this whole area of decision-making significant issues are not far from the surface, we judge it important to affirm the ground on which we stand.

We believe that to give primary significance to the 'Church universal' implies giving primacy to its visible embodiment the 'Church local'. We understand the lineaments of the true Church to be discerned in the local Christian community met week by week for corporate worship, where the pattern of the Cross and Resurrection is displayed by the baptised community as she subordinates herself to the apostolic Scriptures, proclaims the Word, celebrates the Supper, accepts the ministries of oversight and service, and lives out the atonement in travail of love for the world.

Yet in the final analysis the Church is one, whatever the number of its local manifestations. The essential nature of the Church, including the imperatives of mission, presses the local community towards regional, national, international organs for common life, common decision, common action. This pressure is valid and inescapable. Nor should such wider 'conciliar' forms and organs be denied their 'churchly' character. Yet the factor that theologically differentiates the 'Church local' from wider conciliar expressions of Church life remains. It is the regular gathering for corporate worship. Where the common life of a continuing Christian community is regularly subjected to Word and Supper there is the Church most truly and profoundly manifested. Wider conciliar forms are not *in themselves* the fulness of this reality. They live from it and by it. That is why they need to be understood by reference to the conciliar form of the 'Church local' which Baptists know as the Church Meeting.

Herein lies the clue for Baptist attitudes to wider conciliar forms. In their own limited and derivative sense they are precisely 'church meeting'. They are not some higher level of Church order. They are not some superior or more ultimate piece of decision-making machinery. They are means by which the oneness of the Body may find wider expression and prompt united action. In so far as they are truly subject to the Word and truly open to the Spirit they may become means by which the Lord of the Church speaks to the churches.

It is however for the churches to recognise his voice. Any authority which the wider conciliar forms may possess is given to them by the Lord of the Church. Yet because it is *his* authority it cannot be imposed without in the end contradicting its own nature.

Authority is not simply a matter of decision-making at some appropriate point or level. It is also a matter of the recognition and reception of decisions through the whole range of the Church's life.

In this as in other areas, theology and practice do not always coincide. Baptists have not always been faithful to their best insights. Equally, sociological factors have properly to be taken into account where decision-making is concerned. Further it may be objected that all the Commission is proposing is the creation of adequate machinery for common decision-making, and the will to use it. It is however our conviction that no meaningful response at this point can evade the raising of the difficult issues of power, authority and ecclesiology to which we have tried to draw attention.

We believe that the model of diversity in unity adopted by the Commission constitutes the most promising avenue of advance offered in this generation. We would wish to remain in close fellowship and consultation with our partner Churches (Proposition 10), though this cannot be the limit of our Christian relationships. It is our hope that the questions we have posed and the reservations we have tabled will promote discussion and responses which will assist that movement into visible unity in life and mission to the advancement of which the Commission has set its hand.

Document VIII.22

The Proposed English Covenant, 1980

Towards Visible Unity: Proposals for a Covenant (London: Churches' Council for Covenanting, 1980), pp. 9–10.

The five churches which accepted the Ten Propositions drew up a draft Covenant which was published in 1980. Three Anglican members entered a note of dissent. This extract is the Preface to the Report.

We were commissioned by our Churches to draw up a Covenant to promote visible unity between them in life and mission, on the basis of the Ten Propositions, Our many discussions have led us to propose certain actions on the basis of which our

Churches will be able to acknowledge one another as true Churches within the One Church of Christ, and to recognise and accept one another's sacraments, membership and ministries. We have deliberately set the making of the Covenant within an act of worship, to make it clear that our hope is in the living Christ who is Head of the Church, and in the Holy Spirit, the Lord and giver of life.

Questions concerning the ordained ministry have inevitably occupied our attention, and we believe that this Covenant provides an unambiguous way in which the ministries of all our Churches may be incorporated in a new relationship within the historic ministry of the catholic Church to their mutual enrichment. Consecration to the historic episcopate by episcopal ordination and the joint ordination of presbyters according to a Common Ordinal will become the practice of all our Churches from the point of Covenant onwards, and this intention is sealed by the ordination of bishops and presbyters in the Covenant Service itself. We have believed it right, during the initial period of our new Covenant relationship, to recognise existing ministries of oversight exercised in the grace of God by some who have not been ordained as bishops. In the national Covenant Service, and in regional and local services, ordinations are associated with prayers of invocation to the Holy Spirit, in which God's blessing is sought on the new and enlarged ministry which the existing ministers of all the covenanting Churches will exercise within the covenant. Other opportunities are provided for all ministers and Church members to make a similar personal response to the covenant, in association with the bishops of the covenanting Churches.

In the matter of the ordination of women as presbyters or bishops, we have provided for their recognition and ordination in Churches where they do now minister; and at the same time have recognised the position of those who on conscientious grounds cannot accept their ministry. We believe that in the new situation created by the Covenant, there will be many opportunities to explore the diverse ministries of the Churches, including those exercised by women.

The Covenant is a covenant between Churches, and important though the ordained ministries are, we propose to conclude the Covenant Service with an act of Holy Communion in which all may share together as guests at the one table of the Lord. It is as Churches that we offer to one another the sign of reconciliation at the beginning of the Covenant Service, and we provide for a reaffirmation of baptismal promises by all who are present as the climax to the ordinations,. We believe that our recommendations for regional and local services to follow upon the national service will help the Churches throughout England to make the covenant their own and to enter into a new relationship with one another. This relationship must be sealed by commitment to one another by means of the corporate episcopate and common decision-making in particular regions and areas, and we have made recommendations to this end. The Covenant will stand or fall by the will to share in it of the ministers and Church members in every locality.

The Covenant proposed in our report gives our Churches an opportunity for reconciliation which is in true continuity with the catholic tradition of the Church, and at the same time accepts the particular histories of our several Churches, all of which are marked by God's grace and judgment. It will enable the Churches which share in it to demonstrate their unity, and thus to share more effectively in the one mission of Christ to the world. Because we believe visible unity in life and mission to be God's will for his Church, we wholeheartedly recommend this Covenant to our Churches. The Church of England and the Free Churches have worked together for 60 years in the quest for unity: this Covenant represents the next step in that common search for visible unity which we invite our churches to take with hope and joy.

Document VIII.23

To Lima with Love, 1986

M. Thurian (ed.), *Churches Respond to BEM*, vol. iv (Geneva: World Council of Churches, 1987), pp. 218–24.

The Yearly Meeting of the Society of Friends made this response to the World Council of Churches consensus statement on Baptism, Eucharist and Ministry in August 1986. It picks up the characteristic Quaker emphases.

18 In the corporate life of our Religious Society, as in our worship and our own lives, we try to work under the guidance of God. We have to discern the promptings of love and truth in our hearts, and to recognize and respond to God's leadings.

19 Our worship, our practical work and our social lives express the paradox of the homeliness of grace. We worship in total dependence on God's Spirit for inspiration, and with a full awareness of the many ways in which our inadequacy, our self-centredness, and our habits of mind can hinder the movement of the Spirit.

20 We may seem at times to take God for granted. But we know the beyond in our midst; we rely on grace, God's free, sustaining, creative and lively action as we rely on the air we breathe and the ground we walk on.

21 In our experience, God works with those who are true to their deepest nature. Those whom Jesus called friends cooperate with him knowing how he works, and we know the depths of the patterns of love, truth, faithfulness, death and resurrection which he exemplified. We are aware of the life and power of the Spirit of God, maintaining us as a society and as local worshipping communities. We welcome the stress in the Lima text on the work of the Spirit, and know in our meetings the Spirit's less spectacular fruits and gifts.

22 Alongside Friends' stress on the primacy of God's action, we set great store by the centrality of ordinary experience. We agree with the witness of the universal church that mystical experiences are attested by the moral quality of people's lives. The whole of our everyday experience is the stuff of our religious awareness: it is here that God is best known to us.

23 However valid and vital outward sacraments are for others, they are not, in

our experience, necessary for the operation of God's grace. We believe we hold this witness in trust for the whole church.

24 We are not generally drawn to speculative theology. We try as individuals and as a body to be faithful to the truth we have discovered. We prefer not to crystallize our understanding of the truth; our corporate experience is a growing and living tradition.

25 We understand the Bible as a record arising from similar struggles to comprehend God's ways with people. The same Spirit which inspired the writers of the Bible is the Spirit which gives us understanding of it: it is this which is important to us rather than the literal words of scripture. Hence, while quotations from the Bible may illuminate a truth for us, we would not use them to prove a truth. We welcome the work of scholars in deepening our understanding of the Bible. May we offer the comment that occasionally the Lima text shows too little critical discrimination in the evidential use of scripture?

26 We respond to the Lima text in Christian language, but many Quakers would prefer less specifically Christian terminology. We worship, live and work together in unity, however, valuing the variety of expressions of truth which each individual brings.

Baptism

27 We know the power of God's Spirit at work in the lives of people within the community of our meetings. These people may have been drawn into the community by a sudden convincement, a long period of seeking, or have grown up within it from childhood. We also know that we are engaged in a life-long growth into faith, and experience a continuing irruption of grace into our lives which demands and sustains a commitment to a life of discipleship. We recognize this power at work in people of all ages, races and creeds: transforming power which can issue in lives of joy, humility and service. Where these experiences are reflected in the statements of BEM we rejoice at this measure of our unity and are challenged to search for more.

28 The Quaker conviction is that the operation of the Spirit outruns all our expectations. We acknowledge that the grace of God is experienced by many through the outward rite of baptism, but no ritual, however carefully prepared for, can be guaranteed to lead to growth in the Spirit. A true spiritual experience must be accompanied by the visible transformation of the outward life. Our understanding of baptism is that it is not a single act of initiation but a continuing growth in the Holy Spirit and a commitment which must continually be renewed. It is this process which draws us into a fellowship with those who acknowledge the same power at work in their lives, those whom Christ is calling to be his body on earth.

29 It is out of this understanding that we have historically rejected water-baptism, seeing no necessary connection between this single event in a person's life and the experience of transformation by the Spirit. We cannot see that this rite should be used as the only way of becoming a member of the

body of Christ. Nor do we find the use of water-baptism to be an inescapable inference from the New Testament's account of Jesus' life and practice. On the contrary, scripture does not persuade us that baptism as initiation is any more important than circumcision as initiation, since either clouds the issue that neither the correctness of opinion nor religious observance, but only the undeserved grace of God, enables us to walk in faith and be active in love.

30   Part of the meaning of baptism is a proclamation of becoming a member of the church. Entry into membership of the Religious Society of Friends is a public acknowledgment of a growing unity with a community of people whose worship and service reflect, however imperfectly, their perception of discipleship and their recognition of the work of the Holy Spirit in the world., This unity is grounded in the experience of being 'gathered' in the love of God in the silent expectancy of our meetings for worship and in a willingness to surrender ourselves to a corporate seeking for the will of God in such measure as we can comprehend it.

31   We too feel the tensions which divide the wider church over the place of infants and young children within the congregation. We know also that there are those whose membership of the Society may be little more than a formality, while many of the most faithful participants in our meetings do not seek formal membership.

32   Our witness to the unfettered operation of the Spirit must involve a humble confession of our own failings; yet we must testify to the fact that lives which display the fruits of the Spirit have been nurtured within the Society of Friends.

Eucharist

33   We are impressed by the breadth of insight shown in this section into the nature of corporate worship. Many of the aspects noted here are in accord with our own aspirations and experience of Quaker worship. We welcome the interpretation of the eucharist as the gift of God, granting communion between the human and the divine, renewing the members of the worshipping body and binding them together. We too see our worship as a thanksgiving and celebration of the work of God in all creation and for all people, and a recognition of the cost of love and commitment, Particularly also, we welcome the forthright statement of the implications of worship, its implicit call to reconciliation and service in our daily lives and its challenge to us to work for justice in all areas of life; our worship focuses our hope for the fulfilment of God's purpose. Thus although our practice appears very different, we recognize many of the spiritual aspirations expressed in the symbolism of the eucharist.

34   In Quaker worship neither the elements of bread and wine nor any eucharistic liturgy is used. Our liturgy is one of silence and waiting on God for the words that may come, to any one of us, from the depths of that waiting together. We recognize that the words and symbolic actions of the eucharist are experienced by many Christians as a most powerful means of grace, a grace

which shines forth clearly in their lives. Nevertheless, it is our experience that the grace of God is not restricted to any particular form of eucharistic liturgy; the reality of God's presence may be known in worship that retains none of the traditional elements that are central to the life of many churches.

35 In 1928, at a time when parliament and the religious life of our nation were rent with strife on the nature of the Real Presence, London Yearly Meeting wrestled to understand its own experience and expressed it these words: 'In silence, without rite or symbol, we have known the Spirit of Christ so convincingly present in our quiet meetings that his grace dispels our faithlessness, our unwillingness, our fears, and sets our hearts aflame with the joy of adoration. We have thus felt the power of the Spirit renewing and recreating our love and friendship for all our fellows. This is our eucharist and our communion' (*Christian Faith and Practice*, extract 241).

36 We would assert that the validity of worship lies not in its form but in its power, and a form of worship sincerely dependent on God, but not necessarily including the words and actions of Jesus near the end of his live as an invitation to recall and re-enact the self-giving nature of God's love at every meal and every meeting with others, and to allow our lives to be broken open and poured out for the life of the world.

37 We realize that others will have reservations about our open and unstructured form of worship. Absence of form and of structure no more guarantee depth and spirituality of worship than do their presence. Our bold experiment in worship is not always the embodiment of the claims we make for it; nor does it always embody those realities of which eucharistic worship can be a profound symbolic expression, realities which should provide sharpness of focus and nourishment. When we are faithful it does.

38 We fear that separating a particular sacrament and making it a focal point in worship can obscure the sacramental validity of the rest of creation and human life. We fear too the dangers of over-familiarity, of perfunctory or passive repetition of the act and of imagining the act to have power of itself. Admission to the eucharist only of those whose status is considered satisfactory by the church can exclude many sincere seekers after God and for this reason we find it dificult to see conformity to this practice as the true basis of unity in the life and spirit of Christ. The Lima text offers no reassurance on this point. Further, through its failure to acknowledge the experience of those Christian groups which express their commitment in ways other than through a eucharistic form of worship, the Lima text makes us profoundly uneasy.

39 We would wish to unite with all Christians and also with those of other faiths who work for reconciliation and healing in a broken world. Our membership includes those who, whilst ill at ease with orthodox formulations of Christian belief and doctrine, are nevertheless counted among those who do the will of God. As Friends we wish to recognize the divine gifts in those who call God by other names or see their commitment to truth in very different ways from those expressed in the Lima document.

Ministry

40 We respond with warmth and delight to the opening paragraphs which describe the calling of the whole people of God. We know 'the liberating and renewing power of the Holy Spirit' and the call, as members of the body of Christ, to faithful mission and service. The priesthood of all believers is a foundation of our understanding of the church.

41 We turn, then, to the question in §6: 'How, according to the will of God and under the guidance of the Holy Spirit, is the life of the church to be understood and ordered, so that the gospel may be spread and the community built up in love?' We note that the text seeks a 'common answer' to this question. We doubt, not only whether a common answer is possible, but whether it is desirable in the many situations and cultures in which churches find themselves.

42 The text (E29) speaks of Christ as the one who gathers, teaches and nourishes. He is the shepherd, the prophet and the priest. The task of exercising these functions in the world belongs to the whole community of God. We cannot accept those aspects of §11 and §13 which claim these tasks for the ordained ministry. Our own experience leads us to affirm that the church can be so ordered that the guidance of the Holy Spirit can be known and followed without the need for a separated clergy.

43 Paragraphs 9, 10 and 11 make the assumptions that the twelve are the apostles and that the apostles are the authority for ordained leadership. We cannot make these simple equations. Besides the apostles there were many other witnesses of the life, death and resurrection of Jesus, including the faithful women who witnessed all these events. We see in the New Testament churches a variety of structures and leadership roles as the church grew and changed. This gives scriptural support for the many present day patterns and for continuing experimentation and flexibility. Our own founders claimed that our church order was 'gospel-order' and 'primitive Christianity revived'. However, apostolicity for the church is not the restoration of ancient systems, even if these could be discovered. It is, rather, to live in the Spirit in which the apostles lived. This Spirit, which was poured out at Pentecost on all the church, young and old, women and men, continues in our experience to call and empower all members of the church in a variety of ministries.

44 The Spirit has led us from our foundation to recognize the equality of women and men in the people of God. Early Friends taught that the redemptive activity of Christ restored men and women to their position before the fall, as equal help-meets both made in the image of God. Though we have not been immune from influences in the surrounding culture, we have sought to practise this equality in our structures. We know that the Spirit gives as wide and diverse gifts to women as to men and acts as effectively through women as through men. In our mind, a church which does not fully recognize and encourage the gifts and ministries of all its people is imperfectly realising the body of Christ.

45 To be without an ordained clergy is not to be without either leadership or

ministry. The gifts of the Spirit to us include both. For us, calls to particular ministries are usually for a limited period of time, and these gifts pertain to the task rather than the person. In one lifetime a person may be called to a number of ministries, each with its own charism.

46 We identify in our structure *elders* with a responsibility for the spiritual life of the meetings; *overseers* with a responsibility for pastoral care within meetings; and *clerks* who serve administrative needs. At one time we recorded as *ministers* those whose vocal contribution to worship was particularly acceptable. This practice, however, was abandoned after a decision of the Yearly Meeting in 1924.

47 We now recognize a variety of ministries. In our worship these include those who speak under the guidance of the Spirit, and those who receive and uphold the work of the Spirit in silence and prayer. We also recognize as ministry service on our many committees, hospitality and childcare, the care of finance and premises, and many other tasks. We value those whose ministry is not in an appointed task but is in teaching, counselling, listening, prayer, enabling the service of others, or other service in the meeting or the world.

48 The purpose of all our ministry is to lead us and other people into proper communion with God and to enable us to carry out those tasks which the Spirit lays upon us.

49 Throughout our history we have rejoiced in the ministry we have received through 'concerns' formed by the Spirit in the hearts of individual Friends. These concerns may have been for personal service or for the furtherance of some particular insight. Such concerns need to be brought before a meeting for church affairs so that they may be tested by the meeting as a whole. This may ultimately be seen as a leading of the Spirit to which the meeting must be corporately obedient. The discerning of such leading and the subordination to it of individual opinion is a ministry to which we are all called.

50 Like all the church, we have a high calling – to be the body of Christ, to live empowered by the Spirit, to do the will of God. We admit our weaknesses in carrying this out. With our structure we risk failures in understanding and transmitting our tradition, and failures in pastoral care. We do not always adequately support one another. When we appoint people to carry out tasks for us, there is a danger in approaching this in too secular a way, failing to see its significance as an 'ordination' – an occasion when we can and must pray for them to receive the necessary gifts and strength from the Spirit, Paragraph 40 is a help to us on this.

51 We recognize that the different circumstances and traditions of parts of the church have led to different forms of organization. We respect those who have forms different from our own for we acknowledge that what is important in the formal structure is whether it allows people to know and respond to the call of God. However, when we see the emphasis in the text on an ordained, threefold ministry, it arouses in us a number of fears.

Firstly, we believe that without an adequate development of the ministry of the laity there will continue to be an unbalanced relationship between clergy and community, which will encourage the people to depend too much on ordained leadership.

Secondly, we are disturbed at the linking of ordination with authority, for this can legitimize authoritarian leadership and limit the exercise of spiritual authority. We agree with the statement in §16 that authority in the church can only be authentic as it conforms to the model of Christ.

Thirdly, we fear the emphasis on a threefold ordained ministry as an 'expression of the unity we seek and also a means of achieving it'. Such a ministry manifestly is not a focus of unity and has not achieved unity. We regret that the text does not take more seriously the first three clauses of §22 which recognize New Testament diversity, the Spirit-led adaptation of ministries to context, and the gifts of the Spirit with which many forms of ministry have been blessed.

52 What, then, is the focus for Christian unity? It must be Jesus, who calls us not into structures but into discipleship and to follow him in his way. Can we not know that we are one in him when we are faithful to his calling and when we exercise towards one another that greatest gift of love? Can we not rejoice in our diversity, welcoming the opportunities to learn from each other? Can we not seek a recognition of each other's ministries as the work of the same Spirit? That Spirit can, if we are ready to adventure, lead us into ways we have not known before.

Document VIII.24

Baptist–Methodist Agreement on Baptismal Policy within Local Ecumenical Projects

Baptist–Methodist Agreement on Baptismal Policy within Local Ecumenical Projects (Didcot: Baptist Union 1991)

This agreement was reached between the Baptist Union Advisory Committee on Church Relations and the Methodist Church Ecumenical Committee in 1991 'after long consultation'.

A *We recognise the necessity of:*
i) Maintaining the integrity of both Methodist and Baptist understandings and practice of baptism;
ii) Having a flexible and sensitive approach in this very delicate area;
iii) Maintaining and developing good relationships and unity within the congregations of the sharing churches.

B *We note that:*
i) It is the practice of the Methodist Church to baptise infants and to confirm them on confession of faith or, when infant baptism has not occurred, to baptise and confirm believers. In both cases these services make provision for pouring, sprinkling or immersion in water.

ii) It is the practice in Baptist churches to hold a service for infants and their parents (variously known as 'The Dedication Service', 'The Service of Infant Presentation and Blessing', 'The Blessing of Infants', etc) and to administer believer's baptism on the candidate's personal profession of faith in Christ.
iii) Standing Order 800 of 'The Constitutional Practice and Discipline of the Methodist Church' makes clear that 'it is contrary to the principles and usage of the Methodist Church to confer what purports to be baptism on any person known to have been already baptised at any time'.
iv) Whilst welcoming 'Baptism, Eucharist and Ministry' (the so-called Lima Document) as a 'notable milestone in the search for sufficient theological consensus', the BUOB Council in November 1984 dismissed as wholly unacceptable in its present form the statement that 'Any practice which might be interpreted as "rebaptism" must be avoided'. In this way the Council sought to protect the freedom of an individual's 'informed conscience' in matters concerning baptism and to allow for the possibility of a change of conviction here.
v) Whereas 'Recognised and Regarded' (Methodist) ministers are expected to administer infant baptism in appropriate circumstances those with 'Authorised' (Methodist) status have greater flexibility here. This latter category may accordingly be more acceptable to (most) Baptist ministers in Local Ecumenical Projects.

C *Procedures:*

1 Since baptism, whether of believers or infants, is such an important step, any persons involved (candidates or parents of infants) should proceed with the full knowledge of all the options that are available to them. Candidates for believer's baptism and confirmation shall, wherever possible be trained together and shall thus be made aware of the teaching of both churches.
2 It shall be left to the discretion of the Baptist membership to baptise as believers any who have previously been baptised as infants in other churches. In the interests of the unity of the congregation this should not be applied to Methodist members except as provided under 4 below.
3 Whenever a Methodist member wishes to make a public confession of faith (other than through those opportunities normally provided by the services of the Methodist Church) then the Methodist Church Council shall arrange an appropriate opportunity such as The Service for the Celebration of Christian Renewal.
4 If, despite the above provision, any Methodist maintains a conviction about being baptised as a believer, this shall only be after a full consultation between (1) the candidate AND (2) the Baptist minister and Church Meeting and the Superintendent Minister and Church Council. This consultation will, of course, be pastoral in nature and not in the way of a tribunal. In view of SO 800 such a service should not take place unless the Methodist member is willing to have his/her membership transferred to the Baptist roll.

Document VIII.25

Local Ecumenical Partnerships, 1992

Commitment to Mission and Unity: Report of the Informal Conversations between the Methodist Church and the Church of England (London: Church House and Methodist Publishing House, 1996), pp. 25–6.

There were 16,128 Anglican and 6,678 Methodist churches in England in 1995. The table gives the number of Local Ecumenical Partnerships in 1992.

In 1992 there were 767 LEPs listed, of which 200 were then classified as Local Covenants. About half of the LEPs also involve sharing a building according to the 1969 Sharing of Church Buildings Act. The principal involvement of churches is as follows:

	LEPs		Sharing Agreements
Church of England	551		270
of which Methodist-Anglican total		455	
Methodist	631		363
URC	445		277
Of which Anglican-URC total		212	
Of which Methodist-URC total		362	
Baptist	201		103
of which Anglican-Baptist total		142	
of which Methodist-Baptist total		132	
Roman Catholic	129		56
of which Anglican-Roman Catholic total		127	
of which Methodist-Roman Catholic total		92	

Document VIII.26

The United Reformed Church and Local Ecumenical Partnerships

URC, *Reports to Assembly*, 1996, pp. 116–17.

The 1996 Assembly of the United Reformed Church approved a Statement submitted by its Ecumenical Committee on 'The United Reformed Church and Visible Christian Unity'. Section 5 on Local Ecumenical Partnerships illustrates their significance for the Church, since a higher proportion of United Reformed congregations are in LEPs than that of any other church.

5.1 Local Ecumenical Partnerships are a sign that it is possible to be one at the local level. They establish a local unity between Christians of different denominations that is formally recognised by these denominations. Much of the impetus for these developments has come from grass-roots initiatives.

5.2 The idea of a *Church of churches* is a central conviction of the Reformation and an increasingly important insight in recent Roman Catholic ecumenical discussions. It is spelt out particularly clearly in *God's Reign and our Unity*, the 1984 report of the Anglican-Reformed International Commission:

> *The goal is the emergence of reconciled local communities, each of which is recognisable as 'church' in the proper sense; communities which exhibit in each place the fullness of ministerial order, eucharistic fellowship, pastoral care and missionary commitment; and which, through mutual commitment and co-operation, bear witness on the regional, national, and even international levels.*

The aim is

> *for locally recognisable forms of the Universal Church ... something which expresses locally the wholeness of the Catholic Church.*

5.3 Of great significance for the United Reformed Church is its participation in Local Ecumenical Partnerships (LEPs). Two hundred of the three hundred and thirty are joint with the Methodists. There are three United Reformed Church/Methodist United Areas and three regions where the Methodist Church and the United Reformed Church are seeking to work together. Many of our ministers are 'Recognised and Regarded' as Methodist ministers and others have been authorised by the Church of England to preside at communion and, in a few cases, to serve as sole resident minister of an Anglican parish, which is also a Local Ecumenical Partnership.

5.4 For the past twenty years, whilst maintaining its denominational structures and supporting United Reformed churches in England, Scotland and Wales, most of our churches in new areas have been Local Ecumenical Partnerships. The General Assembly of 1993 called upon every district council to engage with ecumenical partners in research aimed at placing a body of Christian people in every locality. Such new congregations, often fast growing and with a young age profile, have produced some fine ecumenical fruit – a new kind of identity, a grass-roots experience of the sharing of different historical traditions, ministry and styles of building, and a shared ministry to the whole community. However, in some difficult frontier missionary situations where most churches are unable to produce spectacular growth or financial self-sufficiency the Local Ecumenical Partnerships share this experience.

5.5 For some United Reformed Churches now in joint churches or Local Ecumenical Partnerships, local unions offered hope of new life to a shrinking, ageing congregation. For some others it was the answer to a crushing burden of building repairs. Inevitably some of these hopes have not been fulfilled. Strong local churches do not often enter into Local Ecumenical Partnerships, but our cross-denominational unions of 1972 and 1981 did mean that all our churches have that experience to offer to the ecumenical movement. There

Church Unity

are also a number of old established Baptist/Congregational union churches, which are now Baptist/United Reformed Church and they have their witness to uniting to share. Where a local church, strong at least in vision and faith, has felt the call to such a united life and has opened itself to the unfamiliar insights of other traditions and exposed its own precious insights to the often puzzled scrutiny of the other partner(s) in this calling, there is a foretaste of God's reign.

5.6 The continued separation of the churches as denominations puts great strain on such Local Ecumenical Partnerships and United Areas. Multiple mailings, the demand for representation on the bodies of each participating church, conflicting systems of ministerial appointment and for the raising of finance are just some of the burdens they carry. The United Reformed Church is committed through the Churches Together in England, Action for Churches Together in Scotland and CYTUN (Churches Together in Wales) through the Methodist/United Reformed Church Liaison Committee, through the financial support for ecumenically appointed ecumenical officers, and through its network of district and provincial ecumenical officers, to easing these burdens.

5.7 The majority of United Reformed Churches are not partners in such Local Ecumenical Partnerships, but almost all are long-standing members of their local councils of churches. After the formation of the new ecumenical instruments in 1990, many of the English councils of churches found a new sense of purpose and turned themselves into *Churches Together in ...* For many of our local churches this represents a serious ecumenical commitment to joint community work, mission, study and worship, and that commitment is often reflected in a local covenant. Some of these covenants have now become stale as the member churches locally, regionally and nationally have failed to take new steps on the road from co-operation to commitment and from commitment to communion. It is significant that the Group for the Local Unity of Churches Together in England decided to devote its 1996 conference to this particular form of commitment.

5.8 It is becoming clear that ecumenical progress now depends more and more on the policy-making bodies at every level and the members and ministers of the 'single denomination' local congregations. Shortage of money and ordained clergy is forcing the pace. In some areas, there is already joint District/Circuit/Deanery consultation on deployment. In others, there are shared appointments of specialists in youth work or social responsibility work. Joint training courses for ordination, post-ordination, lay ministry and youth work are building up a network of mutual understanding and friendship among the leaders of the churches. Grass-roots criticism of the churches' lack of co-operation in response to new legal regulations and their lack of real consultation on matters on every church's agenda, such as new patterns of ministry, homosexuality and ministry, and central restructuring is growing. That there is an increasingly shared spirituality across all churches is evidenced, for example, in the widespread use of Taizé, Iona and Corrymeela worship material. All these existing and potential forms of co-operation, which fall far short of organic union, will, in time, lead the churches to the same hard questions about unity and reconciled diversity which the Local Ecumenical Partnerships are already posing.

Document VIII.27

The United Reformed Church Responds to *Called to be One*

URC, *Reports to the Assembly*, 1997, pp. 97–8.

Churches Together in England urged local churches to discuss the booklet, *Called to be One*, in 1996–97. Section 4 is the most specific part of the United Reformed Church's response.

4.1. Within the overarching commitment of the United Reformed Church to the full, visible unity of the Church, the *Called to be One* process poses some specific and immediate questions and challenges. Most of these were already on the United Reformed Church's agenda, either being tackled with ecumenical partners or alone. Where the latter is the case, the first challenge is to begin to tackle the matter with ecumenical partners.

A. *What do we mean by Church?*

i The United Reformed Church welcomes the challenge to renewal (CTBO 7.6 i) which urges it to rediscover and renew its own traditions. This 25th year of its union is a good time to identify, renew and offer its traditions of corporate discernment through the councils of the church, of shared leadership by ministers and elders, and of the exposition of the Bible in the context of worship. Each of those traditions is, of course, shared with some other members of Churches Together in England. The United Reformed Church needs to explore further how these elements are to be recognised and affirmed in single and multiple-congregation Local Ecumenical Partnerships.

ii. The United Reformed Church is not large enough in this country to be present in every community. Strategic decisions about deployment of ministers and planting and closing of churches have to be taken. More work needs to be done on an ecumenical ecclesiology to inform those decisions.

iii. The United Reformed Church also needs to seek ways to help United Reformed Churches which are not in ecumenical partnerships of any kind to come close enough to other traditions to be able '*to examine one another's traditions*' and '*to explain what it is in other traditions that they find difficult to accept*' (CTBO 7.6ii and iii).

B. *Belonging to the Church*

i. The United Reformed Church understands membership as a calling of the baptised on confession of faith to join with the people of God in worship and

Church Unity

      in service and in corporate discernment of God's will. This calling is expressed primarily, but not only, through the local church.

ii. Today the United Reformed Church is concerned at the growing reluctance of worshippers to become members. It is also concerned at the emphasis on individual commitment and choice at the expense of the corporate calling. A renewed understanding of the Church as a holy people, in the world but not of the world, may be a timely offering to all the churches.

iii. However, the United Reformed Church, through its experience of sharing in parish ministry with the Church of England in various kinds of Local Ecumenical Partnerships, also recognises and appreciates that inclusive understanding of belonging to the Church. More work is needed to try and reconcile the two understandings of membership. In particular, the United Reformed Church will continue, for the sake of those in rural areas, to look at the possibility of meaningful membership of two churches.

iv. The United Reformed Church recognises the difficulties for our partner churches which arise from the varying practices and understandings found in local churches regarding the relationship between baptism, membership and admission to communion. It warmly welcomes the report of the CTE working party on Christian Initiation, Baptism and Membership. A recent URC consultation on *Believing and Belonging* will also contribute to the work which the United Reformed Church needs to do in this area, both within its councils and through the ecumenical instruments.

C. *Authority and Leadership*

i. The United Reformed Church's experience of bringing together a Congregational and a Presbyterian system of authority is worth sharing. It has required a tactfulness on the part of District Councils and a tolerance and restraint on the part of Church Meetings. These have not, of course, always been in evidence. This flexible and sensitive kind of relationship between local and wider church is an offering to the ecumenical pilgrimage.

ii. There has, however, been some confusion about where authority rests in particular matters. The January 1997 meeting of Mission Council discussed a paper on the exercise of authority in the United Reformed Church and asked for more work to be done. The United Reformed Church would welcome an ecumenical working group on this.

iii. Although personal leadership is valued, especially from local ministers and from provincial moderators, the United Reformed Church continues to be convinced that authority must be exercised in councils of ministers and elders and members.

iv. The term *collegial leadership* needs clarification. It could mean an elders' meeting as well as the moderators' meeting. Further work needs to be done between the churches on collegial leadership and its relationship to oversight ministry.

D. Passing on the Faith

i. The United Reformed Church is called, with all other churches, to pass on the faith of the Gospel from generation to generation. It fully recognises that *God's mission is greater than any individual church can grasp* (CTBO A.33) and it believes that division has *made it impossible for Christians fully to know, experience and communicate the life of the one, holy, catholic, apostolic Church* (Basis of Union A.7).

ii A major stumbling block to that mutual acceptance of ministry and eucharistic sharing so necessary to our growing together and to our mission together is our different understandings of how to safeguard the handing on of the faith. The United Reformed Church therefore welcomes the call to the Church of England and the Free Churches (in CTBO 7.9) to consider the renewed understanding of apostolicity to be found in the Porvoo Common Statement. However, it believes the understanding set out in the report of the 1984 Anglican-Reformed Dialogue *God's Reign and our Unity*, and in the more recent Leuenberg discussion document on *The Church of Jesus Christ* should also be part of any further work.

iii. In addition, the United Reformed Church is also committed, with partner churches in Wales and in Scotland, to exploring alternative routes to a mutual acceptance of each other's apostolicity.

5 Conclusion

The United Reformed Church gives thanks to God for the many ways in which it has been enriched, enabled and inspired by the churches who are its fellow pilgrims on the way to the Kingdom. It also acknowledges, with penitence, that it may have contributed to continuing divisions through complacency, prejudice or impatience. It believes the *Called to be One* process is calling the United Reformed Church to the renewal of its life at every level, whether in Local Ecumenical Partnerships or not, with various partners, through all kinds of ecumenical bodies, so that it may faithfully be '*part of what God is doing to make his people one*' (Basis of Union para. 8).

Select Bibliography

Karl Barth, *The Teaching of the Church regarding Baptism* (London: SCM Press, 1948)
D. W. Bebbington, 'Baptists and Fundamentalism in Inter-war Britain', in K. Robbins (ed.), *Protestant Evangelicalism: Britain, Ireland, Germany and America, c. 1750–c. 1950* (Oxford: Basil Blackwell, 1990)
G. K. A. Bell, *Documents on Christian Unity: First Series* (London: Oxford University Press, 1924)
G. K. A. Bell, *Documents on Christian Unity: Second Series* (London: Oxford University Press, 1930)
Charles Booth, *Life and Labour of the People in London: Final Volume: Notes on Social Influences and Conclusion* (London: Macmillan, 1902)
J. H. Y. Briggs, 'She-Preachers, Widows and Other Women: The Feminine Dimension in Baptist Life since 1600', *Baptist Quarterly*, vol. xxxi, no. 7, July 1986, pp. 337–52
C. G. Brown, *The Death of Christian Britain* (London: Routledge, 2001)
R. W. Cleaves, *Congregationalism 1960–1976: The Story of the Federation* (Swansea: John Penry Press, 1977)
K. W. Clements (ed.), *Baptists in the Twentieth Century* (London: Baptist Historical Society, 1983)
K. W. Clements, *Lovers of Discord: Twentieth-Century Theological Controversies in England* (London: SPCK, 1988)
F. Coutts, *The Better Fight: The History of the Salvation Army, Vol. vi, 1914–1946* (London: Hodder & Stoughton, 1973)
R. Currie, *Methodism Divided* (London: Faber & Faber, 1968)
R. Currie, A. Gilbert and L. Horsley, *Churches and Churchgoers* (Oxford: Clarendon Press, 1977)
R. Davies (ed.), *The Testing of the Churches 1932–1982* (London: Epworth Press, 1982)
R. E. Davies, *A History of the Methodist Church in Great Britain*, vol. 3 (London: Epworth Press, 1983)
G. W. Dolbey, 'The Changing Face of Methodism: II. The Methodist Church Act, 1976', *Proceedings of the Wesley Historical Society*, vol. xli, part 4, February 1978, pp. 97–103
C. D. Field, 'The Methodist Local Preacher: an Occupational Analysis', in G. E. Milburn and M. Batty (eds), *Workaday Preachers: The Story of Methodist Local Preaching* (London: Methodist Publishing House, 1995)
W. F. Flemington, *The New Testament Doctrine of Baptism* (London: SPCK, 1948)
H. A. Hamilton, *Family Church in Principle and Practice* (London: 1941)
M. E. Hirst, *The Quakers in Peace and War* (London: Swarthmore Press, 1923)
D. J. Jeremy, *Capitalists and Christians* (Oxford: Clarendon Press, 1990)

Elaine Kaye, 'Constance Coltman – A Forgotten Pioneer', *JURCHS*, vol. 4, no. 2, May 1988, pp. 134–46

Elaine Kaye, Janet Lees and Kirsty Thorpe, *Daughters of Dissent* (London: United Reformed Church, 2004)

T. C. Kennedy, *British Quakerism 1860–1920* (London: Oxford University Press, 2001)

John Kent, *The Age of Disunity* (London: Epworth Press, 1966)

Ronald P. Marshall and Jack Lucas, *Border Experiment – A Report and Evaluation of a Seven Year Experiment in Mission on the Welsh/English Border* (London: Methodist Home Mission Department, 1968)

K. Middlemas and J. Barnes, *Baldwin: A Biography* (London: Weidenfeld & Nicolson, 1969)

D. D. Morgan, *The Span of the Cross* (Cardiff: University of Wales Press, 1999)

J. Munson, *The Nonconformists* (London: SPCK, 1991)

R. Pope, *The Flight from the Chapels* (Cardiff: Wales Synod of the United Reformed Church, 2000)

J. Rae, *Conscience and Politics* (London: Oxford University Press, 1970)

A. P. F. Sell, *Testimony and Tradition* (Aldershot: Ashgate 2005)

A. P. F. Sell, *Nonconformist Theology in the Twentieth Century* (Milton Keynes: Paternoster Press, 2006)

A. P. F. Sell and A. R. Cross, *Protestant Nonconformity in the Twentieth Century* (Carlisle: Paternoster Press, 2003)

J. Smyth, *In This Sign Conquer* (London: Mowbray, 1968)

D. M. Thompson, *The Decline of Congregationalism in the Twentieth Century* (London: Congregational Memorial Hall Trust (1978) Ltd, 2002)

D. M. Thompson (ed.), *Stating the Gospel* (Edinburgh: T. & T. Clark, 1990)

J. Munsey Turner, *Conflict and Reconciliation: Studies in Methodism and Ecumenism in England 1740–1982* (London: Epworth Press, 1985)

Stephen Yeo, *Religion and Voluntary Organisations in Crisis* (London: Croom Helm, 1976)

Index of Persons

Albright, W. A. 279
Anderson, D. 242
Asquith, H. H. 2, 227, 240, 301
Attenborough, J. 27, 28

Bacon, J. C. 365
Baldwin, Mary (*see* Wilson)
Baldwin, S. 268, 281
Balfour, A. J. 219
Baker, E. 43
Baker, H. 83
Barker, R. J. 239
Barlow, J. H. 279
Barnes, J. 269
Barrett, C. K. 212, 340, 369
Barrow, H. 278
Barth, K. 79, 81, 98, 181, 209, 341
Batty, M. 148
Bebb, E. D. 145
Bebbington, D. W. 170
Belden, A. D. 280
Bell, G. K. A. 344, 350
Berry, S. M. 303, 304
Bickerstaff-Drew, Fr 274
Birrell, A. 227, 229
Bissell, B. 60
Blogal, I. 60
Blunkett, D. 225
Bolam, C. G. 169, 207
Bonhoeffer, D. 169, 315
Booth, B. 222, 223, 242
Booth, Catherine 77
Booth, Charles 13, 17
Booth, W. 222, 242
Bradley, Miss 85
Brailsford, H. N. 262
Brodrick, W. St. J. F. 271
Briggs, J. H. Y. 81
Brooke, R. 274
Brown, C. G. 7, 9
Brown-Douglas, C. C. 241
Bryce, J. 227, 277
Buchanan, A. 41

Bunyan, J. 174
Burns, J. 227
Burton, J. 358
Burton, L. 44
Butler, R. A. 223, 246
Butterfield, H. 169, 206

Caird, G. B. 167
Calder, R. 254
Callaghan, A. 261
Callaghan, L. J. 224, 225, 260
Callard, P. 37
Calley, M. 49
Calvin, J. 147, 168, 199
Campbell, R. J. 167, 168, 170, 171, 181
Campbell, T. 382
Campbell-Bannerman, H. 227
Carlyle, T. 178
Carnegie Simpson, P. 239, 240, 241
Carruthers, S. W. 242
Cartwright, Mrs 303
Chamberlain, A. 227
Chaplin, H. 227
Chapman, E. V. 37
Christol, F. 282
Clark, D. 142
Cleaves, R. W. 81
Clements, K. W. 8, 170
Clifford, J. 196, 220, 229, 267, 268, 270, 271, 275, 279
Cole, G. D. H. 262
Coltman, Claud 82, 83
Coltman, Constance 77, 82, 83
Cordingly, B. 37
Cottle, J. L. 316
Coutts, F. 225
Crewe, Lord 230
Cromwell, O. 228
Crosfield, G. 279
Cross, A. 8, 9, 17, 140, 170, 225, 269
Currie, R. 7, 8, 9, 344

Dalaston, G. E. 82

Index of Persons

Darbishire, H. 264
Davidson, R. T. (Archbishop) 176, 222, 230
Davies, R. E. 8, 344, 349
Deeks, D. G. 285
Dodd, C. H. 167
Dolbey, G. W. 225

Eddington, A. S. 168, 194
Edwards, J. 7
Eliott, J. T. 279
Ellis, E. M. 278
Elmslie, W. A. L. 146
Elmslie, W. T. 223, 244, 268, 282, 283
English, D. 61
Evens, G. B. 37

Field, C. D. 140
Fields, G. 36
Fisher, G. F. 6, 14, 93, 340, 341
Flemington, W. F. 79, 81
Forsyth, P. T. 167, 168, 169, 181, 191, 199, 211
Fotheringham, J. K. 241
Fraser, A. H. 241
Frost, B. 36
Frost, R. 316

Garbett, C.F. 249, 251
Gates, E. 77
Gaunt, A. 155, 157
George, A. R. 349
Gilbert, A. D. 8
Gillespie, R. C. 58
Gladstone, W. E. 219, 260
Glover, T. R. 167, 168, 170, 176, 195, 196, 198
Goldman, R. 80
Gordon, E. 77, 88–9
Gore, C. 167, 347
Graham, B. 4, 15, 372
Gramsci, A. 60
Gray, J. 341, 365
Green, F. Pratt 155, 157
Grey, E. 276
Gunton, C. E. 169, 211
Gwatkin, H. M. 347

Haldane, R. B. 227
Hamilton, H. A. 80, 81
Harjuan, T. 282

Harrison, A. W. 246
Harvey, T. E. 279
Hay, W. 196
Hayden, R. 81, 93, 101, 116, 386
Headlam, A. C. 338
Heap, W. 21
Hedger, V. 77
Helwys, T. 67
Herbert, A. P. 296
Heron, A. 310
Hill, C. 49
Hill, M. 44
Hinsley, Cardinal 340
Hirst, M. E. 269, 411
Hitler, A. 223, 263, 268
Hobhouse, E. 271
Holland Williams, G. 316
Hollowell, J. H. 229
Hornabrook, J. 302
Horne, C. S. 220, 226
Horsley, L. 8
Hort, F. J. A. 347
Horton, D. 365
Hough, J. 313
Howarth, A. 267, 271
Howells, G. 197
Hubble, G. 58
Hughes, D. P. 270
Hughes, H. M. 338
Hughes, H. P. 267, 270
Hughes, W. G. 239
Hunter, J. 144
Huxtable, W. J. F. 342

Jacks, L. P. 78
Jenkins, D. T. 169, 209
Jenssen, V. 282
Jeremy, D. J. 9, 17
Jessop, T. E. 369
Johansen-Berg, J. 316
Johnes, M. 303
Jones, B. P. 25
Jones, I. H. 155, 156

Kaan, F. H. 155, 158
Kaye, E. 80, 81
Kelly, C. 1
Kennedy, T. C. 269
Kent, J. 344

Index of Persons

Kierkegaard, S. 169
King Jr, M. L. 298
Kraemer, H. 210
Kruger, P. 270

Lang, C.G. 338
Lansdowne, Lord 295, 302
Laski, H. J. 262
Laud, W. 191
Lawson, J. 221, 237
Learoyd, A. 22
Lees, J. A. 80
Lidgett, J. Scott 220, 229, 231, 246, 295, 301, 338
Lloyd George, D. 2, 221, 227, 229, 278
Lloyd, J. Selwyn 225
Lucas, J. 17, 412
Lumb, R. 247
Lunn, H. T. 270
Luther, M. 160, 161, 168, 178, 179

Macarthur, A. L. 88
McConnell, F. D. 316
MacDonald, J. Ramsay, 240
McIntire, C. T. 206
MacLeod, J. G. 242
McMurray, T. P. 22
Manning, B. L. 168, 191, 200, 202
Marchant, J. 271, 279
Marshall, R. P. 17
Marx, K. 61, 221, 260
Mason, D. 37
Maxwell, J. C. 194
Mayson, C. 60
Meadley, T. D. 369
Mellor, D. 296, 302
Meyer, F. B. 22, 28
Miall, E. 219
Micklem, E. R. 259
Micklem, N. 168, 169, 199, 260, 365
Micklem, T. C. 155, 160
Middlemas, K. 269
Migot, H. 282
Milburn, G.E. 148
Milne, A. 242
Milton, J. 264
Milwood, R. 61
Montgomery, Mrs 22
Moody, D. L. 31

Moody, G. 296
Morgan, D. D. 221, 225
Morley, J. 227
Morris, C. 269, 289, 372
Moule, C. F. D. 315
Moulton, A. (*see* Callaghan)
Moulton, F. 262
Mountain, J. 196
Mudie-Smith, R. 18
Munson, J. 9
Murray, V. 14, 34
Mussolini, B. 263

Newbigin, L. 59
Newton, I. 194
Nicholson, Mrs J. 30
Nicholson, N. 14, 30
Niebuhr, Reinhold 248
Niemöller, M. 254
Nietzsche, F. 237
Norwood, F. W. 280

Oman, J. 168, 187
Orchard, W. E. 82, 83

Paulden, M. O. 77, 83
Payne, E. A. 113, 253, 256
Peake, A. S. 338, 339, 349, 350, 353, 354
Peake, L. S. 353
Peel, A. 223
Penry, J. 25
Perkins, E. B. 357
Perks, R. W. 338
Peters, K. 358
Philippson, J. E. 358
Pilkington, R. 227
Plummer, A. 347
Pope, H. J. 302
Pope, R. 17
Potter, W. H. 259
Phillips, M. W. 221, 260
Pratt, B. M. 316
Preston, R. H. 326
Price, A. Whigham 89

Rae, J. 269
Ramsey, A. M. 2, 342
Randles, J. 227
Rattenbury, J. E. 339, 349
Reid, J. 242

415

Index of Persons

Reid, J. K. S. 342
Reid, R. 227
Richards, L. 82
Rieger, J. 282
Robbins, K. G. 267
Roberts, A. 262
Roberts, E. 25
Roberts, W. 196
Robertson, W. L. 241
Robinson, A. 347
Robinson, J. A. T. 169, 209, 313, 315
Rogers, E. 305, 306, 339, 356
'Romany' (*see* Evens)
Rorke, J. 241
Royle, E. 21
Rupp, E. G. 349
Russell, G. S. 82
Ruston, A. 7

Saddam Hussein abd al-Majid 290
Sankey, I. D. 31
Saunders, M. 16, 56
Scarman, Lord 321
Schleiermacher, F. D. E. 209
Schneider, C. 254, 255
Schomer, H. 254
Schweitzer, A. 176
Selbie, W. B. 77, 83
Sell, A. 8, 9, 17, 140, 170, 225, 269
Shakespeare, J. H. 196, 337, 342, 345
Shaw, G. B. 262
Short, J. 365
Skinner, R. F. 264
Smith, R. ('Gipsy'), 13
Smyth, J. 269, 274
Snaith, N. H. 369
Soper, D. O. 15, 36
Spurgeon, C. H. 195, 196
Stacey, D. 37
Stacey, J. 37
Steel, D. M. S. 298
Stempel, H. 254
Stennett, J. 160
Stennett, S. 160
Stephens, Mr 26
Stephenson, H. 365
Sutcliffe, G. 141

Taylor, V. 168, 204

Temple, W. 222, 250
Tennant, F. R. 168
Thatcher, D. 264
Thatcher, M. H. 225, 262, 320, 321
Thomas, A. 78
Thomas, G. 221, 222, 238
Thompson, D. M. 8, 17, 81
Thorogood, B. 321
Thorpe, K. E. 80
Thurian, M. 397
Todd, Constance (*see* Coltman)
Trevithian, R. 37
Turner, J. M. 344
Turner, K. 37
Twinn, K. 207

Underwood, A. C. 197

Vaughan, Cardinal 226
Vincent, J. J. 16, 60, 372

Walker, M. 140, 160
Walker, R. G. 316
Walton, R. C. 130
Watkins, O. S. 274
Watts, A. 278
Watts, S. M. 254, 365
Wells, H. G. 262
Wesley, C. 31, 155, 339
Wesley, J. 20, 35, 141, 145, 338, 339, 355, 370
White, B. R. 130
White, G. 227
Whitehorn, R. D. 364
Williams, H. 330
Wilson, C. E. 29, 197
Wilson, E. J. 279
Wilson, J. H. 224, 225, 238, 259
Wilson, Marjorie 259, 260
Wilson, Mary 260
Wise, G. 70
Wishart, J. H. 242
Wolverhampton, Lord 145
Wordsworth, W. 140, 264
Wren, B. A. 155, 159

Yeo, S. 13, 17, 412
Young, F. M. 169, 204
Young, K. 141, 299

Zwingli, U. 161

www.ingramcontent.com/pod-product-compliance
Lightning Source LLC
Chambersburg PA
CBHW081146290426
44108CB00018B/2456